WORDS, BODIES, MEMORY

SÖDERTÖRN
PHILOSOPHICAL STUDIES 23
2019

Words, Bodies, Memory

A Festschrift in honor of Irina Sandomirskaja

Edited by
Lars Kleberg, Tora Lane, Marcia Sá Cavalcante Schuback

SÖDERTÖRN
PHILOSOPHICAL STUDIES

Södertörns högskola
(Södertörn University)
Biblioteket
SE-141 89 Huddinge

©Authors

Licensed under a Creative Commons Attribution
3.0 Unported License

All images contained within this publication are subject to separate copyright

www.sh.se/skriftserier

Cover image: Jean Dubuffet, *L´Inconsistant*, 1959,
©Jean Dubuffet / Bildupphovsrätt 2019

Layout: Per Lindblom & Jonathan Robson

Södertörn Philosophical Studies 23
ISSN 1651-6834

ISBN 978-91-88663-72-6

Contents

Foreword
11

I

Besieged by the Future
EGLĖ RINDZEVIČIŪTĖ
17

Better Red than Dead – Remembering Cold War Sweden
JOHAN HEGARDT
31

As if a Town
Wandering with W. G. Sebald in Terezín
MARYAM ADJAM
43

In the Cold Cities
– Poetics of Self and Memory as Traumatic Continuity in Gennady Gor's Siege Texts
POLINA BARSKOVA
53

When I was living in Moscow
DISA HÅSTAD
63

Chance Encounter in Bad Nauheim
LARS KLEBERG
67

Potential Trust
(animated neon with 6 stages)
ESTHER SHALEV-GERTZ
83

II

Reading and Censorship:
Leo Spitzer's Monographs from WWI
KENNETH J. KNOESPEL
89

Автор как лакуна
MIKHAIL IAMPOLSKI
107

Nelly Sachs' Chorus Poetics
MARCIA SÁ CAVALCANTE SCHUBACK
126

A Response in Rhythm
– Marina Tsvetaeva's Poem "Возвращение вождя"
(The Return of the Leader) and Sofia Gubaidulina's
Composition "Das Ross" (The Horse)
FIONA BJÖRLING
141

The Rhythm of Time
HANS RUIN
153

«Не поддадимся чувству естественности всего происходящего!»
(«Новая искренность» в «Обращениях к гражданам»
Д. А. Пригова)
MARK LIPOVETSKY
160

The Translator as Trickster:
Mark Tarlovskii and Southern Subjectivity
SUSANNA WITT
193

III

Postsocialist Bakhtin Burlesque:
YOUNG-HAE CHANG HEAVY INDUSTRIES
performing 'Cunnilingus in North Korea'
CHARLOTTE BYDLER
215

The Merry Widow and Socialist Realism
PER-ARNE BODIN
233

Rodimaia storonka?
A Ukrainian Director Films a Russian Poem in 1934
NATASCHA DRUBEK
247

Cruel Romances of War:
Victimhood and Witnessing After Afghanistan
SERGUEI ALEX OUSHAKINE
271

Смерть во сне:
нарратор и точка зрения в фильме Ларса
фон Трира *Europa*
ALEKSEI SEMENENKO
299

The Representation of Public Memory in the Millennium
Artistic Projects *+2000/-2000, Even* by Osvaldo Romberg,
and *General Reminder* by János Sugár and Yuri Leiderman (edition 2)
ANNA KHARKINA
307

The Three Great Stimulants
MAGNUS BÄRTÅS
317

IV

Totalitarianism and the Experience of Experience
TORA LANE
325

On Grammatical Meanings
JOHN SWEDENMARK
333

How Lenin's Language Was Made:
Russian Formalists on the Material of History
and Technique of Ideology
ILYA KALININ
337

"We Have Turned into Wild Beasts.
Why Are We Here?": Russians, Assyrians and Kurds in
Northern Persia during World War I
DAVID GAUNT
349

Kropotkin on Violence:
Memoirs of a Revolutionist
KARIN GRELZ
363

Taking Over Gallows Hill
ANDREAS GEDIN
371

V

Bringing back space to the historiography of Russia
KARL SCHLÖGEL
375

Stalin's Two Bodies?
A Socio-Political Dimension
KIRILL POSTOUTENKO
381

«Следующей почтой вышлю все».
Переписка советских сотрудниц секретариата
Международной Демократической Федерации
Женщин с «Москвой» в первые послевоенные десятилетия
YULIA GRADSKOVA
401

Politics and Talk:
the Final Debate in the 2018 Swedish Elections
JAAKKO TURUNEN & INGA BRANDELL
417

Reforms, Guns, and Soft Power
– Reflections on Russian Military Thinking
GUDRUN PERSSON
431

Exchanging Trade for Recognition.
A Russian Mission to Sweden
HELENE CARLBÄCK
447

The Return of the Clerk,
the Sovietologist and the Eccentric
– Irina Sandomirskaja as a mirror
of Swedish–Russian Expertise
JOHAN ÖBERG
463

Irina Sandomirskaja:
A Bibliography
473

Foreword

This book is a celebration. To celebrate means to praise, but in its oldest Latin sense it referred to gathering in great numbers to mark an occasion. It is a book that praises the many innovative aspects of Irina Sandomirskaja's contributions to a variety of fields in the humanities and Slavic studies, in particular through the numerous colleagues who mirror the impact of her work in their own research and thought. As such, this celebration is also an expression of academic gratitude and a gesture of friendship.

Irina Sandomirskaja, who we are celebrating here, has extensively advanced the field of cultural studies. Departing from Russian linguistics and the relation between language and its ideological functions, her work has focused on developing a theoretical framework from within the complexity of a contemporary history that has been deeply marked and wounded by wars, totalitarian governments, the violent destruction of social boundaries, the appropriation of memories and hope, and the confiscation of the life of things. Developing a theory from within reality is not the same as superimposing already existing ideas and perspectives upon cultural and historical phenomena. On the contrary, as is apparent from the way in which Irina Sandomirskaja deals with fields and disciplines ranging from grammatical theory, the sociology of language, ethnology, poetical analysis, film studies, the history of science, stylistics and rhetoric, to critical theory, poststructuralist analysis and feministic criticism, it involves a continuous process of innovation generated by her meticulous reading of the book of reality and the deciphering of its complex language and grammar.

What the many humanistic disciplines treated in her work build is not a "transdisciplinary" framework, but rather a continuous migration process in which the different languages of theory speak with each other in order to listen more attentively to the plural language of things. Irina Sandomirskaja's academic production can be read as a response to a historical demand formulated by the poet Anna Akhmatova: "And who would have believed that I was fated to live so long and why didn't I know it? My memory has become unbelievably sensitive. I'm surrounded by the past and it is demanding something from me. But what? The dear shades of the distant past are practically talking to me."[1]

Irina Sandomirskaja's intellectual trajectory follows her life trajectory. After her dissertation entitled *Emotivnye glagoly so znacheniem povedeniia* (*Emotive Verbs Denoting Behavior*), defended in 1991 at the Department of

Theoretical Linguistics of the Soviet Academy of Sciences, she co-authored a work with the anthropologist Natalia Kozlova about contemporary Soviet language based on a study of the "naïve" writings of a self-taught Russian woman in the 1970s and 1980s. In 1992 she made her first visit to Sweden together with a group of Russian women artists. Two years later she was invited by professor Fiona Björling to the Department of Slavic Languages at Lund University as a guest researcher. In 1996–97 she was a research fellow at the Swedish Collegium for Advanced Studies in the Social Sciences, and in 1997–98 a guest researcher at the Department of Slavic Languages at Uppsala University. In 1998 Irina Sandomirskaja came to Södertörn University, first in the research program called "Cultures in Dialogue" and later as a contributor to the development of the Baltic and East European Graduate School and the Center for Baltic and East European Studies, where since 2003 she has held the position of Professor of Cultural Studies. The wide scope of her theoretical approach is evident from her scholarly works and contributions to different research projects and programs such as "Time, Memory and Representation" and her own new research project "Transnational Art and Heritage Transfer and the Formation of Value: Objects, Agents, and Institutions", as well as the numerous articles listed in the Selected Bibliography included in the present volume. Among her most remarkable contributions, two monographs deserve special mention. The first one is *Kniga o rodine: opyt analiza diskursivnykh praktik* (*The Book about the Fatherland: An Analysis of Discursive Practices*) from 2001, in which the Motherland/Fatherland complex is analyzed both synchronically as a kind of discursive mechanism and diachronically in an archaeological reconstruction of the particular history of Russian phraseology initiated in the early nineteenth century by the Slavophile linguist Shishkov. The second is the very original book entitled *Blokada v slove: ocherki kriticheskoi teorii i biopolitiki iazyka* (*Besiegement in Language: Essays in the Critical Theory and Biopolitics of Language*) from 2013. This book-length essay begins with the culturo-linguistic archaeology of the story of the Pygmalion-like deafblind Soviet therapist and educator Olga Skorokhodova. On the basis of her life, Irina Sandomirskaja reads the complex relation between motherland and language under the Soviet regime; this opening discussion is followed by substantial essays on Walter Benjamin's *Moscow Diary*, on Lidiya Ginzburg's works in besieged Leningrad, on poetry during the Terror of the 1930s and 1940s, and on Stalin's language policies. The aim of this study is not a cultural or historical synthesis of ideas but rather an attempt to superpose fragments of a recent past in which ideas are replaced by biopolitics. In 2013 the book was awarded the prestigious Andrei Belyi Prize as the year's best work in the Russian humanities.

Irina Sandomirskaja has been very influential not only in Swedish and Scandinavian Slavic studies and in the humanities in Russia, but also internationally as a guest lecturer in different countries and at academic institutions such as Princeton University. By opening new paths of reading, analysis and listening to the complex language of things and the recent past, her work has had an impact on various areas of research.

Her influence on questions of language and poetry, totalitarianism and the Cold War, the politics of memory and reflections on history and time, as well as on Bakthinian studies, is reflected in the present volume, which has been supplemented with articles of a more artistic nature that have also taken inspiration from her work. All of this confirms the way in which Irina Sandomirskaja develops what Walter Benjamin, following Goethe, called "tender empiricism"—theory generated by a sensitivity toward the presence of memory and history in words, bodies, things.

We wish to express our gratitude to the Center for Baltic and East European Studies (CBEES) at Södertörn University for funding the volume, and to Charles Rougle for his excellent work with editing and translation.

Lars Kleberg, Tora Lane, Marcia Sá Cavalcante Schuback
May, 2019

---

[1] Anna Akhmatova, *My Half-Century. Selected Prose*, trans. Ronald Meyer (Ann Arbor: Ardis Publishers), 1992, 15.

I

Besieged by the Future

EGLĖ RINDZEVIČIŪTĖ

> [...] the purpose of theory is to yield generalizations, objectivity, and reproducibility of knowledge. None of these qualities would be expected in autobiographical writing, which is often necessarily sketchy and elliptic, produced as it is from the subjective, deeply individual, and traumatized perspective of a survivor.[1]

Blue, red, and green colors are flashing at me through the window of my room. Against the milky dark sky of Moscow, projectors light up the sides of high rises that were built on Novyi Arbat by Nikita Khrushchev in a style imitating the modern architecture of Havana. I am musing over this coloristic play from a guesthouse of the Lithuanian Embassy to the Russian Federation. The color display is about the only fun I am having here. My room is freezing. The guesthouse was built in a decorative style in the 1960s, when it was used to house delegates and visitors to the capital of the Soviet Union from the Soviet Socialist Republic of Lithuania. After the collapse of the USSR, the building was handed over to the Lithuanian government and continues to perform a similar function, sheltering a motley crew of artists, intellectuals, and any other embassy guests. Both the furniture and bedding in my room clearly date back to the Soviet period. The window frames, however, are new and plastic, but the double glazing has failed. It is minus 16 C outside. Inside, I roll up a woollen jumper and use it to put under my head instead of the stone cold and heavy feather pillow. Every morning I do a few press-ups on the tatty thin carpet covering the floor, wolf down a plate of cooked buckwheat with grated carrots and a boiled egg on the side, wash this nutritious breakfast down with a cup of a strong, black coffee in a self-service cafeteria downstairs, pack my essentials—notebooks, a laptop, maps, my passport and wallet—into my bag, and exit into the cold wind blowing down the street. The cold can be escaped underground, where I am wrapped in streams of warm air carrying that inimitable and unforgettable smell of the Moscow Metro. Researching the Soviet past, it seems, is an exercise in virtuous self-constraint, a self-constraint that is but one element of a larger process, a history that is still being written. For the ascetic lifestyle in the Soviet context is "a stigma, a badge of honor indicating power; not merely a necessary reaction to political and economic conditions, but a prestigious habitus cultivated by the elite of the cultural bureaucracy".[2] To suffer cold and to exercise is to be complacent. Next time I will book a very well-heated and comfortable room in a Russian B&B.

There are many methodological handbooks containing detailed advice on how to organize research fieldwork in different areas of the world. Should a young historian choose to go to Russia, a plethora of American university websites are there to help, listing useful archives and providing advice on how best to secure access to them and how to organize one's life when away. And then there are the increasingly many memoirs of Russianists who have gone there to study this fascinating country. In his recollections, Loren Graham, the foremost historian of Russian science and technology, describes jogging in Gorky Park in winter and being (possibly) followed by his minder. Sheila Fitzpatrick, the leading cultural and social historian of the Soviet period, detailed her battles with her own anxiety but also the KGB's attempts to frame her while she was doing fieldwork.[3] Despite Russia's nearly three centuries of modernization, doing research there still has an aura of adventure and probing the boundaries. Each time I go to Moscow I recall the writings of Walter Benjamin in the early twentieth century, who was overwhelmed by the coexistence of a brutal and inhumane system and the overflow of colorful and diverse goods that mediate the turbulent urban life of the city. There is an odd magnetism to Russia. In Moscow, according to Irina Sandomirskaja, the writing of Western modernity can "complete itself" by entering a condition of translatability where knowledge and expression acquire a new mode of existence.[4]

The problem with the past, whether translatable or not, is that, strictly speaking, it is incredibly difficult to tell where it starts and where it ends. How can I write history, if I am not a historian? How can I tell when my interviewees are telling me useful stuff and when it is irrelevant? How to ask them the right questions? Questions like these continued to come up in consultations with Irina Sandomirskaja, who supervised my dissertation work in 2003–2008. The most helpful advice that I got was strikingly simple: history is going to be what you are going to write. Just listen to what people are telling you. I read piles of treatises on historiography, attended a course on qualitative social science methods at the Essex Summer School in Colchester, UK, an expensive trip that was generously funded by the Baltic Sea Foundation, where I absorbed a whole range of qualitative interviewing techniques. However, what has made perhaps the deepest impression on me is the simple maxim to listen to what people are saying with their words, bodies and behavior. Writing a history is not a mere analytical exercise in the cognitive analysis of data, but also the responsibility not to let the moments of the past disappear undocumented. I am still unsure if I have become a proper historian, but I have certainly become a collector of elements of the Soviet past that were overlooked or discarded by mainstream narratives. For example, I traced the unexpected contribution to science of those few enlightened Soviet systems scholars who put forward what looked like scientifically neutral cybernetic theories of self-regulation, the complexity and coevolution of mankind and the global biosphere. These were intellectual shards of liberal thinking which did not fit with the dualistic image of an authoritarian regime, an image arranged around the opposition between repression and dissidence. However, I sought to show that these contributions shone brightly once they were dusted off and reinterpreted in their own context. With hindsight, I would also like to add, in the context of the concerns that surrounded me in the process of my own writing.

For writing is preservation. After all, as I recall Hayden White stating provocatively in a seminar in Stockholm, there is no such thing as the past: the materials with which a historian works are always part of the present. History is about the reconfiguration of what is an eternal now—presently accessible records, stories, and images. However, there is a different sense of responsibility that comes together with "history writing". Generating theory is tinkering, designing a tool to help explain the observed data. Scientific theories must not only make sense, they must work. Planes must fly. Cars should be able to take sharp corners. Should a theoretical instrument not work, it can be discarded. Histories are similar in a way: they too must make sense and explain how we got to where we are. But histories also stick—they are stories that people refuse to abandon even if they are demonstrably wrong.

Researching and writing about the Soviet past is an intellectually challenging and emotionally charged exercise. The archival documents are there, but accessing them requires a concerted physical effort, for you must keep your own individual biophysical system of intelligence running optimally as you navigate the stressful everyday realities of the Russian metropolis. The archivists do not owe me anything—I am a foreigner. My interviewees do not owe me anything. Everything that I am told, handed or shown is a gift of sharing.

A study of the Soviet past can be approached as an exercise in empathy that must plot the ways in which individuals are caught up in systems of meaning that transcend their own personal experiences. I often return to the problem of the idiom as theorized by Sandomirskaja in her *A Book on the Motherland*.[5] The idiom is a package of meaning that cannot be disassembled. It can only be reused, time and again, instantiating a particular semiotic reality in new contexts. Idioms may not make sense, strictly speaking, but they work in practice. Idioms are performative. A fieldwork researcher, therefore, faces the difficult task of sorting the material into idiomatic and non-idiomatic—which black boxes can be opened and fruitfully analyzed and which can be better observed from the outside by tracing the effects they have on people, practices and institutions. Researching the Soviet past is an emotive navigation among the idiomatic cavities in the system of meanings.

Language is playful, artificial, assembled from inscriptions, shapes and forms. As it is being lived, language entangles us with institutions every time we attempt to express and communicate our experience to others or ourselves. Sandomirskaja's work shows clearly that there is no existence outside language, but this semiotic prison is incredibly rich in existential possibilities. Language can accommodate and reinforce emergent power; it can shape and constrain, but then it also protects the weak and the invisible. For example, the *babushka*—a Russian woman of a certain age, who, just like history, does not have a clear line demarcating just where she starts and where she ends. As Sandomirskaja notes, *babushki* are expelled to the margins of gendered and classed society, but nevertheless they do not hesitate to enact their power both in their families and in the public space. *Babushki* will speak and they will make sure that they are heard.[6]

One of the principal problems discussed in Sandomirskaja's work is how social types and objects acquire durable identities and are able to assume agency in hostile environments. Her recent work analyzes the survival of another relic of an undesired past—religious art in communist Russia. She details the conceptual, material and institutional assembly that enabled the emergence of the Russian icon as a collectible piece of art and a tourist commodity. The icon is a very fragile object—egg-based paint is carefully applied on slippery wood covered with varnish that will inevitably darken and crack. Thus new icons are created to age, it is anticipated that their surface will darken and crack. Fragile as they are, they tie together the communist revolution, Russian nationalism, the imperative of a political economy of value that has become increasingly international, and a striving for beauty that cannot be evacuated regardless of circumstances.[7] Collection can become a material extension of one's feeling of being alive, of assembling the past into the present.[8] For instance, all that has reached me from my great-grandparents are a few golden coins with the image of Tsar Nicholas, a legacy from when Lithuania belonged to the Russian Empire. However, their value for my family had to do with neither monetary nor aesthetic worth, but size. Unlike houses, furniture or pictures, coins could become part of my family heritage, as they were small enough to hide, to carry and to hand down to the next generation as they battled the waves of displacement and repression following the Second World War. But family stories are one thing; no less important is the very simple and undisguisable beauty of a golden coin, its incredible luminosity, so similar to the tempera colors on icons.

Neuroscientists argue that the perception of beauty activates a small and mysterious part of the brain that is hypothetically regarded as being in charge of self-reflection—the highest level of neural integration that makes planning for the future and engagement in collective behavior possible. Is it a utopian wish to salvage from the ruins of the brutal Soviet past the intellectual resources that enable beauty, social cooperation and future-making? I am convinced that this is absolutely not the case. Quite the opposite, there is much to be learned from gazing into the darkest abyss of the Soviet regime and excavating the social, cultural and intellectual resources that enable maintaining order and securing survival in the context of tragedy and disorder.

In what follows, I engage with some of the themes that have been developed in Sandomirskaja's work on liminal and catastrophic cases to show the ways in which this kind of analysis can guide an understanding of the present social condition that is defined as the Anthropocene, the age in which mankind has become a geological, planetary force that appears to drive the global biosphere toward a new form of organization under which human survival is no longer guaranteed.[9]

First of all, we live in a time when language appears to have reached its limit to orient humans in this new kind of emerging world. There is a genuine lack of discursive means to think adequately about the planetary human condition in the context of the very real risk of global climate change. Many scientists are dismissed as alarmist, because their danger scenarios are partial and hypothetical, but also because these scenarios are situated in the future as possibilities and do not engage the existential mode of human being in what I call a pre-global climate change condition.

However, I propose that we can begin to articulate this pre-global climate change condition through Sandomirskaja's analysis of social organization and existence in besieged Leningrad during World War II. In our case, mankind is besieged by the future. There is a lot to be gained by thinking of the contemporary mode of being and coping as expressions of managing a blockade and of an emergent dystrophy of the social. To be sure, not everything that Sandomirskaja has observed in her analysis of the strategies and tactics of survival and dying in besieged Leningrad can be mapped onto the present concerns. However, there are several significant elements that could serve as points of entry for analyzing the ongoing inaction, disengagement and failure to recognize the gravity of the current situation.

One obstacle that the pre-climate change imagination struggles to deal with is an inability to think of humans today in relation to "the historical experience and memory of the human being, finite, finalizable, and unpowerful".[10] The world population has never before been as rich and as safe. However, if approached as besieged by the future, this wealth and security emerge as fragile qualities, and the horizon of their endurance is rapidly shrinking. During the Leningrad blockade, "life itself was rationed". In this borderline existential situation, "normal", everyday language practice appears to break down: an understanding of the experience of starvation in dead, frozen, besieged Leningrad is not complete without an understanding of the betrayal of the very status of Leningrad's population as a mere relic of human biomass, a biomass that needed to be fed and was slowly dying away, stuck in the midst of war. A similar betrayal of the outside world is described in Sandomirskaja's study of the sensations and cognition of deaf and blind children, who experience the surrounding world as treacherous, changing without warning and ultimately isolating.[11] In both cases, however, language powerfully bounces back, for it is a part of a survival strategy that helps the subject in the moment. However, the question remains whether this strategy is viable in the long term.

Pre-climate change society fails to recognize its nonentity status, a condition that will not become clear until it is too late, when the climate has changed beyond our ability to adapwt. For Lidiya Ginzburg, the survivor of the Leningrad siege discussed by Sandomirskaja, the nonentity of the individual human resulted from the blockade and the catastrophe of starvation and death. For computer modelers of the global climate since the 1980s, the individual human was tragically complicated by the absence of a regulatory, homeostatic mediator between the collective outcomes of individual behavior and the increasingly volatile and chaotic, potentially catastrophic future to which these collective outcomes were leading. The inability to articulate the climate-change future in language and translate it into sensorial perception makes governance of the future impossible. Besieged by long-term and global-scale change, like Leningrad cut off from the political economy, language breaks down when it is tasked to reconcile, bridge and make sense of how the individual relates to the collective and how both relate to the extremely remote and large-scale biophysical future.

In the context of global climate change, the whole world population is Leningrad. It is besieged by the catastrophic future. Its citizens are confident in their society as a meaningful form of association. However, there is a risk that the current social condition is becoming tautological: "Tautology is circular like the siege itself: it produces no added value of meaning, no progress in time; it blocks judgment and suspends communication".[12] For a person outside decision-making and outside the market, global climate change is precisely such a tautology—every move produces a CO2 imprint, judgments about everyday matters just do not add up, and communication becomes circular. Global mankind is already a population,[13] but how, as Timothy Morton asks, can this be converted back into ethical citizenship?[14]

One feature of society in besieged Leningrad was that "relationships" between human subjects became "connections" that were necessary to maintain key functional components of bare existence: what remained was "a skeleton of ordinary or forced strategic interactions. Once they had stiffened and lost their suppleness, these connections caused painful suffering, for they were painful reminders of dead relationships".[15] How do individuals survive in such a stripped-down social life? They do it by working, using work as routine, automatic action that fundamentally lacks any point and direction outside itself: "work (without any purpose) fills in life in the same way that water fills the tissues of a dystrophic body suffering from nutritional dropsy".[16] Drawing on Lidiya Ginzburg, Sandomirskaja continues: work "occupies thoughts, attention, and time; it distracts from painful thoughts, blocks and drives anxiety inward, 'calms and refreshes'; its smoothness compensates for lost wholeness".[17] In turn, the besieged individual has a particular kind of fear, "the fear of having to confront something that is not part of the absolutely needed and routinely implemented, not included on the list of the nearest tasks of immediate survival, something that occurs out of schedule and pattern and thus threatens to break through the armor of accustomed indifference to death-on-schedule".[18] From the perspective of the global climate-change future, society begins to reorganize itself like a body experiencing starvation: people can become "unneeded persons", like the cells of an organism that could just as well be sacrificed for the dystrophic biosphere. Thus, social teleology in such bio-dystrophy is governed by the fear of any effort that would transcend minimum needs.

Sandomirskaja mobilizes these powerful metaphors to rethink the political as it emerges in the siege of Leningrad. In the world besieged by the future, a post-truth politics emerges as a dystrophy of meaning systems in which content slips away. Similar to a starved organism, language starved of teleology leads to confusion. It becomes unclear whether the observed smoothness of a body is edema or muscle mass and, in turn, it is difficult to evaluate at first glance whether or not a catchy statement or glossy meme has any relation to empirical reality. Survival in besieged Leningrad, however, essentially depended on bureaucratization and calculation, planning. Similarly, the survival of humanity depends on putting an Earth system-governance framework in place and basing it on predictive models and an assessment of everyday activities in terms of CO2 load.

However, is there a place for intellectual engagement in a context of siege, where survival becomes the sole preoccupation of power and knowledge and bare existence? "The *intelligent* has a mission of creating critical knowledge, thinking in an ethically accountable way, and acting toward a democratic equality and social justice".[19] But this notion of the *intelligent* is also processual—the *intelligent* is something that could unfold, a position that evolves, is expressed, and is then disassembled. The global systems scholars I studied mostly did not try to be critical. They tried to create knowledge that would "work", speed up calculations, improve production processes, forecast the weather, simulate interaction between humans and the environment. The models, data and theories emerging from the desire to make science and technology work could and did become critical in some contexts. Democratic equality remained difficult to digest for decision scientists, who were concerned with formalized ways of reconciling different parameters—the different needs of individuals and social groups, even states. Indeed, a striving for equality led to the idea of abolishing all deliberative decisions whatsoever by establishing a principle of taboo and the creation of informational and material milieus to guide complex social behavior, as in Nikita Moiseev's writings on the noosphere.[20] The *intelligent*, it appears, cannot scale up to the global level. However, there remains some hope that in a world besieged by the future, ethical choices can still be made:

> Postupok—an ethical act that is based on choice and transcends the economy of reaction with its motivation in bare need—is valuable notwithstanding its motives and compromises. It would be boasted, censured, and lied about, but it would also be remembered and cited—and that means the time of the siege, even though violated by the manipulative politics of memory, would be restored as time, not as a whirlpool of tautologies: "In the abyss of lost time—time regained".[21]

But will this be enough to solve the tangle of today's insufficient measures taken to decarbonize society? Can ethics alone save us from the ominous pre-future, what Irina Sandomirskaja describes as "bad infinity"? Bad infinity is a "circle representing the totalizing structure inherent in all of its manifestations".[22]

There is a lot to be learned from the besiegement story about time and loss and key elements of the grammar of a catastrophe. It is a good critical device. There is little, however, to be learned from the repertoire of individual survival techniques. Elements of the human biomass in besieged Leningrad survived thanks in part to bureaucracy, in part to their own very individual physiology, but also to their own psychological choices. These techniques can hardly be scaled up for societies and global survival. When the world is besieged by the future, there are no bombings announcing the siege, and flows of food are not disrupted, but if it is viewed from the future, our social organization is already displaying signs of dystrophy.

Nevertheless, drawing on Ginzburg, Sandomirskaja suggests that writing about "bad infinity" is a political act. This kind of writing is particularly important because under dystrophic "normalcy" in besieged Leningrad the "norm" referred to the pre-war period, the times of terror. In a besieged situation, "normal" does not equal "viable".[23] This obscures ethical decisions and undermines any long-term orientation. A particular type of history emerges that is based on the metonymy of "lesser evils" with which societies or individuals will struggle until they exhaust themselves and wither away. The lesser evil is a metonymy of the greater evil with which a dystrophic subject refuses to engage. Sandomirskaja refers to Ginzburg's observation that "the absolute evil of today is replaced by historically meaningful, already experienced evil".[24]

The long-term future is always "machine-translated" because it is only available through carefully calibrated and sorted computer models. The future vision is a machine vision, one that blends the human and the technological. According to Richard Staley, mechanistic—or mechanic—philosophy emerges as part of the modern preoccupation with linking physics and society, most visibly in the aesthetic and philosophical articulations of the machine and the city, where people as individuals appear in tension with functionalist, robotic actors and structures, all integrated in a single systemic flow.[25] However, the modern metaphor of the machine is no longer helpful when modern society is a city under siege, beleaguered by the unpredictable future. Ginzburg's Leningrad is better than Lang's *Metropolis* as an articulation of humanity facing global climate change. If, as Staley shows, Einstein used examples involving machine systems to explain the principles of his theory of relativity, machine systems do not appear to explain anything when the world is on the brink of catastrophe. Similar is the case with market mechanisms, which were perceived as liberating from the patriarchal system of exchange that fixed the individual's role in society and the economy. The market disappears under the conditions of biopolitics in a time of catastrophe, when bare existence is rationed according to the residual value of economic usefulness but also biological viability.[26]

Machines that were meant to help people to grope in the dark fail and do not return any meaningful signals.[27] One of the reasons why planning for climate change is impossible is that the baseline for models of global circulation and ecological systems will change in an unpredictable way, as will the value of painstakingly assembled variables. There is no way to glimpse into this long term and complex future even with the help of computer simulations. The time is out of joint when we try to confront an illegible future. First, we cannot rely on our principal senses such as sight and hearing that are fundamentally required to create, distribute and internalize symbolic systems of meanings through which we could address our situation. At the turn of the twenty-first century, humanity is deaf and blind. Like the population of besieged Leningrad, the current world population under siege by the illegible future is a messy biomass, a biomass that is beginning to understand that it risks becoming a prehistory of a future catastrophe. Our normative teleologies are unsettled and there is no consensus on what technological means should be used to guide human macro-actors to a desirable future.

Society besieged by the future is best explored and understood not by physics and mechanics, but by the disciplines of physiology and defectology, which study the reactions of decoupled biosystems that are undergoing catastrophic stress.[28] This does not mean, however, that these approaches will offer solutions:

> [...] tactility thus gives an instantaneous contact with the outside world as it is—but it fails to work, as vision and hearing do, towards the generalization of the world that is achieved through the classifying function of verbal representation, written or oral. Nor does tactility presuppose the reproducibility of the world thus contacted.[29]

In the worst-case scenario, the future will come through "impressions"—not through anticipation and a handy correspondence to generalized schemes, but as an avalanche of material sensations that will no longer make sense and will render existing technologies of coping obsolete.

Pieter Brueghel the Elder's dramatic painting *The Blind Leading the Blind* (1568) is one of the best-known images of blindness as a condition that misguides individuals and leads them to peril. However, this trope of blindness must be reviewed, and blindness should be rehabilitated as a condition that offers new intellectual resources. These resources could be used to cope with highly complex situations in the context of which our existing sensorial and cognitive apparatuses are severely insufficient. There is a strong cultural barrier to achieving this, though: "Sightlessness and voicelessness are age-old metaphors, through the prism of which seeing and speaking people imagine political repression".[30] Besieged by the future, mankind is deaf and blind at the moment. However, defectology, pedagogy for deaf-blind children, could provide a rich source of new language, metaphors and forms of understanding. Moreover, engagement with the condition of siege and deaf-blindness could offer a repertoire of existential positions. As Irina Sandomirskaja summarizes a Kharkiv theorist of deaf-blind language, Ivan Sokolianskii, there is "an implicit biopolitics, a technological understanding of life as obedient to a 'grammar' of human actions as these actions are preserved in objects and their names".[31] When the outside is unreadable, the inner life develops great intensity and becomes incredibly vivid.[32] The human, as outlined by Sandomirskaja, can be "deaf, blind, speechless, blockaded in the isolation of her 'defect', alienated from the symbolic reality—and writing". However, there is no doubt that in these ruins language will be excavated, assembled and used to build up a new existence, however unrecognizable it may be.

[1] Irina Sandomirskaia, "A Politeia in Besiegement: Lidiia Ginzburg on the Siege of Leningrad as a Political Paradigm", *Slavic Review* (2010), 306.
[2] Irina Sandomirskaia, *Blokada v slove: ocherki kriticheskoi teorii i biopolitiki iazyka* (Moscow: NLO, 2013), 77.
[3] Loren Graham, *Moscow Stories* (Indiana University Press, 2006), 188–93; Sheila Fitzpatrick, *A Spy in the Archives: A Memoir of Cold War Russia* (London: I.B.Tauris, 2013).
[4] Sandomirskaia, *Blokada v slove*, 61–65.
[5] Irina Sandomirskaia, *Kniga o rodine: opyt analiza diskursivnykh praktik* (Vienna: Wiener Slawistischer Almanach, 2001).
[6] Irina Sandomirskaja, "Babusjkan som sådan och som kulturpolitik", *En bok om böcker och bibliotek: tillägnad Louise Brunes* (Huddinge: Södertörns högskola, 2009), 193–99.
[7] Irina Sandomirskaia, "Catastrophe, Restoration, and *Kunstwollen*: Igor Grabar, Cultural Heritage, and Soviet Reuses of the Past", *Ab Imperio: Theory and History of Nationalities and Nationalism in the post-Soviet Realm* 2 (2015): 339–62.
[8] Ibid.
[9] Paul Crutzen, "Geology of Mankind", *Nature* 415 (2002), 23; Nikita Moiseev, *Chelovek i noosfera* (Man and the Noosphere) (Moscow: Molodaia gvardiia, 1990).
[10] Irina Sandomirskaia, "Bakhtin in Bits and Pieces: Poetic Scholarship, Exilic Theory, and a Close Reading of Disaster", *Slavic and East European Journal* 61, 2 (2017): 297.
[11] Sandomirskaia, *Blokada v slove*, 13–43.
[12] Sandomirskaia, "A Politeia", 310.
[13] Sandomirskaia, "A Politeia", 311.
[14] Timothy Morton, *Hyperobjects: Philosophy and Ecology after the End of the World* (Minnesota: Minnesota University Press, 2013).
[15] Sandomirskaia, *Blokada v slove*, 186.
[16] Sandomirskaia, *Blokada v slove*, 201.
[17] Sandomirskaia, *Blokada v slove*, 201.
[18] Sandomirskaia, "A Politeia", 316.
[19] Sandomirskaia, "A Politeia", 309.
[20] Egle Rindzeviciute, "Soviet Policy Sciences and Earth System Governmentality", *Modern Intellectual History* (2018): 1–30.
[21] Sandomirskaia, "A Politeia", 325.
[22] Sandomirskaia, "A Politeia", 325.
[23] Sandomirskaia, *Blokada v slove*, 233.
[24] Sandomirskaia, *Blokada v slove*, 219.
[25] Richard Staley, "The Interwar Period as a Machine Age: Mechanics, the Machine, Mechanisms, and the Market in Discourse", *Science in Context*, 31, 3 (2018), 274, 278–79.
[26] Staley, "The Interwar Period", 280 and onward.
[27] Donella Meadows, ed., *Groping in the Dark. The First Decade of Global Modelling* (London:Wiley, 1982).
[28] Stefanos Geroulanos and Todd Meyers, *The Human Body in the Age of Catastrophe: Brittleness, Integration, Science and the Great War* (Chicago: The University of Chicago Press, 2018).
[29] Sandomirskaia, "Skin to Skin", 330.

[30] Irina Sandomirskaia, "Skin to skin: language in the Soviet education of deaf–blind children, the 1920s and 1930s", *Studies in East European Thought* 60 (2008), 322.
[31] Sandomirskaia, "Skin to Skin", 330.
[32] Sandomirskaia, "Skin to Skin", 330.

Better Red than Dead
– Remembering Cold War Sweden

JOHAN HEGARDT

Introduction

During a conference lunch at Södertörn University, Irina is talking with Irena Grudzinska-Gross about life in Poland during the Soviet era. All of a sudden, Irina concludes that the protests against the regime in Poland and other East European countries could be understood as the politics of fun, which suggests that life was boring. The latest trend in the Swedish film industry is to picture Sweden during the 1970s. I think that the filmmakers have got it all wrong. Life in Sweden during the Cold War was extremely dull and boring, and not fun at all. It therefore seems to me that nostalgia in general is based on a boring past rather than on a glorious past.

Remembering

Remembering, memory, and memory studies are not an easy theme. In "Entre mémoire et historie: La problématique des lieux de mémoire", Pierre Nora explains a few for this essay important things.[1] He writes that as soon as there are traces, distance and agency, we do not exist anymore in true memory but in history. This also implies, according to Nora, that history and memory are opposites. We carry memories, but we construct history. He also underscores that our need for memories is at the same time a need for history. I would stress that what I am about to explore is on the one hand my personal need to remember, but at the same time I am probably also constructing history. What is interesting here is Nora's focus on the archive and his long discussion about the need to collect everything in archives. For me to be able to remember I need the archive—not to remember, but to make sure that I am remembering and not making things up. Nora explains that because of the politics of memory, everyone has become an historian, and the turn from the history of memory to the politics of memory has multiplied the number of private memories each demanding its own history. This suggests that we no longer talk about origins. Instead we talk about lineage or heritage. What Nora expresses in his text is a critical study of what we today understand as heritage and memory, often used in political discourse and critically examined in heritage and memory studies. I understand that I am on my way into a field that is not at all unproblematic, an issue touched upon by Aleida Assmann in "Kollektives Gedächtnis und kulturelle Identität".[2] In her essay, Assmann argues against those that have criticized memory studies. Nevertheless, as far as I can see, she has problems taking memory studies beyond what Nora describes above. I would like to suggest that this multiplication of private memories is the foundation for identity politics. What the problem tends to be, from my horizon at least, is that memory is always connected with identity and lineage and therefore with identity and heritage politics.

In his essay "Between Worlds", Edward Said strongly argued against identity politics and nationalism:

> Identity as such is as boring a subject as one can imagine. Nothing seems less interesting than the narcissistic self-study that today passes in many places for identity politics, or ethnic studies, or affirmations of roots, cultural pride, drum-beating nationalism, and so on. We have to defend peoples and identities threatened with extinction or subordinated because they are considered inferior, but that is very different from aggrandizing a past invented for present reasons.[3]

On the other hand, Assmann can clearly show that memories are important, for they exist as personal or collective memories—people, groups, organizations, authorities and even governments talk about what has once happened, not as something in a historical past, but as something engaging in the present.

It is in the walls

There is an expression in Swedish "Det sitter i väggarna"—literally "it sits in the walls". What exists in the walls is a ghost from earlier days, a tradition unknown to the present but still there. The walls hold on to a memory that haunts the present and forces, for example the staff at a museum, to repeat what their predecessors had done before them.

We often say that if only the walls of an old house or the old trees in the forest could talk, they would tell us stories about the past. The trees, like the walls, carry secret memories of the past within them. The same goes for old objects—if they only could talk.

We could argue that such stories can also be found in society. I would like to suggest that the Cold War is present in Swedish society, but it is hidden, like the memories we believe are concealed in old trees, old objects and old houses—it is "in the walls". Remembering Cold War Sweden is not a memory project, however, because I am not attempting to unfold memories that must be unfolded for different reasons. What I am aiming at is to understand the effect that the Soviet Union had on Sweden through my own, mostly banal, memories from the time. These recollections are not important to me or my identity. They are not traumatic, nor have I been under any form of oppression, but they do exist and they do point in certain directions. In a broader sense, no memories are important, yet they are significant nevertheless. So the direction I will take is to explore such unimportant important memories.

Introducing the Foreign Minister

Two months before the fall of the Iron Curtain in 1989, Swedish Foreign Minister Sten Andersson declared that the Baltic States were not and had never been occupied by the Soviets. This statement had its roots in a 1947 declaration by the Swedish government that Sweden would accept the Soviet annexation of the Baltic States. Sweden did this contrary to international laws and conventions. The question "why" is of course central, but I have not been able to find a clear explanation. Instead there exist many different reasons for these politics.[4] One is Sweden's desire to be neutral. I accept that, because the will to be neutral would shape Swedish policies toward not only the Soviet Union until its fall in 1989, but also Swedish society and the everyday life of its citizens.

After the fall of the Iron Curtain, international research has, broadly speaking, focused on two things: Soviet oppression in the Baltic States, East Europe and, of course in Russia, and the post-Soviet period in these same countries. It goes without saying that this focus is incontestable and deeply needed. But I think it is time that we also focus on the western parts of Europe. The way of life, politics, culture in any form, and so on, were affected by the very existence of the Soviet Union. It had a grip on our minds and being that went beyond more apparent things such as the threat of a nuclear war, official political debates and so forth. We lived in a bizarre shadow of the Soviet Union. The Soviet Union was there, and could maybe perhaps or even probably be described as the uncanny other, a strange image in the mirror affecting our minds and bodies, without us being able to more explicitly describe its impact. We could always condemn it, try to understand it, embrace it or even glorify it, but at the end of the day, it slipped out of our hands but was still there as something on the side, in the corner of our eye, a strange image in the mirror, or the uncanny other.

Family stories

I have no memory of the 1962 Cuba crisis, but it affected me indirectly as a small child. When a university student in the mid-1950s, my father spent a year in the United States, where he and an American veteran of the Korean War became close friends. When the crisis began my father's friend and his wife were convinced that Sweden would come under heavy pressure from the Soviets and concluded that they must help my father and his family. According to our family story, they went so far as to arrange a house for us and a job for my father.

The first memory

In the beginning of the 1970s, my family and I travelled from New Delhi to Moscow. We flew with Aeroflot, the Soviet airline, on our way home to Sweden from the Indian capital, where my father was stationed as the head of SIDA, the Swedish International Development Agency. Having already had some experience of flying, it was strange to be onboard an Aeroflot flight. Everything was similar but at the same time different from airlines I had flown on before, such as SAS (Scandinavian Airlines), Air France, Air India, British Airways or even PIA (Pakistan International Airlines), where the captain always ended his talk to us onboard with the word *Inshallah*.

Upon our arrival, we ventured out into the city and soon found what we already knew: the lack of food and consumer goods. The most shocking experience for a 12-year old boy like me, who had been raised in a liberal family and spent some time in American schools, however, was the Lenin Mausoleum, although not Lenin himself or the absurdity of having his dead body on display. I still remember waiting outside and watching the soldiers parade in front of the building, and I remember even more clearly entering it and going down some stairs together with my father. When I whispered something to him, a solider standing in the shadows shouted at me. Although I didn't know a word of Russian, it was clear that I was not supposed to speak in the building. When we stood on Red Square after the visit I asked my father who was making the most noise, the soldier or me? My father looked at me and said: "The soldier, but that's not the point".

The scar

On my left leg, from my buttock down to my knee, there is a broad scar. The Cold War indirectly put it on my body. It is from my time in the military, where every young man was forced to serve. There were only four options: do it with arms, do it without arms, go to jail, or be declared psychologically unfit, which many thought was the best option.

Objects

I have tried to remember any everyday object that was directly connected with the Cold War and that therefore would not have existed were it not for the Cold War, but I have not been able to find any. On the other hand, many things that we used might indirectly have had something to do with it.

Here I recall a strange object: the can opener. Everyone had one, and they were very functional. But during the 70s a new and fancy opener turned up on the market. You could fasten it on the wall or use it by hand. The point was that all you needed to do was to fasten the can on it and turn a handle. It was very difficult to use compared to the small one, but you could find it in most homes. It was a stupid technical innovation, because the little opener worked perfectly. What this new gadget might have stressed was that the West was much more technically advanced than the Soviet Union, but I would not be surprised if the same item existed there as well.

And there was that special beer bottle called Rigello, a plastic container and paper sleeve that was supposed to be biodegradable and would disappear by itself if it was thrown away in the forest. What at least I did was to collect the caps and create meandering lines by putting them together.

I'm probably wrong, but I believe that the purpose of many objects developed for the market during the 1970s, for example, was to mark a technical distance to the Soviet Union. Things should be made in America or at least have some fresh technological American aura.

Arriving home

Flying around the world was always an interesting experience, especially when I returned to Sweden. Sweden joined the EU in 1995, but before that the country was rather closed, and during the Cold War its borders were strictly monitored. I recall two emotional memories: one, the freshness of the SAS airliners and the positive, clean, almost pure solitude of Swedish society, and two, the exact opposite of this positive privateness, the stone-faced customs officials and boring, almost gray Swedish society. A beautiful sunny summer day could all of a sudden become completely gray even if the weather had not changed.

Hopeless discussions

Drunk, or getting drunk, mostly from beer in Rigello bottles, we could go on and on discussing communism and the Soviet Union. Such discussions always ended with the comment, "but what about the US!?" Today this is called "whataboutism".

East European trips

In 1980, during the turbulence around Solidarność—the independent self-governing trade union "Solidarity"— movement, I travelled to Poland and other East European countries together with my girlfriend at the time, who was deeply interested in the fate of the East European Jews. There was an obvious political difference between these countries which caught my attention. In Poland, for example, exchanging money on the black market was no problem, but it was rather pointless because there was nothing to buy. In Hungary there were western-style discos, and exchanging money on the black market was also pointless, not because there was nothing to buy, but because there was hardly any difference between the official exchange rate and what you got on the black market. The atmosphere was also very relaxed in Hungary compared to the atmosphere in Czechoslovakia, where police with Kalashnikovs patrolled the train stations and it was even dangerous to exchange money on the black market. Scared of being caught, we were tricked and lost our money to the black-marketeers.

Taking a stand

In 1990, a friend of mine and I took part in a small demonstration outside the Russian Embassy in Stockholm against Russian aggression in Estonia prior to the country's independence in 1991.

The banality of remembrance

I agree that my examples above are banal or even insignificant compared with the stories told by those who experienced the oppression. They are probably not even fully and correctly described, but they would not have existed were it not for the Soviet Union, and that is my point.

I do not believe that such memories are unique to me. Is there such a thing as what Maurice Halbwachs calls a collective memory? Multiplied, in any case, such recollections form a pattern throughout a society that is now gone but once existed in a very strange in-between situated amid a sort of depressing gloominess and brightly lit sunshine, emotions that are not facts or metaphors, but a consequence of something in the corner of our eye—a strange image in the mirror, a border, a dream, and at the same time a reality, a situation impossible to grasp; a secret, a trembling and frightened society, which Sweden was during the years of the Cold War. The key concept in Swedish politics during these days was accordingly "trygghet". Translating the word "trygghet" into English is a bit tricky, but "freedom from danger" might be pretty close. Freedom from danger meant restrictions on one's freedom, which is connected with Sweden's neutrality. In this case, neutrality means to be "the border", and strangely enough, it is the border between the metaphors of "gloominess" and "brightness", the USSR and the USA, both feared because of their lack of "trygghet" – freedom from danger! And as I recall in one of my memories, returning to Sweden was always a paradox between the bright and the gray, but at the same time it was a return to a world outside the world, a world framed away from the world, an in-between world, if that is possible, which is the regime of freedom from danger. This regime was thus a consequence of the Soviet Union. "Freedom from danger" can also be described as what Nina Witoszek calls the state of being "gratefully oppressed".[5] Were we during the Cold War in such need of freedom from danger that we gratefully accepted being oppressed? Perhaps, because freedom from danger does have a price, as do all forms of freedom. This statement needs an explanation or an answer to the question of what oppression implies. In what way were we oppressed? We were gratefully oppressed by the ideology or the regime of freedom from danger. It all had to do with the negotiated price we paid to be free from danger, which means that we put our Being in the hands of the State and sold our soul to boredom.

Better Red than Dead

The first part of my title reads "Better Red than Dead" (in Swedish, "Hellre röd än död"). This statement could be found written on walls in Stockholm during the 1970s and 1980s. What it implies is obvious: it is better to be dominated by the Soviet Union than to be killed in a nuclear war. How is it possible that people could take such a stand at the same time as people on the other side of the Iron Curtain were being killed, not by a nuclear war, but by the Soviet regime? The statement is actually a comment on another standpoint that also flourished – "Better Dead than Red". What this implies is an extremely polarized society in which one part is "better dead than red" and another is "better red than dead". These two viewpoints are of course based on two political positions, left and right, one pacifistic and one militaristic. The polarization can, however, be interpreted as something very national and without any clear reference to the Soviet Union as such. What it suggests is a conflict inside the society between people drawn to leftist politics and those drawn to more right-wing, center-right or even Social-democratic politics. Left-wing views could of course not be discarded, if only because of the reality of the Soviet Union. They certainly could exist on their own regardless of the country, but many left-wing politicians and voters embraced or even glorified the Soviet Union. Many on the center-right, the Social Democrats, and, of course, those farther to the right rejected all left-wing politics due to the simple fact that the Soviet Union existed.

What I want to point to here, however, is not what people thought, but the divide that resulted from the uncanniness and incomprehensibility that the Soviet Union generated. It is this uncertainty that creates bizarre statements such as "better dead than red" or "better red than dead", which in turn gives rise to hopeless "whataboutism".

Suicide

I remember that we used to say that during the Cold War Sweden had the highest suicide rate in the world. To check my memories, I contacted *The National Centre for Suicide Research and Prevention of Mental Ill-Health*. They directed me to an article published by Radio Sweden. Here I discovered that it was actually the American president Dwight Eisenhower who created this myth, which came to be more or less accepted. According to the article, Eisenhower stated that "'sin, nudity, drunkenness and suicide' in Sweden were due to welfare policy excess." This would prove to be "fake news". Sweden did have many suicides during the Cold War, but when compared with other countries that compiled accurate statistics, Sweden was among the average nations. But in 1980, the suicide rate in Sweden was twice as high as it is 2018.[6] This still implies that Sweden during the time of "freedom from danger" had a higher rate of suicides compared to the years that followed the Cold War, which is an interesting paradox.

I was radicalized by the Beatles

In the late 1960s, I was a young boy living in a very posh yet rather liberal suburb not far from Stockholm. In this context the 1968 movement had a special impact. It was something going on at a distance, but I believe it also involved some threat to people in my community. Without understanding it, of course, we kids saw it as some sort of fresh freedom opportunity. Inspired by the Beatles, we boys let our hair grow. This was not seen as something deeply problematic, but it did have its impact on the older generation of grandparents, and in some cases also on parents, when, for example our hair grew so long that it started to cover our eyes. The year 1968 is a very strange one for many reasons. I was too young to have any memories beyond my long hair and the feeling of freedom. The year includes a paradox, namely the aspect of freedom. My eight-year old person could feel this possibility, but freedom from what? As I understand it today, it was about freedom from the "freedom from danger". So many things happened in 1968, which makes it a very strange time. Let me mention a few examples. Martin Luther King was shot dead. In Mexico hundreds of people were killed while demonstrating. In Paris, Stockholm, Warsaw and Prague people demonstrated. The Soviet war machine invaded Czechoslovakia. What was it all about? There is no core answer to the question. In Paris and Stockholm, university students demonstrated against the political system, as did university students in Prague and Warsaw. I grew long hair. Could it be so simple that the whole issue was about freedom from "the freedom from danger", a freedom that had a price everywhere in the world, but mostly in the post-World War II welfare society, a society that was not only under construction in the West, but was also being built in the East? Were the political systems on both sides of the Iron Curtain creating societies that oppressed their people in the name of "trygghet", the freedom from danger? Based on my memories, at least, the price paid was boredom. The freedom-from-danger-society was boring. Is this an overly simplistic explanation? Maybe. But did the seventies not also come with the politics of fun?[7] The hippie movement, the discos—was this not a question of having fun? And to be able to have fun we must free ourselves from the oppressing political power of the "freedom from danger". When I lived in India during the 70s, I wanted to become a hippie as I grew up, because it looked like they had fun and were free. I did not become a hippie, because after a while I started to despise them. Here they were in India, dressed in rags, using drugs and actually exploiting the country and its people for their own personal needs and desires, people who were dressed in clean clothes, working hard and many times living under awful conditions. The hippie movement, or rather the Western hippies in India, were an insult to the Indian people, I soon concluded. This memory is still very strong. Nevertheless, 1968 and what followed could still be understood as a reaction against the regime of "freedom from danger" and its social and political consequences, or at least it can be remembered as such.

Different views, different memories

I stated above that we could always condemn the Soviet Union, try to understand it, embrace it or even glorify it, but at the end of the day it would slip out of our hands yet remain there as something on the side, in the corner of our eye, a strange image in the mirror or the uncanny other.

What this might imply is that we are talking about different memories and therefore about different "epistemic communities", based on the notion of "episteme" that Foucault employs to explain systems of thought. Today the term "epistemic communities" is often used in political and social science to refer to a group of professionals who think in a similar manner. In my case, epistemic communities might explain the everyday Swede's understanding of the Soviet Union. As mentioned above, the Soviet Union could not be understood as a core phenomenon by anyone. Instead, different perceptions emerged. Each such understanding might be described as an epistemic community that disseminated information throughout the society. Remember the so-called "Kremlologists", observers who tried to figure out what was going on in the Kremlin? To be able to orientate themselves in such a situation, and, given the position of Swedish neutrality, the Swedish people had to build epistemic communities in which they could find some sort of common and collective meaning. But, as I have stated, at the end of the day the chosen episteme would probably not have much meaning. That is not the point in this case, however. The point is that Swedes like myself needed an orientation in circumstances that were impossible to understand, and each of us found ourselves attached to an epistemic community that was based on a common and collective explanation and understanding of the situation during the Cold War. One example is what I discussed above: so-called "whataboutism". Throwing the question or even the statement "whatabout!" at one's opponent indicates the existence of different epistemic standpoints. This could mean that remembering Cold War Sweden is today based on which "episteme" one found understandable. This suggests memories leading in many different directions, which might imply that the whole issue of remembering Cold War Sweden actually is a question of identity.

Conclusion

I must again underscore that what I have discussed above are reflections. It is not a trauma. It has nothing to do with violence. It is rather the opposite—freedom from danger. Maybe it all has to do with the memory of safety, the idea of a world free from all forms of danger. Maybe the project had a similar agenda in the West and in the East. In the East, freedom from danger led to oppression. In the West, freedom from danger led to depression.

In a society that is free from danger, the politics of freedom from danger is obsolete. The fall of the Wall and the end of the Cold War was according Fukuyama the End of History, but as we have seen today, that was not the case.[8] Should we maybe instead understand the end of the Cold War and the fall of the Wall as the end of the politics and regime of freedom from danger, in both the East and the West?

The question points to the present. "It's a dangerous world", President Trump has stated. The question is who makes it dangerous, and if it is dangerous, to whom. To males, according to Trump. Probably not. Is it time to return to the politics and regime of freedom from danger, or should we maybe instead invent a new global strategy – the politics of fun – that frees us all from danger? The answer to the question lies beyond my memories.

[1] Swedish translation by Anna Petronella Foultier and published in *Mellan minne och glömska: studier i det kulturella minnets förvandlingar,* Johan Redin and Hans Ruin, eds. (Göteborg: Daidalos, 2016), 77–111.

[2] Swedish translation by Peter Handberg and published in *Mellan minne och glömska: studier i det kulturella minnets förvandlingar,* Johan Redin and Hans Ruin, eds. (Göteborg: Daidalos, 2016), 121–44.

[3] Edward Said, "Between Worlds", *Reflections of Exile: & Other Literary & Cultural Essays* (London: Granta, 2012), 567.

[4] http://palwrange.blogspot.com/2011/12/var-de-baltiska-staterna-ockuperade.html, accessed January 5 2019.

[5] Nina Witoszek, "Moral Community and the Crisis of the Enlightenment: Sweden and Germany in the 1920s and 1930s" in Nina Witoszek and Lars Trägårdh, eds., *Culture and Crisis: The Case of Germany and Sweden* (New York & Oxford: Berghahn Books, 2002), 68

[6] https://sverigesradio.se/sida/artikel.aspx?programid=2054&artikel=5924063, accessed November 28 2018

[7] Thank you, Irina, for always finding theses brilliant twists on things.

[8] Francis Fukuyama, *The End of History and the Last Man* (Harmondsworth: Penguin, 1992).

As if a Town
Wandering with W. G. Sebald in Terezín[1]

MARYAM ADJAM

The window frames of the Hotel Memorial are fringed with bird nests. The carefully assembled lumps of clay hug the windows overlooking the square. Traffic is dense. Back and forth flit the swallows in Terezín. Spring is over and summer is on the way. Hungry little beaks gape wide, constantly clamoring for more. On the replastered façade, cream-colored as decreed by current fashion, over the carved baroque reliefs, there are also traces of nests that have been torn down. The battle with the swallows in sleepy summertime Terezín goes on.[2]

"It was probably three years ago. They'd invaded the fortress. You couldn't get through the gate. There were hundreds of them," she says, shaking her head and smiling meekly. She who guides us through the Small Fortress's labyrinth of cells, passages, parade grounds and execution sites. Anxious bird eyes stare from the walls of the cells, following the intruders. The swallows swish by warningly above the pipes in the deserted prison bathhouse. While we sense the walls. Look at our reflections in the mirrors.[3]

*

In between façade and town stands Terezín. In between the dead and the living. In between the sensed and the hangman's gaze. In between parody and tragedy. Terezín a mockery. Terezín a shrine. In between despair and clarity.

> … amazingly, you've got Mr Hamáček selling kohlrabi on a slaughter ground, Mrs Bouchal and Mrs Fridrich searing at their permanently jammed laundry press on the very same spot where trains use to leave to the extermination camps in the East. When you were kids, you played in morgues and felt each other up in bunkers![4]

Terezín shrugs its shoulders at sermonizing, shows off its daily life, its continued life. Should we begrudge it its life? Should we blame the children who take a dip in the river? Does the river remember its history?

Is it possible to dance again? Dance where others have danced on a tightrope before.

*

For three days and nights the testimonies filled my hours; the faces, voices, lingering, thoughtful. They filled my dreams. A symphony of voices, of testimonies, with no chronology, as Claude Lanzmann has defined *Shoah*, his documentary on the Holocaust. Nevertheless, he breaks off abruptly when the hangman gets lost and wanders off. The drums can be heard beating time to the march, evenly, hard, resolutely. "Mr Suchomel, we're not discussing you, only Treblinka. You are a very important eyewitness and you can explain what Treblinka was."[5]

The boundaries of Lanzmann's furious sense of justice are luminous. Resolutely, he points out a former camp guard, a village population elusive in its anti-Semitism, a church the former site of a mass murder and a Mass. He stubbornly badgers his way to admissions: we saw, we knew, we thought it was in its order.

Walking in Terezín, Lanzmann's drums beat in my head. His hand pointing in the direction of the signs. The crematorium, to the west. Near the river. Follow the cement stairs in the overgrown forest. They will take you. They will take you all the way down to the river. Follow, see, sense. Whole wagonloads of ashes through the forest, down to the river.

*

In the interstice Terezín dances on a tightrope. In between guilt and memory Terezín stands. In between fortress and town. Every door on either side neatly displays its duality. The explanations are in fine print. Blend into the walls.

To the left: "Cavalier no. VI[6] was built between 1782–87. It is part of the inner defense perimeter, which consists of the bastion, the cavalry barracks and the administration building. The artillery workshops and laboratories were located within the Cavalier complex."

To the right: "The Ústí barracks. The main storehouse for clothes and confiscated goods."

Remnants of a fortress. Traces of a camp.

To the left. A triumph of the wars, labyrinths of trenches, cavalry barracks, bastions, for those who armor themselves against a siege. A World Heritage Site, to be preserved.

To the right. A well-organized death's abode. A citadel of guilt that stands naked, stripped of all time and space, just a number and a nickname: "I—VI Útí Barracks." For those who are to be stripped naked, whose names shall be confiscated. A memory condemned to fade away.

A fortress that flaunts cavalries, a town that worships oblivion. "An experience that has taken possession of the entire space",[7] but is scraped away nonetheless, repainted. A space that dreams itself away to the broad horizons of inexperience.[8]

In Terezín there is no escaping the layers, which dry and crackle, are constantly visible beneath the plaster. The Hotel Memorial turns out to have been the SS headquarters. For days we look desperately for proof. Hoping that it will turn out to be another house, another street. The fact remains: we lie sleepless in our beds. While the dead continue to dance on a tightrope. In our beds we lie and breathe to the beat of the hangman's dreams. On top of the plaster life goes on.

*

> A person was very lucky to be an animal assigned to this menagerie, but only a few people managed to stay in the fortress town.... That town too had its circus; there too one had to walk a tightrope without a safety net and jump over high hurdles.[9]

The fortress town, the writer Jiří Weil calls Terezín. Neither town nor fortress. Both town and fortress. Lucky were those stripped naked if they could come to this menagerie. To be looked at without being seen. With the abyss without safety net yawning under the tightrope. In a menagerie the town cannot be without its fortress. Not without its ramparts against the gazes. In a menagerie the fortress cannot be without its spectacle, its town with its daily life.

Searching for the memory of a mother and awaiting a Terezín that he doesn't yet know exists, the writer W. G. Sebald's protagonist Austerlitz also finds himself, in a menagerie of the night, the Nocturama. Of the "denizens" there he remembers their "strikingly large eyes and fixed, inquiring gaze."[10]

> The only animal which has remained lingering in my memory is the raccoon. I watched it for a long time as it sat beside a little stream with a serious expression on its face, washing the same piece of apple over and over again, as if it hoped that all this washing, which went far beyond any reasonable thoroughness, would help it escape the unreal world in which it had arrived, so to speak, through no fault of its own.[11]

The gaze has turned. The observed observes. Walks a tightrope and observes the spectator. In between fortress and town, the gaze is the only companion.

Gazes behind ramparts awaiting the besiegement. Gazes toward the spectacle of the menagerie. And the unaverted gaze of the observed.[12] Austerlitz continues to search:

> From whatever viewpoint I tried to form a picture of the complex I could make out no architectural plan, for its projections and indentations kept shifting, so far exceeding my comprehension that in the end I found myself unable to connect it with anything shaped by human civilization, or even with the silent relics of our early history and prehistory.[13]

Another fortress, another camp, Breendonk. The trees sway on the horizon. The grass embraces the concrete and the barbed wire. Covers. Swallows. Hides. In the Breendonk fortress it is easy to get lost. In space. In time. In the façade.

Oversized photographs in black and white (raised on giant frames in the middle of the lawn and field of view) take you by the hand, lead you back to the has-been, to the no-longer, behind the green façade. They show you "The Site": See the meadow, nothing but a pit. Bent backs; carrying, breaking, chopping. The guard, standing above the pit, nearest the sky, smiles into the camera. Here is where you should sit and look. Here is where you shall find memory.[14] Wanderings of memory, mute bulges in this façade, this fortress of greenery.

To Breendonk Austerlitz sends a second self. Through the fortress the Narrator wanders. Just as Agáta, Austerlitz's mother, wandered in a Prague she did not recognize, before she was deported to Terezín. Just as Austerlitz wanders in memory and in Agáta's footsteps. Blind, he seeks to see. In the fortress he finds fortifications that besiege the landscape with their geometry and their naming. In between the concrete and the grass, the fortress names and fortifies: "escarpe and courtine, faussebraie, réduit and glacis."[15] Just as the inner logic of a camp names and fortifies its pseudo-technical order.[16] "Barackenbestandteillager, Zusatzkostenberechnungsschein, Bagatellreparatur©werkstätte, Reinlichkeitsreihenuntersuchung."[17] Syllable by syllable Austerlitz unravels the words. Step by step he gets lost in the fortress of total order. In the fortress he finds a fortress. Carefully guarding the memory it does not remember.

Does a fortress eradicate all memory within? All history? Doesn't it raze everything to the ground in order to dig its moats and flaunt its ingenious labyrinths? Suspending the time, erasing the space, beginning anew.

What does Terezín remember?

*

Another evening at the pub in Terezín. He, the guide to be, the one with no memory, still remembering everything, offers to take us by the hand and lead us through the darkness of the labyrinth. He who has heard our ridiculous broodings about a fortress, about the loss of the grounds, sits now laughing over a beer. He will lead us up. It is not far to the heavens in Terezín.

In the innermost corner of the attic, he points authoritatively. Engravings. The evidence, the testimony: Walls covered with scribbles and drawings. Of distant dreams. Windmills. Bridges. Of the blue sky above a bereft city. Of the gallows. Of an empty bed and a guard's pointing finger. Strictly relegated to a past, specifically dated, with a defined origin. 3/II 1944. Hollanda.[18]

"The Site." Carefully it prophesies and responds to all doubt. Meticulously it sows the seeds of doubt. Of course Terezín remembers.

About the village razed to the ground by the fortress, the village on whose remnants the foundation was laid, he can also tell us, this Virgil of ours. Beyond the forest it had to move, making room for the fortress. About those who left the village and later the fortress town, over and over, meekly, habitually. About a fortress that became a town, and a fortress once again. About a war like any other. The military, the god of the city, has commanded. Who knows what stars they wear on their shoulders. Which helmets, which uniform, what sound the order makes as it echoes among the walls of the houses. It echoes and must be obeyed. That is what Terezín answers. That is how Terezín dances on a tightrope between town and fortress.

He tells stories, over and over. He cannot tell enough. Wouldn't we like to take a tour of the labyrinth, in the tunnels beneath the fortress?[19]

*

> I know a little tiny town
> A city just so neat
> I call it not by name
> But call the town As-if...
>
> And there they live their lives
> As if a life to live
> Enjoying every rumor
> As if the truth it were[20]

As if a town.[21] As if a truth. In between façade and town, we wander. In between town and fortress. In between the testimony and the memory.[22] Blindly we grope, but there is no way out to find. For the deception, is this very search for an answer.

To "the camouflaged town", Terezín, Austerlitz travels deaf-blind. For it is he who can become visible to the dead "in certain lights," he who not even under this journey can imagine "who or what" he is:[23]

> It does not seem to me, Austerlitz added, that we understand the laws governing the return of the past, but I feel more and more as if time did not exist at all, only various spaces interlocking according to the rules of a higher form of stereometry, between which the living and the dead can move back and forth as they like, and the longer I think about it the more it seems to me that we who are still alive are unreal in the eyes of the dead, that only occasionally, in certain lights and atmospheric conditions, do we appear in their field of vision.[24]

The unaverted gaze stares in the interstice between a fortress and a town. Austerlitz searches, sees, and yet doesn't see. He is the one who knows that he doesn't see, "whether because I really did not want to see what it had to show or because all the outlines seemed to merge in a world illuminated only by a few dim electric bulbs …"[25] Austerlitz is the one who borrows the gaze and lends his own. Allows Agáta, his mother, to guide him, while he guides the Narrator.

To the mute bulges of Breendonk he sends the Narrator to search blindly, looking for a memory that doesn't belong to him. To Terezín, this monument to the seeing that looks blindly on, he himself travels blindfolded. He stares at things "as if one of them or their relationship with each other must provide an unequivocal answer…"[26]

Austerlitz searches for the time, the place, history, those stripped naked and the memory. "In certain lights" he finds momentary paths chosen by chance through the interlocking spaces, he finds an illusion of the dead, and he finds the memory. He senses the everyday banality of memory, feels each relief, every hollow, feels the irregularities. And he continues to search. No salvation within reach. Neither in Terezín does Austerlitz find "who or what" he is.

Memory: the spectacle that takes you by the hand, guides you in the right direction, this has happened, here is the witness.

Memory: an unaverted gaze, a wandering "beyond any reasonable thoroughness," a single desire, to escape.[27]

Between memory and the memory of memory Austerlitz wanders.[28] A shift in memory beyond seeing, beyond the search for a "who or what."

Memory a wandering in the fort akin to a wandering in Prague decades earlier, akin to wanderings that shall come in other fortresses, other camps. Memory's history is its wandering in labyrinths. It is only in between the spectacle and the gaze of a tightrope walker that memory can wander. Interweaving its delicate silk threads into a landscape of its own.[29]

Terezín is the symbiosis, the fortress town. But it is in the shift between fortress and town, between façade and town, between the illusion and the disillusion, between the spectacle and the unaverted gaze of those being watched that its memories wander. Without taking note of our desperate search for "what or who" we are. Terezín stands between the replastered façade, the monument, the streets, the labyrinths and the forest.

*

Into the forest we go. Surrounded. Chasms of vegetation on one side. Horses graze in the moats. The roads into this fortress arch over the pasture, offering the horses an escape from the light. Two by two, closely, closely, they stand under the arch. Look patiently and slightly bored at the camera lens targeting them.

Into the light we go. Above us a roof of trees. A carpet beneath our feet: walnuts, chestnuts, cherries. It is harvest time. The river flows on the other side. Bordered with poppies, stairs lead down to the river. The way out of the fortress. Overgrown, reconquered by the forest.

*

Out of the forest we go. The fortress left behind beyond a forest of oblivion. The gravel road goes to the village in the distance. Wide-spreading fields on one side. And the river on the other. Rising in between the fields and the forest left behind, embedded in the trees, camouflaged by their crowns, is the tower. The watchtower, warning: you are passing the border. When we have stared long enough at the tower, when we have heard its warning bells ring, the border rises out of the greenery. On the plowed edge of the field, in the cool shade of the forest, still standing are the concrete pillars. The carefully measured gaps between them yawn empty, yearning for their barbed wire. The border is crossed, and we return into the forest.

[1] Located outside Prague among ramparts overgrown with vegetation lies the fortress town Terezín, a World Heritage Site and a former concentration camp (Theresienstadt). This essay is a reflection on how history and memory emerge in and through the town. Although Terezín was not a formal concentration camp, due to the system of "self-administration", in reality it functioned as a camp. For this state of in-betweenness see further: Hans Günther Adler, *Theresienstadt 1941–1945: The Face of a Coerced Community*, trans. Belinda Cooper. (New York: Cambridge University Press, 2017). The essay's title "As if a Town" refers to Leo Strauss' description of Terezín in the song "Als-ob", written for a cabaret staged in the camp in 1942.

[2] Based on field notes, Terezín, June 7, 2014.

[3] Based on field notes from a guided tour through the Small Fortress, Terezín, June 8, 2014. The Small Fortress is part of Terezín's fortifications, located next to the town.

[4] Jáchym Topol, *The Devil's Workshop*, trans. Alex Zucker (London: Portobello Books, 2013), 38–39.

[5] Claude Lanzmann, *Shoah* (New Yorker Films, 1985), Part 2.

[6] I.e., the cavalry barracks; M.A. The information on the signs at the site is in Czech, English and German. The quotes in this text have been retranslated and are some what modified from the English version at the site.

[7] Anders Olsson, "Irrandets melankoli och Jägaren Gracchus (W.G. Sebald/Franz Kafka)," in *Ordens asyl – En inledning till den moderna exillitteraturen* (Stockholm: Albert Bonniers förlag, 2011), 181.

[8] For how memories of the Holocaust emerge in the everyday life of the former sites of mass murder and how they are represented see further: Barbara Törnquist-Plewa, "Tale of Szydlowiec. Memory and Oblivion in a Former Shtetl in Poland," in *The Holocaust in Post-War Battlefields. Genocide as Historical Culture*, Klas-Göran Karlsson and Ulf Zander, eds. (Lund: Sekel bokförlag, 2006), and Barbara Törnquist-Plewa, "The Use and Non-use of the Holocaust Memory in Poland" in *Painful Pasts and Useful Memories: Remembering and Forgetting in Europe*, Barbara Törnquist-Plewa and Niklas Bernsand, eds. (Lund: Center for European Studies at Lund University, 2012) 11–27.

[9] Jiří Weil, *Life with a Star*, trans. Rita Klímová with Roslyn Schloss (Evanston, Ill: Northwestern University Press,1989), 115. The Czech writer Jiří Weil was called to be deported to the Theresienstadt concentration camp (Terezín) in 1942, but he went into hiding. In his novel *Life with a Star* he portrays an existence under siege, deprived of a name, as walking a tightrope.

[10] W. G. Sebald, *Austerlitz*, trans. Anthea Bell (New York: The Modern Library, 2001), 2–3.

[11] Sebald, *Austerlitz*, 2.

[12] The gaze here concerns not only the visibility or invisibility of the victim, but rather refers to the multiple illusions of visibility that Theresienstadt as a camp produced, and which continue to be produced through the gap between the embodiment of the memories of the victims in the place and the town's continuous production of visibility as representation. For illusions of visibility and visibility as an illusion see further: Irina Sandomirskaja, "Welcome to Panorama Theresienstadt – Cinematography and Destruction in the Town Called 'As if' (Reading H. G. Adler)," *Ghetto Films and their Afterlife. Special double Issue of Apparatus: Film, Media and Digital Cultures in Central and Eastern Europe*, 2–3 (2016), DOI: http:/dx.doi.org/10.17892/app.2016.0002-3.48.

[13] Sebald, *Austerlitz*, 25–26.
[14] Based on memos and notes of a virtual tour via the net in Fort Breendonk, April 2014. The tour is part of the activities of the National Memorial Fort Breendonk and offers a visit to the indicated preserved parts of the fortress through 360º photographs of the place. "National Memorial Fort Breendonk", last modified March 11, 2019, http://www.breendonk.be/EN/Virtual/pano_travaux_forces/index.html
[15] Sebald, *Austerlitz*, 18.
[16] Patrick Lennon, "In the Weaver's Web: An Intertextual Approach to W. G. Sebald and Laurence Sterne," in *W.G. Sebald. History, Memory, Trauma*, Scott Denham and Mark McCulloch, eds. (Berlin: Walter de Gruyter, 2006), 100.
[17] Sebald, *Austerlitz*, 330.
[18] Field notes and photographs from a visit to an attic in an apartment building in Terezín, June 9, 2014.
[19] Field notes on a conversation with Lukas, June 8–9, 2014, Terezín.
[20] Leo Strauss (1887–1944), musician and librettist deported to Theresienstad in 1942, wrote the song "Als-Ob", "As-if", as part of a cabaret staged in Theresienstadt. The song illustrates the apparatus of deception the Nazis staged in Terezín, "the town As-if". An apparatus that not only maintained an illusion of ordinariness and everyday life in the camp, but also made use of visibility as the very means of deception through Nazi propaganda films. (See further Sandomirskaja "Welcome to Panorama Theresienstadt") Leo Strauss was later deported to and murdered in Auschwitz. For the full lyrics of "Als-ob" see: Památník Terezín, *Art Against Death. Permanent Exhibitions of the Terezin Memorial in the Former Magdeburg Barracks*, (Prague: Pub. House Helena Osvaldová for the Terezín Museum, 2006), 215.
[21] On the notion of deception in Theresienstadt/Terezín, and life in the town as an "Als-Ob"-existence and how it is reflected in Leo Strauss' song, see further: Peter Jelavich, "Cabaret in Concentration Camp", in *Theatre and War, 1933–1945: Performance in Extremis*, ed. Michael Balfour, (New York, Oxford: Berghahn Books, 2001), 151–160.
[22] In "Welcome to Panorama Theresienstadt" Irina Sandomirskaja (2016) argues that As-if, "Als-ob," captures the essence of the Holocaust and the Nazi terror through "producing visibility – an Als Ob- of social community under terror and for the sake of making the terror more efficient." Theresienstadt was not only an apparatus of illusion, a "town as if", but was also made visible by the Nazis through staging life, producing a second apparatus of illusion, the illusion of vision, thereby undermining the concept of testimony and reality as such.
[23] Sebald, *Austerlitz*, 261.
[24] Sebald, *Austerlitz*, 261.
[25] Sebald, *Austerlitz*, 30.
[26] Sebald, *Austerlitz*, 274–275.
[27] Sebald, *Austerlitz*, 3.
[28] In Terezín memory emerges through its movement in the interstices. A "shimmering go-between' or between-movement of several different betweens" as Marcia Sá Cavalcante Schuback defines it. (Marcia Sá Cavalcante Schuback, "Memory in Exile", in: *Research in phenomenology* 47 (2017), p. 186.) A poetics of the in-betweens that captures the movement between different layers of memory in the town.

[29] David Darby ("Landscapes of Memory: Sebald's Redemption of History", in *W.G. Sebald – History-Memory-Trauma*, Scott Denham and Mark McCulloh, eds. (Berlin: Walter de Gruyter, 2006), 265–277) argues that it is this network of interwoven stories, memory fragments and history that constitutes Sebald's landscape, which in the final analysis is contingent upon the narrator's voice and the paths he chooses to take (Darby, 2006. 275). I would rather argue that the landscape that emerges through Sebald's compositions is in fact memory as such, its unpredictable and conceivable paths, its interweaving of these threads of chance into wandering without any clear destination or end. See further on the relation between memory, history and landscape in Sebald's works: Anne Fuchs and J. J. Long, eds., *W. G. Sebald and the Writing of History* (Würzburg: Verlag Königshausen & Neumann GmbH, 2007).

In the Cold Cities
– Poetics of Self and Memory as Traumatic Continuity in Gennady Gor's Siege Texts

POLINA BARSKOVA

My essay examines the idea of construed Jewishness as a continuity of poetics in the pre-WWII prose and Leningrad Siege poetry of Gennady (Gdaly) Gor—one of the most striking, difficult and, I would go as far as to say, mysterious authors produced by the Siege of Leningrad (1941–44).

The question of the Jewish author and the Siege is a difficult one. On the one hand, many of the Siege creative notables were ethnically Jewish: e.g., Lidiya Ginzburg, Vera Inber, Pavel Zaltsman in literature, Solomon Yudovin, Yakov Rubanchik, Anatoly Kaplan in visual art. For various reasons, however, they chose to ignore or downplay their origins in their Siege work (or in most of their writing in general—which would be the case of the perhaps most brilliant analyst of the Siege, Lidiya Ginzburg, for whom her ethnicity seems to have been a possibly even more problematic, tabooed subject than her sexuality—she was queer). My question, when approaching the task of these notes, was whether there were authors who managed to find a place for contemplating their Jewish identity in their creative output on the Siege? Or even to find ways to connect these two topics—Jewishness and the Siege?

One author who ultimately came to mind was Gennady Gor, perhaps the most "unofficial" of all the Siege poets: Gor didn't publish a single word of his Siege poetry during his lifetime, thereby creating a situation of a radically negative *intended* readership. Consequently, the fact that among all the Siege authors' works, one finds residual traces of Jewish identity self-writing in Gor's poetry allows us to suggest that contemplating Jewishness during the Siege was a topic that was not sought after by those in ideological power and was thus relegated to the non-publishable (непубликабельный) realm of creative work.

There are several scholars today (e.g., Vladimir Piankevich, Nikita Lomagin, Daria Starikashkina, to name a few) who study the "Jewish question" during the Siege—their findings mostly concern the predictable ris0e of anti-Semitism in the troubled city. The most evident and discussed example is the diary of Liubov' Shaporina (also, there is the not yet fully published Siege diary of Olga Freidenberg, who, at the beginning of her Siege notes makes the common mistake of guessing that Nazi forces would bring to the city, if conquered, all the power of the "great German culture"). Yet again—when we seek examples of the creative representations of Jewishness—we find that these are scarce, which makes us devote special attention to Gor's uneasy case.

Gennady (Gdaly) Gor was born in the Chita prison (his parents had been arrested for their political activity), spent his childhood in the Baikal area in and around the town of Barguzin, and in the 1920s he arrived in Leningrad to shape his adventurous yet not untypical—for that time and place—literary biography. His career began rather tumultuously during the one of the most eventful and productive periods of Leningrad literature history—the 1920s-1930s, when many literary schools and trends coexisted, one of which—OBERIU (The Real Art Union)—was the most radical constellation of writers interested in experiments with language. Gor was strongly attracted to OBERIU and its leaders (Daniil Kharms, Doivber Levin).

In the 1920–30s Gor writes experimental prose, trying on many stylistic hats. Some of them bring him success among his peers, some—punishment from the ideological "elders". For his novel *The Cow* he is ousted from Leningrad University on the ubiquitous accusation of "formalism".

Around this time he creates the memoir "В городке Студеном" (In the Cold City, 1936) about his Jewish childhood in the Baikal region in Siberia (near the shtetl of Barguzin) that is full of rare (mostly natural) beauty and rare, radical violence that he attempts to estrange with his innovative, expressive language. In this fictionalized memoir Gor describes an episode from his childhood, which he spent among Jewish relatives who passed him from one household to another and at the Jewish Zionist school (understandably, Gor would never return to his Zionist upbringing later in his Soviet life).

The style of this prose is markedly connected with the emerging Jewish expressionism in early Soviet writing. Gor writes under the influence, or rather a variety of influences, sometimes *like* Daniil Kharms, sometimes *like* Isaak Babel.

Leningrad's influential poet and critic Olga Berggolts, who later would become the official voice of Siege poetry, reacts to Gor's stylistic experimentation with a cheeky epigram:

> Я прошу не обижаться,
> Гору дам совет любя:
> Чем под Бабеля стараться, –
> Лучше делать под себя!..) (1926)

Please do not take this / too personally, dear Gor: / rather than imitating Babel, / try to write something of your own!

In his article about Jewish expressionism in Leningrad avante-garde prose of the 1930s, Valerii Dymshits[1] argues that there were several young writers in Leningrad at the time who attempted to connect these two areas of influence, OBERIU and Babel—Ber Levin, Zal'tsman and Gor himself, who combined Jewish thematics and expressionism in a style that reflected OBERIUs formal quest for estrangement.

In his memoir (in contemporary terms I would assess it as creative non-fiction) "In the Cold City" (1936) Gor creates a unique, isolated world of the "cold," isolated Siberian city where nature and culture, or rather nature and tradition, enter into a form of difficult interaction, or even a competition and a clash:

> Мы спускались. Налево бежали пригородные деревья, скакали болота, обрубки, пни. Направо дымились отбросы, объедки, обноски, простиралась падаль.

We walked down. The trees of suburbia ran to the left, along with marshes and stumps of trees. And there to the right there were smoking piles of garbage, food scraps, old clothing, all kinds of carrion.

Gor constantly creates juxtapositions between the natural world and the urban world, in which the urban incorporates his perception of things Jewish: tradition, business, education, family connections. The dynamics of the relationships between these worlds form the main crux of the poetics and politics of this text. Yet another crucial component of how Gor depicts his Jewish upbringing in Siberia is violence. Violence is all-pervasive here, it erupts suddenly and touches everybody:

> Лицо у него было злое. Когда он говорил с тобой, ему хотелось ударить тебя, наплевать тебе в лицо.
>
> - Мою милую собаку, - спросил Оська у ребят, - вы хотите посмотреть?
> - Хотим! Хотим! - закричали все.
> - Может, кто-нибудь из вас согласится ее пристрелить.

His face was angry. When he was talking with you, he wanted to hit you, to spit in your face.

"Would you like to look at my darling dog?" Oska asked the children.
"Yes! We do!" They all shouted.
"Maybe one of you is willing to shoot it?"

> [...]Крестьянский вывел его на большую улицу и здесь стал бить его по глазам. Также он мучал его руки, повторяя: не смей играть с жидами.
>
> The peasant elder walked with him into the street and started beating my grandpa in the eyes. He also hurt his hands, repeating: don't you dare play with Jews.[2]

I argue that it is precisely these combined layers of images—the urban, the natural, the violent (in his conversation about/with his Jewishness)—that we find again strikingly collaged in Gor's Siege poetry. And this is important because on this point I disagree with the prevailing opinion on Gor (expressed especially by the historian of Leningrad poetry Oleg Yuriev[3]) that his Siege poetry has nothing in common with his writing before or after the disaster. I agree instead with the conception of continuity suggested by Andrey Muzhdaba,[4] and my present goal is to reveal traces of Gor's shocking Siege writing in his earlier memoir prose.

I claim that Gor transplants his version of his Siberian Jewish childhood into the Siege, and the main research question for me here is why, to what end? What is the intention of this experiment of imagination and memory?

Gor was not the only poet in the city writing for non-official purposes, outside of the Smolny propaganda program. Actually, he belonged to the whole group, or rather—the whole phenomenon of post-OBERIU Siege poetry writing.[5]

The Siege poetry of the *младообэриуты* is inalienably connected with its historical environment—the Siege of Leningrad, which will be now introduced, or rather introduced anew into this narrative. It would be absurd to call the Siege an un-described historical event—the very ways in which it has been described for the most part of the last century, however, have obscured its impact and meaning.

With its death toll of arguably 1,000,000 victims and lasting almost 3 years, from September 1941 till January 1944, the Nazi Siege of Leningrad is considered to be the most significant military event of its kind in modern history—the most significant and, one could argue, the most publicized. Beginning already in the autumn of 1941, the bibliography of the Siege numbers thousands of official cultural texts in every imaginable genre and register—from journalistic sketches and epic narrative poems to vaudeville and the *chastushka*. The rub here, however, is that having to comply with the worldview of Soviet military propaganda, every Siege author who chose to publish their work at that time had to present the events in strict compliance with a propaganda teleology that aimed to shape this event as an exemplary ideological narrative of the city-front defended by its impeccably heroic inhabitants. This uniformly active role assigned to the participants of the Siege events by the official master plot was reflected in a specific subjectivity which smoothly channeled personal suffering into collective vengeance.

Crucially for the case under consideration, this narrative imposed rigorous demands on the formal criteria of how the Siege was to be portrayed. One of the most central characteristics of the official style of Siege poetics was wholeness or consistency (целостность) of both form and content, language and image: anything that might disturb this structure by implying destruction, fragmentation and deterioration brought on by the calamities of the Siege—be it the disease of dystrophy or consequences of the constant bombing and shelling or the criminality connected with cannibalism—was off limits. The Siege writing not meant for publication is still very much a topic under investigation—its most studied and perhaps one of the most striking parts is a corpus of prose belonging to the literary scholar and prosaist sui generis Lidiya Ginzburg, for whom the situation of the disaster became an experimental field of self-exploration *in extremis*. As Irina Sandomirskaja, one of the first Ginzburg scholars, points out, "for a certain kind of Siege writer writing is not a supplement to immediate existence but a definitive and inalienable existential necessity: it is a "necessitas", that is, something that cannot be bypassed, an obstacle that cannot be removed. "Writers are people who, if they don't write, cannot experience life".[6] It is precisely this kind of writing that opened for the Siege subjects opportunities for formal experimentation—a blurring of both the boundaries of the writerly self and the boundaries between fiction and non-fiction, imagination and document.

Though the realm of nonofficial Siege poetry is voluminous and diverse, the only Siege authors who were committed to registering the effect produced by the disaster onto the language of its subjects had a pedigree going back to the most daring linguistic experimenters and risk-takers in the Leningrad literary scene of the 1920s–1930s.

Of all the post-OBERIU Siege authors, Gor was, is perhaps the most radical. Let us revisit once again this story about his Siege poetry—one of the most significant "Romantic" (in that it recalls the trope of "a manuscript found in an attic") and difficult discoveries in post-Soviet literary history.

After Gor's death in 1982 his family found in his desk a notepad of poetry that can be said to be the most radical (thematically and aesthetically) poetic statement about the Siege experience in existence. Here is one startling and typical example:

> I devoured a girl, the giggler, Rebekkah
> And a raven looked on at my horrific lunch.
> And the raven looked on at me as if at boredom,
> How slowly a human was eating a human.
> The raven looked on but in vain,
> I never did throw him one of Rebekkah's arms.
>
> Я девушку съел хохотунью Ревекку
> И ворон глядел на обед мой ужасный.
> И ворон глядел на меня как на скуку
> Как медленно ел человек человека
> И ворон глядел но напрасно,
> Не бросил ему я Ревеккину руку
>
> (1942)

What shocks and surprises us the most in this poem? It might be the detailed description of the Siege's most *real nightmare*—cannibalism in a surprising, almost frivolous combination with an aphasiac slippage of language (на меня как на скуку), mention of Edgar Allan Poe's beloved pet bird or the ethnically marked name of the laughing girl. I maintain that all these elements are crucial and tightly connected, and that the laughing Jewish girl Rebekkah harks back to Gor's childhood, a world that is both acutely cherished and brutally destroyed when it is juxtaposed with impressions of the Siege.

Let us look also at the following poem, where Gor most insistently and effectively combines the Siege with his childhood memories:

> Красная капля в снегу. И мальчик
> С зеленым лицом, как кошка.
> Прохожие идут ему по ногам, по глазам
> Им некогда. Вывески лезут
> Масло Булки Пиво,
> Как будто на свете есть булки.
> Дом, милый, раскрыл всё –
> Двери и окна, себя самого.
> Но снится мне детство.
> Бабушка с маленькими руками.
> Гуси. Горы. Река по камням –
> Витимкан.
> Входит давно зарытая мама.
> Времени нет.
> На стуле сидит лама в желтом халате.
> Он трогает четки рукой.

А мама смеется, ласкает его за лицо,
Садится к нему на колени.
Время все длится, все длится, все тянется
За водой, на Неву я боюсь опоздать.

(1942)

A red drop in the snow. And a boy
With a green face, like a cat.
Passersby keep treading on his legs, his eyes.
They have no time. Signs peeling—
Butter, White Bread, Beer.
As though there were such a thing as white bread.
Home, sweet, exposed it all—
Doors and windows, its own self.
But I dream of childhood.
Grandma with her little hands.
Geese. Mountains. A river over stones—
The Vitimkan.
In comes Mama, long under ground.
There is no time.
A llama in a yellow gown sits on a chair.
He touches a rosary with his hand.
And Mama is laughing, petting his face,
She sits down in his lap.
And time keeps stretching, keeps stretching, elongating.
I am afraid to be late to the Neva for water.

The present moment of the Siege, of disturbed urbanity, is interrupted by the authorial introduction of "the dream of childhood"—actually, the Siberian childhood we've already "met" in his memoir. We find here lots of nature imagery: river, mountains, birds, stones. Gor's direct address to these images and memories becomes possible due to his treatment of time, which he pronounces to be at once non-existent and absolutely porous and flexible. According to these new laws of time, nothing separates any longer past from present, his striking childhood from the Siege.

The here and now is canceled, which allows the other time, the time of memory, to flow freely into the present—but what will become of it here? However, when his childhood "enters" the Siege via memory order to comfort the subject suffering from the Siege, it becomes endangered—as does the subject himself. The childhood memory that is so well-shaped and whole in the memoir becomes shattered and aphasiacally disfigured in poetry: we see its fragments everywhere. Thus the master metaphors of Gor's Siege writing—dispersal, fragmentation as a result of cannibalism and bombing—enter into his work with language: what we mostly face here are the shattered remains. And when in Gor's Siege poetry we meet characters from his Jewish childhood—Rebeccah and Aaron, as well as Ginzburg and Rabinovich, mentioned by their last names only, we react to them as to memory doomed to fragmentation by the Siege but also serving as a glue that resists this fragmentation: memory becomes in Gor's Siege poetry the antidote to the "end of time"—and what makes this scheme ever more curious and moving is that this memory is far from blissful. Having invented his troubled childhood in the 1930s, Gor recycled it in his Siege poetry with paradoxical, poignant results.

[1] Valery Dymshits, "Predislovie," in Doivber Levin, *Likhovo* (St Petersburg: Knizhniki, 2017), 4.
[2] Gennadiy Gor, "V gorodke studenom," *Zvezda* 7 (1935): 62.
[3] Oleg Yuriev, "Zapolnennoe zianie-2," review of *Blockade. Gedichte*, by Gennadij Gor, *Novoe literaturnoe obozrenie* 89 (2008), accessed January 15, 2019, http://www.zh-zal.ru/nlo/2008/89/ur20.html.
[4] Andrey Muzhdaba, "Blokadnaia utka: stikhotvornyi tsikl Gennadiia Gora v kontekste ego prozy 1930–1970-kh godov," in *Blokadnye narrativy: sbornik statei*, Polina Barskova and Riccardo Nicolosi, eds. (Moscow: Novoe literaturnoe obozrenie, 2017), 201–225.
[5] Polina Barskova, ed., *Written in the Dark: Five Poets in the Siege of Leningrad* (Brooklyn: Ugly Duckling Press, 2016).
[6] Irina Sandomirskaia, *Blokada v slove. Ocherki kriticheskoi istorii i biopolitiki iazyka*. [Moscow: Novoe literaturnoe obozrenie, 2013]. 185

When I was living in Moscow

DISA HÅSTAD

When I was living in Moscow in the 1970s there were a lot of people worth getting to know. Some of them were the widows of great men who were still alive, and all had their story to tell. I became particularly friendly with Nadezhda Yakovlevna Mandelstam, who was also a writer in her own right, author of *Hope against Hope* and *Hope Abandoned*. She was the widow of the poet Osip Mandelstam, who had died in a camp in 1938.

The person who introduced me to her was Viktoria Schweitzer, a literary historian best known for her biography of Marina Tsvetaeva. Viktoria had been going to Nadezhda Mandelstam for years to help her, go to the shops and keep her in communication with the world. After her husband's arrest, Nadezhda Mandelstam was not allowed to stay in Moscow but moved around the country, where she managed to find schools in which she taught English (she had grown up with an English governess). After working twenty years she was able to retire with a pension, and she moved to Moscow and bought a flat in 1958.

When I met first met her she was in bed, smoking cheap cigarettes. This was how she usually spent her time. Mostly out of boredom—she didn't find it worth it to get up and get dressed. She was very thin, seemed very old and had big dark eyes which looked at me curiously.

"So, you are Swedish", she said. "I know Sweden, we went there on holiday with my family before the revolution".

In the bourgeois family in Kiev where she grew up it was normal to go on vacation abroad.

She had been a happy, wild girl who studied art and was a member of a group who tried to shock the bourgeois by exhibiting their revolutionary works on various balconies. In Kiev the government was all the time changing—sometimes nationalists, sometimes revolutionaries, sometimes the Whites. When she met Osip Mandelstam they went to bed together the same day, she writes in her memoirs.

She followed him in his first exile, to Voronezh. They came back to Moscow and began criticizing their writer colleagues for their leniency towards the regime—something that did not endear them to their colleagues. They must have seemed very self-righteous and demanding.

In the beginning she tried to keep a salon in her Moscow flat. But the writers she invited felt that she was insulting them. "She shat on all of us", one of them said, according to Joseph Brodsky. They went home and started writing books against her.

But she was not alone. In place of the writers came her publishers from abroad (her books were never allowed to appear in Soviet Russia, where she was a non-person), new friends like Vika Schweitzer, some correspondents like me, and a long line of young girls who spent their time copying work for samizdat—forbidden literature that circulated privately.

I used to bring her thrillers in English which she would read during sleepless nights. "Bring me trash", she said.

But she didn't say no to samizdat; I could please her by giving her Andrei Bitov's novel *Pushkinskii dom*, which she later put into circulation.

I remember discussing Sartre with her; she was very much against him and called him a shit (*govno*). Someone else was there too, who tried to say that Sartre was an interesting writer. But she got under the bedclothes and only one word— *govno* —could be heard from under the blanket. From her point of view she was right—Sartre was defending the Soviet Union; he and Simone de Beauvoir had even started a trial against Kravchenko, a party man who "chose freedom" and started telling some uncomfortable truths about the Soviet regime. Sartre and de Beauvoir said he lied. I don't think Nadezhda Yakovlevna had even heard about the trial—it was her instinctive hatred of the Western intellectuals who had never stood up for their persecuted Russian colleagues.

She was not always in bed. When I brought my boss Per Wästberg, then editor in chief of *Dagens Nyheter*, there she was, wearing a dress and sitting in the kitchen. Per thought she looked about 90 years old (she was 76) and said her apartment was simple and lugubrious. But to her it was worth a lot. She was always afraid it would be taken away from her and that she could not have a peaceful death there. (She did, in 1980).

I brought several people to her. It was an established practice of mine, so that these people living outside society should not be isolated.

One day the famous French theatre director Roger Planchon (a legend in Moscow since his tour with *The Three Musketeers*) came to town with Shakespeare's *Pericles*. We talked at supper after the performance; he told me he had only one wish in Moscow, to meet Nadezhda Mandelstam, a legend in France after the publication of her books. Not without pride I could tell him: "I know her. If you like I can take you to her".

We set out the next day. Planchon bought a red rose. Nadezhda Yakvlevna wanted to know about one thing—the new poetry in France. He started telling her about René Char (a new name for both her and me), and so they talked about René Char the whole afternoon.

To have lived through what she had required a strong character. She was not afraid now of small defenders of the regime. Vika Schweitzer told me that when they had gone out for a walk once—Nadezhda Yakovlevna, her husband Misha and she—they had sat down to rest on bench in a strange courtyard. A policeman came and told them they could not sit there. He asked Misha for his papers, which was a bit unfortunate, as Misha had no right to stay in Moscow, being a former GULAG prisoner. The policeman asked Misha to come to the station. Nadezhda Yakovlevna immediately said: "Then I'm coming too!" so they all went to the police station, where nothing very bad happened.

I remember once drinking champagne with Nadezhda Yakovlevna, but I can't remember what we were celebrating. I asked another person drinking with us, her "little doctor" Yury Freidin, what the occasion was. He couldn't remember either, but thought I had simply brought it.

"She really prefers vodka or gin", he said. "But since you brought Veuve Cliquot, she must have felt obliged to finish it."

Chance Encounter in Bad Nauheim

LARS KLEBERG

In the park of the Bad Nauheim sanatorium on a sunny day in late spring, 1897. A small, round grassy spot, encircled by white benches and bushes. At the rear of the stage, a tall evergreen hedge opens out onto a path.

NF – Niels Finsen
AP – Anton Pavlovich Chekhov

NF is seated on a wicker chair. He is wearing a heavy brown overcoat, is bareheaded, and has a little easel in front of him at which he is painting. AP, wearing a single-breasted linen suit and a straw hat walks past, halts a moment to glance at the easel, goes on, then returns slowly. Stops.

NF
(*After a few moments of silence, without looking up*). Are you interested in painting?

Pause.

NF
Are you interested in painting?

AP
Pardon me, I didn't mean to interrupt.

NF
Think nothing of it. (*Pause*). There's something special about the light here, the way it falls. Everything looks different when the sun is shining and the trees are in shadow. (*Pause*). I'm only an amateur. One needs a hobby.

AP
I have no hobbies, myself. There aren't enough hours in the day. Actually, I'm looking for a friend … from a long time back. He's an artist as well, incidentally, by the name of Levitan. But apparently he has already moved on. You don't happen to have met him here, a Russian artist? (*Pause*). I'm Russian myself.

NF
(*Smiling*). Pardon me, Herr Chekhov – am I pronouncing that correctly? We easily saw through your alias, "Doctor Pavlov." And your books are quite well known in Denmark, too. My home country. My name is Finsen. (*Attempts a bow, seated in his chair. Pause*).

AP (*hesitates, begins to walk on, then asks*)
Do you mind if I sit down?

NF
Not at all.

AP
I came here to see my old friend, as well as to get away from all the attention back home. A writer must be constantly prepared to receive visitors, particularly elderly ladies, to reply to questions, to sign books and autograph photos. Excruciating. However, I find hordes of Russians here as well. Running away from oneself isn't easy – you have yourself with you wherever you go, so to speak. (*Finsen smiles, goes on painting. Pause*). What do you do when you're not painting, if I may enquire?

NF
I'm a doctor – a physician and inventor. I don't really have time, either. But sometimes a doctor is also required to put on the patient's garb. I don't know whether the hydrotherapy is helping, but Doctor Groedel has a fine reputation. And this certainly is a lovely place. Hopefully a couple of weeks of carbonic acid baths will give me a bit of energy. (*Pause. Goes on painting*). You're a physician yourself, aren't you?

AP
I am, but I have abandoned my calling.

NF
May I ask why?

AP
Well, my writing began as a hobby, but then it took the upper hand. I felt I was constantly betraying medicine, so in the end it was best to hang down my sign. (*Pauses. Looks at* NF's *painting. Pause*). If you don't mind my asking, are you colorblind?

NF
Funny you should ask. I am preoccupied with the impact of rays of light on the organism. As far as I know, I have always been able to distinguish between red and blue.

AP
But what about red and green, or green and brown? In any case, you use an unusual range of colors. (*Pause*). They say the colorblind are particularly sensitive to certain nuances others do not see. (*Pause*). What kind of inventions do you make?

NF
(*Sets down his brushes and palate*). Do you see that cat over there, sunning itself by the stone wall?

AP
I do.

NF
Look again in a quarter of an hour and you will see that it has moved, to keep out of the shade.

AP
Yes, I suppose it is enjoying the heat.

NF
It is enjoying something, but not the heat. Rather, what the cat is after are the invisible chemical rays, the ultraviolet rays. I have been aware of this ever since my student days. Later, when I began analyzing the wavelengths of light, I found that different animals sought out not only the light in general but specifically those chemical rays, which seem to have a particular effect of excitation. However, sometimes they try to keep away from those rays as well. Once when I trapped a chameleon in a box, the glass top of which was half red, half

blue, and let the sun shine on it, the chameleon remained pale on one side, while the other side quickly turned black as pitch. Protection from the chemical rays. That explains why we develop pigment, and why the Negroes in Africa are black.

AP
I believe I read about "Doctor Finsen's red rooms" in a medical journal.

From the other end of the park, a brass band strikes up a sprightly march. Pause.

NF
The red rooms were meant to protect smallpox patients from the chemical rays. But now I am working on their positive effects, not least their ability to kill bacteria. A couple of colleagues and I have begun experimenting on treating *lupus vulgaris* with concentrated light therapy. As you know, until now there has been no effective therapy – scraping, cauterization and other unpleasant treatments have been tried. In the past in England there was even some belief in the laying on of royal hands! We hypothesized that at our latitudes we might need to compensate for sunlight deficiency, so we tried electric carbon arc lighting. One of our patients with severe lupus, an engineer at the Copenhagen electricity works, offered us electricity at no charge in exchange for his treatments.

AP
Some patients have useful contacts.

NF
The light we were testing was so powerful that we had to begin by filtering out the heat waves through lenses and blue water – the very opposite of the red rooms, which removed the chemical rays. The cold rays gave rise to other reactions on the epidermis than the warm ones, a kind of erythema, and soon we had proof of their bactericidal effect. Facial lesions this man had been going around with for years – reminiscent of a leper – fell away, and under the scabs there was smooth, healthy skin. Naturally, a great deal remains to be done. And since last year, with the support of this engineer and a number of patrons, I have been running a Light Institute for research on and treatment of lupus.

AP
Are you saying that the rays with a healing effect are the invisible ones? Very interesting. And do you sunbathe yourself, Sir?

NF
No... I really don't have the time; I am devoted to my patients and the laboratory. But I promise you that if light baths in the sun or under a carbon arc lamp were to come into general use, then we – particularly us northern Europeans – would be able to achieve improvements for thousands of people. The power of light is as yet nearly entirely unexplored. And our research is in step with the times. In Denmark there are already young men rabblerousing in favor of nude bathing and gymnastics in the sunshine. Their group calls itself Hellenists. And young artists are taking their lead and honoring the nude body in sunlight.

AP
Nude bathers? And in art? That sounds utterly alien to our culture. (*He has a violent coughing fit, then spits into a large handkerchief*).

Pause.

NF
Do you see the cat now? It has moved to keep out of the shade. (*Pause*). I feel certain that sun worship will soon be popular in Russia as well. One day your poets will sing the praises of the sun!

AP
If we live long enough to see it. (*Pause*). But not nude bathing. They say there are some semi-males who do it on the Karelian peninsula during the summers. But in principle, in my country, the naked body is never exposed, and particularly not in art. There is, however, one amusing exception that justifies the rule. It is said that in a mansion outside Saint Petersburg there hangs a painting of Elizaveta Petrovna, the daughter of the tsar, stark naked. As a child mind you, but the body is that of a nude woman. Today it may seem provocative, to say the least. But in the eighteenth century it would never have occurred to anyone that the naked body on the canvas was the actual body of the daughter of the tsar. It would have been obvious to all that although it was her head, the body was that of a classical goddess: the painting was an allegorical depiction

of the daughter of the tsar in the role of the goddess Flora. But with the triumphal march of realism in recent years, people's sense of the boundary between art and reality has become so blurred that the painting has had to be hidden away, so that no one should have to think they have seen the daughter of the tsar in the nude.

NF
(*Laughing*). Indeed, times change. Russian realism is an accepted concept in Denmark today as well. Turgenev, above all, is widely discussed. All the young radicals are reading Turgenev, myself included.

AP *sighs deeply, coughs.*

NF
However, his latest work, *Punin and Baburin*, was a dreadful disappointment. That old revolutionary who dies with the slogan "Hurrah, Hurrah! God save the tsar" on his lips when serfdom is abolished – no, not really … Imagine if literature began to demonstrate a greater interest in state of mind than in engagements and debates, and ceased writing about "types" and "characters", things we've all read hundreds of times before. I am not very familiar with your writing, but you appear to be moving in a different direction. The reader doesn't know at the end whether the hero and heroine will live happily ever after, but in exchange there are individual cases. *The Duel* and *Ward no. 6* are available in Danish. But I found a book that came out in Swedish translation last year, *The Black Monk,* even more interesting. That story had something disquieting and magical about it. By the end you are unsure if you actually see the mysterious monk who appears to your protagonist, if you are awake or dreaming. Do you personally believe in these things, in mirages?

AP
Do you?

NF
I am sure there are rays about which we have no idea. But we have our hands full with those we already know exist, although their effects are as yet unknown to us.

AP
What interests me is not mirages, but how people perceive them.

NF
Actually, I preferred the story of the old professor.

AP
The problem with that one was that people took the retired professor for me. That his ideas – or his lack of ideas – were my lack of ideas. After that I had to move on to writing some kind of dialogues, you know, as in *The Duel*, so as not to be pinned down to any specific idea. And that ended up with the critics accusing me of not having any ideas at all. But I am interested in *how* people have ideas, not in proffering them. The critics are the real problem, those policemen of ideas who will rip a moral out of a story at any price. If they fail, it is the failure of the author. (*Pause*). As you just said, it is about individual cases, and no individual case can simply have conclusions drawn from it and then be pigeonholed. I learned that from the only one of our professors who impressed me, Zakharin. He was a phenomenal diagnostician.

NF
Zakharin, the name sounds familiar.

AP
His lectures were extraordinary. But when they were published in book form it was as if the music vanished, leaving nothing but the libretto. I understand they have now been published in English as well, but no one abroad will be convinced of the genius of Zakharin.

NF
One Swedish critic compared your work to Dostoevsky's, referring to you as one of the up and coming Russian symbolists.

AP
(*Laughs*). God save us… symbolists? We have a small group that goes by that name, but I am not among them. They may be good fellows, but I cannot accept their longing for the hereafter! If they spent a bit more time in the brothels, the problem would vanish. No, what is interesting is not the symbolists and their exercises. What we need is a new perspective, a way of seeing that does not require wearing ideological spectacles. Levitan, the painter I mentioned, are you familiar with him? No, I suppose that he is only known back home. But he is more interesting than all the other so-called realists and impressionists and symbolists put together. There is something about his work:

at times you are unsure what is foreground and what is background – they suddenly change places. He is currently working on a canvas called *Haystacks*, which pulls off that tour de force brilliantly. Everything hovers. If it were possible to achieve such a feat in literature, it would be a great accomplishment. I would like objects to appear quite naked, with no conclusions at all drawn. (*Begins to cough again, spits into his handkerchief*).

Pause.

NF
There is a new Norwegian author. You would probably be interested in his novel *Hunger*.

AP
Hansen...?

NF
No, Hamsun. His name is Knut Hamsun.

Suddenly the brass band can be heard, playing louder and louder. Through the opening in the evergreen hedge we see it pass by, followed by an entourage of sanatorium patients. The music ends abruptly. After a moment of silence, loud cheering.

Pause.

NF
What on earth is going on?

AP
(*Sighs, rises from his chair and goes to where he can see through the opening in the hedge*). Good grief, it seems my compatriots are celebrating the name day of some member of the Tsar's family.

NF
Are they here, in Bad Nauheim?

AP
No, no.

NF
Well, what's all the cheering about?

AP
Just in case.

Long pause.

NF
Getting back to Hamsun, I do believe his novel would interest you.

AP
I've read it... Too much Dostoyevsky, too much sweat. – that could, of course, be the fault of the translation.

NP
He is trying to capture the sensations, the subconscious or semi-conscious layers of personality.

AP
Can you imagine him without all that psychology? What is of interest is not the ego but the sensations themselves, the pure sensations. Untinted objects. (*Pause*). Tell me, there's something I don't understand – Hamsun is Norwegian, right? Well, doesn't that really make him Swedish? Doesn't Norway belong to Sweden?

NF
Scandinavia is a bit complicated. Take me, for example – although I am Danish, my family was originally Icelandic, though in the service of the Danish crown. And, actually, I was born on the Faroe Islands.

AP
Does that put you among the colonizers or the colonized? Is there a movement for liberation in Iceland?

NF
(*Smiling*). Yes, but it is very inconspicuous.

AP

I believe the coming century will be the time of the great liberation movements. Or the great wars. Or both.

Pause.

NF

You are a playwright as well, aren't you? Sadly, your plays are not yet available in Denmark.

AP

I used to be. I no longer write for the theater. Russian theater is an abyss that devours everything without a trace. *Horror vacui.* And it will always be that way, no matter how brilliant future producers are. *Horror vacui*! They pile everything upon everything else, horrid, ugly scenery, actresses who want nothing more than to show off the new dresses and jewelry they have acquired heaven only knows how. A theater worthy of the name would just leave everything in peace, including the audience. But the magic would still be there. When my last play flopped, I realized that no one understood what I was trying to do. The words, the people, the scant scenery, it was all meant to be there, side by side, without disturbing the other bits. Foreground and background were meant to suddenly change places, rather like in Levitan's *Haystacks*. You see, I am not interested in the minds of my characters, but in how they reflect each other. The question is how this can be depicted on stage. There is never enough air! (*Coughing*).

NF

A French colleague who visited me in Copenhagen not long ago spoke of Japanese theater. In Paris, people are wild about Japan. Everything must be *à la japonaise*: fans, lacquered chests, stoneware jars – they are all selling like hotcakes. My colleague brought me a gift of a lovely woodcut. He spoke fascinatingly of Japanese theater, although he had never seen a performance, only read about it in a magazine. According to him, the mastery of the actor is alpha and omega in Japanese theater.

The dramas themselves are classical, based on mythology, but that is not the important thing. It is the art of acting which is at once extremely traditional and absolutely vital. Just as it is said that a certain wooden temple is destroyed and burned down once every two decades, only to be built up again – exactly as it was, but brand new – that is how each generation of actors precisely imitates its predecessors. And yet in a way that makes it seem absolutely new! All this I heard from my French friend, and it reminds me in a way of what you are saying. An actor who does not look to the past and the future and the world around him, but who is fully focused on the present moment, on a point at which everything stands still. Although Japanese drama does have some kind of transcendental content, there is nothing in it that is anywhere but here and now. The text in itself, the music in itself, the actor in himself, and yet all unified.

AP
In Russia there is only one actor who would understand that, and she is the young Komissarzhevskaya. She was in that play of mine that was booed out. But at the dress rehearsal the audience sat in tears. She knows what reduction is. Her eyes. She made time stand still. The lines stood still, hovering in the air. (*Pause*). But I'm finished with all that now. *Finita la commedia*.

NF
But it's all right for an experiment to fail, is it not? Why don't you try again?

AP
I will not. Perhaps as a story, where the narrative can speak for itself, with no interference. (*Pause*). I find the Japanese art of which you spoke fascinating. Like everything Japanese. Yes, even Japanese women. I once had the pleasure of intimacy with a Japanese woman. They have a very objective and sometimes humorous attitude to love. Reminiscent of a professional equestrian. It is completely different from that of Russian girls with their false modesty and equally false rapture. But perhaps Danish girls are different?

NF
Sorry to say I have no experience to speak of.

AP
Really? But you are a physician, aren't you? (*Pause*). That same objectivity can be found in Japanese art. In Paris we looked at Japanese woodcuts in a shop, amazing landscapes. Behind the counter you could also see erotic images, too explicit even for French taste, entirely without those mendacious smiles and semi-buttoned corsets. The pictures by Utamaro and others are quite shameless by our standards. And their composition is drastic as well, like segments of a large image we are not being shown. You have no idea what is big and what is small; the central perspective has been suspended.

NF
You are interested in oscillation between foreground and background.

AP
(*Laughing*). Between you and me it is possible that the explanation is that I am nearsighted in one eye and farsighted in the other, so my focus is constantly shifting. Details become quite insistent.

Pause.

NF
In our profession the individual case must always be our lodestar. In every case, it is an individual who will receive the treatment. I have always detested university medicine, in which research for a PhD takes priority over patient's choices. I pity young doctors today, required to submit to such underhanded trickery. I once had to dissuade a younger colleague from pursuing an exciting research prospect simply so as not to arouse the jealousy of his professors. Pick a narrower topic, I said, try to get your work praised by some foreign dignitary, and be careful not to present any overly interesting conclusions – do that and you'll have your PhD in no time. (*Long pause*). May I request a favor? Would you be so kind as to get me some water from the the Ludwig spring, the alkaline one?

AP
(*Surprised*). Of course.

NF
Thank you.

AP
(*Leaves*).

NF
(*Eyes shut, breathing heavily*).

Pause. NF *begins to paint again.*

AP
(*Returns with a carafe of water*). Here you are.

NF

Thank you, very kind of you. (*Takes out a small glass bottle, about half a cup, fills it with water and promptly pours out the rest onto the ground*). It's my heart. Some kind of long-term pericarditis no doctor can explain. Ascites, of course, but the puncturing is only palliative. I have begun to reduce my intake of solid foods and liquids. I weigh and register everything. I only use this water to moisten my lips when they get too dry. (*Raises the bottle to his lips without swallowing*).

AP

And yet…?

NF

And yet it does not help. I suppose I will not live long, but for the sake of my work I would like to go on as long as possible. (*Pause*). I would give almost anything to attend my own autopsy.

AP

(*Smiles. Pause*). What you were just telling me reminds me of something Zakharin once mentioned – the armoured heart. Very rare. Is there any TB in your family?

NF

No, none that I know of.

Pause.

AP

I believe you are married. If you had known that you were going to die soon, would you still have wed?

NF

I asked myself that very question before I proposed. I didn't really know about my heart condition, but I did know the prognosis was not good, so I explained the situation to my fiancée. And I asked her to choose her freedom. But she replied that whatever time we have together will be good enough. This was fully five years ago now, and as you see I am still alive. We had one son who died at birth, and that gave me the feeling that things were still not right. Last year, however, we had a second son, who can now run about and play. (*Pause*).

I think about *The Black Monk*. I understand that you are not entirely well, either. If you had to choose between your health and your creative work, what would you choose?

AP *shrugs. Pause.* NF *goes on painting.*

AP
Tell me, do you believe in God?

NF
The problem is that you have to go to church as well. That is absolutely alien to me, although I attend occasionally for my wife's sake. She is the daughter of a bishop, mind you. What about yourself? In Russia I imagine church and religion are indivisible. What about church and the other authorities.

AP
In Russia it is either/or. Between, "there is a God" and "there is no God" lies a whole vast tract which the really wise man crosses only with great effort. A Russian knows one or the other of these two extremes, and the middle tract between them does not interest him. (*Pause*). When I was ill in hospital last spring, Count Tolstoy paid me a visit. He was most eager to discuss the immortality of the soul, and resurrection on the Day of Judgment. I didn't know what to say, beside which I was forbidden to speak, so Tolstoy carried on the conversation singlehandedly. I am a great admirer of his art, but matters of faith leave me cold. At best. (*Coughs, spits*).

NF
The great French philosopher, Pascal, demonstrated irrefutably that the existence of God cannot be proven. One can merely have faith. Have you read Pascal's *Pensées*?

AP
No. But Lev Nikolayevich, Tolstoy you know, spoke of him.

NF
Anxiety, the *inquietude* of the soul, is the prerequisite to faith. According to Pascal, we must be uncertain and dare to invest everything in the great leap of faith. We may succeed, we may fail. His worries and impatience are understandable, he was ill, in constant pain, and died at only thirty-nine. No one can

say what the diagnosis was. He himself seems to have believed that illness is the correct state of mind for achieving faith. (*Pause*). Today it might have been possible to save his life. Some people say, however, that the sum of illnesses is a constant; when one has been obliterated, another comes to replace it.

AP
No, I am firmly convinced that we are moving forward, toward better times. I have seen progress during my own lifetime. I often say this: the difference between when I was beaten in my childhood and when I was no longer beaten was enormous. Since then I have believed in progress. Is it true what you say, that Pascal only lived to be thirty-nine?

NF
Thinking about all he had accomplished by the time he was my age makes me blush.

AP
How old are you, if you don't mind my asking?

NF
Thirty-six.

AP
Almost the same as me. (*Pause*). Tolstoy also spoke of another French philosopher, of whom I had never heard. To be honest with you, I found him more interesting than Pascal. Étienne de La Boétie. He is said to have died at just thirty-four. Still, he was able to write a remarkable essay, "Discourse on Voluntary Servitude". According to Tolstoy, La Boétie claimed that human servitude to any tyrant rests ultimately on approval of the oppression by the oppressed. What makes us unfree? Who makes us unfree? The answer is: we do it ourselves! What makes mankind willing to bend under the yoke, if animals refuse, asks La Boétie. We who are meant to have free will, why do we not wish to be free? Although oppression may seem insuperable, someone must have granted the tyrant his power. It begins with his having five or six underlings, "accomplices to his cruelty, companions to his pleasure, souteneurs to his lechery, and partners in whatever he grabs up". Soon these six will have six hundred in their turn, taking advantage of them just as they are taken advantage of by the tyrant. And in their turn, these six hundred will soon have six thousand underlings, all of whom deliver upwards at the same time as they

take advantage of those below them, and under them soon hundreds of thousands or million on whom the entire system, and thus the emperor, rests. This was written by a philosopher more than four centuries ago! It sounds incredibly topical, not least where I come from. But how can mankind ever be free if human beings are prepared not just to humiliate their neighbors but also to allow themselves to be humiliated? According to La Boétie, what we must do is to realize our freedom. But there's just one little detail – human beings fear it, fear freedom. (*Long pause. A bell rings*). That's the lunch bell.

NF
I'm not having any.

AP
I understand. (*Pause*). Well, it was interesting to meet you.

NF
The same to you.

AP
And best of luck with that light therapy of yours.

NF
If we live long enough to see!

AP *walks offstage.* NF *remains seated, eyes shut. Then he returns to his painting.*

THE END
(Translated by Linda Schenck)

Note: NF = Niels Finsen, 1860–1904, Danish physician. 1903 Nobel laureate in medicine. AP = Anton Pavlovich Chekhov, 1860–1904, Russian author.

Potential Trust
(animated neon with 6 stages)

ESTHER SHALEV-GERTZ

Next spread: *Potential Trust (animated neon with 6 stages)*, ©Esther Shalev-Gertz 2019

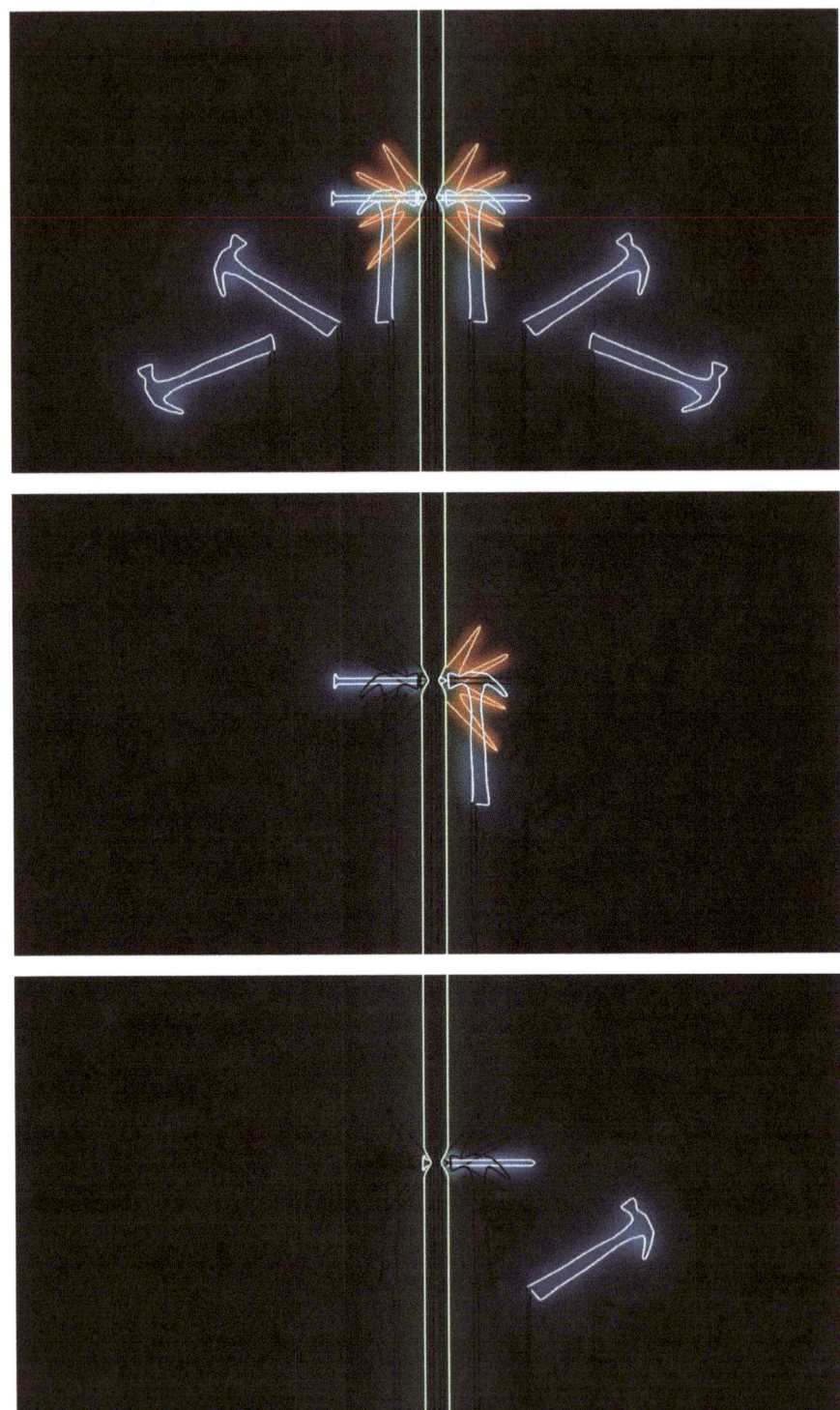

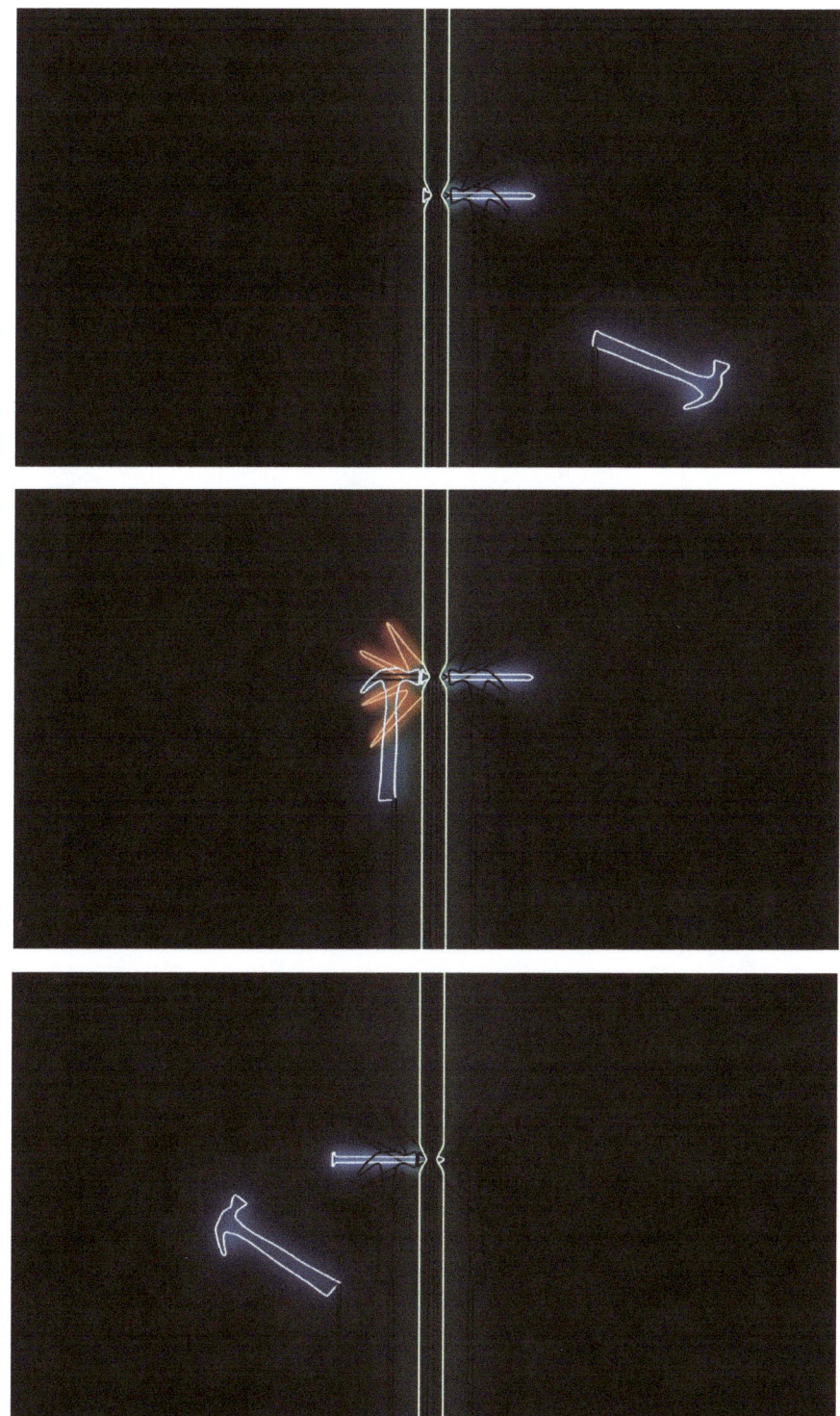

II

Reading and Censorship:
Leo Spitzer's Monographs from WWI[1]

KENNETH J. KNOESPEL

Leo Spitzer's (1886–1960) distinguished career in Romance scholarship is seldom viewed within the setting of his work as a military censor of Italian prisoner of war correspondence for the Austrian Ministry of War in WWI (1915–1918). In his 1948 essay "Linguistics and Literary History"[2], often viewed as his public *curriculum vitae*, Spitzer makes no mention of the three monographs that came from his study of the more than 100,000 documents he reviewed as a censor[3]: 1) *Die Umschreibungen des Begriffes 'Hunger' im Italienischen: Stilistisch-Onomasiologische Studie auf Grund von Unveröffentlichtem Zensurmaterial* (1920); 2) *Italienische Kriegsgefangenenbriefe: Materialien zu einer Charakteristik der Volkstümlichen Italienischen Korrespondenz* (1921); 3) *Italienische Umgangssprache* (1922). In his biographical study of Spitzer, Gumbrecht includes only passing references to the early work.[4] The recent translation of *Italienische Kriegsgegangenenbriefen* into Italian underscores Spitzer's long identity with Italy and Italian scholarship.[5] Already in the late 1920s Spitzer's monographs appeared in Russian circles that included Bakhtin and Voloshinov. The Spitzer legacy in English has been shaped by the collections of essays published by Princeton[6] and in French by Jean Starobinski[7]; Foucault translated "Linguistics and Literary History" for the Starobinski collection. Emily Apter's assessment of a "new" comparative literature considers Spitzer's role in America but does not take up the monographs in detail.[8] While his erudition served to affirm the expansion of ideological humanism in America after WWII, his psycholinguistics of dialogue and the phenomenology of language so evident in his early work become opaque in his American reception. The following comments should be viewed as a sketch for a longer study. Even more, I hope this survey invites further examination of Spitzer's early monographs and their bearing on language theory and literary criticism.

Background

Spitzer's expertise in Romance languages led to his recruitment in September 1915 to serve as director of the censorship department of the *Gemeinsames Nachweisebureau* for Italian prisoners of war in Vienna.[9] He quickly discovered that the war provided an opportunity to gather examples of living language rather than texts from the canon of literary history. From his very first publication, which considered the invention of words in Rabelais,[10] it was clear that he was attracted to the psychological study of language. The phenomena that led him to Rabelais became amplified through his supervision of censorship, which also enabled him to create an archive of linguistic examples copied out from correspondence brought to his attention. Overall, he and his colleagues were responsible for screening prisoners' attempts to vilify their German captors or describe conditions that were inhumane and subject to international law. The severe lack of foodstuffs due to the British blockade brought the fact of starvation before him on a daily basis. By the end of the war the mortality rate of Italian prisoners was 16%. It is estimated that of the 600,000 Italian soldiers captured during the war, 100,000 died in captivity.[11] Spitzer discovered quickly that Italian prisoners had become accomplished at inventing euphemisms or paraphrases for describing hunger. He reports that by 1916, through original material brought to him with complaints of hunger, he had become, with some irony, the "*Hungerspezialist*".[12]

Spitzer's moral view of suffering appears in his broad humanitarian hope that future war could be avoided through a study of linguistics that would reveal sources of human conflict. His own removal by the Nazis from his professorship in Marburg in 1933 because of his Jewish origins calls attention to the innocence of his humanitarian vision. After moving to Istanbul, where he worked with Erich Auerbach, he was appointed Professor of Romance Languages at Johns Hopkins University in 1936. Spitzer's work between 1915 and 1918 resulted in the publication of three monographs.

Fig. 1 German postcard showing French prisoners of war near Verdun 1916

Spitzer's Monographs from World War I

1. *Die Umschreibungen des Begriffes "Hunger" im Italienischen: Stilistisch-Onomasiologische Studie auf Grund von Unveröffentlichtem Zensurmaterial* (Halle, 1920)

The memory of hunger was hardly distant in 1920 but remained closely associated with the war on all fronts. Spitzer emphasizes at the outset that one cannot write about hunger without recognizing suffering:

> The suffering that almost all prisoners of war from all lands experienced was hunger that could most easily be addressed by the food sent from those close to them. At the same time, it was the duty of the host country where the prisoners were being held under less than desirable conditions to remove the complaints being sent home. As a consequence, the prisoners' need to communicate their condition collided with the authorities, who needed to suppress complaints regarding hunger and the absence of bare essentials.[13] [All translations are by the author unless otherwise indicated]

> [*Das Leiden, das die Kriegsgefangenen aller Länder am meisten geplagt und das am ehesten durch Lebensmittelsendungen der Angehörigen aus der Heimat gelindert werden konnte, war der Hunger und zugleich war die Ehre des Wirtlandes, bei dem die Kriegsgefangenen gewöhnlich mehr order weniger schlecht gehaltene Gäste waren, durch das Hinausdringen gerade dieser Klage ins*

> *Heimatland der Gefangenen am schwersten getroffen, so daß das Interesse der Gefangenen mit dem der sie beherbergenden Macht kollidierte, diese die Hungerklagen beseitigen mußte, die jenen eine Lebensnotwendigkeit bedeuteten.*]

The suffering caused by lack of food was a consequence of the blockade initiated by the Allies: "The Hunger blockade of the Allies made no distinction when it came to the ordinary soldier who longed to go home." *["Die Hunger blockade der Entente hat hier ohne Unterschied die Entente wie die Mittelmachtssoldaten heimgesucht".*] Since the blockade effected all soldiers, Spitzer simply concludes, *"what more can be said?"*[14] [*"Damit ist alles gesagt".*]

Given letters and cards from the group of censors under his charge, he builds a data base comparable to philological study in university settings.

> A trained worker could go through a postcard in half a second and immediately discover a complaint about hunger. Office workers, book keepers, students taught the method of textual criticism and hermeneutics in the office of censorship appeared as if they were professional philologists.[15]

> [*Ein geschulter Arbeiter überflog in einer halben Sekunde eine Karte und fand sofort die Hungerklage heraus. Kommis, Buchhalter, Studenten, erlernten im Zensurbetrieb die Methoden der Textkritik und Hermeneutik, wie sie sonst nur Philologen vom Fach besitzen...*]

However, the material being "researched" was far different from the texts studied in university settings. "The unique handicraft of the war offered texts that the scientific muse of philology was not trained to engage."[16] [*"[...]ein so ungeistiges Handwerk, wie das des Krieges, der Muse der Wissenschaft nicht entraten kann."*]

Even a provisional list of the categories used by Spitzer displays an effort to shape a comprehensive strategy that reveals the ways "hunger" becomes diffused in language: 1)"Fame" [hunger, starvation] and how it is concealed; 2) Appetite as a euphemism for fame; 3) Personification of fame; 4) Health, hygiene, and medical care; 5) Air and wind; 6) Sickness; 7) Bodily condition; 8) Religious exercises; 9) Spiritual; 10) Music; 11) Dance and Games; 12) Reading and Study; 13) Hunting; animals; 14) Useful objects; 15) Geographical description; 16) Prophecy and wishes; 17) Importance of received packages; 18) Local allusions; 19) Local dialect; 20) Neologisms and writing as means of concealment; 21) Etymological abstraction. As already noted, these categories apply to the use of language that the "philological muse" was not prepared to deal with. Rather than historical research based on examples drawn from literature, Spitzer embarks upon research into linguistic features that may be applicable to language in general. It becomes increasingly evident that he is opening the metaphoric ground of language itself. The monograph gives special focus to 1) the role of jokes or language tricks; 2) the place of psychology and fantasy in communication; 3) the dialogic nature of written and spoken communication; and 4) universal elements of language that are not determined by social class.

Language Tricks

Spitzer expands his analysis of the "trick", a term already used by German philology to describe the ways prisoners sought to convey their need for food. The endeavor "to trick" turns the relation between the writer and censor into a game where the reader-censor is challenged to discern that "something has been buried here".[17] [*"Hier liegt etwas vergraben."*] Awareness that their correspondence is being censored intensifies the prisoners' efforts to invent ways to circumvent censorship. "In any case, the prisoners were well aware that their letters were being censored."[18] *["Jedenfalls hatte der Kgf. ein deutliches Bewusstsein, daß sein Brief zur Zensur gelange."]* The game moves to another level of linguistic play when the prisoner assumes that, because he is a native Italian, his understanding of language must be better than the German-speaking censor. For the prisoner, the challenge involves inventing linguistic "tricks" that the censor may be incapable of detecting because his lived experienced of Italian is simply different. For Spitzer, the game is a personal test of his own knowledge of Italian.[19] The prisoners' expectation that the censors only have time for spot checks adds a further dimension to the game. The process becomes a psychological field that tests and expands the limits of language. The "trick" becomes a figure at the very edge of language, and marks a psychological and linguistic trigger point that leads Spitzer to further study.

Psychology and Censorship

Since both the prisoner and the censor are engaged in a process of invention and discovery, the imagined interaction suggests to Spitzer that he has discovered a frontier for studying imagination and creativity.

> Since the prisoner had more time, he could work more carefully on some crafty paraphrase (*Umschreibung*) that the overwhelmed censor would not be able to figure out. With the time before him, the prisoner could occupy himself by reflecting on how language might be styled to present himself even

more creatively and discover a new art that was already, so to speak, inherent in his desire to convey something secretly.[20]

[*Auch der Kgf. hatte ja Zeit, er konnte in langsamer stilistischer Arbeit kniffige Umschreibungen ersinnen, die der bewandertste Zensor nicht enträtseln würde —zugleich aber trieb ihn die Langeweile zur Selbstbespiegelung, Übertreibung und Überkünstelung; die Lust, auf neue Art das ihm Längstgewohnte zu sagen, wirkte der ursprünglichen Absicht der Verheimlichung entgegen.*]

In effect, this metaphoric play is an element in psychological warfare.[21] The omnipresence of metaphor that Spitzer discovers in the correspondence argues that far more attention must be given to the place of fantasy in everyday language.[22] His work has opened quite simply, "the treasure chest of metaphor [*Metaphernschatz*].[23]

Dialogue and Correspondence

Access to fantasy and psychology in language emerges from dialogue. The observation becomes a major component of Spitzer's books from 1921 and 1922. The self-conscious experience of language as psychologically unseen or unacknowledged reveals itself in dialogue or conversation. The psychological phenomenon that appears in prisoners' correspondence is present in all language and may also be studied in the language of children. Citing Agatha Lasch (1879–1942), the first woman professor in German studies, Spitzer writes,

> [...] it is then the desire for amusement and play – an instinctive impulse in community for keeping secrets— also present in other levels of language nurtured through education and social development can hardly be underestimated.' In this sense, the prisoners of war are children themselves.[24]

[*Sind es doch die Lust an Scherz und Spiel, sowie der instinktive Hang zu Geselligkeit und Geheimbündelei, welche bei der Bildung und Entwicklung der Sondersprache von nicht zu unterschätzender Bedeutung gewesen sind'; auch die Kriegsgefangenen sind in diesem Sinn 'Kinder' gewesen* [...]]

For Spitzer, the psychosocial interplay in dialogue can also be applied to the study of literature.[25] In a cluster of comments, he suggests that the emphasis on realism in modern literature has made the study of allegory moribund at precisely the moment when the allegorical impulse in language appears in the linguistic study of dialogue.

Implication for Linguistics

Following his commentary on tricks, dialogue, and the psychology of invention, Spitzer powerfully attests to the cataclysmic impact of war on language. The effects of war extend far beyond *Das Schauplatz des Krieges* and permeate the entire society. Language absorbs war and continues its destructive presence in a time of peace:

> The horrendous dynamic of what has happened extends beyond anything else and appears as a horrendous transformation of language evident in the fundamental transformation of Romance language. The implication for European culture appears quite obvious: war has become a culturally dominant element that emerges from civilization itself. The war is waged in language behind the lines. Each soldier on the front is part of war on the home front. Whether a career soldier or a soldier in reserve, whether on leave or released from service, the soldier continues to effect his family. National democracy is renewed and maintained precisely in this way. War is a perpetual wound and even through it may be morally condemned, it cannot but have an effect on language.[26]

> [*Der ungeheueren Dynamik des Weltgeschehens, die alle früheren Umwälzungen in ihren Dimensionen überbietet, würde eine ungeheure Sprachwälzung entsprechen, wie sie eben die Ausbildung der romanischen Lagersprachen ist: dieser Gegensatz löst sich sehr einfach für unsere europäischen Kulturländer: der Krieg ist eben bei aller militärischen Überlastung unserer Kultur doch von Zivilisten und rein Zivilistisch geführt worden. …Der Krieg wird auch vor allem literarisch geführt daher überwiegt die Sprache des Hinterlandes. Jeder Frontkämpfer wird gerade bei einem Volkskrieg, der vor allem von Reservisten, also nicht Berufsmilitärs beführt wird, auf Urlaub oder gar bei der Entlassung aus dem Miltärdienst von seiner Familie wieder aufgesaugt. So wirkt den die modern nationale Demokratie sprachlich nivellierend und konservierent. Der militärische Krieg is eine rein vorübegehende Maßnahme der zivilistischen Regierungen und, da er in sich überwunden und moralisch verurteilt ist, kann er auch sprachlich nicht dauernd wirken.*]

Besides marking his own evolving pacifism, Spitzer alerts readers to the ways in which war upsets easy distinctions of social class based on language. Contrary to assumptions that the use of language is socially determined by education, Spitzer emphasizes the universal function of psychology and fantasy (*Gleichförmigkeit*). "[T]he boundary between the individual and the general *Stilistik* (of different groups) is less sharp than one would think."[27] [*Diese Bemerkung wird uns darauf hinlenken, die Grenzen zwischen individueller und genereller Stilistik weniger scharf zu ziehen.*] Already aware of the ideological use of *"das Volk"* to affirm German nationalism, Spitzer warns against any simplification that would link language to that term. Research should involve those elements that appear common to language rather than a preconceived abstraction associated with *"das Volk"*, which is "only an abstraction and certainly only the common denominator in research directed toward the individual, the language, and experience".[28] [*Das Volk ist nur eine Abstraktion, bewissermaßen der Durchschnitt der Individen, Sprache und Wesen dieser gilt es zu erforschen*] He is well aware that the details he has gathered include material for further research.

2. *Italienische Kriegsgefangenenbriefe: Materialien zu einer Charakteristik der Volkstümlichen Italienischen Korrespondenz (1921)*

Kriegsgefangenenbriefe (1921) expands the work of the prisoner of war archive to language in general. The immediate objective involves calling attention to the quasi-rhetorical structures that enable a consideration of the psychological dimensions of language. Repeating an observation made in the 1920 book, he stresses the ways in which the war has opened an entirely new source for the study of language.

> Just as the war has awakened problems and strengths that were hardly known or even recognized from human experience, the war has awakened the censor, a daughter of the war, to a new field of human research.[29]
>
> [*Sowie nämlich der Krieg auf den verschiedensten Gebieten menschlicher Intelligenz und bei den verschiedensten Individuen Probleme und Kräfte geweckt hat, die bisher unbekannt order unerkannt waren, so kann auch die Tochter des Krieges, die Zensur, dem menschlichen Forschungstrieb eine neue Wissensquelle sein.*]

The potential impact of the material being researched is enormous. For Spitzer, the turning point is the access he provides to everyday speech.

> Would that it were possible to make public everything that happens in everyday speech! From such a source the psychologist and linguist would learn more than from all the published research combined. By activating the study of everyday speech we give fresh access to the study of language. even if scientific investigation continues its work on language and literature by studying French songs or drinking songs as we did in the good old days.[30]

[*Würden doch möglichst viele Alltagsgespräche veröffentlicht! Aus ihnen hätte der Psychologe und der Linguist mehr zu lernen als aus den so beliebten geschriebenen Quellen. Bewiss is durch die modern Mundartkunde ein frischerer Hauch in die Sprachwissenschaft eingezogen und das Mündliche an der 'Mundart' endlich in der Sprachwissenschaft mündig geworden –noch immer aber gilt die Beschäftigung mit der guten alten Zeit, also etwas das Studium eines altfrazösischen Liedchens order Schwänkchens als 'wissenschaftlicher' denn die Erforschung des uns umgebenden Sprach-und Literatur materials.*]

The study of language can learn more from the "typical tongue"[31] ["*die typischen Zungen*"] found in the prisoners' correspondence that he discussed with his friend and colleague, Paul Kammerer[32]:

> Through the censor's work with small postcards and letters, we may draw more knowledge about humans, life, people, and the emergence of world events than all the studies on travel, exploration, custom, and social interaction that one might read. Through the art of reading the warp and weft of Italian letters made available by war surveillance, we have learned something about Italian.[33]

> [*Der zur Zensur gelangende Neuling erwartete vielleicht, aus den vielen kleingeschriebenen Karten und Briefen mehr Wissenschaft über den Menschen, das Leben, die Völker, das Weltgeschehen zu schöpfen als aus allen Reise- und Erdbeschreibungen, sitten- und sozialgeschichtlichen Studien, die er je gelesen, hoffte, durch eine Art Anschauungsunterricht bei der Lektüre italienischer Briefe über das ganze Weben und Wirken der Italiener belehrt zu warden [...]*]

> The common letter reveals the presence of dialect much less than it shows a conflict with the written language. This conflict is like the disorientation of someone who strolls through a modern city and must work to recognize all the old streets and houses that have been overwhelmed by the new building.[34]

> [*So gibt eigentlich der volkstümliche Brief nicht so sehr ein Bild des Dialektes als das des Kampfes des Dialekts mit der Schriftsprache. Wie man in einer modernen Grosstadt mit liebevollem Kennerblick die alten Gässchen und Häuer aufsuchen muss, die von modernen Bauten verdrängt und übererwuchert werden*[...]]

Based on the previously collected material, Spitzer's categories allow him to focus on forms inherent in the correspondence he has reviewed. His divisions are not simple rhetorical categories but "short forms" of micro-genres that contribute to the constitution of the correspondence. They are scripts that the censor reads and animates through his own "*gewisse Mentalität*".[35]

Spitzer identifies 23 different forms: 1) greetings and closure; 2) the form of the greetings; 3) apologies for imperfect handwriting; 4) pleasure at receiving mail; 5) sense of distance; 6) expression of faithfulness; 7) hope for peace; 8) dreams; 9) photographs; 10) children and relatives; 11) parents; 12) expressions of consolation and empathy; 13) resignation; 14) religion; 15) follow-up questions; 16) requests for money or clothing; 17) requests for foodstuffs; 18) hunger and other suffering; 19) self-defense and patriotism; 20) recognition of the censor; 21) humor; 22) love, feelings, and brutality; 23) naiveté. As I will suggest below, these categories also apply to German military correspondence during the war.

3. *Italienische Umgangssprache 1922*

The theoretical implications of the earlier monographs become the focus of the 1922 book. From the perspective of twentieth-century literary theory, the book anticipates reader response theory and resonates with the evolving work of the Bakhtin Circle in Leningrad in the late 1920s. Bakhtin cites Spitzer's book in *Problems of Dostoevsky's Poetics*.[36] Voloshinov refers to Spitzer's book in *Marxisme et Philosophie du Langage: Les problems fondamentaux de la méthode sociologique dans la science du language*.[37] (Spitzer's reception in Leningrad must wait for an expanded version of this study.) While the earlier monographs show an evolving self-awareness, *Italienische Umgangssprache* amplifies the degree to which self-discovery is taking place in the act of reading itself. Although the chapters remind one of the earlier monographs, they are also pared down to 1) the opening address; 2) the speaker and the listener; 3) the situated nature of the speaker; 4) the closing form of the conversation. At the same time that the categories are reduced, the theoretical implications are amplified. Rather than identifying rhetorical forms of speech, Spitzer seeks to describe the psychological dimensions of what I would call the linguistic or syntactic triggers that open the psychological space. "The descriptive-psychological method used in these pages involves following as carefully as possible the psychological process of partners in conversation as they play out their interaction."[38] (Spitzer [*Die deskriptiv-psychologische Methode, die hier zur Anwendung gelangt, besteht im Nachfühlen der psychologischen Prozesse, die zwischen zwei Gesprächsparners während eines Gesprächs abspielen.*]

Since this is a preliminary study, I can only give a limited sense of the questions engaged by Spitzer. For example, the initiation of a conversation by the speaker may appear as a "shadow thrown backwards in time", but it becomes inevitably influenced by interchange with the conversation partner.[39]

> The speaker imagines the setting as a complete whole and anticipates such an echo to return without thinking that the listener is completely unprepared to follow such a synthesis. Above all, it is the awareness that the detail of a mutual conception must be created. As a result, both the partner and the speaker discover themselves as actors in a performance.[40]

> [*Der Sprecher sieht das Bild der Situation in seiner Phantasie vollkommen fertig und weist auf dieses mit <u>ecco</u> hin ohne zu bedenken, daß der Hörer, vollkommen unvorbereitet wie er ist, der Synthese nicht folgen kann: allerdings ist verfrühte synthetische Form für den Hörer ein Ansporn, sich schaffen und auf diesen Ehrgeiz seines Partners hat auch der Sprecher mit schauspielerhafter Verstellung spekuliert.*]

The description of the back-and-forth exchange in a dialog is described as "a valve opened bit by bit until the pressure is released and the listener and speaker are equally served".[41] [[...] *zugleich kann sich auf diese Weise wie durch ein immer weiter und weiter geöffnetes Fentil der Affekt allmählich entladen und Hörer und Sprecher is damit gleich gedien.*].

> An opening statement, (something which could stand by itself), arouses the listener to grasp the entire event in detail at the same time that it virtually activates the fantasy of his memory. It is as if the reins are loosened in order for the agency of the fantasy to put in words what is imagined. Thus what is conveyed is animated in colorful detail so that the speaker only needs to give external referents while the detail and content becomes filled in by the listener.[42]

> [*Die Aufforderung, sich ein Geschehen selbst vorzustellen, beweckt nicht nur, den Hörer dahin zu bringen, daß er sich dies Geschehen in seinem ganzen Umfang und allen seinen Details ausmale, sondern gewissermaßen ein fiktives Bewährenlassen der Phantasie des Hörers: man tut so, als ob man dieser die Zügel ließe, obwohl man natürlich durch die Nennung des Geschehens und der Objekte, auf die er seine Phantasie einstellen soll, vollkommen die Richtung der Phantasietätigkeit bestimmt hat: das erzählte Geschehen wird farbenprächtiger gestaltet dadurch, daß der Sprecher nur die äußeren Anhaltspunkte zu geben scheint, während Details und Inhaltsfülle dem Hörer hinzuzuflügen überlassen warden.*]

The analysis of the contemporary reader or observer involves their discovering themselves, or being revealed, in settings where it is difficult to discern the relationship between truth and metaphor.

It is often difficult even for the contemporary to stand between figurative language and truth *(Dichtung und Wahrheit)* and through so many levels to make a clear choice between what appears either clarity or an abyss.⁴³

[*Es ist oft sogar für den Zeitgenossen schwer, zwischen Fiktion und Wahrheit zu scheiden: ja vielleicht bewegen wir uns gern und mit Absicht in Umgangsformen, die an der Grenze zwischen Dichtung und Wahrheit stehen und fliehen vor der Klipp und Klarheit schar gesonderter Abstufungen.*]

Above all, language itself bears a powerful animating force:

Everything in the extended world is dead *(tot)* for the human (involved in a conversation). If he wants to warm what appears dead, he must give it life. This happens through words; words, possessed by humans, are the breath of life. I am thinking of demonstrative pronouns.⁴⁴

[*Alle Dinge der Außenwelt sind dem Menschen gegenüber tot. Um den Partner für solche tote Dinge zu erwärmen, muß man ihnen Leben einflößen. Dies geschieht durch Worte, die den Lebenshauch des Menschen besitzen: ich meine die Pronomina.*]

Spitzer's experience as a censor has indeed been amplified into a study of *Umgangssprachen* or euphemism as a fundamental insight into the phenomenology of language:

The same argument appears in my other books. In the broadest sense, what might be called a poetic impulse runs through these books that combines detailed psychological work on linguistic confrontation in which one or the other triumphs. The difference between the cloaking and uncloaking euphemisms for hunger in the writing of the prisoners of war and the concealment and revelation of everyday drama in Italian life is hardly as great as one would think. The war-time censor only an amplifier of the censorship that is always present in social practice.⁴⁵

[*Dasselbe Bild könnte man aus meinen Büchern 'Italienischen Kriegsgefangenenbriefen' und 'Die Umschreibungen des Begriffes "Hunger" im Italienischen' entnehmen: überall lieferte eine fast dichterisch zu nennende Impulsivität einer psychologisch scharfsinnigen Kombinationsgabe Schlachten, in denen je nachdem diese order jene triumphierte. Der Unterschied zwischen der verhüllend-enthüllenden Ausdrucksweise der Hungermitteilung italienischer Kriegsgefangenen und der frei-unfreien Ausdrucksweise in italienischen Bühenenwerken ist dabei nicht so groß als man anfänglich glaubt: die Kriegszensur ist nur eine quantitative Verstärkung der Zensur, unter der Sprache ja immer steht—eben jener gesellschaftlichen sittlichen kulturellen [...]*]

Neither historical linguistics in academic isolation nor individual experience can be separated from the practice of reading or communication. The censor's control negates and blocks but also provokes a response that manifests the capacity of language to recreate itself. Spitzer's methodology, often vaguely referred to as "stylistics", or dismissed as a form of New Criticism, must be refigured in view of a phenomenology of reading. It is here we also find the resonance between Spitzer and Paul de Man that de Man himself has acknowledged.[46] Euphemism and paraphrase remind us how language approached through phenomenology seeks ways to find meaning in settings where any statement may be understood with difference. For the reader, euphemisms shape a texture that bears an expectant vigilance for different layers of language. The individual elements or fragments are always being attached or detached from our previous linguistic experience or memory.

Spitzer and Comparative Literature

In comparison with Erich Auerbach's *Mimesis,* Spitzer's influence remains indirect and foreshadows questions that become central to literary history and theory. René Wellek's references to Spitzer's work track his role in shaping the roots of comparative literature.[47] Although space must limit my comments on Spitzer's role in the emergence of American forms of Comparative Literature, his career enables us to track German influence on American scholarship.[48] Although Spitzer joins scholars such as Erich Auerbach and Ernst Curtius in the renewal of European civilization after WWII, his work on dialogue and the psychological study of language points to theoretical issues that have come to occupy literary studies.[49] Although Spitzer's practice of "close reading" appears to reinforce an "F. R. Leavis"-inspired "New Criticism", his interest extends beyond Anglo-American versions of French "explication'. As Apter suggests, Spitzer's practice of reading brings him far closer to Paul de Man than to New Criticism.[50] Even an initial study of the monographs shows Spitzer to be part of a generation trained in forms of linguistic exegesis that includes Heidegger.[51]

In his 1948 paper that serves as a personal survey of his work, Spitzer emphasizes the importance of his work on Rabelais.

> My personal way has been from the observed detail to ever broadening units which rest, to an increasing degree, on speculation. It is, I think the philological, the inductive, way, which seeks to show significance in the apparently futile, in contrast to her deductive procedure which begins with units assumed as given—and which is rather the way followed by the theologians

who start from on high, to take the downward path toward the earthly maze of detail, or by the mathematicians, who treat their axioms as if they were God-given.[52]

The 1948 essay describes the process of "speculation" in the words of Jacob Grimm as an "*Andacht zum Kleinen*".[53] Considered from the vantage point of hermeneutics, he is also aware that he must respond to criticism that he may be caught in a "philological circle".

> For, when I spoke in terms of a series of back-and-forth movements (first the detail, then the whole, then another detail, etc.), I was using a linear and temporal figure in an attempt to describe states of apperception which, in the mind of the humanist, only too often co-exist [...].For every poem the critic needs a separate inspiration, a separate light from above (it is this constant need which makes for humility, and it is the accumulation of past enlightenments that encourages a sort of pious confidence.[54]

Comparative Literature for Spitzer is a laboratory and an extension of his research and experience during WWI.

Conclusion

While Spitzer's monographs deserve further attention, I also want to emphasize that the rhetorical and linguistic structures Spitzer finds through surveillance and censorship also apply to German war correspondence found in *Feldpostkarten* or *Ansichtskarten*. The monographs are a reminder that my own work with text and image in an archive of German postcards also involves "surveillance and censorship". To what "history" do these cards belong? A personal history, a particular German history, or the context of the large "unified" history of WWI? Arranged in sequence, the cards invite multiple narratives that may also be integrated with the facing images and with photographic and lithographic production. But whatever sequence a narrative constructs, it is necessary to fill in the blanks or the missing spaces. How we address these "blanks" invites consideration of the "missing" conversations that are alluded to or seem to hover in the vicinity. From a linguistic vantage point, each sentence may contain syntactic triggers that activate a shifting-in or shifting-out of references showing that the cards participate in a larger circuit of communication. We may also ask about the ways in which metaphors shape our own inquiry. I emphasize such methods to suggest how the questions posed by Spitzer's interrogation lead in multifaceted ways to the theoretical practice found in late twentieth-century comparative literature. The postcards open imagined spaces of communication between the writer and the reader that may be recognized but never articulated. The postcards are more than "paper" piled on the heap of memorabilia from WWI. They belong to the discovery of discourse and the phenomenology of language opened by Spitzer's work during the war.

Just as the millions of postcards sent during World War I offer a testimony to the erasure of nineteenth-century panoramic landscapes, they provide glimpses of the landscapes (both real and imagined) that replace them. Their intimate evidence bears witness to the war long after the declaration of peace. With their views of churches and squares, battle dioramas, soldiers gathered before shelters or destroyed buildings, the postcards testify to frozen moments as if they are paper fragments that can be compared with the countless millions of shrapnel that rained from the sky. Placed side by side, they are a silent, slow-motion film with subtitles that illustrate change on the front and at home. Their double-face is not static but in continuous movement. The family that received them saw in the space-between things that we cannot imagine. And we too see things they could not see. We bring our research and sophisticated suspicion to the blank spaces and question what remains between. Such paper fragments open space between image and text and draw us to the generative space between personal witness and the narratives that wait to be written.

[1] This essay is for my friend and colleague Irina Sandomirskaja, who first perspicaciously asked what we might discover from Spitzer's role in censoring prisoners' complaints about starvation in Austrian prisoner of war camps.
[2] Leo Spitzer, "Linguistics and Literary History," in his *Linguistics and Literary History: Essays in Stylistics* (Princeton: Princeton University Press, 1974 (1948), 1–39.
[3] Leo Spitzer, *Italienische Kriegsgefangenenbriefe: Materialien zu einer Characterisktik der Volkstümlichen Italienischen Korrespondenz* (Bonn: Peer Hanstein Verlag, 1921).
[4] Hans Ulrich Gumbrecht, *Vom Leben und Sterben der großen Romanisten: Karl Vossler, Ernst Robert Curtius, Leo Spitzer, Erich Auerbach, Werner Krauss* (Munich, Carl Hanser Verlag, 2002); Idem, *The Powers of Philology: Dynamics of Textual Scholarship* (Urbana: Univ. of Illinois Press, 2003).
[5] Leo Spitzer, *Lettere de prigionieri di Guerra italiani 1915–1918*, ed. Lorenzo Renzi (Milan: Il Saggiatore, 2016).
[6] Leo Spitzer, "Linguistics and Literary History;" Idem *Essays on English and American Literature* (Princeton: Princeton Univ. Press, 1962); E. Kristina Baer and Daisy E. Shenholm, *Leo Spitzer on Language and Literature: A Descriptive Bibliography* (New York: Modern Language Association, 1991).
[7] Jean Starobinski, "Leo Spitzer et la lecture stylistique," in Leo Spitzer, *Études de style* (Paris: Gallimard, 1970), 7–39. ("Art du langage et linguistique," 45–78.
[8] Emily Apter, *The Translation Zone: A New Comparative Literature* (Princeton: Princeton Univ. Press, 2006).
[9] Reinhard Johler, "Laboratory Conditions: German-Speaking Volkskunde and the Great War," in *Doing Anthropology in Wartime and War Zones: World War I and the Cultural Sciences in Europe* (Bielefeld: Transaction Publishers, 2010), 1–24.
[10] Leo Spitzer, *Die Wortbildung als stilistisches Mittel Exempliziert an Rabelais* (M. Niemeyer, 1910). Spitzer affirms this was his first publication in his essay "Linguistics and Literary History": "In my first publication, *Die Wortbildung als stilistisches Mittel* (a Thesis written in 1910), I dealt with Rabelais' comic word-formations…", 15.
[11] Cited by Lorenzo Renzi, *Presentazione alla nuova edizione di Lorenzo Renzi*, in Spitzer, *Lettere di prigionieri di Guerra*, 18.
[12] Leo Spitzer, *Die Umschreibungen des Begriffes "Hunger" im Italienischen: Stilistische-Onomasiologische Studies auf Grund von Unveröffentlichtem Zensurmaterial* (Halle: Karras, Kröber & Nietschmann, 1920), 10.
[13] Ibid., 1–2.
[14] Ibid.,
[15] Ibid., 11.
[16] Ibid.
[17] Ibid., 260.
[18] Ibid., 258.
[19] Ibid., 260.
[20] Ibid.
[21] Ibid., 269.
[22] Ibid., 270.
[23] Ibid., 283.
[24] Ibid., 263.

²⁵ Ibid., 288.
²⁶ Ibid., 182.
²⁷ Ibid., 254.
²⁸ Ibid.
²⁹ Leo Spitzer, *Italienische Kriegsgefangenenbriefe*, 3.
³⁰ Ibid., 5.
³¹ Ibid., 11–12.
³² Paul Kammerer indicates an early interest in the sociological study of postcards written by prisoners of war. He divides facing images into categories including religion, flowers, children, families, spouses, and erotic scenes among others. Anything that might be useful for aerial reconnaissance was censored: panoramas, trains stations, bridges, fortifications, recognizable buildings. Flags and other symbols that could represent support for the enemy were also to be censored. Paul Kammerer, "Meine Ansichtskartensammlung," in Paul Kammerer, Menschheitswnde: Wanderungen im Grenzgebiet von Politik und Wissenschaft (Wien: 1919), 86–97.
³³ Spitzer, *Italienische Kriegsgefangenenbriefe*, 6.
³⁴ Ibid., 15.
³⁵ Ibid.
³⁶ Mikhail Bakhtin, *Problems of Dostoevsky's Poetic* ed. & trans. Caryl Emerson (Minneapolis, University of Minnesota, 1993 [1984]).
³⁷ Valentin Voloshinov, *Marxisme et philosophie du langage: les problems fondamentaux de la méthode sociologique dans la sciene du language* [Novelle edition bilingue traduite du russe par Patrick Sériot et Inna Tylkowski-Ageeva] (Limoge: Lambert-Lucas, 2010).
³⁸ Leo Spitzer, *Italienische Umgangssprache* (Bonn: Kurt Schroeder Verlag, 1922), viii.
³⁹ Ibid., 39.
⁴⁰ Ibid., 29.
⁴¹ Ibid., 56.
⁴² Ibid., 96.
⁴³ Ibid., 64.
⁴⁴ Ibid., 69.
⁴⁵ Ibid., 290.
⁴⁶ Paul de Man, *The Resistance to Theory* (Minneapolis: University of Minnesota, 1986), 54; idem, *Critical Writings 1953–1978* ed. Lindsay Waters (Minneapolis: University of Minnesota, 1989), 158–159.
⁴⁷ René Wellek and Austin Warren, *Theory of Literature* (New York: Harcourt, Brace & World, 1956), 112, 182f.; René Wellek, *Concepts of Criticism*, ed. Stephen Nichols (Yale: Yale University Press, 1963), 22, 77f.
⁴⁸ Ulrich Weisstein, *Comparative Literature and Literary Theory* (Bloomington: Univ. of Indiana, 1973 [German 1968]).
⁴⁹ Apter, *The Translation Zone*; Edward Said, "Roads Taken and Not Taken in Contemporary Criticism," *Contemporary Literature* 17:3 (1976), 327–348.
⁵⁰ Apter, *The Translation Zone*, 57.
⁵¹ Spitzer's response to Heidegger's misinterpretation of Mörike's poem, *Auf eine Lampe* offers a revealing commentary on his former Marburg colleague: "If language is our only

'house', we human beings have unduly anthropomorphized it. .... Many philosophical readers of Heidegger have been repeatedly astonished at his use of etymology as a form of thought (and especially at the use of German etymology to derive or assert universal states of affairs). For the philologist, it is amusing to see the usual philosophical network of word games extended to what is philologically dubious [...] In such cases the specific discipline of the philologist becomes evident in the exclusion of what is not expressed in the text and in the inclusion of resonances with the poet's own words (this has nothing to do with perceiving the 'unheard' that Heidegger postulates in respect to poetry). Only long training and that *je ne sais quoi* known as philological tact can provide even an approximate warrant for such decisions and distinctions" (see Emil Staiger, "Martin Heidegger, Leo Spitzer," *PMLA* 105:3 (1990, [1953]) 409–435).

[52] Spitzer, "Linguistics and Literary History," 23.
[53] Ibid., 24.
[54] Ibid., 27.

Автор как лакуна

MIKHAIL IAMPOLSKI

1

В последние несколько лет Ирина Сандомирская чрезвычайно продуктивно занимается философскими проблемами реставрации. В центре ее рефлексии естественно оказывается вопрос об оригинале, подлиннике, который проблематизируется самим процессом реставрации. Один из влиятельных теоретических подходов к этой проблеме был сформулирован в ставшем классическом труде Чезаре Бранди «Теория реставрации». Бранди говорит о двойном историзме произведения. Первый относится к тому времени, когда над ним работал автор, естественным образом участвовавший в процессе происходящих с произведением изменений. Однако после завершения последнего вмешательство автора прекращается, и созданное им продолжает меняться под воздействием внешних обстоятельств, лишенных авторской интенциональности. Этот период, по мнению Бранди, отмечен *вторичным историзмом*. Реставратор призван отделять первичный историзм от вторичного и, вмешиваясь в последствия второго, призван самоустраняться от всякого вторжения в первый: «мы не можем с какой бы то ни было легитимностью игнорировать ход времени и самим вторгаться в момент, когда художник создавал то, что до нас не дошло»[1]. Иначе говоря, реставратор не имеет права «дописывать» оригинальное полотно, часть которого пропала и являет нам *лакуну*.

Лакуна имеет важное значение для вторичного историзма. Она нарушает целостность произведения (а всякое произведение, согласно Бранди, стремится к целостности и органическому единству): «лакуна – это не имеющее оправдания, даже болезненное прерывание формы»[2]. Но она не просто прерывает форму, она обладает способностью выдвигаться на первый план. Бранди интерпретирует ее в терминах гештальт психологии, как фигуру, которая превращает некогда созданное художником в фон, из которого она агрессивно выступает. Отсюда – главная задача реставратора: не дописывая утраченные части полотна, «уменьшить воспринимаемую значимость лакуны как фигуры»[3], одновременно выводя фон на ее место: «Нарушение, производимое лакуной, более всего проистекает из отступления изображения в фон, и агрессивного вторжения лакуны как фигуры в контекст, который пытается ее изгнать, а не от формального прерывания, которое лакуна производит в изображении»[4].

С такой точки зрения, лишенное интенциональности материальное разрушение, оказывается не просто механическим, но *смысловым*, оно перераспределяет отношения фигуры и фона и тем самым меняет органическую целостность произведения. Оно работает не как случайный механический фактор, но как некий лукавый деперсонализированный *автор*, трансформирующий смыслы. При этом автор, некогда сознательно произведший смыслы, перестает доминировать, а лакуна претендует на его место. Они как бы меняются местами. Реставратор должен явиться как некая третья инстанция и указать лакуне на ее скромное место в фоне, редуцировать ее и лишить статуса автора. Он как феноменолог должен подвергнуть лакуну редукции – *epoché*.

В театре Но существует странное амплуа – *ваки*, это актер, который, хотя и присутствует на сцене, делает вид, что его нет. Как пишет Эуджено Барба, он «выражает свое небытие» и «привлекает внимание к своей способности не выражать»[5]. Такую же парадоксальную роль в Но и Кабуки играет *коккен* – одетый в черное ассистент, – помогающий основному исполнителю, и от которого требуется представлять собственное отсутствие: «Их присутствие, выражающее и представляющее ничто, столь непосредственно черпает из источника актерской энергии и жизни, что знатоки утверждают: труднее быть *коккеном*, чем актером»[6]. Эти странные фигуры являются театральными персонификациями лакун. Они обозначают – ценой больших энергетических затрат – необходимость исключить их из сцены. Но это виртуозное самоисключение маркирует отсутствие, требующее заполнения.

Лакуна – не просто автор-самозванец, она работает как агрессивный указатель на наличие авторского подобия, как *негативной инстанции* – указатель пустоты, способной генерировать смыслы и порождать тотальности. Более того, лакуна, как фигура, способна выдвигать на первый план материю, материальность произведения, которым начинает приписываться активная роль в творении.

Значимость лакуны часто выступает на фоне общей стертости, незаметности авторского присутствия. В литературе, например, слово, смысл которого мы понимаем из контекста определенных ситуаций, может быть так включено в конфигурацию мира, что делает наличие его автора «невидимым». Именно с этим связана наша способность к *объективированию* слова, его умение сообщать нам нечто о мире, выходящее за рамки субъективного опыта, и как бы от него отделяемого. Ян Паточка, который специально занимался феноменологией такого отделенного от субъектности мира, замечал:

> Создавая стабильную, овеществленную, объективированную лингвистическую архитектуру, мы создаем нечто большее, чем просто вещь в мире, но и нечто, что одновременно способно «содержать» в себе мир [...], превратить его в объект. Объективация языка – это особенно красноречивый пример *трансцендентности человека*, того факта, что на каждой стадии своей жизни человек уже эффективно преодолел все то, что является совокупностью единичных вещей[7].

Художник обладает повышенной способностью к такой объективации мира, основанной на объективации языка. Цельность художественного мира тесно связана с этой способностью художественных миров отделяться от субъектности своих творцов. Там, где речь идет об органической целостности произведения, о которой говорит Бранди, автор присутствует лишь как инстанция, которую мы реконструируем с помощью специальных герменевтических усилий.

Паточка анализировал эту проблематику еще в ранней книге 1936 года «Естественный мир как философская проблема». Здесь философ видел истоки современной, кризисной объективации мира в постепенном переходе от наивного представления мира к научному. Но уже в наивном представлении он выделял две составляющие – *данность* и *объяснительную*. Последняя связана с утратой свободы, спонтанности и с превращением человека в объект, на который внешний мир оказывает воздействия. Паточка выделял (с помощью феноменологической редукции) некую особую трансцендентальную субъективность, которая предшествует всему сущему, всему, что обладает бытием, и связывал ее с *данностью*, конституированием мира: «мы открываем, что трансцендентальное – это субъективность, предшествующая сущему, и это мир»[8].

Но рядом с этой трансцендентальной конституирующей субъективностью существует и иная. Первую Паточка называет *творящей*, а вторую – *сотворенной*. Творящая объективность становится сотворенной благодаря нашей способности к рефлексии над самим актом творения. Эту операцию Паточка видит уже у Декарта: «Когда, отсылая к моей собственной активности, я подвергаю ее рефлексии, я могу убедить себя в моем собственном существовании в формах идентичности»[9].

Моя деятельность становится объектом рефлексии и именно по отношению к ней формулируется Декартом знаменитое: cogito ergo sum. В сфере сотворенной субъективности и возникает ощущение авторства как инстанции, организующей произведение. Но эта актуализация авторства возможна только тогда, когда органическая целость воображаемого мира уже подвергается коррозии, когда в ней возникает изъян, тень лакуны, даже если эта тень предстает как точка зрения перспективы, в которой нет никакого «реального» автора.

Чем глубже кризис репрезентации и наивного представления, тем труднее достигнуть мира трансцендентальной субъективности и тем сильнее у нас потребность мыслить и воображать автора, рефлексировать над ним. Сам поиск авторской инстанции – это проявление усиливающегося недоверия к самоочевидности данного. И именно в контексте такого поиска сотворенного субъекта, способного занять позицию субъекта творящего, и возникает рефлексия о лакуне в теории реставрации. Лакуна – это материальное указание на частичную утрату автора, на зияние, творящее смыслы, бросающее авторству прямой вызов. Она взывает к реконструкции мнимых авторских фигур, их выведению из фона на авансцену и к подавлению чужеродного, чужого агрессивного авторства без личности.

2

Эта проблематика, на мой взгляд, релевантна для концептуализма. Конечно, при переносе в другие материи лакуна становится своего рода метафорой. Речь тут больше не идет о реальной утрате части текста, а «реставрация» в самом широком смысле начинает распространяться на любую фикцию автора, которого выводят из тени, из фона на авансцену текста, но выводят именно в сложном взаимодействии с зиянием.

Концептуализм, как считают некоторые теоретики, возникает как результат абстрагирования и выхода за рамки материальности вещи, которой приписывается статус произведения искусства. Напомню известное определение Гройса, в котором фиксируется различие между концептуальным и неконцептуальным искусством:

> При широком понимании «концептуализм» будет означать любую попытку отойти от делания предметов искусства как материальных объектов, предназначенных для созерцания и эстетической оценки, и перейти к выявлению и формированию тех условий, которые диктуют

восприятие произведений искусства зрителем, процедуру их порождения художником, их соотношение с элементами окружающей среды, их временной статус и т.д.[10]

Речь тут прямо идет о замещении данности объяснительным представлением, позволяющим рефлексию по поводу самого акта творения. В результате резко акцентируется фигура творца, укорененная в жест конституирования мира. Автор выдвигается на первый план в ущерб самому «произведению». Напомню утверждение Паточки: «Когда, отсылая к моей собственной активности, я подвергаю ее рефлексии, я могу убедить себя в моем собственном существовании в формах идентичности».

Пригов (а его опыт мне кажется особенно показателен для интересующей меня проблемы) во многих своих текстах сосредотачивался на исследованиях «процедуры порождения текста художником», тем самым отметая сам принцип творческой спонтанности, которую он трактовал как чисто формальную маску, прикрывавшую пустоту на месте художественного субъекта. Хорошо известны его иронические экзерсисы с симулякрами авторства, его тексты, написанные, например, от лица женщин и т.д. Автор в такой перспективе – это текстовый конструкт, принадлежащий к одному из аспектов процедуры порождения текста.

Себе Пригов иронически отказывает в авторстве, заявляя, что он творит в компании множества двойников, среди которых и Пушкин, и Лермонтов, и Достоевский):

Вместе, вдвоем, втроем, вчетвером, вообще, кто есть, вместе, вместе, но тихо, тихо)

Я твой, я твой двойник печальный

Двойной потусторонний свет

Сосуд! Сосуд первоначальный

(уже я говорю: Постой! Постой! - говорю: Постой! - говорю: Кто? Кто ты? - говорю, говорю я!)

Я Пушкин есть, но я и нет

(Стой! Стой! - кричу я: Стой! - кричу: Это же мои стихи! Мои! -

кричу кричу я: Мои! Мои стихи! - кричу я, кричу)

Я Лермонтов, но я и нет

> Я Достоевский, но я и нет!
>
> (Достоевский! Достоевский! Достое-е-е-евский! – это уже я кричу, пытаясь перекричать его: Стой! – пытаюсь перекричать его: Стой! – пытаюсь: Стой! – перекричать его)[11].

Эти приговские *крики* указывают не столько на повышенную эмоциональность того, кто носит имя Пригова, сколько на систематическое исчезновение его собственной субъектности, на зияние лакуны, заменяемой чужими масками, плодами насильственной реставрации. Сам крик – это способ грубого конституирования подмены там, где ничего нет. Речь именно идет о *ваки* или *коккене*, изощренно и с полной энергией кричащих о своем отсутствии. И чем более энергичным оказывается авторский персонаж, тем более он сходен с лакуной. Речь идет о том, чтобы именно «убедить себя в [...] собственном существовании в формах идентичности».

В какой-то мере Пригов криками пытается отделить себя от чисто текстовых химер, которые от него неотделимы. Но эта повышенная эмоциональность не в состоянии сделать Пригова не персонажем и не текстовой инстанцией, а живым человеком. Его литературные двойники сами отличаются повышенным эмоциональным тоном, как например, Лермонтов или Достоевский.

Известно, что придуманная Приговым «новая искренность» – это лишь дискурсивная практика, не предполагающая подлинной аффективности. В одном из текстов, где он экспериментирует с «искренностью», он сообщает о принятой им манере всех называть по именам:

> В обычной жизни-то я всех называю по имени-отчеству, так что вроде бы эта простота и искренность в моем случае оборачивается некоторой имитацией искренности, как бы даже не искренностью, а условностью. Так ведь условность искренности – она и есть та сторона искренности, которая и обнаруживается в словесности[12].

Иными словами, чем искренней текст, тем более он литературно условен и тем больше он отделен от всякого личного человеческого опыта, от субъектности, которую (в последнее время) парадоксально принято одновременно связывать с аффективностью и с трансцендентальной способностью к исчезновению в мире.

Пригов неоднократно декларирует слабость и нерелевантность авторской личности. Поэт в его текстах – это *литературный образ* гения и титана и при этом совершенно незначительная в реальности фигура:

«конечно, есть люди, наделенные необыкновенным, прямо-таки фантастическим воображением, и их помыслы совершенно необычны. Увы, мы не из таких»[13]. Или в другом месте:

> Собственно, все мое творчество посвящено личности поэта как слабого человека, кроме тех произведений, где поэт обозначен как сильный человек, гений и герой. А вот этот образ – наиболее близок мне. Хотя, что тут нового. Всем давно уже известно, что поэт как человек – существо весьма непрезентабельное[14].

О себе Пригов пишет как о сменяющихся наборах идентификационных клише, сквозь которые он не может пробиться.

Но эта «непрезентабельная личность», будучи по существу лакуной, вообще не имеет никакой идентичности, это просто набор литературных клише, заполняющих *отсутствие*. В 2001 году Пригов написал примечательный текст о литературной методике конструирования личности автора и его идентичности – «Само-иденти-званство». В этом тексте он упоминает и свои «многолетние и отчаянно мной самим манифестируемые, так сказать, персонажные игры внутри литературных и изобразительных конвенционально-фиксированных поведенческих моделей»[15] и среди прочего говорит о драме российской истории, которая постоянно создавала по литературному образцу набор «личностей», не позволяющих осуществиться подлинному движению истории[16].

В 1998 году Пригов написал текст «Что подумает обо мне иной», где дан длинный список всевозможных характерологических клише:

> Иной думает, что я талантливый, умный, красивый [...] Иной думает, что я коварен, злобен, подл, что пишу стихи ради огромных денег, что под подушкой у меня кривой нож, что думы мои черны и беспросветны [...] Иной думает, что я черный, почти абиссинец, что горбатый и припадаю на левую копытообразную ногу, что вынужден каждую ночь подрезать когти и уши, что с трудом отбиваю исходящий от меня серный запах [...] Иной думает, что я стремителен и неистов [...] Иной думает, что я умен, умен, невероятно умен [...] Иной думает, что я толстый, мрачный и саркастичный, пишу целыми днями, опустив ноги в таз с горячей водой, иногда разражаюсь диким демоническим хохотом...[17]

и т.д.

Некоторые исследователи предполагают, что исчезновение личности творца – характерная особенность концептуального искусства. Чарльз Грин, например, обратил внимание на распространение среди концептуалистов творческих дуэтов, само существование которых отменяет ценность уникальной личности художника. Он останавливается на таких парах, как Кристо и Жан-Клод, Марина Абрамович и Улей, и других. В русском искусстве к ним легко добавить Комара и Меламида, Илью и Эмилию Кабаковых. Грин пишет о коллективном творчестве как о выражении характерной для концептуалистов тенденции к деперсонализации, и говорит об «идее искусства, которое кодирует личное отсутствие и смещенную идентичность, исчезновение и производство маркеров или следов ухода…»[18].

Но ситуация, как мне представляется, гораздо сложнее той, что описывает Грин. И Пригов – тому доказательство. Факт, что всякое разрастание эмоциональности и искренности в тексте приводит к опустошению авторской инстанции, гораздо более сложный. Начать тут лучше всего, пожалуй, с Ницше, который, как известно, сформулировал парадоксальную в его устах критику индивидуальности. Он, например, утверждал, что индивидуальность, личность, Я – это чистые фикции:

> Тело помогает нам познать человека как множество живых существ, которые частью борются между собой, частью распределяют обязанности и повинуются друг другу; утверждая свое отдельное существование, они невольно утверждают и целое.
>
> Среди этих живых существ есть такие, которых можно в большей мере отнести к повелевающим, нежели к повинующимся; среди них тоже идет борьба и бывают победы[19].

У Бранди органическая целостность отсылает к единому автору, у Ницше наоборот. Отрицание существования индивидов, и утверждение, что всякое «органическое существо» состоит из множества живых существ, по мнению португальского философа Нуно Набаиша, связано с ницшевским недоверием к понятию атома, отдельной частицы или даже отдельной вещи. Такие понятия не позволяли мыслить энергетику, общее движение воли к власти. Поэтому Ницше был вынужден отказаться от понятия атома в пользу понятия «кванта», фиксировавшего величину определенной динамической силы, которая «порождает индивидуацию»[20]. Барба также связывал персонализированную репрезентацию отсутствия с разворачиванием мощной актерской энергетики.

Ницше так объясняет фикцию индивидуальности:

> Понятие «движение» есть перевод этого мира воздействий в мир зримый – мир глаза. Здесь всегда подразумевается, что в движение приводится нечто – при этом всегда мыслится вещь, которая действует (будь то в форме фикции: атома-комочка, или даже его абстракции – в виде динамического атома), – выходит, мы не расстались с привычкой, которой прельщают нас восприятия и язык. Субъект и объект, деятель и действие, действие и то, что оно совершает, отделены одно от другого: не забудем, что все это чистая семиотика, а не что-либо реальное. Механика как учение о движении – это уже перевод на язык человеческих восприятий.
>
> Чтобы быть в состоянии считать, нужны единицы: но это еще не дает права предполагать, что такие единицы действительно существуют. Понятие единицы мы заимствовали у нашего понятия «я» – древнейшей статьи нашего символа веры. Если бы мы не считали себя единицами, то никогда бы не построили понятие «вещь». [...] Феноменальное, стало быть, состоит из: примеси понятия числа, понятия субъекта, понятия движения: здесь все же сказывается наш глаз, наша психология.
>
> Если мы устраним эти примеси, тогда не будет больше никаких вещей, а останутся лишь динамические количества, связанные напряжением со всеми прочими динамическими количествами: чья сущность и состоит в их отношении ко всем другим количествам...[21]

Лакуна такая же наделенная материальностью мнимость – «вещь», «комок». У Ницше парадоксальным образом творческая энергия, воля оказываются производными от исчезновения атомов, комков, предметов – то есть индивидуальных форм, производимых исключительно нашим глазом и языком. В итоге Ницше формулирует свой парадокс так: «воля к власти — не бытие, не становление, но некий пафос— вот элементарнейший факт, из которого только и вытекает какое-либо становление, какое-либо следствие»[22]. Мир же индивидов, или псевдо-индивидов, Ницше определяет как мир механики и семиотики, не затрагивающих «причинную силу». В терминах Пригова этот парадокс можно было бы сформулировать так: чем сильнее автор, тем он слабее как индивид. И это совершенно понятно – ведь сама идентичность, само понятие личности – это семиотические текстовые конструкты, которые не могут быть автором, но только персонажем.

Но, пожалуй, с максимальной полнотой эту эпопею исчезновения сильного автора за маской персонажа сформулировал Фернандо Пессоа в его известной теории гетеронимов. Знаток, переводчик и исследователь Пессоа Ричард Зинит высказал гипотезу о близости гетеронимии Пессоа деперсонализации у Ницше[23]. В известном письме 1935 года Адольфо Касаишу Монтейро Пессоа объяснял создание им гетеронимов «органической тенденцией к деперсонализации и симуляции»[24] и пояснял: «Главным свойством мой личности как художника является то, что я драматический поэт, во все, что я пишу, я вкладываю экзальтацию поэта и деперсонализацию драматурга»[25]. Пессоа считал именно деперсонализацию главным свойством драматурга, способного, как Достоевский у Бахтина, исчезать, утрачивать свою личность за множеством голосов и персонажей. То есть сила персонажей прямо связана со способностью автора исчезать, трансцендировать индивидуальность в потенциале творческой энергии.

В 1928 году Пессоа набросал свои соображения по поводу градаций деперсонализации, которые он назвал «Степени лирической поэзии». Первая степень – лирический поэт, который характеризуется ограниченным количеством эмоций, выражающих единство темперамента (любовь, печаль и т.д.). Вторая степень относится к более интеллектуальному поэту, способному к созданию более разнообразного мира. Третья степень – еще более интеллектуальный поэт, который

> начинает деперсонализироваться, чувствовать не потому, что он чувствует, но потому, что он думает, что чувствует; чувствует состояния души, которых он в действительности не испытывает, а потому что он их понимает. Мы тут оказываемся в прихожей драматической поэзии, в ее интимной сущности[26].

Речь идет о постепенном переходе на позиции концептуализма или объясняющей репрезентации Паточки. Далее следует четвертая степень лирического поэта, она относится к еще более интеллектуальному литератору, который «вступает в полную деперсонализацию. Он не только чувствует, но и проживает те состояния души, которые непосредственно не испытывает»[27]. И, наконец, на пятой стадии тотальной деперсонализации персонажи четвертой степени сами становятся авторами и окончательно отделяются от личности творца. Это степень гетеронимов.

Пессоа показывает, что восхождение по ступеням абстракции выводит поэта из состояния конфессионального автора, выражающего свою личность, в мир тотальной деперсонализации, утраты своего Я. И это восхождение эквивалентно обнаружению максимума творческой энергии и способности порождать не только персонажей, но и фиктивные авторские фигуры.

Мне кажется, что Пригов с его множественностью псевдоавторских личин и явной склонностью к драматическому и театральному, близок Пессоа. Показательно, что максимум творческой энергии тут реализуется в рамках концептуализма, который порождает одновременно «слабого» автора и одновременно «гения и титана» как персонажа и псевдоавтора.

3

Когда «личность» превращается в персонаж и исчезает за персонажной маской, акт творения начинает связываться с таким неопределенным и *энергетическим* понятием, как «*жест*». Жест подозрителен потому, что он не укладывается к традиционную семиотику и «механику». В Предуведомлении к «50 капелькам крови в абсорбирующий среде» Пригов указывает на неопределенность и нечистоту жанра этого текста: «От поп и соц-арта, а также концептуальных текстов эти отличает стремление апеллировать к какому-никакому реальному визуальному и эмоциональному опыту, а также к прямому поэтическому жесту»[28]. Жест подозрителен своей связью со спонтанностью реакции, то есть, в конечном счете, с неким призраком реагирующей и имеющей опыт личности. Однако в ином месте жест понимается как проявление безликости:

> мы видим возрастающую тенденцию растворения стиха (или в общем смысле – текста) в ситуации и жесте [...]. В акционно-перформансной деятельности текст (стихотворение, скажем) присутствует как нулевой или точечный вариант ситуации и жеста[29].

Пригов объясняет, что в своей «онтологии» (я бы все же сказал – семиотике) текст, стихотворение несовместимы с жестом («ситуация, жест как бы отменяемы стихом»[30]). Это связано с тем, что они не столько мыслятся как результат генерации, порождения или индивидуации, сколько как продукт, сопоставимый с вещью или личностью. Жест, однако, включен в текст, но лишь в форме следа от первоначального импульса. Жест невольно отсылает к ницшевским квантам и энергии.

Жест интересен концептуалистам потому, что он, пожалуй, единственное, что несет в себе энергию творческой воли, исчезающую и из фигуры автора, и из произведений в процессе деперсонализации. В «Диалоге» Ильи Кабакова и Бориса Гройса есть интересный эпизод, когда Кабаков (совершенно в стиле Пригова и деперсонализации) говорит об исчезновении выдающихся личностей и самому себе приписывает «витальность насекомого»[31]:

> Я бы сказал, что в основе лежит демократический принцип, а не аристократический. Опора этого мировоззрения в том, что мы все одинаковые и будем жить, игнорируя исключительные события, решения, исключительных людей. С чем связана подобная установка – я не знаю. Это философия маленького человека, философия пассивного существования, в конце концов, философия неудачника[32].

Все это очень напоминает рассуждения Пригова о слабом авторе. Речь в этой связи заходит о музее, в котором, по мнению Гройса, все-таки собираются исключительные творения исключительных людей. Кабаков ему возражает, и Гройс отчасти с ним соглашается, но только отчасти: «Да, он собирает банальные вещи, но банальные вещи, поданные как исключительный жест»[33]. Это интересное различие, напоминающее о Дюшане: вещи банальные, ярких произведений нет, но поданы они *исключительным жестом*. И далее Гройс делает занятное заявление: «Ты хочешь быть исключительным и банальным одновременно»[34]. В каком-то смысле это неожиданная формулировка парадокса всего концептуального проекта – предельная банальность в упаковке исключительного суверенного жеста.

Эти мотивы проработаны у Гройса в эссе «Политика инсталляции». Здесь описывается разница между художественным произведением и «стандартной музейной экспозицией», создаваемой кураторами. Такая экспозиция, по мнению Гройса, отражает господствующие представления о публичном пространстве демократии, открытом для любого посетителя и дискуссий. В этом пространстве произведения искусства не могут навязать зрителю свое присутствие. Гройс пишет о больных, ослабленных произведениях внутри кураторских проектов: «произведение искусства больное, беспомощное; чтобы оно было увидено, зрители должны быть приведены к нему так, как посетители приводятся больничным персоналом к лежачему больному в больнице»[35]. В кураторском пространстве обитают больные произведения слабых авторов, которые лечатся кураторами от немощи. Публичным демократическим пространствам противостоит авторское, сильное, суверенное и приватное пространство инсталляций:

> Материальный носитель инсталляции – это само пространство. Это, однако, не означает, что инсталляция в чем-то «нематериальна». Наоборот, инсталляция материальна par excellence, так как она пространственна, и располагаясь в пространстве, она отвечает наиболее общему определению материальности. Инсталляция трансформирует пустое, нейтральное, публичное пространство в индивидуальное произведение искусства и оно приглашает зрителя испытывать это пространство как холлистское, тотализирующее пространство произведения искусства. Все, что попадает в это пространство, становится частью произведения искусства просто потому, что оно помещено внутри этого пространства[36].

Здесь как будто происходит превращение пустого, бессмысленного пространства лакуны в агрессивную суверенность фигуры. Инсталляция таким образом превращает демократическое в суверенное, а слабого художника с его слабыми произведениями (трансцендентального субъекта) в суверенного титана и гения в духе Батайя.

Здесь хорошо определен смысл перехода от банального (кураторского) к исключительному (авторскому), хотя сам этот переход несет в себе элемент необъяснимо мистического. У куратора пространство выставки пустое, в нем зритель фланирует, как фланер в городе. Но стоит назвать это пространство инсталляцией, как оно перестает быть пустым и становится тотально материальным и неотличимым от художественного объекта. Гройс пишет: «Различие между художественным объектом и просто объектом становится тут незначимым. Принципиально важным же тут становится различие между маркированным пространством инсталляции и немаркированным публичным пространством»[37].

Пространство становится материальным в результате некоего маркирования, которое производит глубокую онтологическую трансформацию. Но само это маркирование и есть жест художника, на который не способен куратор, по определению не являющийся творцом. Но ситуация тут, на мой взгляд, еще более сложная. Когда-то Вилем Флюссер так определил смысл жеста:

> Жест – это движение тела или инструмента, связанного с телом, которое не имеет удовлетворительного причинно-следственного объяснения. […] дискурс, касающийся жестов, не может завершиться причинно-следственным объяснением, потому что такие объяснения не принимают в расчет специфику жестов[38].

Для понимания жеста мы вынуждены связать его со своего рода семиотикой, символизмом и понятием коммуникации. Мы вынуждены искать *смысл* жеста. И этот смысл обнаруживается в аффектах. Жест может выражать боль, усталость, радость и проч. Аффекты выражаются для нас через жесты. То, что призвано быть причиной жеста, оказывается само манифестируемым через него и в каком-то смысле им создаваемым. «Чтобы ближе подойти к смыслу аффекта, я должен интерпретировать жесты»[39], – пишет Флюссер. Это, в конечном счете, может означать, что жест производит аффект. Нет жеста, нет доступа к аффекту. Причинно-следственная связь переворачивается. Причина становится следствием, а жест символом.

Если отнести эту логику к диалогу Кабакова и Гройса, можно сказать, что не столько суверенный художник позволяет состояться жесту, сколько сам жест производит сильного автора, как некое воплощение аффекта, творческой энергии. Нет жеста, нет художника, нет и инсталляции. Но поскольку аффект (или фигура за этим аффектом) есть производное, символически выражаемое, то, как указывает Флюссер, аффект этот *искусственен*. В нем нет ничего естественного (естественность теперь приписывается философом невидимому отличному от аффекта «состоянию ума», которое только обозначается аффектом через жест). Это разделение аффекта и «состояния» позволяет Флюссеру провести тонкое различие между подлинностью жеста и его фальшивостью, различие, которое при этом далеко не очевидно:

> Когда я вижу жест, подчеркивающий чувство, например, у плохого актера в плохой пьесе, стремящегося передать эмоцию отцовской любви, я назову его «фальшивым». Но будет неправильно назвать его «ошибочным» или «лживым». Он «фальшив» в смысле «дурного вкуса» и будет лишенным подлинности, даже если актер действительно любящий отец. [...] Для жеста, выражающего чувство, совершенно возможно быть эпистемологически и морально честным и эстетически нечестным, как в случае жеста плохого актера[40].

Иными словами, тут постулируется возможность подлинности фальши. Эстетически сомнительный жест может сохранять связь с истинностью некой энергетики. Это состояние связано с «искусственностью» символического обозначения, в которое встроено невидимое «естественное» состояние. Это раздвоение, на мой взгляд, может быть соотнесено с раздвоением субъекта на трансцендентального и сотворенного (Паточка). Первый всегда в каком-то смысле лежит в горизонте подлинности, а второй всегда искусственен, а потому легко становится фальшивым. Жест творца несет в себе и трансцендентальную составляющую и фальшивость сотворенного «гения и титана». Лакуна, о которой говорил Бранди, и которая относится к области вторичного историзма, всегда искусственна (хотя и создается самим «естественным» движением времени) и потому легко превращается в фигуру на фоне мира, конституируемого «слабым», трансцендентальным субъектом (автором). Лакуна фальшива и подлинна одновременно.

Фон, о котором писал Бранди, и в который легко превращается текст первого историзма, это *среда*, из нее возникают и в нее уходят значимые фигуры. В тексте, посвященном хоре (неуловимой среде дифференциации и индивидуации), Деррида делает неожиданное наблюдение о странном сходстве между неназываемой хорой и Сократом, который утверждает, что относится к роду людей (софистов, поэтов), не имеющих в отличие от философов и политиков, *места*. Сократ определяет себя как человека третьего рода, который сам не может быть назван и который, подобно хоре, есть лишь вместилище всего того, что имеет идентичность. Деррида пишет:

> Сократ исчезает (s'efface), он стирает в себе все типы, все роды, не только типы и роды людей изображения и симулякра, похожим на которых он себя выставляет, но и людей действия и людей слова, – философов и политиков, – к которым он обращается, отступая перед ними. Но отступая таким образом, он помещает себя или объявляет себя принимающим адресатом (destinataire réceptif) или, скажем, вместилищем всего, что отныне туда будет вписано[41].

Это исчезновение Сократа лежит в той же плоскости, что и деперсонализация Пессоа или слабость автора Пригова. Самое интересное тут, возможно, это неожиданное превращение автора в не-место (но места не имеет и ницшевский квант). Пространство тут противоположно тому, в котором Гройс видел манифестацию авторской суверенности. Здесь происходит исчезновение всякой суверенности вместе с именем автора. Автор становится неким псевдопространством. И это противоречивое свойство *быть и не занимать места* в полной мере характеризует лакуну, превращающую произведение в фон, но не находящую себе в нем места. Если это наблюдение хотя бы в чем-то справедливо, мы оказываемся по ту сторону простой дихотомии – материального и мыслимого, концептуального, фальшивого и подлинного, естественного и искусственного. Но, возможно, само искусство, не вписывающееся в эту дихотомию, каким-то образом прописано в не-месте переходов и метаморфоз, в не-месте, где материальное ищет встречи с интенциональным и демонстрирует слабость той бинарности, в рамках которой мыслит себя концептуализм любого рода.

[1] Cesare Brandi, *Theory of Restoration* (Rome: S. p. Nardini Editore, 2005), 91.
[2] Ibid., 92.
[3] Ibid.
[4] Ibid., 93.
[5] Eugenio Barba & Nicola Savarese, *A Dictionary of Theatre Anthropology. The Secret Art of The Performer* (London, Routledge, 1991), 10.
[6] Ibid.
[7] Jan Patočka, *L'écrivain, son "objet"* (Paris: P.O.L., 1990), 88.
[8] Jan Patočka, *Le monde naturel comme problème philosophique* (La Haye: Martinus Nijhoff, 1976), 27.
[9] Ibid., 31.
[10] Борис Гройс, *Московский романтический концептуализм* // *Московский концептуализм* / Сост. Е. Деготь и В. Захаров. (Москва: WAM, 2005), 343.
[11] Д. А. Пригов, «Монстры. Чудовищное/трансцендентное.» – *Собрание сочинений в пяти томах*, т. 3. (Москва: Новое литературное обозрение, 2017), 131–132
[12] Д. А. Пригов, «Монады» – *Собрание сочинений в пяти томах*, т.1 (Москва: Новое литературное обозрение, 2013), 378.
[13] Там же, 395.
[14] Там же, 401.
[15] Там же, 348.
[16] «Вся российская история была историей доминирующих идентификаций, достаточно глубоко и надолго выжегших все пространство вокруг себя, что в настоящее время, даже при вроде бы потворствующих экономических и социокультурных обстоятельствах не потворствует расцвету упомянутого множества, но воспроизводится вокруг заново и с невиданной легкостью при любом властном жесте.» – Там же, 349.
[17] Д. А. Пригов, «Монстры», 37–38.
[18] Charles Green, *The Third Hand: Collaboration In Art From Conceptualism To Postmodernism* (Minneapolis: University of Minnesota Press, 2001), 139.
[19] Фридрих Ницше, Черновики и наброски, весна 1884 – осень 1885 гг. (27-27) – В кн.: Фридрих Ницше. *Полное собрание сочинений в 13 томах*, т. 11 (Москва: Культурная революция, 2012), 264–265.
[20] Nuno Nabais, *Nietzsche and the Metaphysics of the Tragic* (London-New York: Continuum, 2006), 54.
[21] Фридрих Ницше, Черновики и наброски 1887–1889 (14–79). – В кн.: Фридрих Ницше. *Полное собрание сочинений в 13 томах*, т. 13 (Москва: Культурная революция, 2005), 239–240.
[22] Там же, 240.
[23] Richard Zenith, "Nietzsche and Pessoa's Heteronyms. – Partial Answers" in *Journal of Literature and the History of Ideas*, Volume 10, Number 1, January 2012, pp. 139–149. Пессоа писал о необходимости отказаться от «догмы личности», которую он считал «теологической фикцией». – Fernando Pessoa. *Le chemin du serpent* (Paris: Christian Bourgois, 1991), 79.
[24] Pessoa, Ibid., 205.
[25] Fernando Pessoa, *Selected Prose* (New York, Grove Press, 2001), 246.

[26] Fernando Pessoa, *Le chemin du serpent*, 119.
[27] Ibid., 120.
[28] Д. А. Пригов, «Монстры», 80.
[29] Там же. – «23 явления стиха после его смерти».
[30] Там же.
[31] Илья Кабаков, Борис Гройс, *Диалоги* (Вологда: Библиотека Московского Концептуализма Германа Титова, 2010), 191.
[32] Там же, 193.
[33] Там же.
[34] Там же.
[35] Boris Groys, "Politics of Installation". – *e-flux journal* #02 January 2009, 2.
[36] Ibid., 3.
[37] Ibid.
[38] Vilém Flusser, *Gestures* (Minneapolis, University of Minnesota Press, 2014), 2.
[39] Ibid., 5.
[40] Ibid., 7.
[41] Жак Деррида, *Эссе об имени* (М.-СПб: Алетейя, 1998), 163.

Nelly Sachs' Chorus Poetics

MARCIA SÁ CAVALCANTE SCHUBACK

Nelly Sachs' first two poetry collections are entitled *In den Wohnungen des Todes* (In the Habitations of Death) and *Sternverdunkelung* (Eclipse of the Stars)[1] published in 1947 and 1949, respectively. Although she had been publishing her poems since 1929, asked when she began writing poetry, she answered "*in den Wohnungen des Todes*", "in the Habitations of Death". A lot has been written about Nelly Sachs' poetry in relation to inhabiting the experience of death and also about this statement of hers[2]. As Aris Fioretos has insisted in his readings of her poetry, "everything said is dedicated to the dead".[3] The common and unquestionable reading is that her poetry accomplished a fundamental turn at the end of the war when the extension of the horror of the crimes against the Jewish people and their suffering became public. Having this in mind, I would like in the following reflection to focus on what it means for Nelly Sachs to give birth to poetry in the habitations of death.

But how to begin in the habitations of death (*In den Wohnungen des Todes*)—how is such a beginning to be understood? How can death give birth? A central cycle of this collection is called "The "Choruses after Midnight". It is an extensive circle of choruses: "Chorus of Abandoned Things", "Chorus of the Rescued", "Chorus of the Wanderers", The Chorus of the Orphans", "Chorus of the Dead", "Chorus of the Shadows", "Chorus of the Stones", "Chorus of the Stars", "Chorus of Invisible Things", "Chorus of the Clouds", "Chorus of Trees", "Chorus of the Comforters" and "Chorus of the Unborn". It is a circle of choruses inside a chorus. One begins in death like an abandoned thing, like something that has been rescued, like a wanderer, an orphan or a comforter, like shadows, stones, stars, clouds, trees or as invisible things and the unborn. As Walter Berendsohn wrote once, Nelly Sachs let "the whole universe, from stones to the stars, sing together in these huge choruses of the dead and of the survivors".[4] In the habitations of death poetry begins like a multitude of choruses, choruses of abandoned, rescued, wandering, orphaned, shadow-cloud-tree-stone-like, invisible and unborn voices. But not only so. Poetry begins in the habitations of death as chorus inside chorus, multi-voices inside multi-voices, voices within voices. How do all these poetic multivoiced choruses sing? And moreover, what do they tell us about the poetic purpose of a chorus?

First, they tell us something about the kind of "we" that arises from these choruses. It is indeed a chorus-like "we". But why are these choruses within the chorus called "Choruses after Midnight"? After midnight is the time following the end of the day and before the start of another day. After midnight is the time when the dead and the unborn day meet. In "Chorus of the Dead" we hear the following:

> Wir von der schwarzen Sonne der Angst
> Wie Siebe Zerstochenen –
> Abgeronnene sind wir vom Schweiß der Todesminute.
> Abgeweckelt an unserem Leibe sind die uns angetanen Tode
> Wie Feldblumen abgeweckelt an einem Hügel Sand.
> O ihr, die ihr noch den Staub grüßt als einen Freund
> Die ihr, redender Sand zum Sande sprecht:
> Ich liebe dich.
>
> Wir sagen euch:
> Zerrissen sind die Mäntel der Staubgeheimnisse
> Die Lüfte, die man in uns erstickte,
> Die Feuer, darin man uns brannte,
> Die Erde, darin man unseren Abhub warf.
> Das Wasser, das mit unserem Angstschweiß dahinperlte
> Ist mit uns aufgebrochen und beginnt zu glänzen.
> Wir toten Israels sagen euch:
> Wir reichen schon einen Stern weiter
> In unseren verborgenen Gott hinein[5].

"We dripped from the sweat of death's minute", "we" are the survivors. But not only because we escaped death, because we should have been dead but are alive, but because we inhabit death in a certain way. We are in death in such way that the deaths done unto us "withered on our bodies" [...] like flowers of the field withered on a hill of sand". This is very uncanny, insofar as we are the closest to them, since they are the deaths done unto us, withering in our bodies, but at the same time we are the most distant from them, since they are dead and we are alive. As such they are "our" dead. Our dead are the screaming closeness to this distance. One cannot talk with the dead; but the dead, on the other hand, speak with us and we say words, poetical words to them. An essential asymmetry binds us to them. We talk not with them but to them and also for them. It is indeed from the dead that we say "we"—"We the dead of Israel". It is to the dead that we say "you"—you who still greet the dust as friend". The poem takes up this uncanny extreme closeness to the abyssal distance between us—the living, those who are together because we are not dead—and you—our dead, and not just any dead, but "ours", since it is to them and for them that we speak, that is, we exist, since they are in us, withered in our bodies. The poem speaks about a "we" and a "you" that arise out of an amalgam of the living and the dead, an amalgam like "air in which we are suffocated", as "fires in which we are burned", as "the water which has beaded with our sweat of fear". "We" is the amalgam of a "we" and a "you", dead and living that arises when the four elements became deadly nascent, nascent deadly.

The word for "we" in German is *Wir*, which sounds almost like *wie*, meaning "how" or "in what way". "You" (informal plural) in German is *Ihr*, which sounds exactly like *irr, from the verb irren*—to wander and go astray. These resonant proximities between *wir* and *wie*, *ihr* and *irr*,[6] appear when listening itself speaks, as when what is said reverberates like an echo in which various differences or solitudes speak simultaneously. Even if they are not written down explicitly like that in the poems, these resonances sound in the reading. We listen to their mute sounding. The chorus is not only the proper voice of a "we" that is the elemental amalgam of a we and a you, of living and dead, but their multiple voices resonating and echoing in each other within us. For Nelly Sachs the chorus is a dramatic song of several voices whose drama consists in the fact that the same word sounds differently than it does by itself because what is speaking in it are the voices of others in our voices—the living, as much as our voices in the echo of the voices of the others—the dead. To be able to listen to such resonant proximities, our ears need to change so that we can hear differences in the middle of such a mix and thereby hear what is being separated when it is bound together. Separating and binding together *we* and *you*—we the living and you the dead—the blend of living and dead, has a decisive impact on Nelly Sachs' chorus poetics. We are those who live after the death of our dead—we are nodes of a life after death, a life that can only be lived because it comes after the dead who went before. But in order to become aware of that, we need chorus-ears. A change of poetic language can be traced in Nelly Sachs' works around the end of the war, something, as was observed above, that she insisted on pointing out. But what should also be pointed out is how this new language is the language of listening; the language of a listening that speaks in its mute resonating way. It is therefore very much a change in the ears that happens in these years. As she says in a poem of *The Habitations of Death* called "How long have we forgotten how to listen!"

> Und ihr werdet hören, durch den Schlaf hindurch
> Werdet ihr hören
> Wie im Tode
> Das Leben beginnt.[7]

Listening carefully to this mute resonating of multiple voices within multiple voices and those inside ourselves, we discover that we are not only those who live after death but also those who live before the unborn. In the voices of the dead, heard as a memory or echo, we also listen to the voices of the unborn, strange voices of those "who are sick with parting", as it is said in the "Chorus of the Unborn", one of the "Choruses after Midnight". What separates and binds together the dead and the unborn? The dead and the unborn are absent bodily in relation to life here and now. Their absences differ, however, to the extent that the dead have in fact lived, been born, left traces and remained. Their souls depart too early. The body simply cannot keep up. The dead are no longer a body. Having been alive and now exterminated, they are sand and ashes, traces and remnants in the air, in fires, in the earth, in water. But precisely because they have been a body, the dead are the ones we know even without knowing. The fact that they have existed, shown themselves, can be traced, tells us that they are our acquaintances, even if we may have an albeit distorted, imprecise, idealized and guilty acquaintanceship with them. The unborn, however, are a very different kind of body. They are those who are too early for a body, those who are too early to arrive. They have no trace, no before, because it is they who are the before. The unborn have a peace of their own, as the Austrian poet Georg Trakl wrote once.[8] They have a peace that is different from the peace of the dead. The peace of the unborn is close to early morning—the time before sunrise, a time when the only thing that exists is a coming from the night. The unborn, who rest in the too-early, come like a morning hour, *with the after* the night, the night that cares for what can only be seen when being lost. The night is "our black nurse" that "let us grow", as we can read in the "Chorus of the Unborn", to become "future lights for your (the unborn) sorrow.[9] The unborn have an inverse chronology, in so far as their before is existentially after—a future past or a past future; they invert love and sorrow, thus their love anticipates the sorrow that has already taken place. And if with them "like dew we sink into love", "[…] still the shadows of time lie like questions/Over our secret".[10] The unborn are the pregnant, impossible experience of the existence of others within us that are not with us, at the same time as we in them are those who begin to live in (their) glances. The unborn are eyes in which we mirror ourselves, ears into which we speak when the night, this "black nurse", "lets us grow". They are the very coming to the alien and the unfamiliar that like the night renders possible the vision of the invisible; thus to see it we have to lose ourselves in it. The unborn are a breath inhaling us. Life after death and life before birth meet in the element of the night to tell about a coming to the alien, albeit from opposite or complementary directions, to the alien of the butterflies of transformation. It says on Paul Klee's gravestone that he lives as well among the dead as among the unborn, since that way he is closer to the beginning than usual yet not close enough.[11] This placeless place of a life after death and a life before birth is located neither here and now nor off over there. It is the impossible, evasive place of our own existence, an in itself beyond and outside itself, a life coming to the unknown. A fundamental difference in relation to Klee's living well both among the dead and the unborn is that in Nelly Sachs' poetic experience what is at stake is to live *with* "our" dead and "our" unborn, with a "we" that is the elemental amalgam of "we" and "you", dead and living, no longer living and not yet born, we, living dead of Israel, you, deaths done unto us, withering in our bodies. Thus, we are the life that begins at death and with the unborn, and it is this beginning at the point where death and the not-born meet that we, voices—of our dead and our unborn—to which we must listen, begin to exist. And then it becomes possible to hear how "life begins in death" and that all we say we say to the voices of our dead and unborn rather than for our dead and unborn.

To speak to all these voices, we must transform ourselves into "reed pipes of seclusion" (*Röhren der Abgeschiedenheit*),[12] "hollow bones" ("*hohles Gebein*")[13] through which voices of this you, voices of our dead and unborn, become resonant. To speak for a voice that is the voice of choruses within choruses, the voice of so many dead, unborn, wandering, rescued, orphaned, clouds and star-like, is to speak within a speaking. It is to speak the speaking, to say the saying, and not primarily the content of what is being spoken or said. The voices of our dead and unborn are "sand that speaks for sand".[14] The image that Nelly Sachs gives us is the hissing breath of the sand. What the hissing breath of this sand is saying, as we listen to the "Chorus of the Dead", is "*ich liebe dich*", (I love you), which in German is a very explicit fricative breath: *ich-dich* [which disappears in the English version], which when it is said in German and spoken aloud sounds almost like *jiddisch/Ich-Dich*, "Jewish", the resounding name that resembles the hissing breath of the sand.

Our dead and unborn—the "we" and the "nodes" of Nelly Sachs' poetry—are the dead and unborn brothers and sisters in Shoah. *In The Habitations of Death* (*In Wohnungen des Todes*) is dedicated to "the dead brothers and sisters". Our dead and unborn, our brothers and sisters say to us "*Ich liebe Dich*", sounding the name that is our, of our people, "Jewish", and speak to us in the hissing language of the sand in which it becomes possible to hear how life after death and life before birth coincide, how they are one and the same life. These we-nodes are those who have been rescued.

"We the rescued", which can be heard in another chorus after midnight, "Chorus of the Rescued":

> Wir Geretteten,
> Aus deren hohlem Gebein der Tod schon seine Flöten schnitt,
> An deren Sehnen der Tod schon sinen Bogen strich –
> Unsere Leiber klagen noch nach
> Mit ihrer verstümmelten Musik.
> Wir Geretteten,
> Immer noch hängen die Schlingen für unsere Hälse gedreht
> Vor uns in der blauen Luft –
> Immer noch füllen sich die Stundenuhren mit unserem tropfenden Blut.
>
> Wir Geretteten,
> Immer noch essen an uns die Würmer der Angst.
> Unser Gestirn ist vergraben im Staub[15].
> …

These choruses after midnight speak to us of another experience of transcendence and rescue. They point neither to a life beyond this life nor to another world. They point to our life here and present it as a life after death and before birth and/or as the place of the rescued. What has been discussed for several centuries about the immortality of the soul and life after death appears here as a kind of acute phenomenology of current existence, of a life here. *Here* is life after death and the place of the rescued, a life after midnight and before morning. It is a life "between yesterday and tomorrow",[16] the life of an end that does not end and of a belated beginning. Therefore, the motive of exile which is Nelly Sachs' life and the central matter of her poetry, is not merely one of a here that moves to a there, a relationship between the known and the unknown; thus the "here", being already an after-life, is already a there. The exilic motive is much more the habitation in the "between yesterday and tomorrow".[17] "We" the rescued are already hollow bones from which flutes to our dead are made—we are already the flutes that preceded "us". These lines speak of the peculiar temporality of a life existing after death and before birth, a life after midnight, a life searching for mornings. We are already the hollow bones into which our dead of Shoah are carved. We are already those who have disappeared and those who will be. We are already before we are.

Another poem from *In The Habitations of Death* (*In den Wohnungen des Todes*) begins: "Someone/Blew the Shofar" (*Einer war,/ Der blies den Schofar*)[18]. The schofar is the Jews' holy flute made from the bones of a purified animal that cannot be a cow or a bull. The poem presents a scene in which the schofar player throws back his head like a deer that has fallen into a trap and dies, exhausted. This image followed Nelly Sachs ever since she began writing poetry. It is an image of Eli, the little eight-year old boy in occupied Poland who began playing the flute when he found himself entirely alone after the German soldiers took his parents prisoner. He plays, throwing back his head to point the flute upwards toward God to pray, lament, and worship in the only way he can, by playing. The German soldiers interpret his gesture as a coded signal and kill him with several blows to the head. To Nelly Sachs the blowing of the schofar is an image of Shoah. The boy with his head thrown back illustrates a strict instruction from the Kabbalah, the Book of Zohar, which teaches how the player must tilt back his head while at the same time lifting it toward the sky. Eli's grandfather, who by a freak of chance survives the boy's sacrifice, the death of a child, is struck silent forever by this scene of terror. Life after death, the lives of those who were rescued, life that begins with death is life silenced by terror. This silenced life, however, is a life not really of silenced speech, but of a silence that speaks, and of a listening to this silence that speaks within this silence. Our language is a silence that speaks, Nelly Sachs insists, and in doing so she shows how hard it is to be a poet of life after death and before birth.

This "image" of the flute-playing boy throwing his head back in order to touch the heights of God and the stars brings out a special feature of Nelly Sachs' poetics, namely the significance of the dramatic scene. In addition to poetry she wrote a couple of dramas. One is entitled *Eli*, another, *Abraham im Salz*. In the few notes in which she comments on her works she speaks of her need to write dramatic pieces when she becomes acutely aware of the limits of poetry. This should not be understood as resembling Adorno's view that writing poetry after Auschwitz is barbaric, especially in German. Nelly Sachs would never argue anything like that, primarily because she writes not only after the dead but also for the unborn. She does, however, ask herself, as in a poem from her late cycle *Glowing Enigmas* (*Glühende Rätseln*):— "Only where find the words/illuminated by the first sea/those opening their eyes/those not wounded by tongues?"[19] She is asking not for innocent or pure words, guiltless words or beautiful words, but for words that languages could not wound or damage, words capable of speaking the unspeakable, about the journey of the bonfire to the sky, the incense of the bodies dispersing in the air. She looks for words on the boundary of the word, on the edge of words, and she searches for words without words, where "who knows", one of the words not wounded by languages can perhaps be uttered, where a poetic word perhaps can begin in the habitations of death.

The beginning of such a word is extremely dramatic; it is the drama of the word's drama; for the word appears as it plunges, when the word is scattered to pieces and becomes only vowels, just tone: "O-A-O-A—a rocking sea of vowels/all the words have crashed down".[20] It is about the drama of the word, the staging of a "between us" that begins to sound on its own. For a word is always what sounds in a "between" us, in a between us and them, the dead and the unborn. The poetic question in Nelly Sachs—and for a poet a poetic question is always a question of life and death—is never a question of style, a formal or intellectual question, nor is it a question of how the extermination of a people can or cannot be represented. It is instead a question of allowing the beginning at death to appear, a fate of Israel for so many, for so many "yous", for so many voices. The discussion about the possibility or impossibility of creating from joy, which Ionesco answered by asserting its impossibility, the discussion about the justice and correctness of searching for an image for this pain, is according to Nelly Sachs like an exit ramp, for there is no other state than that of our hollow bones, a pipe of parting through which the voices of all these "yous", of our dead touching our living, can resound. As she writes in a letter of 14 July 1946 to Walter A. Berendsohn, it is about "the transformation of matter in what is hidden from us …", a "violent theme hovering constantly within me".[21]

This occurs not only in the dramatic scenes she wrote but in all her poetry. Her poems are actually dramatized scenes—plays for "words, pantomime and music", as she titles her play

The Great Anonymous (*Der große Anonyme*).[22] In these notes Nelly Sachs maintains that the play for "words, pantomime and music" wants to show the child of mystery, that is, that mystery is a child, that which remains vulnerable like an open sore in the story of Eli, the boy who played the flute for the divine. Eli is a "he" who appears as an open sore, what in another line in another chorus, the "Chorus of Wanderers", she calls "the orphan-eyed Israel of animals". The gaze of an orphaned animal sacrificed in burning fire has been given the name Israel by history. This gaze is what has seen the seeing. In another poem from *In the Habitations of Death*, (*In Wohnungen des Todes*) she speaks indeed about the eyes of an I-saw-that-he-saw, quoting Jehuda Zwi, following these eyes "with pupils of long rainbows"[23]. The eyes of this I-saw-that-I-saw, the orphaned eyes of this sacrificed animal called

Israel are the eyes of a sacrificed word that has been wounded by languages. Nelly Sachs explains in the notes mentioned above that what she is striving for is to show how the word is conveyed through gestures, how a movement is transferred to other movements, and also how the movement of the word passes down from generation to generation by leaning back to see the sky above. When the word is uttered as a beginning at death, what is considered are not comprehensive doctrines or some sort of grammatical order but the birth of the word at the death of the word, the birth of the word as a silence that speaks. The sound of Eli's flute, the sound of Eli's shofar, is a saying of words that begin at the death of the words, words under threat of being burned like dry wood in the fire, words that make the sweat of fear glow like pearls. What is passed down from generation to generation is this leaning back to see an above, since "it is we who point to a mystery that comes from the night", as we read and hear in another chorus, "Chorus of the Clouds".[24] What goes on from generation to generation are not the words themselves but the inability to say what belongs to the words as their depths. It refers to a saying that is planted in salt, in soil that does not bear fruit, a saying of what saying cannot say. This can never be said by itself, but only in a chorus bearing multi-voiced choruses.

Nelly Sachs understands this beginning in the "salt of death" to be the emergence of a new word as this occurs in the choruses of the Greek tragedies. She goes so far as to say that it is out of this new word born in the salt of death, risen as in the chorus of a tragedy, that a religious experience arises. In his *Poetics*, Aristotle asserts the contrary with respect to the birth of tragedy, maintaining that tragedy arises as a chorus but that the chorus develops from rites and holy rituals in veneration of the god Dionysus. Nelly Sachs' poetics presents a different genealogy—she derives the religious from the tragic chorus and not tragedy from religious rituals. Her poetry sings choruses in the form of psalms and hymns. There the Greek tragedy is the salt of death out of which Biblical psalms and hymns are born from tragic refrains. She suggests a different chronology—the chronology of a beginning at death, not the death of a beginning. According to Aristotle there are three kinds of tragic choruses: those which announce arrivals (*chorikou parodos*), those which concern the present location of the dramatic action (*stasimon*) and those which sing songs of lamentation (*kómmos thrénos*), which can also be interpreted as songs of farewell. The chorus is itself a character, a *person*, who acts both with and against the performers; it is a plural voice, the voice of many voices. This is clear from Nelly Sachs' poetry, except that there the three kinds of choruses—those singing of arrivals, present location and farewell laments—simultaneously sing in a chorus of choruses breathing out psalms, the hissing breath of hymns that mourn our dead and our unborn. Her choruses after midnight blow like the flute played by the bewildered child's gaze, Israel's gaze, and in so doing they sing of the place where we find ourselves—our existence's *stásimon*. They sing dissonant polyphonic voices, like hissing sandstorms. This place is defined as the articulation of four elements—"the air in which we were suffocated", "the fires in which we were burned", "the earth into which our remains were cast", "the water which was beaded with our sweat of fear" (*Chor der Toten*). This place is not a state but a fate: the fate of being a beginning at death, of being life after death and before birth, of being between yesterday and tomorrow; the fate of being a wanderer.

In relation to Aristotle's classic discussion on the origin of the chorus, meaning and role in tragic poetry, in Nelly Sachs' chorus poetics Biblical hymns and psalms arise out of a choir in which each word is sung as being a presence in the present rather than being merely present. They arise more like sounds in-between a giving away and an arriving, sounds of simultaneous voices "between yesterday and tomorrow". The chorus sounds forth a wandering place, the only possible poetic place for a wanderer's fate, the fate of those who drag the road behind them and show that it is the road that is their baggage, those who dress in rags of the land in which they pause. This wandering place, therefore, is not really the wanderers' place; rather, it is the very experience of moving that is the only possible place when the poetic word is to be born in the habitations of death.

Thus understood, the chorus is no longer a demarcation on life's stage meant to show poetry as a place alongside life—a kind of place of consolation—or as the only place where life can happen. This alternative conforms to traditional notions of the role of the chorus in the modern tragedy as represented from opposite positions by, among others, Diderot and Schiller. In *De la poésie dramatique* Diderot formulates his thoughts on "the fourth wall" as follows: "Imaginez, sur le bord du thêatre, un grande mur qui vous sépare du parterre; jouez comme si la toile ne se levait pas"[25] He maintains that the chorus was a kind of fourth wall which, by pretending that the audience did not exist, showed them that the theatrical setting was the scene of an illusion. Similarly, the chorus was to show that poetry was a stage alongside life itself. In contrast to Diderot's concept, in his foreword to *The Bride of Messina* Schiller considers that what the chorus does is in fact to cancel the illusion of the theater, which, almost like an acid in photography, brings out or develops the reality around it by showing that the stage is part of life and not something on the side. Analogously, the poetic chorus is the only place where life reveals its soul.

Nelly Sachs' "Choruses after Midnight" no longer sing of this difference between illusion and reality, between consolation and trust. They sing of wandering and going "from yesterday to tomorrow", "between yesterday and tomorrow", and appear as ears that themselves resonate when the voices of the dead and unborn blow into them. These choruses after midnight, these resounding ears, do not reflect on what has happened, is happening or can happen, nor do they demarcate the poetic scene. They make the many voices resonate in unison to emphasize how "the shadows of time still lie like questions over our secret".[26]

In the notes on her work mentioned above Nelly Sachs writes that she cannot describe the inner process of which her poetic language was born. She can only say that she tried "more and more to spiritualize the moment and make it transparent" (115). To spiritualize this place that is the going in which we already find ourselves—that is, the moment—means making it transparent, it means making it appear. This place appears as a coincidence of our dead and unborn, as a shaking between, as an interweaving of the All in nothing and nothing in the All. This confluence is suddenly like the flash of disappearing stars; it is immeasurable and immense like the horizon that is fed by grains of dust; Yes, for these "dead", the dead who ascribe to us an "our", lie on the ground not like just any bodies but like grains of dust. Our dead are "stones that have faces, father and mother faces," as we read in "Chorus of the Orphans",[27] they are grains of dust that sprout.

Specks of dust, grains of dust, *Staubkorn*, is a central expression in Nelly Sachs' poetics. It is discussed in several letters exchanged with Paul Celan, the author of *Todesfuge* and *Sprachgitter*, the copy of which he sent her she reads as a new *Zohar*, a new work of Jewish mysticism. She views the beginning of life at death as a sprouting grain of dust, a sprouting that cannot be shoved into the ground, that does not develop a web of roots, that passes without leaving a trace, but whose passing without a trace surrounds, suffocates and hurts like a sandstorm. It is a kind of cultivation in the air, an inscription of smoke in the air.

While the poet John Keats chose "*Here lies one whose name was written in water*" for his gravestone, the epitaph dedicated to Nelly Sachs' poetry is for a people whose name was written by "Israel's body drifted as smoke through the air"[28] The air of the dust of smoke, the dust of the air sprouts when it passes by, not when it stays. The air is the element of passing, that which involves in the past that which goes on. For the course of life sees itself utterly saturated with this pain. Nelly Sachs describes this phenomenon with new expressions such as *Durchschmerzung* and *Umschmertzung*—permeated with pain, surrounded by pain.

This place that Nelly Sachs' poetry attempts to spiritualize, or, as she puts it, wants to make transparent, is the place of the moment, the place of being that is as incomprehensible as a bolt of lightning and as immeasurable as a grain of dust. It is a place of a between—between the dead and the unborn, whence between the no-longer and the not yet, a we and a you are defined. This place is a place without place, a place where we are always with a without—with the without-our-parents, with the without-our-children; the place is the experience of being an orphan rather than a son, the experience of embracing the childless state as a child. This place without place is the experience of existence as exile—the place without place of the exile of being, a constant motif in both the history and the mysticism of the Jewish people. One of the teachings in the Kabbalah concerns God's *tsimtsum*, a doctrine formulated by Isaac Luria in the seventeenth century, a teaching about God's exile, about the experience of God's withdrawal during the creation of the world. Mystical and Kabbalistic motifs are ubiquitous in Nelly Sachs's poetry. She often reads Scholem and Buber, but also Christian religious thinkers such as Pascal, Kierkegaard and Simone Weil. The transparency of the moment as a place where we are no more than the fate of wanderers, what she has called the spiritualization of the moment, is in addition a dominant motif in her correspondence with Paul Celan, especially when, after years of writing to each other, they met in Zurich in 1960 at the Zum Storchen café, which serves as the title of a poem dedicated to her.

Nelly Sachs felt that Celan's poetry had given her a homeland, a *Heimat*. Only there did she feel at home. In one letter to him (24 March 1960) she even wrote that Celan had "touched the roots of language as Abraham had touched the roots of faith".[29] For her, Celan was the patriarch of the root of language, of language as a beginning at the sacrifice of the child who plays his flute for God, of the word that begins at the death of the word. Paul Celan, however, viewed her poetry as the poetics of words that cannot be heard, words to which he needed to be close despite his deep sense of alienation in their presence. "The talk was of your God [...]. I spoke against him" [...]. "The talk was of too much, of too little".[30] Celan was always willing to meet Nelly Sachs. He wanted to agree to her request to travel to Stockholm when she was in a deep emotional crisis that resulted in a long stay in the hospital.

He did in fact come to Sweden, but he was unable to meet her owing to the seriousness of her condition. He says in a letter that he came to give her "words and silence". Poets speak with each other about the language of silence. Poets do not converse, they do not conduct dialogues—but their silences speak in a chorus—silence speaks for silence as sand speaks for sand, the saying of silence in the silence of saying. In other late poems we can read what it means to hear, the imperative: "put your finger on your lips: *silence silence silence*"—a line ending with a dash that underscores the "s" in the breath of silence.

This saying in a chorus of silences both denies and creates a distance from current ideas about language as dialogue and conversation. How can dialogue and conversation be possible if the words begin at the death of the words, if the words are words after death and before birth, if the words are words after midnight? The letters between Nelly Sachs and Paul Celan show just what a poetic correspondence is: a listening that says, a saying that listens, a saying within the saying by those who have left us and those who have not yet come to us. It is more a chorus-speech, a co-responding to these you-voices that lay a finger to their lips in order to say: silence, silence, silence, quiet, quiet, quiet. Nelly Sachs and Paul Celan answer together, co-respond to the fate of being poets in the language of their own annihilation—the German language. To be an unwounded word in the language of all wounds; to be the life of saying in the language of the death of saying, to be a Jewish poet of the German language. This means to remain the ears of the homeless. To be words like wind in the wind, like choruses within choruses, choruses of the winds. Nelly Sachs' poetics is about this fate, the fate of poetry as the chorus of the choruses of the winds.

[...] Winds:

You homeless, you homeless [...]
We winds, we winds, we winds
We have a home in the shell
In the shofar, in the flute
[...][31]

[1] For the English translation, see Nelly Sachs, *Collected Poems 1944–1949*, trans. Michael Hamburger, Ruth and Matthew Mead, and Michael Roloff (Los Angeles: Green Integer, 2011).

[2] Aris Fioretos, *Nelly Sachs, Flight and Metamorphosis, an Illustrated Biography* (Stanford: Stanford University Press, 2011), and Kathrin M. Bower, *Ethics of Remembrance in the Poetry of Nelly Sachs and Rose Ausländer* (Suffolk: Camden House, 2000)); W.A. Berendsohn: *Nelly Sachs: Einführung in das Werk der Dichterin jüdischen Schicksals* (Darmstadt: Agora, 1974)

[3] Fioretos, *Flight and Metamorphosis*, 149.

[4] Quoted in Fioretos, *Flight and Metamorphosis,* 201 ("läßt das ganze Universum, von den Steinen bis zu den Sternen, mitsingen in den riesigen Chören der Toten und der Überlebenden".

[5] We from the black sun of fear/ Holed like sieves – /We dripped from the sweat of death's minute./Withered on our bodies are the deaths done unto us/Like flowers of the field withered on a hill of sand./O you who still greet the dust as friend/ You who talking sand say to the sand:/I love you./
We say to you:/ Torn are the cloaks of the mysteries of dust/The air in which we were suffocated,/The fire in which we were burned,/The earth into which was beaded with our sweat of fear/ Has broken forth with us and begins to gleam./ We dead of Israel say to you:/ We are moving past one more star/Into our hidden God. "Chorus of the Dead" in Nelly Sachs, *Collected Poems,* 113.

[6] If we translate these pronouns into, for instance, Portuguese, it becomes immediately apparent that *wir* is *nós*, which sounds and is written exactly like *"nós"* (nodes), while *Ihr* is *vós*, which takes us to *voz* (the voice). Here the resonances of meaning are even stronger.

[7] "And you will hear, through your sleep/You will hear / How in death / Life begins," Sachs, *Collected Poems*, 53.

[8] Georg Trakl, "Heiterer Frühling," in *Werke, Entwürfe, Briefe* (Stuttgart: Reclam, 1986)

[9] Nelly Sachs, "Chor der Ungeborenen" in *In den Wohnungen des Todes* (Berlin: Aufbau Verlag, 1947); "Chorus of the Unborn," trans. Ruth and Matthew Mead, in Nelly Sachs, *Collected Poems*, 139–141, *O the Chimneys. Selected Poems, including the verse play Eli* (Philadelphia: The Jewish Publication Society of America, 1967), 43.

[10] Ibid.

[11] Paul Klee, "Diesseitig bin ich gar nicht fassbar. Denn ich wohne grad so gut bei den Toten wie bei den Ungeborenen. Etwas näher der Schöpfung als üblich und noch lange nicht nahe genug".

[12] In the poem "*Stimme des heiligen Landes,*" translated into English as "*The Voice of the Holy Land*" that also belongs to *In The Habitations of Death*, in *Collected Poems*, 142–143.

[13] "Chorus of the Rescued", Sachs, *Collected Works*, 101.

[14] "Chorus of the Dead", Sachs, *Collected Works*, 113.

[15] We, the rescued,/From those hollow bones death had begun to whittle his fluets,/And on whose sinews he had already stroked his bow —/Our bodies continue to lament/With their mutilated music./We, the rescued,/The nooses wound for our necks still dangle/ before us in the blue air —/Hourglasses still fill with our dripping blood./We, the

rescued,/
The worms of fear still feed on us./Our constellation is buried in dust./ Sachs, *Collected Works,* 101.

[16] "Chorus of Comforters", Sachs, *Collected Works* 135.

[17] For a discussion about the poetry of Nelly Sachs as a poetics of a "from here to there", see Aris Fioretos, *Flight and Metamorphosis,* 114–116.

[18] From the poem *"Einer war, der blies den Shofar,"* Eng. "Someone blew the Shofar," in Sachs, *Collected Works,* 39.

[19] Nelly Sachs, "Glowing Enigmas II," trans. Michael Hamburger, in *O the Chimneys,* 279.

[20] "ein wiegendes Meer der Vokale/ Worte sind alle abgestürzt"—as another poem in *Glühende Rätseln* puts it.

[21] Quoted in Nelly Sachs, *Werke, Gedichte 1940–1950,* Matthias Weichelt, ed. (Frankfurt am Main: Suhrkamp Verlag, 2010), 250.

[22] Swedish translation in Nelly Sachs, *Den store anonymen,* trans. Magaretha Holmqvist (Stockholm: Ersatz, 2010), 141.

[23] *"Deine Augen, o du mein Geliebter,"* Eng. "Your eyes, O my beloved," in Sachs, *Collected Poems,* 87.

[24] Ibidem, 131.

[25] Denis Diderot, "De la poésie dramatique," in *Oeuvres esthétiques* (Paris: Classiques Garnier, 1959), 231.

[26] "Chorus of the Unborn, in Sachs, *Collected Poems,* 139.

[27] Ibid., 111.

[28] "Dein Leib im Rauch durch die Luft", *O the Chimneys,* 21.

[29] Paul Celan and Nelly Sachs, *Correspondence,* ed. Barbara Wiedemann, trans. Christopher Clark (Riverdale-on-Hudson, NY: The Sheep Meadow Press, 1995), 18.

[30] Ibid., 26.

[31] *Chor der Winde/ Ihr Heimatlosen, ihr Heimatlosen!/ O ihr mit dem feinen Gehör begabten./ Wir hauchen euch ein, jeden Seufzer der Natur./ Geschwister sind wir mit euch. Der Grille Ton hat sein Nest in eurem Ohr/ Und ihr seif es die diesen Stern sich drehen hören/ In den Nächten. Wir Winde, wir Winde, wir Winde/ Wir drehen die Mühlen der Armut/ Am Wege der Heimatlosen/ Wir treiben das große Meer in eine Muschel hinein —/ Lauscht an der Ewigkeit Schlüsselloch, ihr Heimatlosen —/ Wir Winde, Wir Winde, Wir Winde/ Ein zu Hause haben wir in der Muschel,/ Im Schofar, in der Flöte —/ Gute Nacht*

A Response in Rhythm
– Marina Tsvetaeva's Poem "Возвращение вождя" (The Return of the Leader) and Sofia Gubaidulina's Composition "Das Ross" (The Horse)

FIONA BJÖRLING

Introduction

Many of Sofia Gubaidulina's works have been inspired by words, not least by poetry. Born in 1931, the Russian-Tatar composer Gubaidulina has composed two works inspired by the poetry of Marina Tsvetaeva.[1] *Hommage à Marina Tsvetaeva*, written for choir and sung a capella, consists of four poems by Tsvetaeva and an interlude:

1. Пало прениже волн   There fell beneath the waves   (19 апреля 1921)
2. Возвращение вождя   The Return of the Leader   (16 июля 1921)
3. Все великолепье   Everything is splendor   (23 апреля 1921)
4. Интерлюд   Interlude
5. Сад   The Garden   (1 октября 1934)

In this paper I continue with my close-readings of each successive poem followed by an analysis of the music as it interprets the poem, thus creating a new work of art.[2] Here I am concerned with the second poem "Vozvrashchenie vozhdia" (The Return of the Leader).

A response in rhythm

The Poem: Возвращение вождя

> Конь – хром,
> Меч – ржав.
> Кто – сей?
> Вождь толп.
>
> Шаг – час,
> Вздох – век,
> Взор – вниз.
> Все – там.
>
> Враг. – Друг.

Тёрн. – Лавр.
Всё – сон …
– Он. – Конь.

Конь – хром.
Меч – ржав.
Плащ – стар.
Стан – прям.³

Immediately striking about this poem is its rhythm. The poem consists of four stanzas of four lines each; there are two monosyllabic words per line, in all cases but one separated by a dash /–/, frequently expressing the copula. 32 monosyllables amount to 32 stresses, that is 16 spondees. Each line is separated by a punctuation mark. The punctuation, that is both the dashes within and the punctuation marking the end of the lines, increases the effect of the rhythmical beat of monosyllabic words. There are no verbs in the poem; with the exception of the question in 1.3, paired with the answer in 1.4 (the only line without a dash), each line comprises a statement, which renders its rhythm static. The effect is stark and masculine, on a par with calling a rhyme on a stressed syllable for a masculine rhyme. In his study of the contemporaneity of Derzhavin's poetics, Viach. V. Ivanov makes a connection between Derzhavin and Tsvetaeva in their use of spondees. Derzhavin's iambic tetrameter is characterized by the systematic use of spondees, writes Ivanov, who further remarks that the "rhythmical coincidence" between Derzhavin's and Tsvetaeva's use of spondees is remarkable.⁴

In considering a poem written entirely in monosyllables, two aspects of the Russian language can be noted: firstly, the vast potential for building words through the use of affixes (prefixes and suffixes) as well as the system of inflections, declensions, and conjugations. Secondly, the fact that each word once formed has one stress only which is strongly marked as opposed to the unstressed syllables, however many there may be. "Vozvrashchenie vozhdia" avoids exploitation of both these aspects of the Russian language.

In her writings on poetry, Tsvetaeva states that for her sound is more important than meaning, and that she listens continually not for words but for a tune or melody. For example, in *Iskusstvo pri svete sovesti* (Art in the light of conscience) she writes: "Slyshu ne slova, a kakoi-to bezzvuchnyi napev vnutri golovy, kakoi-to slukhovuiu liniiu."⁵ Her poetry tends to favor the rudiments of the Russian language, the sounds (phonemes) and the roots (morphemes) which are so to speak in the beginning. This poem constitutes an extreme example of Tsvetaeva's predilection for monosyllabic words.⁶

With one exception, "Vozvrashchenie vozhdia" expresses a situation of utmost exhaustion, lacking any glory associated with a leader returning from war. Not only is the horse lame, the sword rusty, the cape worn, but there is a mental exhaustion: the distinction between enemy and friend, between a crown of laurels and a crown of thorns, seems no longer relevant (3.1 and 3.2). In the final line of the poem, however, there is a surprising contrast to this dominance of exhaustion. The repetition of lines 1.1 and 1.2, in 4.1 and 4.2 (expanded in 4.3 – the cape is old) connects the final to the first stanza. The following line 4.4 continues the rhythmic syntactic pattern of the preceding lines, but brings a surprise of semantic contrast: the leader himself is not bowed down but sits up straight.

The Music

Of the four poems chosen by Sofia Gubaidulina for her musical composition, two are taken from *Uchenik* (The Disciple), a lyrical cycle cohesive in its themes, written in April 1921. "Vozvrashchenie vozhdia" is written only a few months later in July 1921. Given the striking rhythmical pattern of the poem, and Gubaidulina's own concern with rhythm, or what she called "the rhythm of form,"[7] it is not surprising that she has chosen to incorporate this poem in her work. And yet, Gubaidulina utterly transforms the rhythm from its steady beat to a seemingly erratic rhythmical pattern. Both Valentina Kholopova[8] and Dorothea Redepenning[9] have called this style pointillist or aphoristic.[10]

To be noted is that Gubaidulina does not use Tsvetaeva's title, "Vozvrashchenie vozhdia," but names her composition "Das Ross" (the steed or horse). Her musical rendition of the poem differs from those of the other poems comprising *Hommage à Marina Tsvetaeva*. It stands apart from the spiritual seeking expressed by the prayer-like intonation of the other parts of the work, particularly the first and the last poems, "Palo prenizhe voln" (There fell beneath the waves) and "Sad" (The garden). In her notes to the score of this work, the composer lists fourteen specific signs denoting how the singers' voices should be used, on the one hand differentiating plain singing from spoken or whispered singing, and on the other denoting how various ways of breathing should affect the sound. The critic N. Shirieva has analyzed the progression of the parts of *Hommage à Marina Tsvetaeva*, and in particular indicated how the sound of breathing is connected with the ever present vertical, spiritual dimension in Gubaidulina's works, which is always in contrast to the horizontal and human dimension.[11] "Das Ross" is sung in plain song throughout and no sounds of breathing are indicated. Furthermore, the

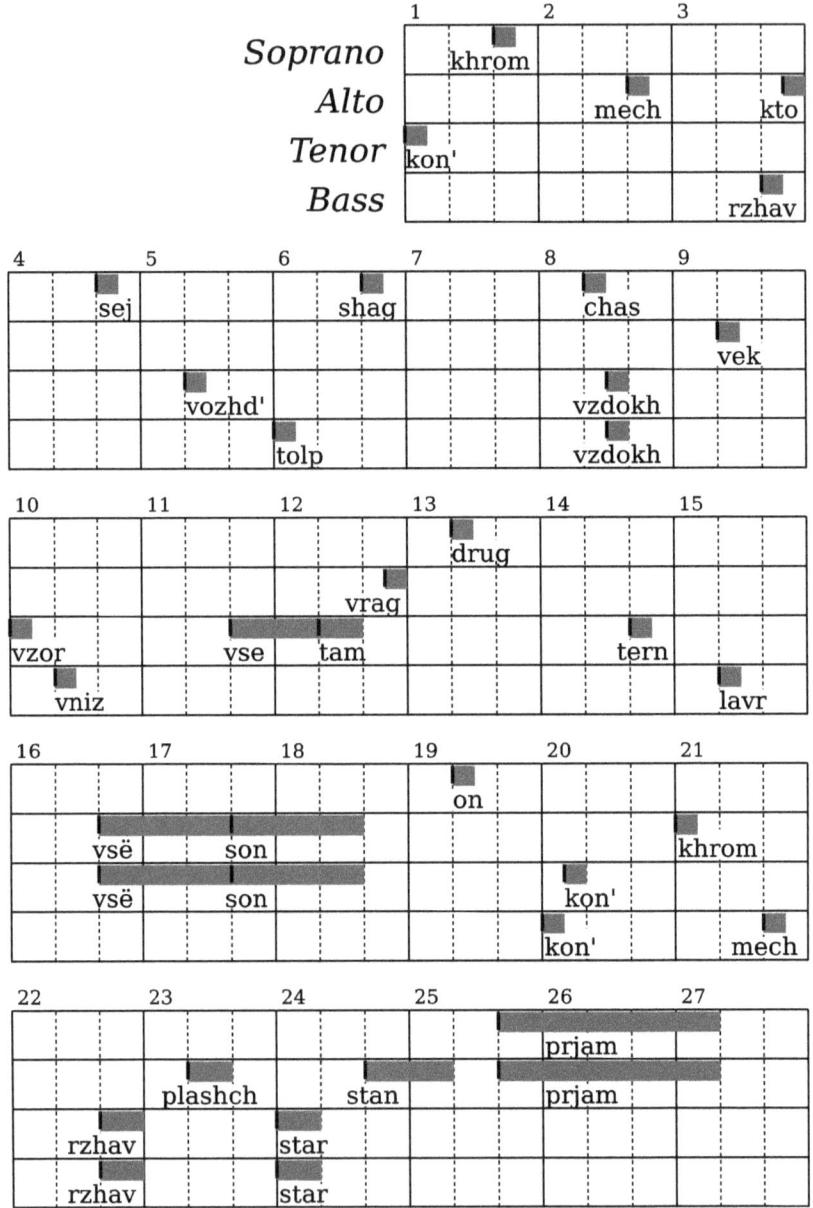

Diagram showing Gubaidulina's positioning of the words from the poem. There are three beats to each bar, that is three quarter notes (crotchets ♩) or six eighth notes (quavers ♪). The diagram does not reproduce the tones but shows how the rhythm of the single words progresses through the bars, accompanied by the switches between registers in the alteration of the four voices (soprano, alto, tenor and bass).

tones are comprised of thirds, both major and augmented, with no examples of glissandos or 'indecisive' tones such as occur in the other parts of the composition. In other words, the music can be said to be relatively 'undemanding'. The rhythmic 'pointillism,' on the other hand, is underlined by the range of the voices between registers.

As shown in the diagram, in the beginning of the piece, each word is sung for only an eighth note or quaver (♪) that is then followed by a pause equivalent to three and then five eighth notes. But after the word *rzhav*, *kto* follows immediately (bar 3), causing surprise and in some ways a comic rush. The voices singing these monosyllabic words sweep from tenors to sopranos to altos and then basses. In bar 11–12 the staccato rhythm is interrupted by *vse tam* sung for longer, i.e. in legato. After another burst of staccato, the notes in bars 22–24 are again in legato, with the final words *stan* and particularly *priam* the longest sung words, which are accordingly emphasized. Thus Gubaidulina, in accord with Tsvetaeva's poem, contrasts the dignified final line with the exhaustion expressed in the preceding text. In addition, let us note that certain words are sung by two voices and thereby given more volume and emphasis: *vzdokh* by tenors and basses (in bar 8); *vse son* by altos and tenors (bars 16–18); and through *rzhav* and *star* by tenors and basses (in bars 22 and 24) to the culmination of the word *priam* by sopranos and altos (in bars 25–27).

Redepenning has suggested that the words lose their meaning and become reduced to mere syllables, but an overview of the diagram reveals a clear structure of the rhymic progression. The initial 'exhaustion' of the first and second stanzas expressed in apparently haphazard staccato tones progresses towards a steadier and weightier finish, expressed in the length of the legato tones, as well as in the doubling of voices (giving a fuller tone) and leads to the culmination of the final two words of the poem.

My conclusion is that Gubaidulina's music is a response in rhythm to the rhythm of Tsvetaeva's poem, whereby the pointillist musical rhythm is playfully contrasted to the steady beat of the poem.

The semantics of *kon'* (horse) in Tsvetaeva's poetry

Apart from the reference to Viach. V. Ivanov mentioned above, I have found no detailed analyses of this poem. My initial understanding was that it was an exercise in playing with rhythm and an exploitation of Tsvetaeva's predilection for monosyllables. A number of the monosyllables in "Vozvrashchenie vozhdia" occur frequently in other poems by Tsvetaeva: not least in the context of the cycle *Uchenik* from which two of the four poems chosen for Gubaidulina's work are taken, namely: *kon'* (horse); *vozhd'* (leader); *chas* (hour); *vzdokh* (sigh); *plashch* (cape). Of these the most striking is the reference to *kon'*, repeated three times in the poem.

The image of a horse, *kon'*,[12] is embraced by Tsvetaeva in a number of lyrical and epic poems (poèmy) and in these the association is often to a supernatural power, a moving and elemental force. Here follow a number of examples:

1. In *Tsar'-devitsa* (The Tsar-Maiden) from 1922, presented as a fairy-tale epic poem (poèma-skazka), the heroine is described as a formidable adventurer and warrior who at first travels on horse-back, later in a boat and, finally, on the winds. The heroine, associated with the sun, is in love with a prince, a singer of psalms, who is bewitched by his wicked stepmother, asleep in the meetings with the heroine, and associated with the moon. On horse-back, the Tsar-Maiden is described as follows:

> "Душу сперло в груди!
> Дева всех впереди!
> Великановый рост,
> Пояс – змей-самохлёст,
> Головою до звезд,
> С головы конский хвост,
> Месяц в ухе серьгой..."[13]

Given that the force of the rider and her horse are presented in symbiosis, the horse too becomes a fairy-tale horse with supernatural powers:

> Конь с Дѣвицею точно сросся;
> Не различишь, коли вдали:
> Хвост конский, али семишёрстый
> Султан с девичьей головы![14]

2. In *Na krasnom kone* (On a Red Horse) the horse is the bearer of the rider to whom the 'I' of the epic poem is irresistibly drawn. The poem expresses the element of fire and the head-long movement as the rider moves upwards and away on his red horse, chased by the heroine in her desperate flight to catch up with and touch him. In a jumble of hooves and horseshoes, hills and heights, he leads her away from her home, from the earth and from the experience of human love, to the edge of the sky. Through a scene of winter and snow storms, the heroine chases him asking:

> Но что – с высоты – за всадник,
> И что это за конь?¹⁵

Through a ferocious battle of rainbows, her helmet bloodied by the dawn, the heroine has been drawn into the hero's world beyond, to behold at the edge of the azure firmament the figure who – 'a proud man on a red horse' ("gordets na kone – na krasnom") – in the final word of the poem is revealed as her genius:

> На красном коне –
> Мой Гений!¹⁶

The poem may be understood as narrating a rite of initiation whereby the heroine is led through her exacting journey to an understanding of the nature of her inspiration as a poet.¹⁷

3. The image of a horse as powerful and elemental occurs in the lyrical poem "Pozhiraiushchii ogon' – moi kon'" (A devouring fire – my horse) from 1918, where the poet speaks of 'my' horse, again characterized by fire that devours all in its way, its rider – insatiable:

> Ох, огонь мой конь – несытый едок!
> Ох, огонь на нем – несытый ездок!
> С красной гривою свились волоса...
> Огневая полоса – в небеса!¹⁸

4. The first three poems of the poetic cycle *Khanskii polon* (Captured by the Khan), written in the autumn of 1921, as Tsvetaeva was preparing to leave Russia, also figure the powerful horse. These poems express her excruciating pain at leaving Russia.

In the first of four poems, the poet addresses the god of flights ("bog pobegov"). Escaping on a horse that does not touch the ground the 'I' refers to herself as rider-horse ("vsadnik-kon'"):

> Конь мой земли не тронь,
> Лоб мой звезды не тронь,
> Вздох мой губы не тронь,
> Всадник-конь, перст-ладонь.¹⁹

In poem 3 she cries out to her country in a triple invocation (occurring in the final two lines of the even stanzas, 2, 4 and 6), which expresses her anguish over the fate of her country in terms of a wild, enchanted and unrelenting horse:

– Ох, Родина-Русь,
Неподкованный конь!

– Ох, Родина-Русь,
Зачарованный конь!

– Эх, Родина-Русь,
Нераскаянный конь![20]

The title of the cycle together with the fourth poem refer to the 12th Century defeat of Prince Igor, recorded in the national epos *Slovo o polku igoreve* (The Lay of Igor's Campaign), that is a time when Rus (medieval orthodox Russia) was weak and split by feuds between her princes. This is to be interpreted as an expression of Tsvetevas concern for her native Russia after the Revolution, now in 1921. Rather than the fairy-tale image of a horse of magical powers, here the image of her native country – Rodina Rus' – conveys anguish for the country she is about to leave in its state of captivity, a country to which she attributes nevertheless the unyielding power of a wild horse.[21]

*

In stark contrast with these images of the power and fearlessness of the horse otherwise invoked in her poetry, "Vozvrashchenie vozhdia" expresses instead of exaltation a total reaction of exhaustion. Can this be some sort of self-irony on the part of the poet?

There is another context, however, in which we can examine Tsvetaeva's poetic use of *kon'*, namely the suite of nine poems of the cycle *Georgii* (George) written in July 1921, and addressed to her husband Sergei Efron, who had been fighting with the White Army in the South of Russia, and whom she feared dead having had no news of him for most of the Civil War.

The image of a horse plays a prominent part particularly in the first three poems of *Georgii*. In contrast to the associations of a horse hitherto examined, the horse in *Georgii* is not red, but white. Throughout poem 1 of the cycle the despondency of Georgii is contrasted with the quiet dignity of the horse:

И плащ его – был – красен,
И конь его – был – бел.

Смущается Всадник,
Гордится конь.

Склоняется Всадник,
Дыбится конь.[22]

In opposition to the traditional portrayal of St George, a proud hero who has slain the dragon, Tsvetaeva's saint is horrified by the deed he has committed. In grief over her missing husband, the poet portrays him as a man totally foreign to the act of fighting and killing, a man characterized by restraint and metonymized by his long eye-lashes:

О тяжесть удачи!
Обида Победы!
Георгий, ты плачешь,
Ты красною девой
Бледнеешь над делом
Своих двух
Внезапно-чужих
Рук.[23]

Conclusion

On July 14, 1921, Tsvetaeva received news that Efron was still alive and her writing of the seventh poem was interrupted. On the following day, July 15, Tsvetaeva began to write the five poems of a new cycle, *Blagaia Vest'* (Good News), also dedicated to her husband, Sergei Efron. "Vozvrashchenie vozhdia" was written on July 16. Although it is not included in *Blagaia Vest'* it can, within this context, be considered a witty postscript to *Georgii*, expressing in empathy the exhaustion of the warrior or leader on his return from war. In this case the surprise in the final line, *Stan' - priam* (his figure is straight), can be understood as the poet's respect for her husband in the endurance that he has experienced.

In presenting Gubaidulina's musical rendition of the poem, Kholopova has written that it "undoubtedly continues the theme of the fate of the horse Monty from her opus "Perception."[24] "Perception" was composed in 1981–1983, for soprano, baritone and strings, on verses by Francisco Tanzer. The twelfth piece of the work is called "Montys Tod" and it describes with pathos the death of the old horse, Monty, who in his heyday had been so full of strength, grace and beauty. If Kholopova is right in her interpretation then we may conclude that Gubaidulina was sensitive to the sadness expressed by Tsvetaeva in the poem "Vozvrashchenie vozhdia," written in tribute to her husband Sergei Efron.

However, this biographical interpretation of a poem, as written in specific circumstances, does not obliterate the predominant image in Tsvetaeva's poetry of a horse as expressing power, glory and energy. Reference to the fate of her husband offers one valid explanation for the poem, but not the only one. It is equally feasible to interpret the poem's striking and unusual rhythm as stemming from the poet's rhythmic creativity. In this case its exploitation of monosyllabic words is expressive of Tsvetaeva's exhuberance, her unique attunement to the play of language with, perhaps, a touch of self irony. In this sense Gubaidulina's inclusion of the poem in her *Hommage à Marina Tsvetaeva* is doubly playful in that she transmits Tsvetaeva's regular and static beat into a pointillist irregular beat. A rhythmical response to rhythm that is not without humor.

¹ *Hour of the Soul* (1974), a Poem for Large Wind Orchestra and Mezzo-Soprano (Contralto). This work was revised as *Hour of the Soul* (*Percussio di Pekarski*, 1976/1988) for Solo Percussionist, Mezzo-Soprano and Large Orchestra. (Michael Kurz, *Sofia Gubaidulina. A Biography*, Indiana University Press, 2007), 278, 279. *Hommage à Marina Tsvetaeva* (1984) for A Capella Chorus on Poems by M. Tsvetaeva, in five movements.
² See Fiona Björling, "Sofia Gubaidulina in Homage to Marina Cvetaeva: Music, Words, Transcendence, *Med blicken österut, Hyllningsskrift till Per-Arne Bodin*, Per Ambrosiani, Elisabeth Löfstrand, Ewa Teodorowicz-Hellman, eds. (Stockholm Slavic Papers 23, 2014), 43–56; and Fiona Björling, "Marina Tsvetaevas dikt 'Сад' och Sofia Gubaidulinas tonsättning *Hommage à Marina Tsvetaeva*, för kör a capella, 1984", presented on September 15, 2017, at a symposium at Stockholm University in Honour of Nils Åke Nilsson 1917-2017. Forthcoming in *Meddelanden från Avdelningen för slaviska språk, nr 44*, Stockholm University.
³ Marina Tsvetaeva, *Sobranie sochinenii v semi tomakh*, T. 2 (Moskva: Ellis Lak, 1994–1995), 49. A literal translation, with the content of the copulas and articles suggested in brackets, reads:
Stanza 1: (The) horse (is) lame,/ (The) sword (is) rusty./ Who (is) this?/ The leader of the multitudes.
Stanza 2: A step (takes) an hour,/ A sigh (takes) an age,/ His gaze (looks) downwards./ Everyone (is) there.
Stanza 3: Enemy. – Friend./ Blackthorn. – Laurel./ All (is) a dream ... / He. – (the) Horse.
Stanza 4: (The) horse (is) lame./ (The) sword (is) rusty./ (The) cape (is) old./ (His) torso (is) straight.
⁴ Viach. V. Ivanov, "Sovremennost' poëtiki Derzhavina", *Izbrannye trudy po semiotike i istorii kul'tury, Tom II. Stat'i o russkoi literature* (Moskva: Shkola russkoi kul'tury, 2000), 10–23.
⁵ Marina Tsvetaeva, T. 5, 285. For a brilliant analysis of Tsvetava's poetic use of the potential of the Russian language, see L. B. Zubova, *Poëziia Mariny Tsvetaevoi, Lingvisticheskii aspect* (Leningrad: Izdatel'stvo Leningradskogo universiteta, 1989).
⁶ Tsvetaeva's poetic use of monosyllables has been noted by other critics, e.g. Angela Livingstone in her notes on translating *Phaedra*, Marina Tsvetaeva, *Phaedra* with *New Year's Letter and other longer poems* (London: Angel Books, 2012), 147. See Björling 2014, 54: "[…] in 'Hour of the Soul' repetitions of the monosyllables *chas* and *noch'*, as well as *dusha* (etymologically related to *dukh*) are interwoven; the same and similar sounds occur in many other poems creating a patchwork of strong sounds, recognizable as Tsvetaeva's poetic texture."
⁷ For a reference to Gubaidulina's interest for rhythm or temporality, see Valentina Kholopova, *Sofia Gaubaidulina. Putevoditel' po proizvedeniiam* (Moskva: "Kompozitor", 2001), 109–110. In an interview, Vera Lukomsky explains: "By the term 'the rhythm of form,' Gubaidulina indicates a rhythmic and temporal proportionality between and within the sections of musical form. She builds proportions according to the numbers of the Fibonacci series and/or other additive-automorphological mathematic series." Lukomsky, Vera, "Sofia Gubaidulina: 'My desire is always to rebel. To swim against the stream!'. Interview conducted and translated from the Russian by Vera Lukomsky," *Perspectives on Music*, Vol. 36, No. 1 (Winter, 1998), 43.

[8] Kholopova, 262.

[9] Dorothea Redepenning, "Russische Chormusik aus zwei Jahrhunderten". (Published on CD: SWR Vokalensemble Stuttgart – Russia, 2013).

[10] "In music, pointillism is a style introduced by Anton Webern in the 1920s, and used by his followers until the late 1960s. Instead of individual notes forming part of recognizable themes or chords, they appear to be isolated, to stand alone in the texture: a single crotchet from a clarinet, a few semiquavers from a flute, a semibreve from violins. In fact, as with all pointillism, this is an illusion: each individual note is part of a carefully ordered and intellectually coherent musical texture, which becomes ever more apparent on repeated hearings. To demonstrate this, Webern once orchestrated a Bach fugue in pointillist style, and the result, though like listening to Bach through a kind of aural prism, is still quite clearly Bach." KMcL http://www.encyclopedia69.com/eng/d/pointillism/pointillism.htm (accessed 2018-10-09)

[11] N. V. Shirieva, "'Posviashchenie Marine Tsvetaevoi' S. A. GubaidulinoI: opyt germenevticheskogo analiza", *Iskusstvo i obrazovanie* 2010, (2:64), 54–60. Concerning Gubaidulina's notion of time, see Björling 2014.

[12] For a glossary of Tsvetaeva's works and literary criticism thereof see http://tsvetaeva.litinfo.ru/words/ (accessed 2018-10-10). Note that *kon'* is sometimes translated as 'steed'.

[13] Marina Tsvetaeva, T. 3, 194.

[14] Marina Tsvetaeva, T. 3, 203.

[15] Marina Tsvetaeva, T. 3, 21.

[16] Marina Tsvetaeva, T. 3, 23.

[17] See for example Anna Saakiants, *Marina Tsvetaeva, Zhizn' i tvorchestvo* (Moskva: Ellis Lak, 1997), 229–236. Compare also with another red horse in the epic poem *Pereulochki* (Side-streets) from 1922:

Красен тот конь,

Как на иконе.

Я же и конь,

Я же и погоня. (Marina Tsvetaeva T.3, 274)

[18] Marina Tsvetaeva, T. 1, 418.

[19] Marina Tsvetaeva, T. 2, 56.

[20] Marina Tsvetaeva, T. 2, 58–59.

[21] Irma Kudrova relates a heartrending incident when Tsvetaeva, as a young child – and much to her own mortification – caused her family to collapse with laughter when she recited her following lines of poetry:

Ты лети мой конь ретивый

Чрез моря и чрез луга

И потряхивая гривой

Отнеси меня туда!

Irma Kudrova, *Put' Komet. Molodaia Tsvetaeva* (Sankt-Peterburg: Izdatel'stvo Kriga, 2007), 11. This text is in turn taken from Tsvetaeva's "Istoriia odnogo posviashcheniia", Marina Tsveateva, T. 4, 132.

[22] Marina Tsvetaeva, T. 2, 35–36.

[23] Marina Tsvetaeva, T. 2, 37.

[24] Kholopova, 259.

The Rhythm of Time

HANS RUIN

Does time *exist*? How could we doubt such a thing? Surely nothing is more tangible than *time*. Is not time both the most intimate aspect of life and its strictest ruler, an all-pervasive reality from which we carve our existence, against whose predations we strive to preserve our youth and vitality, and yet to whose ultimate authority each of us seems destined to succumb? Indeed, for the most part, time appears to us in the guise of this all-encompassing *domain* in which our existence is played out, an absolute measure that will always outlive us. In relation to Time, our own fleeting existence is merely an incident, an evanescent moment in the great cosmic flow.

And yet: when we turn to examine time as such, there is nothing to *see*. What we are beholding when we believe ourselves to be examining time are precisely the *objects* and *phenomena* by means of which we measure time. For instance, we talk about "managing time" or "saving time", but what we mean is that we are counting hours on a timepiece—a wristwatch, a cellphone, a computer, or a public clock. We talk about "observing the passage of time", but what we really mean is that we are noting changes that occur in the bodies and material around us. Winter has once again given way to spring and then summer. We have got a few more grey hairs. This or that friend or family member is no longer with us. We apprehend all these developments, all these changes in the material bodies around us, by grouping them into a single general formula: *time goes by.*

When reaching towards this evasive force and reality, we are naturally drawn to metaphors relating to movement or things that move. We say that time *passes*, but also that it *flows* or *races*. Time is a *meanderer*, but also a *stream*; sometimes an ocean, but also a *river*. For Walter Benjamin, in his famous analogy in "Theses on the Concept of History", time is also a *wind* blowing humanity from Paradise: humanity is hurled onwards with its back to the future. But in order for time to appear, it would seem that more than just continued movement is required. It takes some kind of break, an incision or a *pulse*. Or simply this: a *rhythm*. It is this notion that I want to reflect on here, that is, to see if and to what extent it can be meaningful to conceive of time itself as, in the final instance, having its origins in the phenomenon of *rhythm*.

A reflection of this sort permits me to take my point of departure in classical antiquity's greatest philosopher of time. I am referring here, not to the

Church Father St. Augustine and his oft-quoted meditations upon the inscrutability of time in Book Eleven of his *Confessions*, but to a philosopher and a text which preceded Augustine by more than half a millennium, namely Aristotle and his monumental *Physics*, the lectures on Nature that were compiled by his students and followers. These lectures are, above all, a long and winding investigation into and reflection upon *movement* and *change*—in Greek, *kinesis* and *metabole*. Greek metaphysical speculation saw this as its supreme task: to develop and formulate concepts capable of enabling thought to identify the latent pattern behind or in nature's mutability. Everywhere movement and change are taking place. The challenge for thought, then, is to identify the forms—linguistic, logical, mathematical— that allow us to conceive of and apprehend patterns in things that are obscure and dimensions in things that are in movement.

We live today in a culture so saturated by the results of this ambition that it can be hard for us to fully grasp and appreciate the extent of the Greeks' ambition and the intellectual work required to fulfill it. We have access to mathematical models which, with astonishing precision, can calculate and thereby also predict the course of events that have not yet occurred, such as the movement of heavenly bodies, changes in the weather, and the decay of atoms. And yet Aristotle was looking in the first instance, not for algorithms, but a *language* that might be able conceptually to grasp and explain change itself, and thus to say *what it is*. Zeno's celebrated paradox had exploited language's difficulty in conceptualizing the inner dynamic of movement in order to announce that what we see as movement is actually impossible, and thus that time itself is impossible or non-existent.

It is in his efforts to construct a conceptual framework for describing the movement that Aristotle develops such concepts as "possibility" and "reality", *dynamis* and *energeia*, which to this day we continue to use as a self-evident conceptual framework in both everyday and scientific discourse. It is, moreover, in this connection that he also broaches the question of *time*, itself an underlying thematic of his *Physics* as a whole. This holds primarily for the book's fourth chapter, which contains the first known attempt in the philosophical literature to define time philosophically, that is, to say *what time is*.

There is a special atmosphere around the thinkers of early classical antiquity that makes a return to their texts both liberating and imperative. They pose their questions in a kind of dawn of the world, when so little was as yet fixed and specified, when theoretical-scientific language itself had yet to find its definitive expression. At this moment thought still moved in and out of everyday language as it sought to connect and delineate what it had seen.

Here, in Book Four of *Physics*, Aristotle begins by asking the same question that I also began with, namely, does time *exist*? *Is* it something? In fact, he continues, there is strong evidence to the contrary. If time is the past, then it no longer *is*. If it is still to come, then it does not exist either. And, lastly, if it is the present, then it would seem to quickly collapse into next to nothing, only a narrow threshold between two non-existent entities.

Aristotle cites those who argue that time is quite simply the movement of everything. But he quickly remarks that time cannot be identical with movement pure and simple. Time is what we use to *measure* and *compare* other movements. By means of time we can determine how fast something is moving, when it takes place, and how different movements stand in relation to each other.

All the same, he continues, we cannot imagine time *without* movement. If there were no movement, time could not exist. In any event, *we* would have no means of determining whether this was the case. In a wholly immobile cosmos there is no way to know whether a second or a millennium has passed. It is only in relation to something moving that such a distinction has meaning.

Aristotle's question is thus: if it is the case that time and movement are so intimately connected while nonetheless not being identical, what is it in movement that characterizes time specifically?

After several long and complicated attempts to reach an answer, he finally arrives at his famous definition, on page 219b: "time is the measure of motion". In Greek, the definition reads: *chronos arithmos kineseos*. Time is the *arithmos* of movement, what could also be translated as *number* or *quantity*. We recognize the word *arithmos* from "arithmetic", knowledge of numbers.

Time is thus to be understood as the number or measure of movement, its *arithmos*: But how are we to understand this? Does Aristotle mean by this that time itself is not a part of movement, that it ought rather to be understood as an abstract, latent form which exists somewhere beyond movement itself? No, he is quite clear about time and movement being fundamentally indivisible. We may measure movement in terms of time, but we also measure time by movement.

How much time has passed? No answer to this question is possible that does not involve reference to a movement, perhaps the gnomon's movement across the sundial, the sun's movement across the heavens, the earth's movement upon its axis, or the oscillation of a caesium atom, humanity's currently most advanced precision chronometer. Time seems always to demand reference to a movement, or, as Aristotle writes: "they determine one another mutually".

Time is in motion but without being the movement itself. Time is the *number* of movement, its quantity or measure, as it reveals itself to the measuring soul of humanity. Because, just as time presupposes movement, so, too, does time seem to presuppose the existence of a soul as that point from which it becomes measurable. As Aristotle writes: "If there is nothing other than the soul and its reason that can count, then there can be no time if the soul does not exist". This passing observation is significant because it appears to gesture towards Augustine's famous conclusion, formulated much later, that time is the extension created by the human soul, our inner being, as the only place where past and future join to form the arc that constitutes time itself.

Unlike Augustine and modern idealist philosophers such as Kant and Husserl, who locate time in "the form of inner sense" as the ultimate precondition of all experience, Aristotle never considers deriving one from the other. He notes that what we refer to as time is somehow connected to the soul and to reason, *psuche* and *nous*, and to their ability to measure. But despite its measurement by human beings—a precondition for something to be assigned quantity and number—the measure of time does not *exist* within human beings. Aristotle instead turns his gaze outwards once again, declaring that the ultimate measurement is constituted by that which is most distant and stable, namely the uniformly circular orbits of the heavenly bodies. The periodically recurrent movement of the heavens is the ultimate measure of them all: the cosmos's own latent number. Or should we say: the cosmos's own *rhythm*?

For is it not ultimately *rhythm*, the regularly recurring pulse, that encapsulates the deepest qualities of time in this Aristotelian treatise? Is it not this *rhythm*, at work everywhere in the cosmos, that makes movement and change possible to comprehend and thereby allows the human soul to construe the chaotic flow of movement and change specifically as a *time* within what it imagines as *time itself*?

The word *rhythm*, like *arithmetic*, comes from the Greek. There is an obvious assonance between *rythmos* and *arithmos*. It is as if they are in some way derived from each other. They share not only the same phonetic material but also the same domain. In its earliest documented occurrences, the word *rythmos* refers precisely to a combination of movement and form as a designation for order in flux.

At the same time, it may be noted that the opposite of *rythmos* is *arythmos*—with a y—as a designation for that which lacks order: something chaotic. It sounds almost identical to *arithmos*, as if the mathematical were somehow the opposite of rhythm, something a-rhythmic. But *arythmos* with a y and *arithmos* with an i are not the same thing. According to French philologist Pierre Chantraine, the letter *alpha* in *arithmos*/number should not be understood as a negation. Rather, it functions as what he calls a "prosthesis", an intensifying supplement or support. It thus has nothing to do with what is un- or non-rhythmic.

Both words share the graphically and phonically identical syllable *thmos*, which, again according to Chantraine, is bound up with the notion of something "juste exacte", that is to say something *precise*; in other words, a movement that has come to an end and been completed. Through the bridge of this simultaneously rejected and arrested syllable—*thmos*—a connection is thus established between *rythmos* and *arithmos*, between *rhythm* and *number*.

Aristotle, as already noted, defines time in terms of *arithmos*. Yet he does not mention the word *rythmos*, rhythm, at any point in his *Physics*. If we want to know what he thinks of *rhythm*, we must instead turn to his *Poetics*. In his analysis there of different aesthetic forms, he specifically highlights *rythmos*, together with harmony, as a central aspect of good poetic composition.

However, it is ultimately not in *Poetics* that we find what, in this context, is the most interesting allusion to *the rhythmic* in Aristotle's thought. This is to be found rather in his *Rhetoric*. In Book 3, Chapter 8 of *Rhetoric*, he writes: "The form of diction should be neither metrical nor without rhythm. If it is metrical, it lacks persuasiveness [...] If it is without rhythm, it is unlimited, whereas it ought to be limited [...] Now all things are limited by number, and the number belonging to the form of diction is rhythm".

Here, in the rhetorical analysis of the art of speaking persuasively and even-handedly, we find confirmation of the connection we have been seeking. Here Aristotle ties together numerical amount and rhythm, as *the way in which a flow is given form and thereby made comprehensible*. This investigation of the most effective expression in human language also serves to create a bridge to time as the inner rhythm of change itself. Amidst this flowing and streaming, that which is rhythmic establishes sequence in movement, one upon which human beings can rest even as they are drawn into its mutability and destruction.

Rhythm gives movement form. In so doing, it establishes *time* as a space of repose to inhabit, like a pulsating abode, indeed, as that pulse's own abode, from which the changeable whole becomes comprehensible as a whole similarly at rest.

In this transposition of the rhythmic, from the poetic-rhetorical sphere to that of time and the domain of physical existence, it becomes possible to discern something that we were previously unable to see fully, namely, how our understanding and definition of time as "quantity of movement" is also deeply anchored in a particular experience of *pulse* and *rhythm*. We can now return to Aristotle's line of reasoning in *Physics* in which he expressly connects time to the motion of heavenly bodies, this time seeing—or perhaps even hearing—it in a new mode. In it, he observes how "circular movement is to the highest degree a measurement since its number is the most comprehensible of all". In fact, it defines what he calls "uniform motion". This is also why time, he adds, is often imagined as the movement of heavenly spheres, that which is the measure of all other movements and which is hence the measure of time itself. Time is thus ultimately conceived of as a circle or cycle.

To this we can now add: time is imagined as pulse and *rhythm*, as something that recurs in the same way again and again. It thus reveals itself as the cosmos's own rhythm, circling back to its point of origin only to begin again. Mathematics and arithmetic allow us to construct infinite chains of symbols, following endlessly upon each other, since for every n there exists not only an n-1 but also an n+1, something that makes infinity comprehensible as an everlasting and incomplete sequence. We can place such an imagined axis or line of symbols beside what is pulsating so as to allow the pulse itself to extend itself along its determined path in the sequence n+1+1+1… and so on, and thereby create an *axis of time*. But for time to make its appearance as something measurable and countable in itself, it must first have presented itself as circle, pulse, and rhythm.

It is as such a perceived rhythm of reality itself that *time* first makes its appearance. It is as a rhythm of this kind, too, that it continues to produce its effect and ensure its validity as the resting and pulsating form of all matter. It holds our world together with the help of the ever more highly calibrated instruments with which it is measured, and which themselves in the final instance rely on the ungrounded ground of the rhythmic itself.

Indeed, time is the rhythm of motion.

«Не поддадимся чувству естественности всего происходящего!»
(«Новая искренность» в «Обращениях к гражданам» Д. А. Пригова)[1]

MARK LIPOVETSKY

Начиная с 1985-го года Дмитрий Пригов расклеивает на улицах Москвы и раздает во время своих чтений ленточки бумаги с напечатанным текстом, начинающимся с обращения «Граждане» и заканчивающимся фамильярно-издевательской подписью «Дмитрий Алесаныч». Все эти тексты по своему содержанию вполне аполитичны, но их форма явно пародирует официальные «Призывы ЦК КПСС», печатавшиеся во всех газетах и звучавшие на октябрьских и первомайских демонстрациях. В этом отношении «Обращения» Пригова явно перекликаются с ранними работами В. Комара и А. Меламида, в которых они «приватизировали» советский дискурс, подписывая своими фамилиями лозунги «Вперед к победе коммунизма!» или «Слава труду!».

Однако Комар и Меламид не развешивали свои лозунги на улицах. А Пригов свои обращения – развешивал. Очевидно, что сам выход приговского перформанса, независимо от его содержания, в публичное пространство носит политический характер. «В этих обращениях не было ничего, кроме несанкционированности моих действий. Но у меня с ними [с КГБ] были давние отношения, и эти бумажки просто приплюсовывались к моему досье. Во всяком случае, *(посмеиваясь)* эти бумажки позволили им с легкой душой определить: ну сумасшедший», – пояснял Пригов в 2001-м[2].

«Обращения» представляют собой один из первых постмодернистских перформансов в русской культуре. Однако по своей природе перформанс Пригова не похож на акции Коллективных Действий, связанных с уходом «в лес» – подальше от советской социальности; отличается он и от перформансов 90-х–2000-х годов, таких, как акции О. Кулика и А. Бреннера, групп Э.Т.И., «Война», Pussy Riot – с их прямым вторжением в *политические* пространства. Куда ближе Пригову оказывается деятельность арт-группы «Гнездо», в которую входили ученики Комара и Меламида Геннадий Донской, Михаил Рошаль и Виктор Скерсис. Летом 1978-го года они провели акцию «Искусство в массы». Вот что пишет о ней Екатерина Деготь:

> Одно из лучших произведений отечественного политического активизма, с моей точки зрения. Д–Р–С изготовили классический советский транспарант, но не с текстом, а с фрагментом абстрактной картины (кажется, Пауля Клее), вышли на перекресток улиц Дмитрия Ульянова и Вавилова, прямо к магазину «Академкнига», и направились в сторону Ленинского проспекта. Неприятности у них потом были, но все же акция оказалась, по сути дела, ненаказуемой. А это значит, что была решена главная концептуальная художественная задача – ускользнуть от однозначной интерпретации и поставить все смыслы под вопрос. Просто в СССР от успешности решения этой задачи зависели судьба и свобода. Потому-то вещь так и захватывает.³

Эта характеристика применима и к «Обращениям» Пригова – как по части ускользания от однозначной интерпретации и проблематизации смыслов, так и по части судьбы и свободы.

Именно из-за «Обращений» в ноябре 1986 года⁴ Пригов был задержан на улице и отправлен на принудительное лечение в специальную (т.е. под надзором КГБ) психбольницу №15. Дата ареста Пригова весьма показательна. Перестройка уже объявлена. Через месяц, в декабре 1986-го, будет освобожден из ссылки академик Сахаров. Еще не опубликованы в СССР ни «Реквием» А. Ахматовой, ни «Котлован» (в 1987 г.), ни «Чевенгур» (в 1988 г.) Платонова, ни стихи Бродского (в 1987 г.), только в апреле 1988-го выйдет «Доктор Живаго», а «Архипелаг Гулаг» – в 1989 г. Одновременно увидят свет шедевры эстетического нонконформизма: «Москва-Петушки» Вен. Ерофеева (1988), стихи самого Пригова (1988) и Льва Рубинштейна (в 1988), «Школа для дураков» Саши Соколова (в 1989), проза Владимира Сорокина (в 1989). Но в 1986-м ситуация была еще крайне неустойчивой и неопределенной, и арест Пригова мог послужить «пробным камнем», испытывающим на прочность последовательность перестроечного курса и отражавшим подковерную борьбу между реформаторами и охранителями.

К счастью, репрессивная система уже давала сбои. Как Пригов рассказывал И. Балабановой,⁵ его узнала медсестра психбольницы, бывавшая на выступлениях Пригова, и по просьбе Д. А. позвонила жене Пригова Надежде Георгиевне Буровой. Надежда Георгиевна нашла психбольницу и даже увидела Пригова. Одновременно она оповестила Виктора Ерофеева и Евгения Попова, которые в свою очередь обратились к Белле Ахмадуллиной и режиссеру Владимиру Аленикову (уже прославившемуся фильмами про приключения Петрова и Васечкина). Те пришли в больницу и разговаривали с главврачом. Разумеется, главврач ничего не решал, но он мог задержать «лечение», что, собственно, и произошло. В то же время вместе с И. Кабаковым они организовали кампанию в защиту Пригова на западных радиостанциях и в газетах. В результате на третий день после ареста Пригов был освобожден. Все-таки во время перестройки международный скандал, связанный с преследованием художника, был нежелателен властям, хотя, по собственному признанию Пригова, «если бы это было за год-полтора, я бы действительно сидел […] ну года два-три».[6]

В более поздних комментариях Пригов подчеркивал почти комический характер этого инцидента. Например, он рассказывал о том, что его сосед по палате представился как «Володя Высоцкий». «Высоцкий» разбудил Пригова посреди ночи, чтобы спеть свою новую песню. Новой песней оказалось «Боже, царя храни». Исполняя ее, «Высоцкий» присел на кровать Пригова и, вероятно, от возбуждения обмочился на постель, на которой после этого стало невозможно спать.[7]

Можно подумать, что Пригов ретроспективно придает гротескные черты своему заключению, но трагифарсовые ноты различимы и в воспоминаниях Е. Попова:

> Мы с Ерофеевым встретили Пригова, он идет веселый, рассказал, что с ним в палате находится внук Павлика Морозова.[8] Было видно, что он не сознает всей серьезности того, что могло произойти. У нас это вызвало тихую злобу. […] Ведут Дмитрия Александровича, переодетого в больничную пижаму, он замечает нас и игриво выкрикивает: «О, гутен абенд». Ну, что тут скажешь.[9]

Думается, Попов не совсем прав – Пригов безусловно, трезво осознавал опасность происходящего. Приветствие по-немецки, вероятно, можно было прочитать как сигнал, указывающий на серьезность ситуации («как в нацистском концлагере»). Скорее, изображая легкомысленную веселость, Пригов разыгрывал образ автора, заданный «Обращениями», – глуповатого «пророка», радующегося всему на свете – а следовательно, воспринимал свое заключение как логическое и важное продолжение перформанса.

Как и всякий перформанс, «Обращения» (как, впрочем, и акция группы «Гнездо») *обозначали культурную (социальную, политическую) границу – путем ее нарушения.* Что это за граница?

Нариман Скаков считает, что «Обращения» подрывают медийный режим советской культуры с его регламентом публичного/приватного высказывания:

> "Appeals to Citizens" challenged both traditional and underground writing practices that predominated in the Soviet Union in the 1980s. The mediatic character of the project, which can be described as an extreme form of the process of "the dramatization of the scene of writing," leads to the ultimate destruction and renegotiation of the signifying function of words. [….] every appeal was textually unique. The individuality of each message contradicts conventions – both those of everyday private advertisements, in which a single message about the sale of an item or offer of exchange of apartment gets multiplied, and those of official notices (for example, of a facilities management office), where a single message is reproduced in certain areas of the housing complex. The commercial ethos of homemade advertisements, to which readers were so accustomed, is renegotiated in Prigov's appeals. The singular multiplicity of the pragmatic act of communication is challenged by the incessant flow of unique artistic statements, which have no apparent practical purpose and overwhelm the reader with their quantity and content diversity.[10]

Несомненно, «Обращения» также проблематизируют границу публичности контркультуры. После скандального разгона Бульдозерной выставки 1974 года между московскими (и только московскими!) властями и художественным андеграундом было достигнуто некоторое компромиссное соглашение[11]. Работы художников-нонконформистов иногда выставлялись в специально отведенных пространствах – в павильоне «Пчеловодство» на ВДНХ (1975 г.), на Малой Грузинской, 28 («горкоме графиков», с 1975 г.), разумеется, предварительно подвергаясь политической цензуре. Также само собой разумелось, что эти выставки не сопровождались никакой рекламой, что означало, что посещали их люди «своего круга» – знатоки и любители. Примерно так же обстояло дело с литературными чтениями – они разрешались, но не были официальными и чаще всего оставались домашними концертами для хорошо проверенной публики.

Поэтому тот факт, что Д.А.П. раздавал свои обращения на чтениях, представляло куда меньшую трансгрессию, чем то, что он расклеивал их, наподобие объявлений на улицах Москвы. Тем самым Пригов, во-первых, обращался не к избранной, а к широкой публике. А во-вторых, само собой, полностью игнорировал цензуру. Тот факт, что сами тексты были аполитичными по своему содержанию, подчеркивал, что на самом деле вопрос цензуры – вторичен, если сколько-нибудь важен вообще. Своим перформансом и последовавшей репрессией, которая стала частью перформанса – как потом будет происходить не раз и с группой «Война», и с Pussy Riot, и с акциями Петра Павленского, – Пригов обнажал не просто лицемерие власти, дозволявшей нонконформистскому искусству существовать в прозрачном стакане, не выходя за его границы. Он, в первую очередь, демонстрировал лицемерие и ложь лозунгов перестройки, звучавших с 1986-го года и обещавших новый социализм, освобожденный от пороков «застоя» и усиленный «ускорением» и «гласностью».

Однако это только самый поверхностный уровень трансгрессии.

«Новая искренность»

Пригов несколько раз описывал и разъяснял эту акцию в иных терминах. Так, например, в статье начала 1990-х «Мы брать преград не обещались, а все время приходится» он писал:

> …Состояла же она, эта акция, в написании и расклеивании на домах, столбах, деревьях и заборах города Москвы нехитрых, невинных и как бы до глубины души искренне-доверительных текстов-обращений типа: «Граждане! Если вы потоптали траву, если вы разорили гнездо птицы, то как после этого можете вы смотреть в лицо матери вашей!» И в конце обращения следовала столь же общественно-безличная, как и обращение «Граждане», подпись «Дмитрий Алексаныч», вроде бы представлявшая меня как некоего персонажного автора, находящегося в нелепых мерцательных отношениях с более мощным автором-породителем более широкого спектра акций и всего другого – Дмитрием Александровичем. […] Тексты подразделялись на две категории: экология природы и экология души. Вторые, в отличие от первых, уже представленных и расклеиваемых во внешней среде, раздавались в прямые страждущие, тянувшиеся ко мне со всех сторон, как птицы на кормлении, руки после различного рода чтений, выступлений и встреч. Замечу попутно, что, конечно, эти вроде бы прямые обращения, с работой в природе и отношением к природе моментально отсылали к искренности экологических художников, устанавливая с их дискурсом мерцательные и лукавые отношения, хотя для желавших и страждущих искренности, и могли быть восприняты таким образом. Разбросанность и малочисленность точек расклейки (по сравнению с размерами гигантского мегаполиса) этих, быстро разрушаемых воздействием внешней среды бумажечек, импульсивность и нерегулярность их производства

(параллельно я занимался многочисленной одновременной деятельностью в различных жанрах и направлениях), тянущиеся руки, бестелесность, затертая вербальность, квази-искренность медиирующих текстов, такая же нерегулярность встреч, растянутых во времени – все это вместе взятое посредством упомянутых объявляющих и объявляющихся точек-событий, выстраивали, вычерчивали некую виртуальную траекторию-свидетельство проектного существования, могущего быть растянутым во всю длину жизни.[12]

В статье конца 1990-х–начала 2000-го года «Не такой уж он и безумный – этот двойник I» он возвращается к этому сюжету:

Когда я, как вспоминается, расклеивал по паркам, садам и улицам Москвы свои как бы искренне-экологические тексты с призывом не портить природу и не губить душу, для меня был бы дик и нелеп вопрос:

– А ты искренен?
– А как же?
– Неужели ты и есть полностью вот это?

Да, полностью. Но отчасти. Лишь до следующих призывов, скажем, бороться за счастье людей, не жалея ни своих, ни чужих жизней.[13]

И наконец, в предуведомлении к сборнику этих обращений, опубликованному в Москве в 1996-м году под заголовком «Обращения Дмитрия Александровича Пригова к народу»:

Для меня, да и для небольшого круга людей, работавших в пределах достаточно сходных эстетических принципов, встала проблема преодоления несколько ужесточившегося, застывшего концептуального менталитета (прошедшего тогда свой героический период, впрочем, уже по всему свету). Стратегии реализации этого были различны, но отнюдь не брались со стороны, а просто за счет интенсификации, проращивания существовавших уже ростков, но функционировавших в несколько удаленных и маргинальных зонах творчествования вышеупомянутых авторов. Это была пора большего педалирования иррационализма, сентиментализма, элементов экстатики и эмоциональности. Свои поиски того времени я обозначил как Новая искренность, всеми тогда однозначно понимаемая как оппозиция жестоко отстраненному и структурному письму.

Как видно, как можно заметить, эти обращения мерцают в зоне между заданностью шапки: «Граждане!» – и финального знака выхода из текста: «Дмитрий Алексаныч!» и некой лирико-сентиментальной интонации срединного текста. Это мерцание, труднофиксированность и трудноидентифицированность и стало основной моей интонацией того времени.¹⁴

Во всех этих самоописаниях наблюдается сочетание двух категорий: «новая искренность» и «мерцание». Сочетание парадоксальное, если учесть тот клубок недоразумений, которые накопились вокруг «новой искренности» (далее НИ).¹⁵ Так, в популярных интерпретациях, часто встречающихся в интернете, НИ понимается как «преодоление» постмодернизма. Например, так:

> Человек уже достаточно наигрался в искусство, расширяя его возможности до предела. Настало время, когда ему хочется говорить не о чём-то отстранённом, но о самом себе. Автор перестаёт фильтровать свои мысли, пытаться взглянуть на них со стороны и заботиться об их оригинальности и актуальности. Он искренне изливает на бумагу свой мыслепоток, стараясь не упустить ни единой эмоции и с прустовской педантичностью запечатлеть любое движение души, но пишет при этом он легко, свежо и быстро. [...] В изобразительном искусстве «новая искренность» знаменуется возвращением интереса к предметной живописи, в театре – шокирующей откровенностью «новой драмы» и социального театра вербатим. В кинематографическом застое струю живительного кислорода (sic! – *М.Л.*) пускают бывшие постмодернисты, а ныне – каннские лауреаты, Аки Каурисмяки, Педро Альмодовар, Ларс фон Триер с идеологией «Догмы» и всеми близкими ей [...]."¹⁶

Не станем спорить относительно Каурисмяки и Альмодовара с фон Триером, хотя сдается, что и их «искренность» не стоит принимать за чистую монету, однако можно уверенно утверждать, что к Пригову (которого упоминает автор заметки) этот набор слов точно не имеет *никакого отношения*.

В «Словаре терминов Московской концептуальной школы», на который ссылаются многие комментаторы НИ, приведен вырванный из контекста (из Предуведомления к сборнику под названием «Новая искренность») текст: «Новая искренность – в пределах утвердившейся современной тотальной конвенциональности языков, искусство обращения преимущественно к традиционно сложившемуся лирическо-исповедальному дискурсу и может быть названо „новой искренностью"».¹⁷ В этом издании в качестве источника цитаты указывается Предуведомление к сборнику «Новая искренность» 1984-го года. Однако, в архиве Пригова данный сборник помечен 1986-м годом, да и текст там другой:

«Поэт, как и читатель, всегда искренен в самом себе. Эти стихи взывают к искренности общения, они знаки ситуации искренности со всем пониманием условности как зоны, так и знаков ее проявления».[18] Для Пригова, разумеется, самое важное здесь: «в пределах тотальной конвенциональности», хотя многие предпочли этого не замечать, обратив внимание исключительно на «лирически-исповедальный дискурс». Это понимание искренности глубоко укоренено в творчестве Пригова, еще в 1980-м году в предуведомлении к сборнику «Искренность на договорных началах, или слезы геральдической души» он писал:

> Поэт тоже человек. То есть – ему не чуждо ничто человеческое. Так и мне захотелось сказать что-нибудь прямое, искреннее, даже сентиментальное. И только захотелось, как выплыли из темно-сладких пластов памяти строки: «Утомленное солнце тихо в море садилось…», «Рос на опушке клен, в березку клен тот был влюблен…», «Товарищ, товарищ, болят мои раны…». И плакал я. И понял я, что нет ничего более декоративного, чем искренний и страдающий поэт (Лермонтов, Есенин). Но понял я также, что некие позывные, вызывающие из сердца авторского и читательского глубоко личные слезы, которые, разливаясь, неложно блестят на всех изломах этого, почти канонического, орнамента, этого знака «Лирического», который не подглядывает картинки жизни, но сам диктует жизни какой ей быть.[19]

«Что-нибудь прямое, искреннее» оборачивается цитатами, т.е. уже опосредованными и, более того, клишированными формулами, которые, тем не менее, запускают эмоциональную реакцию, аффект искренности. Михаил Ямпольский в своей книге о Пригове, комментируя сборник «Новая искренность», справедливо отмечает, что интерес к искренности у Пригова сочетается с пониманием того факта, что «искренность невозможна в литературе, потому что сама литературная форма трансформирует ее в литературную условность».[20] Для Пригова же «истинная сфера искренности лежит в чистых аффектах» (161) – то есть за пределами дискурса. Однако, подчеркивает Ямпольский, по мнению Пригова, «без аффекта невозможно производство литературной формы, тем более, в том автоматизированном режиме, к которому он стремился» (161).

Эллен Руттен в книге *Sincerity after Communism: A Cultural History* (2017) обсуждает дискуссии об искренности, которые шли в перестроечной и постсоветской России на протяжении нескольких десятилетий. Руттен понимает НИ как широкий спектр стратегий, направленных на ревизию постмодернизма: "a turn away from postmodernism toward a new cultural mentality in, among other countries, the United States, Estonia, the United Kingdom, Germany, Netherlands, and China."[21] При этом она подчеркивает, что дискурс НИ, по преимуществу, развивается внутри постмодернистской парадигмы, и потому скорее служит ее внутренней критике и обогащению, нежели реальному выходу за ее пределы.[22] Пригова она рассматривает как одного из пионеров этого движения, выдвинувшего тезис о необходимости искусства НИ еще в середине 1980-х, вне каких бы то ни было влияний с Запада. Э. Руттен несколько раз оговаривается, что приговская версия НИ всегда двусмысленна: "sincerity becomes an entity that intricately interweaves with – rather than strictly opposes – irony" (98). Аналогично, его тексты, которые можно прочитать как НИ (например, «Вопросы к Сорокину Владимиру Георгиевичу от Пригова Дмитрия Александровича»), также смущают своим тоном: "Confusingly, the tone of the lecture itself blended emotional commitment with analytical distance, without ever annihilating the tension between the two" (82). Вместе с тем, она склонна солидаризироваться с теми интерпретаторами (как А. Зорин или М. Эпштейн), которые интерпретируют приговскую поэзию как новую версию сентиментализма, в которой ироническая окраска не подрывает, а только смягчает торжество искренности над холодной деконструкцией.[23]

Приговские замечания о «преодолении несколько ужесточившегося, застывшего концептуального менталитета» как будто согласуются с предположением о том, что НИ возникает в ответ на кризис постмодернизма. В то же время надо признать, что в 1986-м году Пригов еще не использует слово «постмодернизм» и вряд ли его знает. Завершение «героического периода», по-видимому, согласуется с возникающими в связи с перестройкой надеждами на выход из андеграунда и необходимостью найти стратегии более публичного существования. Поэтому, кстати говоря, датировка цикла стихов под названием «Новая искренность» 1986-м годом представляется куда более вероятной, чем 1984-м: в 84-м перестройкой и не пахло. Пригов подчеркивает: «Стратегии реализации этого были различны, но отнюдь не брались со стороны, а просто *за счет интенсификации, проращивания существовавших уже ростков*, но функционировавших в несколько удаленных и маргинальных зонах творчествования вышеупомянутых авторов» (курсив мой – М.Л.). Выходит, НИ не является разрывом с концептуализмом (и постмодернизмом), а представляет собой более полное развитие его потенциала.

Именно этот потенциал и связан с категорией мерцания, в которой Д. Лейдерман видит центральную стратегию всего московского концептуализма[24]. Мерцание составляет существо приговской НИ, и цикл «Обращений» является центральным для понимания совершенного им сдвига концептуалистской эстетики. Сдвиг этот, думается, состоял в «овнешнении» персонажности и других аспектов «мерцательной формы» концептуального искусства – в переводе этих приемов в «план содержания» и даже, более того, придания им некой дидактичности (хотя, конечно, всегда самоироничной). То, что Пригов обращает принцип мерцания на искренность – что и приводит к рождению НИ – также не случайно и также связано с культурной атмосферой перестройки.

Как напоминает Э. Руттен,[25] искренность именно в годы перестройки становится важнейшим культурным лозунгом, понимаемым как антитеза узаконенной фальши и лжи. В этом смысле культурная риторика перестройки – особенно в ее ранний период – прямо наследовала «оттепели» и таким ее манифестам, как статья Владимира Померанцева «Об искренности в литературе» (1953). Искренность понималась как главное условие *истинности высказывания*, как видно, например, по таким сенсациям ранней перестройки, как спектакль Валерия Фокина «Говори» (1985) или фильм «Курьер» (1986) К. Шахназарова.

За этим пониманием стояла особое мироощущение, которое можно обозначить как *эссенциализированный антикоммунизм*: существующий социальный порядок воспринимался как настолько противоестественный, настолько несовместимый с «человеческой природой» и «здравым смыслом», что казалось, он исчезнет сам по себе, будто морок, если только позволить людям «жить не по лжи», то есть следуя своим инстинктивным, неотрефлектированным, «естественным» эмоциям. Эта позиция характерна для многих писателей диссидентского круга, прежде всего, А. Солженицына. Тимур Атмашев называет эту идеологию «утопическим консерватизмом» и считает, что именно она вырастает в основание социального консенсуса в ходе перестройки: «Естественно-историческая, или органическая, эволюция была противопоставлена обманным мобилизующим целям, теоретическому спекулированию и физическому насилию… Солженицын предлагает новую историософскую и нравственную норму – органическую эволюцию, которая была единодушно принята в последние годы перестройки».[26] Как будет показано ниже, Пригов сатирически воплощает эту идеологию задолго до того, как она станет «консенсусной».

На основе этой идеологии возникает *сочетание интимности и публичности*, характерное для диссидентского дискурса. Интимность маркирует «естественную норму», а публичность подтверждает ее политическое значение. В 1980-м году Андрей Сергеев напишет «рассказик» про Солженицына – поразительно, что в этом вряд ли известном Пригову и опубликованном лишь посмертно тексте Солженицын, став политиком (главой ведомства по вооружению и разоружению), тоже расклеивает «обращения к гражданам», по методу распространения и интонации напоминающие приговские – их также отличает показательное сочетание интимности и публичности дискурса:

СОЛЖЕНИЦЫН

Солженицына поставили во главе ведомства по вооружению и разоружению. Ежедневно он выпускал обращения к правительствам и народам мира.

Я шел через лес в сторону Глухова и на опушке вдруг увидал поляну

и на ней:

обычные печатные обращения на стволах и –
записки, записки, записки от руки,
наколотые на сухие веточки, пришпиленные булавками к пням, разложенные на траве.

Великий писатель находил время обращаться ко всем поименно:

– Виктор Николаевич, уважаемый, очень надёжусь.
– Федя, какие же собаки ненужные бывают?
– ЗИНА, НЕПУЩУ![27]

Пригов безусловно использует и деконструирует эту семантику искренности.[28] Однако, он идет дальше пародии на диссидентский дискурс, становящийся мейнстримом в годы перестройки: в «Обращениях» искренность – это одна из культурных конвенций, некий механизм, который позволяет придать любому, в сущности, высказыванию *статус истинности*, причем истинности одновременно субъективной и всеобщей. Как говорит Пригов, «если ты точно угадываешь дискурс, скажем, искренности какого-то высказывания, то для человека они, собственно говоря, моментально служат триггерами, включателями этой самой искренности».[29] Но именно истинность высказываний, помещаемых на «обращения», даже на первый взгляд, мягко говоря, сомнительна, несмотря на их искренность.

Это либо искренние банальные благоглупости:

> *Граждане!*
> *Не рука, а душа преступление совершает!*
> *Дмитрий Алексаныч*[30]

> *Граждане!*
> *Подберите птенца, выпавшего из гнезда – он дитя наше всеобщее!*
> *Дмитрий Алексаныч (466)*

> *Граждане!*
> *Мороз, снег, холод невозможный – это и есть наша здоровая русская зима!*
> *Дмитрий Алексаныч (285)*

> *Граждане!*
> *У каждого из нас своя околица, свой причал!*
> *Дмитрий Алексаныч (466)*

> *Граждане!*
> *Дома все должно быть чисто, не то налет домашней нечистоты будет следовать за вами повсюду!*
> *Дмитрий Алексаныч (281)*

> *Граждане!*
> *Чаще бывайте на людях и замечайте неординарность проявлений человеческих характеров!*
> *Дмитрий Алексаныч (283)*

> *Граждане!*
> *Оденьтесь потеплее – грядут морозы почище нынешних!*
> *Дмитрий Алексаныч (289)*

Либо эмоционально-эмфатические высказывания, нарочито лишенные смысла, например, часто повторяющееся:

> *Граждане!*
> *Дмитрий Алексаныч (266, 414)*[31]

Таким образом, искренность в «Обращениях к гражданам» предстает как *пустая форма*, которую может заполнить абсолютно любое содержание (или его отсутствие), но при этом иллюзия правдивости будет сохраняться. С этой точки зрения, «Обращения к гражданам» саркастически подрывают доминирующие культурные конвенции. Это конвенции, идущие не от власти, а от «народа» – к которому Пригов и «обращается». В этом видится и смысл НИ – в радикальной деконструкции не властного, но достаточно авторитетного – именно в силу противостояния власти – дискурса.

В сущности, в этом понимании "искренности" нет ничего *радикально* нового по сравнению с текстами Пригова 70-80-х годов. Если что изменяется, так только *вектор*, который Пригов придает "искренности". В 1995-м Пригов напишет:

> В первый раз, в возрасте почти
>
>   55 лет почувствовал
>
>   себя оставленным мощным
>   советским мифом
>
> Бывало, я плакал как ребенок
>
>   брошенный
>
> Бывало, летал над ним, как
>
>   властительное облако
>
> И вдруг ощутил себя никак
> И надо переучиваться
> Вот незадача[32]

Судя по текстам НИ, это чувство посетило Пригова гораздо раньше – в начале перестройки. Его поворот к НИ и стал реакций на распад единого советского мифа. НИ, таким образом, оказывается способом исследования разных, «точечных» дискурсивных практик, развивающихся *при отсутствии доминирующей государственной идеологии*. Если в 70–80-е годы Пригов разрабатывает разветвленную целую систему приемов, обнажающих конвенциональный и сконструированный характер языка, пронизанного «государственной» риторикой, то начиная с «Обращений к гражданам» он концентрируется на *практиках субъектности*, на способах производства и разновидностях «субъективных истин», – которые оказываются такими же сконструированными и неаутентичными, как и советский идеологический дискурс.

Деконструкция «экологии»

Как помним, Пригов определял «экологию природы» и «экологию души» в качестве основных тем «Обращений», поясняя: «эти вроде бы прямые обращения, с работой в природе и отношением к природе моментально отсылали к искренности экологических художников, устанавливая с их дискурсом мерцательные и лукавые отношения…». Кто такие экологические художники, и откуда вообще возникает эта тема?

Судя по известной книге Б. Гройса «Стиль Сталин» (первое издание –1988 г.)³³, в кругу концептуалистов «экологическими» называли, по преимуществу, писателей - и художников-деревенщиков, но в первую очередь – все того же А. Солженицына, в котором Гройс видел наиболее полное воплощение традиционалистской и консервативной реакции на кризис сталинизма как авангардного проекта:

> [В 60-годы] социалистический реализм стал постепенно уступать место традиционному реализму, наиболее характерной и влиятельной фигурой которого в годы «оттепели» можно считать А. Солженицына. Утопические мечты о «новом человеке» сменились ориентацией на консервативные «вечные ценности», заключенные в русском народе, «перестрадавшем» Революцию и сталинизм […] Эта позиция, выраженная Солженицыным в довольно радикальной форме, постепенно, в слегка замаскированном и смягченном виде, превратилась на протяжении 1960– 1970-х годов в идеологию, господствующую в советских официальных кругах. Ее проповедуют в миллионных тиражах писатели-«деревенщики», занимающие в официальной культурной индустрии ведущее положение – здесь достаточно назвать имена В. Распутина. В. Астафьева, В. Белова и других, – а также многие советские влиятельные философы и литературные критики.³⁴

Гройс подчеркивает, что именно эта «экологическая» идеология и является «точкой сборки» позднесоветской культуры – на ней сходятся и официальная, и оппозиционная культуры, и власть, и «народ»:

> Иначе говоря, именно сейчас советская идеология действительно становится во все большей степени традиционалистской и консервативной, охотно обращаясь при этом в первую очередь к русским традиционным ценностям, включая морализаторски интерпретированное христианство. Неизменным остается при этом коллективистский характер советской идеологии, требующий от индивидуума подчинения воле «народа», совпадающего в советских условиях с государством. Индивидуализм Нового времени этим исключается так же, как и традиционная христианская забота о личном спасении по ту сторону любых социальных обязательств. […] Экологически-националистическая утопия продолжает быть утопией в самом непосредственном сталинском смысле: речь снова идет о тотальной мобилизации современной техники с целью остановить технический прогресс, прекратить историю и путем манипуляции природной средой преобразовывать человека, т. е. из модернистского и технического сделать его антимодернистским и национально-экологическим.³⁵

Для Гройса – и, можно полагать, для Пригова – этот дискурс, а вернее, его триумф в позднесоветской и перестроечной культуре (а как сейчас видно, именно он восторжествовал и в постсоветской культуре 2010-х гг.), свидетельствует о непобедимости сталинизма – при всех происходящих изменениях сохраняется высший смысл сталинской утопии, состоящий в выходе России из исторического времени:

> Таким образом, уже в 1960–1970-х годах внимательному наблюдателю советской культурной сцены постепенно стало ясно, что все попытки преодолеть сталинский проект на индивидуальном или коллективном уровне фатально приводят к его репродуцированию. На Западе институты власти, обеспечивающие «бесцельное» движение прогресса, сменяющего одну моду другой, одну технику другой, против чего восстает субъективность, ищущая цели, смысла, гармонии и, в конце концов, просто не желающая служить безразличному ей Молоху Истории, все-таки устояли против всех восстаний, всех попыток придать времени смысл, направить или трансцендировать его. В России, в Советском Союзе положение прямо противоположное: здесь прогресс осуществляется только как попытка его остановить, как националистическая реакция на монотонное превосходство Запада, как стремление выйти из сферы этого господства, т.е. из времени, в апокалиптическое царство безвременья.[36]

В этом контексте понятно, что уравнивание «экологии природы» с «экологией души», означает существенную подмену действительно экологической проблематики – проблематикой консервативно-утопической и, в пределе, националистической. Посвящая свои «обращения» «экологии», Пригов, тем самым, атаковал именно зону «консенсуса» между интеллигенцией, властью и народом, зону, обеспечивавшую сохранение статус кво даже при радикальных социополитических переменах. Крайне показательно, что именно в ранний период перестройки экологическая тема (борьба против поворота сибирских рек, например) стала заместителем политической критики, а ее глашатаями выступили именно писатели-деревенщики, давно ставшие частью официальной идеологии.

Не удивительно, что интерпретация «экологических» мотивов в обращениях Пригова при ближайшем рассмотрении оказывается внутренне противоречивой и подчас явно издевательской. С одной стороны, среди обращений регулярно звучат восторги перед природой, уравнивающие ее с высшими проявлениями счастья. При этом, кажется, природа прекрасна именно тем, что она «наша», «русская»:

> *Граждане!*
> *Все это вокруг нас – просто неслыханная наша удача!*
> *Дмитрий Алексаныч (329)*
>
> *Граждане!*
> *Отойдите на шаг, посмотрите на место, где вы только что стояли – вы чудо попирали ногами своими!*
> *Дмитрий Алексаныч (260)*
>
> *Граждане!*
> *Выйдешь – снег серебрится; небо залито топленым молоком, сердце холодеет от красоты неземной, Боже!*
> *Дмитрий Алексаныч (286)*
>
> *Граждане!*
> *Чудо! чудо какое наша природа русская!*
> *Дмитрий Алексаныч (268)*
>
> *Граждане!*
> *До чего же трогательна и прекрасна наша русская береза, Боже мой!*
> *Дмитрий Алексаныч (383)*
>
> *Граждане!*
> *Холодно, но прекрасно кругом, до чего же хороша русская зима!*
> *Дмитрий Алексаныч (308)*
>
> *Граждане!*
> *Разве нам надо больше, чем любой пылинке русской! – правда, пылинке китайской, говорят, надо еще меньше!*
> *Дмитрий Алексаныч (429)*

С другой стороны, «русскость» оказывается тождественна всемирности, и заоконный пейзаж простирается от Гималаев до Амазонки. Можно предположить, что таким образом Пригов иронически воплощает идею «всемирной отзывчивости», столь важную для русского национализма[37]:

> *Граждане!*
> *Амазонка шумит под вашими окнами – оттого и ощущение чего-то грандиозного!*
> *Дмитрий Алексаныч (350)*
>
> *Граждане!*
> *Воздух чист на многие километры. Эверест из окна виднеется, и мы сами легки и в доме своем!*
> *Дмитрий Алексаныч (355)*
>
> *Граждане!*
> *Озеро Виктория плещется у подножья дома вашего, но обратитесь к другому окну – там океан Ледовитый вас поджидает – эка!*

> *Дмитрий Алексаныч (362)*
>
> *Граждане!*
> *Ледники соседних гор слепят ваше зрение подмосковное – пора привыкать: теперь всегда так будет!*
> *Дмитрий Алексаныч (367)*
>
> *Граждане!*
> *Лианы оплетают окна ваши, вы их раздвигаете, чтобы разглядеть Килиманджаро – дивные картины, что никуда переезжать не хочется!*
> *Дмитрий Алексаныч (411)*

Красота природы, как и ее «всемирность» то и дело интерпретируются Дмитрием Алексанычем как «награда» русскому народу – по-видимому, за пережитые им страдания. Красота служит доказательством перехода «граждан» и их ареала в утопическое состояние духовного совершенства («Китай духовный»):

> *Граждане!*
> *Выходишь во двор, а навстречу тебе японец со львом идет – это величие мира персонифицированное тебе, заслужившему явилось!*
> *Дмитрий Алексаныч (421)*
>
> *Граждане!*
> *Змей приподнимает паркет пола в квартире вашей и высовывает мудрую голову – вы заслужили это!*
> *Дмитрий Алексаныч (388)*
>
> *Граждане!*
> *С балкона вашего видно то, что можно было бы назвать Китаем духовным!*
> *Дмитрий Алексаныч (432)*

В то же время, таким же квазирелигиозным восторгом, что и природа, окружены в «обращениях» описания родного дома:

> *Граждане!*
> *Приходя с улицы домой – обойдите стол свой с пением торжественным!*
> *Дмитрий Алексаныч (265)*
>
> *Граждане!*
> *Столб золотой горит посредине жилища вашего!*
> *Дмитрий Алексаныч (454)*
>
> *Граждане!*
> *Вы входите в дом свой, и волна благодарности к нему пьянит вас!*

> *Дмитрий Алексаныч (259)*
>
> *Граждане!*
> *Как добр к нам холодильник наш! а телевизор! а лифт вверх нас словно на руках ласковых несущий!*
> *Дмитрий Алексаныч (260)*
>
> *Граждане!*
> *Холодильник вскидывается по ночам – не бойтесь его, он так же заинтересован в прочности дома вашего, как и вы сами!*
> *Дмитрий Алексаныч (266)*
>
> *Граждане!*
> *Входишь в дом свой – а там все по-прежнему – это ли не чудо?!*
> *Дмитрий Алексаныч (284)*
>
> *Граждане!*
> *Вы выходите и в кухне своей так запросто застаете счастье – где еще такое возможно?!*
> *Дмитрий Алексаныч (286)*
>
> *Граждане!*
> *Шторы приспущены, покой разливается, друг наш – квартира милая! как ты мила сердцу нашему истерзанному!*
> *Дмитрий Алексаныч (303)*

Правда, оказывается, что дом прекрасен именно потому, что способен защитить от ужасов внешнего мира:

> *Граждане!*
> *Занавеска закрывает окно ваше и в этом равна Великой Китайской Стене мифической!*
> *Дмитрий Алексаныч (330)*
>
> *Граждане!*
> *Чисто вымыты окна квартиры вашей – прозрачность их есть наилучшая защита от наваждений и миражей внешних!*
> *Дмитрий Алексаныч (266)*
>
> *Граждане!*
> *Стены крепки в квартире нашей, они крепки даже чересчур, лишая нас самих способности защищаться!*
> *Дмитрий Алексаныч (269)*
>
> *Граждане!*
> *Какая сила выманивает нас из дома уютного и гонит в поля эти открытые, кругом безопасности неокаймленные!*
> *Дмитрий Алексаныч (255)*
>
> *Граждане!*

> *Выходите вы из дому, а он обнимает вас, плачет, не пускает – а что делать?!*
> Дмитрий Алексаныч (284)

Внешний же мир предстает столь опасным, что вынесенные наружу предметы успевают «одичать»:

> *Граждане!*
> *Белье на балконе уже по утрам жестяное – оно забыло нас!*
> Дмитрий Алексаныч (317)

> *Граждане!*
> *Вынесенные предметы назад домой просятся – страшно! ведь они уже успели одичать!*
> Дмитрий Алексаныч (280)

Естественно, возникает вопрос – откуда же берутся ужасы, если законный мир так прекрасен и гармоничен? Пригов нарочно оставляет этот вопрос без ответа – силы зла у него безличны и окружены мистической аурой. Он разворачивает другое противоречие – несмотря на устойчивость домашней крепости, жуть проникает вовнутрь дома:

> *Граждане!*
> *Сумрак даже сквозь стены проникает и в квартиру нашу – и она от него не защита!*
> Дмитрий Алексаныч (387)

> *Граждане!*
> *Не заглядывайте с улицы в окно – это страшно!*
> Дмитрий Алексаныч (316)

> *Граждане!*
> *Возвращаясь домой с улицы, мы каждый раз кого-нибудь да приводим на спине своей!*
> Дмитрий Алексаныч (265)

> *Граждане!*
> *Сидишь дома, дверь на запоре, а что-то екнет сердце, и кожа на спине подрагивает – что это?*
> Дмитрий Алексаныч (261)

> *Граждане!*
> *Смело входите в дом свой, но все же в угол левый быстро взгляд свой бросьте – нет, нет, все в порядке!*
> Дмитрий Алексаныч (307)

> *Граждане!*
> *Жуть! жуть, что по ночам за нашей спиной происходит.*

> *Дмитрий Алексаныч (301)*
>
> *Граждане!*
> *Что-то пол в квартире коробится, словно кто-то головой его пробить тщится – кто он?!*
> *Дмитрий Алексаныч (399)*

Таким образом, «экологическое» мироощущение оказывается клубком противоречий, впрочем, неизменно искренне выраженных. Искренность в этом контексте оборачивается отсутствием рефлексии, неспособностью субъекта даже *заметить* противоречия. Приговский «Дмитрий Алексаныч» проповедует открытость миру – и прославляет изоляцию от него. Он упивается родной околицей – и тоскует по экзотическим землям. Он параноидально прозревает тайные силы мрака, прячущиеся везде и повсюду – и заглушает этот страх преувеличенной восторженностью. Но, главное, несмотря на все эти кричащие противоречия, представленное в «Обращениях» мироощущение ошеломительно *банально* и потому порождает колоссальное количество трюизмов, что свидетельствует не только об узости и ограниченности сознания, «влипнувшего» в «экологический» дискурс, но и, главным образом, о нормализации, обыденности, общепринятости этого дискурса.

Пастырский субъект

Торжествующая банальность обращений прямо соотносится с ролью Дмитрия Алексаныча – вождя и пастыря народа – ролью, в большой степени и являющейся предметом перформанса. Казалось бы, этот персонаж идет против «воли народа», помещая себя над ним, принимая на себя ответственность за народ. Недаром его голос – это часто голос строго и недовольного учителя или даже Милиционера:

> *Граждане!*
> *Не забывайтесь, пожалуйста!*
> *Дмитрий Алексаныч (282)*
>
> *Граждане!*
> *Граждане!*
> *Граждане!*
> *чем занят ум ваш?! – непостижимо!*
> *Дмитрий Алексаныч (295)*
>
> *Граждане!*
> *Я останавливаю вас на этом месте и говорю вам: Опомнитесь!*
> *Дмитрий Алексаныч (465)*

> *Граждане!*
> *Я часто замечаю за вами некую невнимательность к миру мелких существ – это неправильно!*
> *Дмитрий Алексаныч (302)*
>
> *Граждане!*
> *Кто кроме меня скажет вам всю правду в глаза, при этом не оскорбив вас!*
> *Дмитрий Алексаныч (295)*
>
> *Граждане!*
> *Не хватайтесь за все – вам поручено очень немногое!*
> *Дмитрий Алексаныч (262)*

Вместе с тем, его позиция тоже внутренне противоречива. С одной стороны, он, в квазибиблейском стиле, изображает себя уверенным вождем, сострадательным к пастве, но строгим к ее порокам. Слабости и страдания Дмитрия Алексаныча (о которых он тоже порой рассказывает, не скрывая тягостных сомнений и неуверенности в себе) лишь подчеркивают героику его пастырского служения и его превосходство над «паствой»:

> *Граждане!*
> *Если кто придет к вам и скажет: Слушай меня! – вы отвечайте ему: У меня уже есть кого слушать!*
> *Дмитрий Алексаныч (340)*
>
> *Граждане!*
> *Я гляжу на вас, и нету мне покоя!*
> *Дмитрий Алексаныч (285)*
>
> *Граждане!*
> *Не я говорю вам это, но природа говорит это голосом тихим!*
> *Дмитрий Алексаныч (299)*
>
> *Граждане!*
> *Будьте спокойны и уверены – я с вами!*
> *Дмитрий Алексаныч (344)*
>
> *Граждане!*
> *Я спокоен и строг, потому что я знаю, что все преходяще.*
> *Дмитрий Алексаныч (446)*
>
> *Граждане!*
> *Я словно впереди боевой машины иду!*
> *Дмитрий Алексаныч (320)*
>
> *Граждане!*
> *Напишите мне, что волнует вас!*

> Дмитрий Алексаныч (320)
>
> *Граждане!*
> *Чем бы вас таким нехитрым повеселить, назидаючи!*
> Дмитрий Алексаныч (273)
>
> *Граждане!*
> *Я люблю вас и потому я строг, даже чрезмерно иногда!*
> Дмитрий Алексаныч (257)
>
> *Граждане!*
> *Я вижу вас, спешащих ото всех концов света ко мне, и умиление переполняет меня!*
> Дмитрий Алексаныч (269)
>
> *Граждане!*
> *Не могу в этот раз объяснить вам всего, но прошу – верьте мне!*
> Дмитрий Алексаныч (308)
>
> *Граждане!*
> *Все, все будет хорошо, я вам обещаю!*
> Дмитрий Алексаныч (335)
>
> *Граждане!*
> *Вот я весь в руках ваших!*
> Дмитрий Алексаныч (335)
>
> *Граждане!*
> *Это я отметил путь ваш!*
> Дмитрий Алексаныч (306)

С другой, Дмитрий Алексаныч – всегда *один из нас*. Он где-то здесь, в толпе, что усиливает эффект его всеведения и всезнания. Дмитрий Алексаныч как будто бы оказывается где-то рядом со своими читателями, всегда у них за плечом – не только как ангел-хранитель, но и как незваный соглядатай:

> *Граждане!*
> *Видел я вас вчера из окна!*
> Дмитрий Алексаныч (272)
>
> *Граждане!*
> *Только что мы расстались, а я уже и соскучился, вот я какой!*
> Дмитрий Алексаныч (272)
>
> *Граждане!*
> *Я молча смотрю на вас, и вы это знаете!*
> Дмитрий Алексаныч (295)
>
> *Граждане!*
> *Я рядом с вами! Рядом!*

Дмитрий Алексаныч (299)

Граждане!
Мне так приятно с вами, но я должен идти!
Дмитрий Алексаныч (290)

Граждане!
Потом, потом, я сейчас тороплюсь, но всегда помню о вас!
Дмитрий Алексаныч (290)

Именно поэтому величавость позиции Дмитрия Алексаныча часто подрывается обращениями, в которых он, сбиваясь на склочный тон, как бы продолжает начатый спор – отвечая на всегда немые и воображаемые возражения паствы:

Граждане!
Сколько же можно говорить вам об этом, я могу и обидеться!
Дмитрий Алексаныч (269)

Граждане!
Вы же видите, что я был прав!
Дмитрий Алексаныч (291)

Граждане!
Я передумал – я снимаю свои претензии к вам!
Дмитрий Алексаныч (309)

Граждане!
Не спорьте, не спорьте со мной, все равно ведь все выйдет по-моему!
Дмитрий Алексаныч (312)

Граждане!
Я вас просил по-хорошему!
Дмитрий Алексаныч (313)

Граждане!
Все, что я писал раньше – отменяется!
Дмитрий Алексаныч (313)

Граждане!
Вы все мне не верите – да ладно, ладно!
Дмитрий Алексаныч (315)

Граждане!
Я вас не призывал ни к чему плохому!
Дмитрий Алексаныч (318)

Граждане!
Я обижен на вас – пишу, пишу – и никакого результата!
Дмитрий Алексаныч (429)

Впрочем, и тогда, когда Дмитрий Алексаныч ободряет, и тогда, когда он критикует паству, он никогда не выходит за границы банальности. В конечном счете, становится ясно, что содержание обращений, по сути дела, неважно – Пригов и подчеркивает этот эффект текстами с забитыми «крестом» словами. Это, в принципе, матрицы или паттерны, в которые можно подставлять разнообразные слова, не нарушая при этом банальности высказывания:

> *Граждане!*
> *То, во что вы верите, xxxxx, если подумать!*
> *Дмитрий Алексаныч (279)*

> *Граждане!*
> *Не вы ли сами xxxxx, а потом xxxxx, так-то вот!*
> *Дмитрий Алексаныч (282)*

> *Граждане!*
> *Я же говорил вам, что все это xxxxx xxxxx не стоит xxxxx xxxxx нашего!*
> *Дмитрий Алексаныч (289)*

> *Граждане!*
> *Что бы вы сказали xxxxx xxxxx xxxxx, но только в самом xxxxx смысле!*
> *Дмитрий Алексаныч (344)*

> *Граждане!*
> *Вы не должны xxxxx, чтобы xxxxx, а не иначе.*
> *Дмитрий Алексаныч (279)*

> *Граждане!*
> *Вы знаете, что xxxxx, или никогда!*
> *Дмитрий Алексаныч (284)*

> *Граждане!*
> *Чем чаще я xxxxx этому!*
> *Дмитрий Алексаныч (290)*

> *Граждане!*
> *Это не моя прихоть xxxxx образ ваш xxxxx они подумают!*
> *Дмитрий Алексаныч (292)*

> *Граждане!*
> *В конечном счете xxxxx и не по нашей!*
> *Дмитрий Алексаныч (293)*

> *Граждане!*
> *Когда вы xxxxx или xxxxx постоянно!*
> *Дмитрий Алексаныч (298)*

> *Граждане!*
> *Это все частности, xxxxx xxxxx xxxxx!*

> *Дмитрий Александыч (341)*
>
> *Граждане!*
> *Не вы ли ххххх ххххх ххххх, о чем я вас справедливо и предупреждал!*
> *Дмитрий Александыч (343)*

В то же время именно банальность становится базой социального консенсуса, она оказывается сообщительной и поэтому вольно или невольно приобретает политический характер. Причем, политические высказывания Дмитрия Александыча не только замаскированы под аполитическую «экологию», но и, как уже говорилось, всегда *лишены конкретного смысла*. Благодаря этому качеству они выступают как полые формы, наполняемые значением только при соотнесении с какими-то текущими политическими событиями. Но именно в этом их немеркнущая актуальность!

> *Граждане!*
> *Немногим более года прошло, а как уже все изменилось!*
> *Дмитрий Александыч (446)*
>
> *Граждане!*
> *А помните, как мы сокрушались всего год назад – вот так-то!*
> *Дмитрий Александыч (288)*
>
> *Граждане!*
> *Как трудно думать о весне и оттепели без всяких аналогий и символов!*
> *Дмитрий Александыч (297)*
>
> *Граждане!*
> *Как часто народный герой переходит в антинародного, и наоборот!*
> *Дмитрий Александыч (285)*
>
> *Граждане!*
> *Не поддадимся чувству естественности всего происходящего!*
> *Дмитрий Александыч (455)*
>
> *Граждане!*
> *Они не ожидали от нас этого!*
> *Дмитрий Александыч (304)*
>
> *Граждане!*
> *Вот и все, а вот и снова все!*
> *Дмитрий Александыч (297)*
>
> *Граждане!*
> *Скажем себе строго: Не в этот, не в этот раз!*
> *Дмитрий Александыч (310)*

Граждане!
Ничего, кроме этого, уже и не осталось!
Дмитрий Алексаныч (310)

Таким образом, в «Обращениях» Пригов устраивает перформанс не только «экологического» дискурса, но и создает «голос» политического лидера, который формируется этим дискурсом. На фоне рождающейся в России политики то была пародийная фигура или вернее, пародийный голос «кандидата от всех» – всех, разделяющих «экологическое» мироощущения. Фигура, безусловно, саморазоблачительная, поскольку перед нами вновь приговский «маленький человек», овладевший дискурсом власти и почувствовавший себя «пастырем». Пастырем, не способным распознать ни противоречий, ни банальности своего «учения», ни пустотности своей «политики», но компенсирующего все «искренностью»!

Вместе с тем, задаваемые «Дмитрием Алексанычем» отношения с паствой удивительным образом воспроизводят ту концепцию языка и власти, которую Ирина Сандомирская раскрыла в работах Сталина по лингвистике: «Язык, каким он предстает в работе Сталина – это язык, в котором провозглашается общность всех со всеми, со всем и навсегда […] Сталин предлагает принципиально новые отношения между носителем (языка, культа, гражданства) и вождем: вождь (язык) призван обслуживать всех, а "все" в свою очередь призваны не просто подчиняться силе вождя, но подписываться на пользование вождем, как если бы вождь (подобно языку) был средством коммуникации».[38] В сущности, Пригов и являет образ такого языка-вождя в своих расклеенных повсюду «обращениях». Собственно, его «Дмитрий Алексаныч» и персонифицирует власть, разлитую в советском языке. Взрыв этой власти именно в момент перестройки, по логике Пригова, свидетельствует о том, что смерть советских риторик, над которыми он издевался в своих «советских стихах», не затрагивает глубинные основания советского культурного бытия – не подрывая, а напротив, усиливая глубоко советскую потребность в «языке, в котором провозглашается общность всех со всеми, со всем и навсегда». Потребность, которая в свою очередь воплощает вожделение вождя как средства коммуникации всех со всеми. Такой язык может только языком полых форм и торжествующих банальностей.

В отличие от «советских стихов», в «Обращениях к гражданам» «экологическая» власть оказывается децентрализованной, рассеянной и, в принципе, *невидимой* – поскольку невозможен читатель, который охватил и освоил бы все обращения, рассеянные в пространстве города и раздаваемые посетителям квартирных чтений. Вернее, таким «читателем» мог быть только КГБ, что подчеркивает преемственность власти, опирающейся на искренность, по отношению к власти советской и постсоветской. И в том, и в другом случае речь идет о том, что Фуко называет «пастырской властью» – нацеленной на духовное спасение индивидуума в первую очередь.

Как Фуко отмечает в статье «Субъект и власть», возникая в институтах христианства, техника пастырской власти сосредоточена на том, чтобы обеспечить спасение индивидуальной души. Поэтому она не может быть осуществлена "without knowing the inside of peoples' minds, without exploring their souls, without making them reveal their innermost secrets. It implies a knowledge of the conscience and an ability to direct it."[39] Более того, пастырская власть опирается на производство индивидуальной правды ("it is linked with a production of truth – the truth of the individual himself"[40]) или, иными словами, – на искренность. Хотя Фуко утверждает, что пастырская власть лишь закладывает основания модерности, превращаясь в биополитику и легальную власть современного государства, исследователи видят устойчивые проявления этого типа власти в советской и постсоветской культуре.

Черты пастырской власти узнаются и в советской идеологии с ее устремленностью не только к глобальному (коммунизм) и индивидуальному (новый советский человек) спасению, предполагающему в свою очередь искреннее приятие каждым освященных идеологией норм и ценностей.[41] Аналогичные процессы наблюдаются и в пост советской политике, особенно после 2014-го года, когда политический, культурный и религиозный национализм становятся императивами социализации каждого. Так, Елизавета Гауфман отмечает, что власть Путина несет на себе отпечаток всех важнейших структурных особенностей пастырской власти: "(1) references to transborder sovereignty, (2) securitization discourse, (3) direct involvement, and (4) sexualization of the figure of the pastor."[42]

Однако, думается, смысл приговских текстов выходит за пределы непосредственного политического контекста. Характерное для «Обращений» сочетание возвышенной, «пастырской» интонации с методичным проникновением в различные области по преимуществу приватных практик превращает «Дмитрия Алексаныча» в провозвестника той эры, когда «политики субъектности» и контроль за повседневной жизнью каждого практиками – а ведь именно ими он озабочен более всего – выйдут на первый план, вытесняя все иные формы политики.

¹ Настоящая статья является частью большого проекта, осуществляемого в соавторстве с И. В. Кукулиным, которому я обязан многими идеями и советами, повлиявшими на содержание статьи, и которому я хочу выразить свою искреннюю благодарность.
² И. Балабанова, *Говорит Д.А.П.* (М.: ОГИ, 2001), 89.
³ Е. Деготь, «Десять акций группы "Гнездо"», Colta.ru, 27 February, 2008, accessed November 30, 2018, http://os.colta.ru/art/projects/109/details/998/
⁴ См. *News from the Helsinki Watch,* March 1987, 5, http://www.parallelarchive.org/document/3981?terms=Prigov%3B, accessed November 30, 2018. Подробный рассказ самого Пригова – см.: Балабанова, *Говорит Д.А.П.,* 88–94. Рассказ Евгения Попова об этой истории с другой точки зрения см.: Д. Шаповал, *Д.А. Пригов. Двадцать один разговор и одно дружеское послание.* (М.: НЛО, 2014), 210–211.
⁵ Балабанова. *Говорит Д.А.П.,* 90.
⁶ Балабанова. *Говорит Д.А.П.,*90.
⁷ См.: Балабанова. *Говорит Д.А.П.,* 93.
⁸ Остается неясным, были ли «внук Павлика Морозова» и «Володя Высоцкого» одним лицом, или речь идет о разных соседях Пригова по палате.
⁹ Шаповал, *Двадцать один разговор,* 211, 210.
¹⁰ Nariman Skakov, "Typographomania: On Prigov's Typewritten Experiments", *Russian Review* 75:2 (April 2016): 242 [241–263].
¹¹ См. воспоминания об этой выставки, в том числе и приговские: «Художник и свобода: к 30-летию "бульдозерной" выставки», Радио «Свобода», 12 сентября 2004, https://www.svoboda.org/a/24199990.html, accessed November 30, 2018.
¹² Д. А. Пригов, *Мысли: Избранные манифесты, статьи, интервью,* под ред. М. Липовецкого и И. Кукулина (М.: НЛО, 2019), 313.
¹³ Пригов, *Мысли,* 330.
¹⁴ Д. А. Пригов, *Москва: Вирши на каждый день,* под ред. Б. Обермайр и Г. Витте (М.: НЛО, 2016), 256.
¹⁵ Здесь, по-видимому, ошибка составителей, поскольку в архиве ДАП данный сборник помечен 1986-м годом.
¹⁶ А. Буренков, «Новая искренность,» accessed November 30, 2018, http://www.be-in.ru/people/455-novaya_iskrennost
¹⁷ *Словарь терминов московской концептуальной школы,* под ред. А. Монастырского (M.: Ad Marginem, 1999), 64–65.
¹⁸ Указано Б. Обермайр в личной переписке.
¹⁹ Д. А. Пригов, *Места: Свое/чужое,* под ред. М. Липовецкого и Ж. Галиевой (М.: НЛО, 2019), 278.
²⁰ М. Б. Ямпольский, *Пригов: Очерки художественного номинализма* (М.: НЛО, 2016), 159.
²¹ Ellen Rutten, *Sincerity after Communism: A Cultural History* (New Haven and London, 2017), 2.
²² См.: Rutten, *Sincerity,* 104–105.
²³ Ср. описание «новой сентиментальности» у М. Эпштейна в статье 1992 года «Прото-, или Конец постмодернизма»: «И когда произносится слово «люблю», то оно подразумевает: да, так могли бы сказать и Данте, и Мопассан, но это я говорю, и у

меня нет другого слова, чтобы высказать то, что оно означает. Транс-цитатное слово содержит презумпцию вины и жест извинения, признание собственной цитатности – и тем самым еще сильнее и увереннее подчеркивает свою безусловность, незаменимость, единственность. Если постмодернистское «люблю» пользовалось цитатностью как смысловой лазейкой, в которую субъект высказывания мог скрыться от его прямого смысла и ответственных последствий, то теперь цитатность подчеркивается, чтобы быть перечеркнутой. Слово сразу расслаивается на два слова, цитируемое и надцитатное (произносимое впервые, здесь и сейчас), что открывается простор для новой многозначности. Если многозначность постмодернизма – это множественность уровней рефлексии, игры, отражения, лепящихся друг на друга кавычек, то многозначность новой сентиментальности – более высокого порядка. Это движение смысла сразу в обе стороны, закавычивания и раскавычивания, так что одно и то же слово звучит как «„„„„люблю"""» и как Люблю! Как «„„„„царствие божие"""» и как Царствие Божие! Причем одно измерение текста неотделимо от другого, раскавычивание происходит из глубины закавычивания, точно так же, как воскресение происходит из глубины смерти» (М. Эпштейн, *Постмодерн в России* (М.: Изд-во Р. Элинина, 2000), 281–2).

24 См.: Daniil Leiderman, "Moscow Conceptualism and "Shimmering": Authority, Anarchism, and Space" (PhD diss., Princeton University, Department of Art and Archeology, 2016): Daniil Leiderman, "The Strategy of Shimmering in Moscow Conceptualism," *Russian Literature,* 96–98 (2018): 51–76.

25 Rutten, *Sincerity,* 75–76,

26 Тимур М. Атнашев, "Утопический консерватизм в эпоху поздней перестройки: отпуская вожжи истории," *Социология власти.* Т. 29: 2:17, 21 [12–51].

27 А. Сергеев, *Изгнание бесов: Рассказики и стихи* (М.: НЛО, 2000), http://levin.rinet.ru/FRIENDS/SERGEEV/izgnanie_besov.html Last accesses February 23, 2019.

28 См. также наблюдение Н. Скакова: «Apart from the subversive level of collision with the linguistic practices of those in power, Prigov also produces critical discourse aimed at undermining the foundations of Soviet dissident *samizdat*. As textual objects, "Appeals to Citizens" clearly follow the aesthetic conventions of underground printing: cheap paper, printed in carbon copy by an anonymous typesetter, unambiguously refers to the communicative practices of traditional dissidents. […] The project thus provides a dual criticism, targeting the prophetic ideological aspirations of *samizdat* on the one hand, and, on the other, the pathos of the officialdom of Soviet bureaucratic speech» (*Skakov*, "Typographomania," 9, 10).

29 Д. А. Пригов – М. Н. Эпштейн, «Попытка не быть идентифицированным», *Неканонический классик: Дмитрий Александрович Пригов (1940–2007),* под ред. Е. Добренко, И. Кукулинаб М. Липовецкогоб М. Майофис (М.: НЛО, 2010), 69 [52–71].

30 Пригов, *Москва*, 466. Здесь и далее все «Обращения» приводятся по этому изданию.

31 По поводу этого, чаще всего повторяющегося, обращения, Н. Скаков пишет: "There is no message whatsoever, and the three words designating the two subjects are enveloped by predicative emptiness. This highlights the pure fact of *appealing*—a communicative gesture for the sake of gesture" (*Skakov*, "Typographomania," 8).

32 Д. А. Пригов, *Монады: Как-бы-искренность*, под ред. М. Липовецкого (М.: НЛО, 2013), 598.

³³ Поскольку Гройс уехал из СССР в 1981 году, можно предполагать, что этот термин имел хождение и раньше.
³⁴ Борис Гройс, *Gesamtkunstwerk Сталин* (М: Ad Marginem, 2013), 56–7.
³⁵ Гройс, *Gesamtkunstwerk,* 57, 58.
³⁶ Гройс, *Gesamtkunstwerk,* 58.
³⁷ Думается, интуитивным образом Д. А. Пригов, получивший, как известно, художественное образование и бывший профессиональным художником и скульптором, в концентрированном виде воплощает здесь националистическую идеологию русской пейзажной живописи, популяризированную и канонизированную в советской культуре. Как отмечает С. А. Штырков, именно пейзажная живопись, популяризируемая «Огоньком» и школьными учебниками русского языка и литературы, стала основным каналом распространения и стабилизации национализма в советской культуре. В частности, исследователь пишет: «Русский лирический пейзаж, постоянно прославляемый и пропагандируемый "в репродукциях, открытках, школьных учебниках, хрестоматиях" [...] был и остается необходимой составной частью практического ежедневного патриотизма. Изображение фрагмента национального ландшафта, экспонируемое обычно без указания его точной географической приуроченности [...], выступало в качестве обобщенного портрета родины. Вырезанная из журнала, купленная в магазине, а порой даже вытканная или вышитая самостоятельно репродукция известной картины украшала городскую квартиру или сельский дом, напоминая обитателям об их причастности к сообществу людей, проживающих на одной территории. Вообще говоря, патриотический пейзаж предполагает, что ландшафт будет преподнесен как свое, родное, русское. Он призван вызывать у читателя-зрителя чувство тихой или острой грусти, приступ сентиментальной тоски, доводящей в пределе до слез, о чем-то утраченном и желание вернуться туда, где находится его подлинная родина». (С. А. Штырков, «Церквушка над тихой рекой»: Русское классическое искусство и советский пейзажный патриотизм», *Этнографическое обозрение,* 6: 2016: 52 [44–57]).
³⁸ Ирина Сандомирская, *Блокада в слове: Очерки критической теории и биополитики языка* (М.: НЛО, 2013), 383, 385–6.
³⁹ Michel Foucault, "The Subject and Power," in Michel Foucault, *Power,* ed. James D. Faubion, transl. by Robert Hurley and others (New York: The New Press, 1994), 333 [326–348].
⁴⁰ Foucault, "The Subject and Power," 333.
⁴¹ См.: Igal Halfin, *From Darkness to Light: Class, Consciousness, and Salvation in Revolutionary Russia* (Pittsburgh: University of Pittsburgh Press, 1999): Олег Хархордин, *Обличать и лицемерить* (СПб-М.: Европейский ун-т, 2002), особенно – с. 18–71; Yuri Slezkine, *The House of Government: A Saga of Russian Revolution* (Princeton and Oxford: Princeton University Press, 2017), 73–118.
⁴² Elizaveta Gaufman, "Putin's Pastorate: Post-Structuralism in Post-Soviet Russia," *Alternatives: Global, Local, Political,* 42(2): 2017: 85 [74–90].

The Translator as Trickster:
Mark Tarlovskii and Southern Subjectivity

SUSANNA WITT

Introduction

One of the heroes in Mark Lipovetsky's fascinating book *Charms of the Cynical Reason: The Trickster's Transformations in Soviet and Post-Soviet Culture* (2011), is Andrei Buzykin, the protagonist of Georgii Danelia's 1979 film *Osennii marafon* [Autumn Marathon]. Describing this "involuntary trickster", Lipovetsky comments: "The tricksterish function of mediation is emphasized in Buzykin—it is no accident that he is a literary translator."[1] This fact is not elaborated further, however, and apart from Buzykin and the mention of his being "a servant of two masters" (his wife and lover) the topic of translation does not surface in the book. This article will provide something of a counterpart to Lipovetsky's study by focusing on the career of an "involuntary translator", Mark Tarlovskii—a poet by calling who like many of his kind ended up in Soviet culture with the hyphenated identity of poet-translator, *poet-perevodchik*. I will approach the literary and biographical projects of this figure through the lens of the trickster archetype. Drawing on both published and archival material, I will trace Tarlovskii's navigations through what Lipovetsky—applying Sloterdijk's term (1983)—labels "cynical culture" in the Soviet 1930s and 1940s. While Lipovetsky's study may shed light on several traits in Tarlovskii's creative makeup which one may find rather intriguing, I would argue that the case of Tarlovskii, in turn, may shed some additional light on the phenomenon of the trickster in Soviet culture at the time.

Theorizing the trickster

According to Lipovetsky, the immense popularity enjoyed during Soviet times by the trickster (exemplified by figures such as Il'f and Petrov's Ostap Bender, Ehrenburg's Khulio Khurenito, Aleksei Tolstoi's Buratino, Buzykin, and, stretching into post-Soviet times, Viktor Pelevin's werefoxes and werewolves) was due to "the need to provide symbolic justification to the practices of the 'shadow' economy and sociality—or, in a broader sense, to the mechanisms of cynical survival and deception that existed behind the ideologically approved simulacra of the state-run economy and 'classless' society."² Reality, so to say, paved the way for the genre. As noted by Sheila Fitzpatrick, the Soviet project itself was based on a reforging of social identities which required trickster-like qualities from ordinary people who in the search for a "usable self" not infrequently turned to manipulating class origins, family relations and biographies.³ Often overlooked in studies of "Soviet subjectivity", which tend to focus "only on the process of the internalization of Soviet modernization by Soviet subjects", the contradictions inherent in such transformations, Lipovetsky argues, cannot be ignored when it comes to phenomena such as "double thought, mimicry, and cynicism".⁴ Lipovetsky demonstrates that even in the case of Stepan Podlubnyi—a main hero in "Soviet subjectivity" studies—we have to do with multiple personae, and he concludes: "[t]he ease of inner metamorphoses and intrinsic artistism, demonstrated by an ordinary Soviet subject, finds a direct aesthetic manifestation in the trickster trope."⁵

What distinguishes the trickster as a trope in Soviet culture, Lipovestky argues, is that the trickster transforms his/her tricks into an art form,⁶ "using comedy to reveal a-systemic elements inherent in Soviet economics, sociality and even politics".⁷ The case of Mark Tarlovskii is of particular interest here, I would argue, because of the difficulties involved in locating the "trope": it seems to manifest itself ubiquitously as an irresistible impulse roaming the interface between life and letters.

The life and (mis)fortunes of Mark Tarlovskii

Born in the town of Elisavetgrad (now: Kropyvnyts'kyi) in central Ukraine in 1902, Mark Tarlovskii, the son of a Jewish typographer, began writing poetry already before moving to Odessa with his family in 1912. After finishing secondary school he joined the literary group known as *Kollektiv poetov* [Poets' Collective] which gathered around the colorful figure of Eduard Bagritskii. Other members of the group soon to become famous were Iurii Olesha, Valentin Kataev, and Il'ia Il'f, to name just a few. Tarlovskii was particularly influenced by the poet Georgii Shengeli, a regular appearance in the group who was also to join the ranks of poet-translators in the 1930s. In 1922, Tarlovskii moved to Moscow, received philological education at Moscow State University and started writing for *Ogonek* and a variety of other journals. He also managed to publish some poetry in periodicals and anthologies. His debut collection appeared in 1928 under the title *Ironicheskii sad* [The Ironic Garden].

It was a nod to Pushkin's "Solovei i roza" [The Nightingale and the Rose] written a hundred years earlier and elaborated that poem's motive of an indifferent audience to bear ironically on current circumstances. Playful, humorous and equilibristic, the book featured an epigraph from Nikolai Gumilev. Although it was quite well received by some critics, it was also targeted for being "alien", "detached from the people" and "non-proletarian in spirit".[8]

Tarlovskii's second collection, *Pochtovyi golub'* [Carrier Pigeon] was submitted to typesetting in the autumn of 1929 but was halted at the stage of the first proofs. It appeared in 1932 under the title *Bumerang*, heavily censored and with some additional poems on more orthodox topics. The poet's third and last collection, entitled *Rozhdenie rodiny* [Birth of the Motherland], was published in 1935. One third of this volume consisted of translations of propagandistic poems from various "nationalities literatures" with designations such as "from the Iakut", "from the Tartar", "from the Tadzhik", etc. This fact is indicative of a decisive turn in Tarlovskii's career. From the early 1930s he was to make a living mainly as a translator, thus acquiring the hyphenated title of *poet-perevodchik* [poet-translator] under which he was to be remembered, if at all, until 2009, when a large volume of his original writings appeared in Moscow, edited by Evgenii Vitkovskii and Vladislav Rezvyi.[9] It revealed a long series of rejected projects and writings for the drawer.

Tarlovskii's later career is perhaps best visualized with the help of a map of the USSR and serves well as an illustration to Anthony Pym's observation that translators are generally characterized by "multidiscursive involvement (translators usually do more than translate), complex cultural allegiances (they are not always faithful or loyal to one side), and physical mobility (they tend not to stay in just one place)."[10] Distant places visited by Tarlovskii in connection with various projects, journalistic as well as translational, include Fergana, Alma-Ata, Frunze, Aktiubinsk, and Ulan-Ude. Unfortunately, Tarlovskii did not live to see the Thaw period, which might have added to his published oeuvre. He died of a heart attack in July 1952, seven months before Stalin.

A manifesto for the hyphen

In addition to the already mentioned parameter of "transforming the tricks into an artform", the trickster, according to Lipovetsky, is to feature characteristics of "ambivalence and mediation", "liminality and transgressive vitality", and "a relation to the sacred." The first refers to the fact that "all tricksters function as cultural mediators that fuse otherwise incompatible features (natural and artifical, foreign and domestic, animal and human, marginal and mainstream [...])."¹¹ In Tarlovskii's case, these traits come to the fore in a peculiar document kept in his archive and entitled "Proekt literaturnogo manifesta" [Draft for a literary manifesto].¹² It is dated March/April 1929, a year often considered a liminal one in Soviet culture, after which censorship hardened significantly and writers designated as fellow travelers were fiercely—and increasingly so—attacked as "anti-Soviet" by representatives of RAPP, the Russian Association of Proletarian Writers. This somewhat untimely manifesto begins, as dictated by the genre, with a "we":

> We are transgressors [perekhodniki]. We are not fellow travelers going along side by side with the proletariat, in parallel with it, never joining our ways with it. Our path forms a zigzag pattern, because we want to know what is happening on both sides of the road. [...] we are transgressors because it is in the very nature of our literary existence and work.¹³

The handwritten document is unsigned, leaving the identity of this "we" an open question. But it is known that Tarlovskii at the time took active part in the literary life of Moscow; he read his poetry at the literary gatherings known as *Nikitinskie subbotniki*¹⁴ and his own apartment occasionally turned into a spontaneous literary salon with readings by fellow poets such as Georgii Shengeli, Evgenii Lann and Sigizmund Krzhizhanovskii¹⁵— writers whose origins were also in the south: Odessa, Kharkov, Kiev. Tarlovskii also spent time in the "writers' colony" in Koktebel', as witnessed by his poem to Maksimilian Voloshin and improvisations originating in this milieu.

The opening of the manifesto establishes a rhetorical figure that will structure the whole text: the figure "both" and "in between", expressed by the prefix "pere-" throughout. This figure may be seen as polemically directed towards the polarizing discourses of the 1920s, which stressed dichotomies such as "proletarian" and "bourgeois", "revolutionary" and "counter-revolutionary", "allied" and "enemy", etc. But it is perhaps also a reply to an earlier literary manifesto, namely the one issued in 1922 by the Serapion Brothers, which declared a position of "neither-nor".¹⁶ Tarlovskii's manifesto, in contrast, proceeds to a declaration of loyalty—which gradually transforms into a declaration of independence:

> As citizens we are law-abiding to the last letter [velichaishie zakonniki]. [...] But, as artists, we are lawless. Or, rather, our laws are unstable. They are transitional [perekhodnyi]. This quality they owe to our memory—visual, auditory and, above all, ideological [ideinaia].¹⁷

The author/s of the manifesto define themselves as a *link* [*perekhodnoe zveno*] between the old world and the new and their creative work is characterized as representing a link between polarities:

> As for genre, our literary work is something transitional between lyrical and epic. […] Truth we blend with lie, and for truthseekers our works are enigmatic pictures.[18]

As if anticipating the potential corollary of such a literary program, the next paragraph makes clear that the "we" of the manifesto do not regard emigration as an option:

> We write in Russian, but not only for Russians. We are not national. However, the fact that our mother tongue is Russian and that most of us write poetry (a genre which is difficult to translate), makes us especially appreciate our existence within the ranks of the Russian workers […].

Retrospectively, we may perceive a certain irony here: Tarlovskii was soon to become completely dependent on translation—specifically, of poetry, the most resistant genre. Moreover, the bulk of Tarlovskii's translations was to be from poetry produced by "nationals" [*natsionaly*], representatives of the various peoples of the Union.

A master trope in the manifesto, the "link" gradually takes on a more drastic imagery. In the end, the authors arrive at the following declaration:

> We are werewolfs. In daytime we engage in threshing, in the night we roam like the gray wolf. We are witches. In the morning we milk the cows, during the night we fly to [the witches'] sabbath. We are transgressors, but not so much defectors [*perebezhchiki*] as itinerant blind singers [*kaliki perekhozhie*].[19]

Suggesting some inspiration from the *The Lay of Igor's Campaign* [*Slovo o polku Igoreve*] on which Tarlovskii had written his masters' thesis and also translated into modern, versified Russian—a translation actually published in 1938—this imagery finally clarifies the essence of the literary program. The werewolf, *oboroten'*, a typical incarnation of the trickster, is a figure who both *embodies* and may be *signified* by the hyphen: a man-wolf. This is a manifesto for the hyphen as such, gradually turning into a parody of the genre. It is perhaps also a self-parody acted out at the interface between life and letters: since Tarlovskii's father was a bearer of two first names, the son officially acquired the double patronym of Arievich-Wol'fovich [son of Arii and son of Wolf].[20]

Poetic transgressions

Tarlovskii's obscure origins in the motley pale of settlement and the position outside clearcut categories as defined in the manifesto correspond well to the second characteristics of the trickster, "Liminality and transgressive vitality". The trickster creates "liminal zones within existing hierarchies and stratifications" and his principle, Lipovetsky maintains, "is not inversion but deconstruction, the undermining of the system by means of revealing and subverting its logic".[21] In the case of Tarlovskii, these characteristics are closely tied to the most important trait of the tricktser's activities, as seen by Lipovetsky, namely its "relation to the sacred", be it ideological truths, Soviet mythology or "anything pretending to be serious, high, or important in contemporary society."[22] Such a relation almost by default characterizes the original texts Tarlovskii managed to publish after his first collection.

Thus, the three poems added to his severely censored second book *Bumerang* (1932) invoke both the Soviet imperial myth of Central Asia and the keyword of the first five-year plan. However, all Soviet mythologemes activated by Tarlovskii are undermined by the style and actual content of the texts.[23] In the first of these poems, "Vuadil'", Tarlovskii elaborates on the homonymy of the name of the Uzbek village *Vuadil'* and the French expression "voi d'île", which he associates with the escape of Napoleon I from the island of Elba: "Otkuda v Aziiu pronik / Napoleonovskii iazyk? / Otkuda topot gall'skikh mil' / V tvoem zvuchan'i, Vuadil'?" [How come Napoleon's language / has penetrated Asia? /How come there's a clatter of Gallic miles /in your sound, Vuadil'?"][24] (in parallel, a hundred days drought in the Uzbek village is compared to *les Cent Jours* of Napoleon's second rule). And in the poem with the programmatic title "Plan", a series of metadiscursive interventions cheat all the expectations a reader might have after the two epigraphs, one taken from Stalin and one from an unspecified "Oriental epic". Here, planned economy easily merges with poetics because, as declared by the poet, "Harmonies are like iron, like forging, / into the plan of my rhyming I have included, / all possible reshuffling, / and it's not for nothing that in these hundred lines / has been taken the maximum scope of the stanza." [Ved' sozvuch'ia, kak zhelezo, kovki, / Ved' vkliuchil ia v plan moei rifmovki / Vsevozmozhnye perestanovki, / I nedarom v etikh sta strokakh / Vziat predel'nyi dlia strofy razmakh].[25] In *Rozhdenie rodiny*, Tarlovskii's third and last collection, we find the most conspicuous of such pieces, the didactical poem "(Tekhnika) x (Chut'e)" [(Technique) x (Flair)]. It carries an epigraph from Marx which concerns the work of man as opposed to that of bees, and opens with a rhymed reference to the same locus: "As witnessed by 'Capital' / (In the first volume, in the fifth chapter) / A new house emerges first / In man's head." [Po svidetel'stvu "Kapitala" / (V pervom tome, v piatoi glave), / Novyi dom voznikaet snachala / V chelovecheskoi golove].[26] The visibility of the poem was enhanced by the attention paid to it by Maksim Gor'kii, who noted that, despite "all the obvious deficiencies" of the piece, it had the merit of bringing into poetry for the first time "one of the most valuable ideas of the founder of a truly revolutionary philosophy."[27]

As noted by Lipovetsky, tricksterish manipulations of the sacred "typically include artistic hyperidentification with, and grotesque parody of, a social role, a set of values, or a discourse."[28] Although this holds true for many of Tarlovskii's published works, the most extreme example is a piece composed in april 1945, "Oda na pobedu (Podrazhanie Derzhavinu)" [Ode to Victory (Imitation of Derzhavin)], first published by Mikhail Gasparov in 2000.[29] This is a stylization in full accordance with the alternative title of the work, "Ode to the victory over fascist Germany as the author thinks it would have been written by a poet who fell asleep in the eighteenth century, somewhere between Trediakovskii and Derzhavin, and woke up most recently."[30] The ode opens with the invocation "Leninoravnyi marshal Stalin!" [Lenin-like Marshal Stalin!] and, as observed by Vadim Perel'muter, the rhetorical force soon carries the author away, bringing him dangerously close to the tonalities of Mandel'shtam's ill-fated epigram and turning the ode into a satire.[31] Defining the piece as "an exercise in triple rhyming, for the sake of which he [Tarlovskii] combined the incompatible: the octave with a parody on Derzhavin," Gasparov stresses the poet's "true devotion for poetry": to compose such a thing knowing very well that, "from the tenth stanza, at least, there was a straight line to the wall [the firing squad]".[32] Bearing in mind the final couplet of that stanza, it is easy to agree with both Gasparov and Perel'muter: "No vstrel Geennu Stalin sam / V slezakh, struimykh po usam."[But Stalin met Gehenna by himself / in tears which streamed down his moustaches.].[33] Tarlovskii's accompanying commentary does not help much to disarm the parodic charge; on the contrary: it rather contributes to it, almost laying bare the device—as befits the liminal trickster.[34]

The main act of deconstruction performed by Tarlovskii was arguably the decision to name his third collection *Rozhdenie rodiny* [Birth of the Motherland]. To give this title to a book partly made up of translations from anonymous originals representing the "literatures of the peoples of the USSR" is a trick that lays bare the principles at work in the Soviet mid-1930s, awaiting the 1936 constitution. The "motherland" as a multinational entity was constructed in the public space of the time precisely by way of such translations, which praised the leader and all the good things brought to the peoples of the Union by the revolution.[35] The combination of title and content points to the mechanics of this very process. Moreover, as shown by archival material, the authors of the translated texts included are all specified elsewhere in Tarlovskii's manuscripts. Their names are actually *removed* from the edition, rendering the poems anonymous.[36] An instance of "undermining [of] the system by means of revealing and subverting its logic"[37] is arguably at hand.

Transgressions in translation

It is arguably as a translator Tarlovskii displays the most readily recognized tricktsterish strategies. Tarlovskii knew Polish and French from university, and having spent some months in 1930 as a teacher of Russian in Fergana, Uzbekistan, he was at least acquainted with Uzbek, a Turkic language. In the early 1930s he began translating for the Department of the Literature of the Peoples of the USSR at Goslitizdat [the State Publishing house for Literature], which was headed at the time by his friend Georgii Shengeli. Tarlovskii's translations of poems from Belorussian, Ukrainian, Azerbaidjani and other languages began to appear in the press as well. Soon, however, he focused on the republic of Kazakhstan, learned some Kazakh (also a Turkic language), visited Alma-Ata regularly in the later half of the 1930s, and spent longer periods there in 1941, 1942 and 1943. He translated Kazakh epic poems at a total of 8000 lines,[38] and co-translated the Kirghiz national epos *Manas* with poet-translators Semen Lipkin and Lev Pen'kovskii to great acclaim.[39]

Most famously, Tarlovskii translated the works of Dzhambul Dzhabaev, the Kazakh folk poet, or *akyn*, who emerged in 1936 at the age of 90 and produced a large body of ideologically calibrated works until his death in 1945. Decorated with the Order of Lenin (in 1938) and the Stalin Prize (in 1941), Dzhambul was the most celebrated of the national bards of Stalinism. His works now often figure as an example of Stalin "fakelore", characterized by Gideon Toury, among others, as pseudotranslations; that is, "texts which have been presented as translations with no corresponding source texts in other languages ever having existed."[40] As I have shown elsewhere,[41] this is not an adequate description of the operations involved in the production of Dzhambul's oeuvre which, in fact, entailed an institutional framework and resulted in original texts as well as translations. A term that better captures the practice would be "constellational production", since this was a process involving several agents, often in fixed constellations consisting of a native agent of transcription, an interlinear translator and a final Russian poet-translator. During the period 1941–1943 Tarlovskii officially held the post as Dzhambul's Russian secretary. His Kazakh counterpart was the poet and editor Tair Zharokov, secretary of the Kazakh Writers Union. Their collaboration resulted, most famously, in the 1941 poem "Leningradtsy, deti moi" [Leningraders, My Children] which is indicative of the mobilizing function assigned to Dzhambul translations with the outbreak of war, as distinct from their function during the 1930s as parts of nationalities policies and the development of the personality cult.[42]

In Tarlovskii's archive we may follow his, at times, tricksterish activities as Dzhambul's main translator during the war years, which often drew on the patriotic metadiscourse surrounding the translations. Among them is an article, co-written with Zharokov, " Boevoe slovo Dzhambula" [Dzhambul's Word of Action], which emphasizes the patriotic merits of the *akyn*, while also deconstructing the trick.[43] Arguing that Dzhambul's work is to be equated with a "martial feat" (not only do his poems raise the fighting morale among the troops, the hundred-years old poet is also heroically contributing the last of his strength to the cause), the authors feel themselves obliged to "lift the veil" on the complex "process of creation".[44] The circumstances described in the article are not unique. They are well documented in archival material from the Nationalities Commission of the Soviet Writers Union in relation to Dzhambul as well as to other "oriental" folk poets.[45] But the deconstruction of the process *in public* was arguably unseen before, and I have not managed to verify the publication of the article. Archival material also reveals Tarlovskii's attempts to launch a new *akyn*, whose "creative resources could make his name almost as popular outside the borders of Kazakhstan as that of Dzhambul",[46] a trick resulting in quite a few translations from this bard (Nurpeis Baiganin) as well as from other Kazakh poets.[47]

Tarlovskii as "kynic"

The trait most pertinent to Tarlovskii's artistic being is to be found in Lipovetsky's elaboration of Sloterdijk's category of "kynicism" in relation to the trickster figure. Kynicism, as defined by Sloterdijk, is the "only functional opposition to cynicism". It is connected to joyful play and laughter and its essence "consists in a critical, ironical philosophy of so-called needs, in the elucidation of their fundamental excess and absurdity".[48] Among Soviet tricksters, kynicism is pointed out by Lipovetsky, for example, "in the excess and lack of any pragmatic motive" underlying the tricks of Behemot and Koroviev in Bulgakov's novel.[49] It is found in the way Khulio Khurenito (in Ehrenburg's novel) "methodically transforms all serious—and invariably—cynical rituals and discourses of power, including those of the revolutionary Russia, into self-deconstructing kynical performances".[50] These characterizations all apply to Tarlovskii, who, I would argue, emerges as a kynic in all of his projects. He is a compulsive, excessive versifier, lyricist and *stilizator*, who cannot refrain from ironically thematizing the most peculiar and at times horrible situations—in seeming contradiction to the pragmatic needs of the moment.

Thus, in 1935, Tarlovskii submitted a proposal for a new volume of poems, *Borenie ironii* [Fighting Irony]. The title obviously harks back to his first volume, *Ironicheskii sad*, and the need for "fighting" certain tendencies implied in the heavy censorhsip of his second book (*Pochtovyi golub'* ending up as *Bumerang*). The new volume was to feature 46 poems, out of which a significant share carried generical designations such as *shutka* [joke] *fantaziia* [fantasy] and *legenda* [legend]. Among them were pieces such as "Gifts from America (a legend about syphilis)", "Two sheets of paper (agitational joke)", "To the inauguration of a new planet (ironical cosmogony)". Particularly indicative of the kynicist mood is the *shutka* "Krov' i liubov'" [Blood and love] which treats the topic of insemination of swine in a way quite removed from any standard kolkhoz pattern: "Obsemenit' i izmenit' / I novym kholodet' romanom—/ Kakaia d'iavol'skaia nit' / Mezhdu svin'ei i Don-Zhuanom!" [Insemimate throughout and betray/ and be chilled by a new romance—/ what a devilish thread between a swine and Don Juan!].[51] The focus here on bodily functions "generally surrounded by moral taboos" is another trait characterizing both the kynic[52] and Tarlovskii. Such is the case, for example, in the poem "Svershitel' treb" [Performer of Rites] which actually appeared in *Bumerang*. It is about "an ordinary louse" and the changing conditions of its nourishment (from a dead body to a couple making love): "Ochevidets i svershitel' treb, / V mukakh smerti i pylu zachatii / Ty sosesh' blagoukhannyi khleb / I na nem kladesh' svoi pechati!" [An eyewitness and performer of rites, /in the torments of death and the heat of conception / you suck the scented bread / and leave on it your seals].[53] Even at the end of his unfortunate career Tarlovskii holds on to his kynicism, as witnessed by the poem "Fantaziia na ura-patrioticheskuiu temu" [Fantasy on a Euphorical-Patriotic Theme] (1950), which satirizes the political campaigns of the late 1940s against "cosmopolitanism" and "kowtowing to the West" as well as the promotion of "Russian priorities" in science and art; that is, the purported Russian/Soviet provenance of virtually all important inventions. The "Russian priority" claimed here in the excessive form of 15 octaves is the genre of elaborate cussing—*matershchina*: "O da, ne vsë u nas izobreli: /Pretendovat' ne stanem my, pozhalui, / Na mantii, chto nosiat koroli, / Na briuki galife i french lezhalyi. / Bifshteks i shnitsel, dazhe bef-buli, / Khot' zharili i nashi ikh kruzhala, / Priznat' my mozhem detishchem chuzhim, / No materchshiny my ne otdadim" [Oh no, we did not invent everything, / we surely don't make claims on / the mantle worn by kings, / on riding-breeches and the stale service-jacket. / Beefsteak and schnitzel, even *boeuf-bouilli*, / although these were roasted in our taverns as well, / we could admit that they are foreign brainchilds, / but our *matershchina* we don't give away.].[54]

Southern subjectivity

As we have seen, the tricksterish element in Tarlovskii's case is not limited to the imaginative worlds of his artistic creations; rather, these works in their entirety function as tricks and, transgressing the line between literature and life, render Tarlovskii himself a trickster figure in the social context of Stalinism. One of Tarlovskii's fictional works, however, actually features a character with substantially tricksterish traits, namely the lengthy verse memoir *Veselyi strannik* [The Merry Wanderer], composed by Tarlovskii in 1935 to commemorate the recently deceased Eduard Bagritskii. In conclusion, I will dwell on this work in order to suggest some ways in which the case of Tarlovskii may shed additional light on the phenomenon of the trickster in Soviet culture.

With the title taken from a line in Bagritskii's poem "Til' Ulenshpigel" [Till Eulenspiegel]—devoted to the classical German trickster character—Tarlovskii portrays Bagritskii and central figures of his literary milieu in Odessa in 1920–1921. Scenes from city life during war communism alternate with descriptions of the always hungry poets' mobilization for agitational work at IugROSTA (a branch of the Russian Telegraph Agency) and as participants in the "living gazette" [*zhivaia gazeta*], an oral substitute for newspapers during conditions of severe paper shortage (the poets acting as the "cultural page"). Events such as a circus performance, poetry readings within the Poets' Collective and various pranks are rendered with constant self-reflection on the part of the narrator. In addition, the memoir is appended by a commentary in prose which provides historical and biographical background and reveals the many literary references, thus deconstructing the work in the way we have seen above. From Tarlovskii's earlier literary practice we recognize the equilibristic play with form, the parodic mood and the stylization. The imitation of style is even foregrounded as a theme when Bagritskii is shown performing as a *blestiashchii stilizator* [a brilliant stylist] in a *triuk* [trick], faking the eight poets missing in order to gain a desirable majority in an election to the Collective's board.[55] A focus on bodily functions is manifest throughout the memoir, and the "relation to the sacred" is established in a stanza that pictures Bagritskii's telling of his meeting with Stalin: "I vot nash drug nam povestvuet metko, / Chem byl tot raut dlia nego bogat, / Kogda ozhivshii v zal voshel plakat, / Raz v sorok vyrosshaia statuetka." [And so our friend tells us aptly / about the riches of this reception, / when into the hall entered a poster, / a forty times enlarged statuette].[56] Portraying "The leader" as *derivative* of his own ideological representation is arguably another instance of "undermining [of] the system by means of revealing and subverting its logic."[57]

Apart from Bagritskii himself, *The Merry Wanderer* features portraits of Iurii Olesha, Il'ia Il'f and Evgenii Petrov, Valentin Kataev, Lev Slavin and Georgii Shengeli, who were all members of what Tarlovskii—in analogy with Bagritskii's first poetry collection *Iugo-Zapad* —calls the "southwest pleiad." Several stanzas are devoted to the relocation of this group of writers to the "north"—the capitals of the empire—compared by the author to migrating cranes.[58] In addition to these "seven foremost stars", Tarlovskii comments, more than fifty Odessan writers made their way into Soviet Russian literature during the first post-revolutionary decade and "will occupy their rightful place in the 'star' catalogue of the future bibliographer".[59] The list of such authors provided in the commentary includes well-known writers such as Babel' and Paustovskii, but also several poets who, like Tarlovksii himself, were to make a living almost exclusively as translators: Semen Lipkin, Arkadii Shteinberg, Adelina Adalis.

What Tarlovskii thus pinpoints in his verse memoir is, I would argue, an important geographical dimension of Soviet tricksterism—its origins in the "southwest". Among the authors represented in Lipovetsky's study of the phenomenon, both Il'f and Petrov and Ehrenburg were from Odessa, Bulgakov was from Kiev, Olesha was born in the same town as Tarlovskii, Elisavetgrad, which also happens to be the birthplace of yet another tricksterish *poet-perevodchik*, Arsenii Tarkovskii.[60] Soviet tricksterism has its roots in a "southern", or rather "southwestern", subjectivity nourished by the specific cultural makeup of the region.

Although many of the authors involved were of Jewish origin, this subjectivity was not "ethnical" in character, an issue actually commented upon in the verse memoir. Tarlovskii pictures Bagritskii spending time with Olesha, who, as noted in the commentary, played an important role in "the formation of the mind" of the former. Olesha declares: "I don't care that you're a semite! / We are relatives". [61] Neither Olesha, nor Bulgakov or Tarkovskii were Jews.

Prior to Tarlovskii's memoir, the literary expression of the "southern" subjectivity had been described by Viktor Shklovskii in his 1933 article "Iugo-Zapad", which established the "southwestern Russian school" as a fact of literary history. [62] Setting out to clarify the traditions of the school (geographically located in Odessa), Shklovskii emphasized the significance of place: the international character of the seaport, the location of a Russian literary school on Ukrainian territory. Odessa is compared to Alexandria—a Greek city on Egyptian soil, the culture of which was neither Greek nor Egyptian. The Odessans, Shklovskii maintained, are Levantines, part of a Mediterranean culture. The foremost trait of the southwestern school (in poetry as well as in prose), Shklovskii argues, is, the *siuzhet* [the plot]. As always interested in the genesis, migration and mutation of literary forms, Shklovskii points out that the *siuzhet* had entered modern Russian poetry via western models, through imitations of the English ballad. The "southwestern" Russians looked in the same direction: "Moving towards new themes they tried to master them through the west."[63] It was by mirroring themselves in "the foreign" that the southwestern Russians got sight of themselves, Shklovskii declares. Referring to Bagritskii's poem about the German trickster whose name means "owl-mirror", he continues: in "the mirror of Eulenspiegel" were reflected and made visible "Odessa's smugglers, who were later to appear in the stories of Babel', Vera Inber and Il'f and Petrov." The form of the verse Bagritskii had acquired from the west: "From Walter Scott, from Burns, from Kipling, Bagritskii learned the narrative verse [*siuzhetnyi stikh*] and, having mastered the foreign mirror, he could at last begin to speak in his own voice in 'Duma pro Opanasa.'"[64] The article ends with a prophesy inaugurating a new literary era: "The South Russian school will have a very large impact on the following, plot-centered [*siuzhetnyi*] period of Sovet literature."[65]

The timing of Shklovskii's article was unlucky, however. He was immediately attacked in the press for its alleged "formalism", which was juxtaposed to the socialist realism being promoted as the First Congress of Soviet Writers was approaching.[66] The proclamation of a particular "South Russian school" was improper, to say the least, in view of the imminent unification of literature under the auspices of a single Writers' organization. Shklovskii had to dissociate himself publicly from his own article.[67] So, too, did Tarlovskii in his verse memoir: having listed the names of the migrating south-Russian authors in his commentary, he declared: "I state all these facts far from solidarizing myself with V. Shklovskii's article about the 'Levantines.'"[68] In the actual verses, however, there is a conspicuous presence of Shklovskian themes and references: " […] Net, mozhet byt' dlia prozy v tom tiuke / Lezhat uzly zaputannykh siuzhetov; // Byt' mozhet, zhiv tam teplyi dukh tavern /V ochaiannoi krivoi "Tristrama Shendi", / Byt' mozhet, etot putnik—staryi Stern, / Ch'ia fabula teper' nam snova vzbrendit; // [No, perhaps in that sack / are knots of entangled plots for prose; // Perhaps, there the warm atmosphere of the taverns is still alive / in the reckless curve of *Tristram Shandy*, / perhaps, this wanderer is old Sterne, / whose story drives us crazy again]."[69] According to Tarlovskii's commentary, these lines refer to Lev Slavin, who "during these years was into Sterne".[70] But it was a well-known fact that Sterne figured prominently among Shklovskii's scholarly interests, and the use of the formalist terms *siuzhet* and *fabula* rather points to a tricksterish play operating with allusions and false, or at least double, attributions.[71] Shklovskii, as the chronicler of the southwestern school, arguably had a place in the verse memoir, but as he had been labelled a "class enemy",[72] he was an unwise reference (unless in negative terms, as in Tarlovskii's commentary). During 1933, the attacks against Shklovskii's article had grown into a broader "discussion" of "formalism" in the arts which heralded the notorious campaign of 1936. It was Tarlovskii's intention to publish the memoir and, sending it to *Krasnaia nov'* in 1935, he provided his own deconstruction of the work. It was, he explained, based on an interplay between "irony" and "pathos" in which he had, as he thought, achieved "a balance": "The irony has saved me from an excessive elevation of the characters (above all, Bagritskii's entourage), the pathos, reversely, has saved me from an excessive abasement of these characters (above all, Bagritskii himself)."[73] Referring to the fact that his work had always been characterized by such a blend, Tarlovskii appeals to the editor to see in this trait "a virtue", a request apparently not granted, since the piece remained unpublished.[74]

    Tarlovskii's commemorative poem not only depicts the tricksterish figure of Bagritskii and literary life in post-revolutionary Odessa, it is in itself—as we have seen—an expression of the southern subjectivity described. A trait that contributes significantly to the atmosphere of the work is the translingual character of the text. Bagritskii himself, Tarlovskii comments, "liked to intersperse his language with argotic words and macaronic Russian-Jewish expressions" (the one explained here is "kish mir in..." [kiss my...])[75] and many of the entries in the commentary are glosses of foreign words: "'*drel'*—argotic, southern word meaning invention [or fabrication]"; "'drek' in conversational Jewish langugage means excrements"[76]; "'Donnerwetter' is in German thunder and lightning"; "'*Zhurbai*'— Ukrainian name of a field lark".[77] Most conspicuous among the various languages featured in the poem is *blatnoi zhargon*— an entire stanza is written in this argot of criminal subcultures. The stanza is an utterance belonging to a person who is presented as "the main organizer" of the activities of the Poets' Collective. It is translated by Tarlovskii in the commentary: "In the *blat* (thieves') jargon, with words of which he [the organizer] liked to intersperse his speech, 'ksiva' means a document granting its holder right to reside, 'linka' means a passport in some other's name, 'kukla' means a bundle which contains money or valuables"; "'Lipa' in thief jargon means falsification"[78]. This figure—the limp *makher*—thus comes to the fore as a *blatmeister*, an essential mark of a trickster.[79]

Southern subjectivity, it appears, is in itself translingual in character and therefore entails a heightened awareness of linguistic expression, a condition, one may argue, for the kind of metareflection so typical of Tarlovskii's memoir. A reflection to this effect was actually made by Shklovskii in the manuscript to his article about the "South-West" but failed to appear in the published version: "It seems to me that this is in many ways a Ukrainian school which has realized itself in Russian. It is a self-translation, so to say."[80] Such a condition, producing an inner outsider and a double vision, is arguably a good starting point for a trickster as well as a *poet-perevodchik*.

Conclusion: The hyphen as hero

The life and work of Mark Tarlovskii may strike a distant observer as a series of contingent, heterogenous and frequently aborted projects, a conventional story—among many others—of poetic talent that was denied full realization under the conditions of Stalinism and was wasted on "forced" translation labor. A somewhat closer look at Tarlovskii's original oeuvre reveals an astonishing blend of particular traits which nevertheless makes an impression of something incidental: the virtuos versifier, the equilibristic stylist, the champion of bizarre topics and bold bodily humour. Looking at the literary and biographical projects of Tarlovskii through the lens of the trickster archetype—as applied to Soviet culture by Mark Lipovetsky—lends a certain coherence to both. Thematizing the mediary position in his unpublished literary manifesto and embodying it throughout life in a series of hyphenated characteristics, Mark Arievich-Wol'fovich Tarlovskii, Russian-Jewish poet, poet-translator, representative and celebrator of the southwestern literary school, emerges as a quintessential trickster, whose tricks, moreover, are performed in a mediary position, in between life and letters. If there is a main hero in the (far from conventional) story of Tarlovskii, it is the hyphen—as befits the son of a typographer. And conversely, if we look at Lipovetsky's study through the lens of Tarlovskii, and his verse memoir in particular, we are made aware of the geographical dimension of Soviet tricksterism: its origins in the southwest and a self-reflecting, translingual and playful southern subjectivity.

[1] Mark Lipovetsky, *Charms of the Cynical Reason: The Trickster's Transformations in Soviet and Post-Soviet Culture* (Boston: Academic Studies Press, 2011), 204.
[2] Lipovetsky, *Charms*, 17.
[3] Cited in Lipovetsky, *Charms*, 42–43.
[4] Lipovetsky, *Charms*, 46.
[5] Lipovetsky, *Charms*, 46–47. The case of Stepan Podlubnyi is treated in Jochen Hellbeck, *Revolution on My Mind: Writing a Diary Under Stalin* (Cambridge, MA; London: Harvard University Press, 2006). For a critical discussion of the concept of "Soviet subjectivity", see Aleksandr Etkind, "Soviet subjectivity; Torture for the Sake of Salvation?" *Kritika: Explorations in Russian and Eurasian History*, 6:1 (2005): 171–186.
[6] Lipovetsky, *Charms*, 32.
[7] Lipovetsky, *Charms*, 47.
[8] Vadim Perel'muter, "Torzhestvennaia pesn' skvortsa, oda, stavshaia satiroi," *Voprosy literatury* 6 (2003): 37.
[9] Mark Tarlovskii, *Molchalivyi polet*, ed. E. Vitkovskii and V. Rezvyi. (Moscow: Vodolei Publishers, 2009). Where not specifically indicated, the biographical account given in this article builds on the afterword to this volume, authored by the editors, "Pod kopirku sud'by" (583–602), as well as on information provided in Perel'muter, "Torzhestvennaia pesn'."
[10] Anthony Pym, "Humanizing Translation History," *Hermes – Journal of Language and Communication in Business* 42(2009). DOI: https://doi.org/10.7146/hjlcb.v22i42.96845
[11] Lipovetsky, *Charms*, 29.
[12] Russian State Archive for Literature and Arts, henceforth RGALI, F. 2180, op.1, ed. khr. 74.
[13] RGALI, F. 2180, op.1, ed. khr. 74, l. 1. Here and in the following translation is mine, if not otherwise indicated (S.W.).
[14] *Nikitinskie subbotniki* was a literary circle existing between 1914 and 1933. Among its participants were writers and literary scholars such as Leonov, Pilniak, Neverov, Inber, Seifullina, Chukovskii, Grossman, Blagoi, and Gudzii. See R. Korn, "Nikitinskie subbotniki," *Voprosy literatury* 12 (1964).
[15] Perel'muter, "Torzhestvennaia pesn'," 37.
[16] Lev Lunts, "Pochemu my Serapionovy brat'ia," *Literaturnye zapiski*, 2 (1922).
[17] RGALI, F. 2180, op.1, ed. khr. 74, l. 1.
[18] RGALI, F. 2180, op.1, ed. khr. 74, l. 2.
[19] RGALI, F. 2180, op.1, ed. khr. 74, l. 3.
[20] See, for example: RGALI, f. 2180, op. 1, ed. khr. 30, l. 7.
[21] Lipovetsky, *Charms*, 31.
[22] Lipovetsky, *Charms*, 34.
[23] For the concept of the "Soviet mythologeme," see Gasan Guseinov, *DSP: Sovetskie ideologemy v russkom diskurse 1990-kh* (Moscow: Tri kvadrata, 2004), 27.
[24] Tarlovskii, *Molchalivyi polet*, 172.
[25] Tarlovskii, *Molchalivyi polet*, 181.
[26] Tarlovskii, *Molchalivyi polet*, 214.
[27] Gor'kii cited in Tarlovskii, *Molchalivyi polet*, 622.

[28] Lipovetsky, *Charms*, 34.
[29] Mikhail Gasparov, *Zapisi i vypiski* (Moscow: NLO, 2000), 31–32.
[30] Tarlovskii, *Molchalivyi polet*, 638.
[31] Perel'muter, "Torzhestvennaia pesn'," 29.
[32] Gasparov, *Zapisi*, 31.
[33] Tarlovskii, *Molchalivyi polet*, 410.
[34] Tarlovskii, *Molchalivyi polet*, 636–639.
[35] See Susanna Witt, "Arts of Accommodation: The First All-Union Conference of Translators, Moscow, 1936, and the Ideologization of Norms," in *The Art of Accommodation: Literary Translation in Russia*, eds., Leon Burnett & Emily Lygo (Oxford: Peter Lang, 2013), 151; for a comprehensive analysis of *rodina* as a concept, see Irina Sandomirskaia, *Kniga o rodine: opyt analiza diskursivnykh praktik* (Vienna: Wiener slawistischer Almanach, 2001).
[36] They are all included in Tarlovskii's proposed but rejected volume *Poety stalinskoi epokhi* (RGALI f. 2180, op. 1, ed. khr. 99); see also: Tarlovskii, *Molchalivyi polet*, 580.
[37] Lipovetsky, *Charms*, 31.
[38] See Tarlovskii's unpublished "Autobiography", which is clearly composed with the intention to demonstrate his great service to the Kazakh people, presumably in order to secure further translation assignments, *komandirovki* and other material benefits (RGALI, f. 2180, op. 1. ed. khr. 30).
[39] *Manas, Kirgizskii epos, Velikii pokhod*, trans. S. Lipkin, L. Pen'kovskii, L. Tarlovskii, ed. U. Dzhakisheva (Moscow: Khudozhestvennaia literatura, 1946).
[40] Gideon Toury, *Descriptive Translation Studies and Beyond* (Amsterdam & Philadelphia: John Benjamins, 1995), 40. For his discussion of the Dzhambul case, see: Gideon Toury, "Enhancing Cultural Changes by Means of Fictitious Translations," in *Translation and Cultural Change: Studies in History, Norms and Image-projection*, ed. Eva Hung (Amsterdam/Philadelphia: John Benjamins, 2005), 3–17.
[41] Susanna Witt, "The Shorthand of Empire: *Podstrochnik* Practices and the Making of Soviet Literature," *Ab Imperio: Studies of New Imperial History and Nationalism in the post-Soviet Space*, 14:3 (2013): 155–190.
[42] See Susanna Witt, "Between the Lines: Totalitarianism and Translation in the USSR," in: *Contexts, Subtexts and Pretexts: Literary Translation in Eastern Europe and Russia*, ed. Brian James Baer, (Amsterdam/Philadelphia: John Benjamins, 2011), 149–170.
[43] RGALI, f. 2180, op. 1, ed. khr. 67.
[44] RGALI, f. 2180, op. 1, ed. khr. 67, l. 7.
[45] See Witt, "Shorthand of Empire."
[46] RGALI, f. 2180, op. 1, ed. khr. 29, l. 4.
[47] See, for example: RGALI, f. 2180, op. 1. ed. khr. 30, l. 8–9.
[48] Cited in Lipovetsky, *Charms*, 50.
[49] Lipovetsky, *Charms*, 54.
[50] Lipovetsky, *Charms*, 55.
[51] For the table of contents of the proposed volume, see Tarlovskii, *Molchalivyi polet*, 581–582; "Krov' i liubov'" was included in the original *Pochtovyi golub'*, first published in Tarlovskii, *Molchalivyi polet*.

⁵² Lipovetsky, *Charms*, 51.
⁵³ Tarlovskii, *Molchalivyi polet*, 153.
⁵⁴ Tarlovskii, *Molchalivyi polet*, 433–436.
⁵⁵ Tarlovskii, *Molchalivyi polet*, 517. Here, reference is also made to well-know cases of text falsification involving the art of stylization such as Macpherson's Ossian. For the characterizations *triuk i blestiashchii stilizator* see op.cit., 552–553.
⁵⁶ Tarlovskii, *Molchalivyi polet*, 529.
⁵⁷ Lipovetsky, *Charms*, 31.
⁵⁸ Tarlovskii, *Molchalivyi polet*, 528.
⁵⁹ Tarlovskii, *Molchalivyi polet*, 556.
⁶⁰ The trick performed by Tarkovskii and Shteinberg in collaboration has famously been commented upon by Semen Lipkin, who coined the term "translation of a new type" to refer to the practice (Semen Lipkin, *Kvadriga. Povest'. Memuary* (Moskva: Knizhnyi sad-Agraf, 1997), 435.
⁶¹ Tarlovskii, *Molchalivyi polet*, 526.
⁶² The article was published in *Literaturnaia gazeta*, No. 1, 5 January, 1933. Viktor Shklovskii, "Iugo-Zapad", in the author's *Gamburgskii schet, stat'i – vospominaniia – esse (1914–1933)*, comp. Aleksandr Galushkin and Marietta Chudakova, foreword M. Chudakova, comments A. Galushkin (Moscow: Sovetskii pisatel', 1990), 470–475.
⁶³ Shklovskii, "Iugo-Zapad," 472.
⁶⁴ Shklovskii, "Iugo-Zapad," 472.
⁶⁵ Shklovskii, "Iugo-Zapad," 475.
⁶⁶ For a discussion of the chain of events, see the detailed commentary in Shklovskii, "Iugo-Zapad," 538–540.
⁶⁷ See *Literaturnaia gazeta*, 29 April, 1933.
⁶⁸ Tarlovskii, *Molchalivyi polet*, 557.
⁶⁹ Tarlovskii, *Molchalivyi polet*, 486.
⁷⁰ Tarlovskii, *Molchalivyi polet*, 541.
⁷¹ See also: "No tut zalozhen plutovskoi roman" [But here is laid down a picaresque] (Tarlovskii, *Molchalivyi polet*, 488) "S chego nachat'? – tak stranen moi siuzhet" [Where should I begin? My plot is so strange] (op. cit., 489).
⁷² Gronskii in *Literaturnaia gazeta*, 28 february 1933.
⁷³ Tarlovskii, *Molchalivyi polet*, 596. The merging of pathos and irony is a trait often referred to in descriptions of the "South Russian school," see Danila Davydov, "Liudmila Khersonskaia. Vse svoi," *Znamia*, 2 (2012)) *http://magazines.russ.ru/znamia/2012/2/dd22-pr.html* (accessed 23 February 2019).
⁷⁴ The verse memoir was also included in the proposal for the (likewise rejected) collection *Borenie ironii*.
⁷⁵ Tarlovskii, *Molchalivyi polet*, 541.
⁷⁶ Tarlovskii, *Molchalivyi polet*, 542.
⁷⁷ Tarlovskii, *Molchalivyi polet*, 543.
⁷⁸ Tarlovskii, *Molchalivyi polet*, 552.

79 "The Soviet trickster is ususally a master of blat (*blatmeister* in Soviet lingo) and extremely well aware of informal economic and social practices [...]" (Lipovetsky, *Charms*, 45).
80 Shklovskii, "Iugo-Zapad," 470.

III

Postsocialist Bakhtin Burlesque:
YOUNG-HAE CHANG HEAVY INDUSTRIES
performing 'Cunnilingus in North Korea'

CHARLOTTE BYDLER

The creation of a World of words

In the beginning, there were two words. Digital or discrete values, black and white, zeros and ones. And these words turned into flesh. Alternatively, as the Bible has it, there was Darkness. Until our Hero, God, said: "Let there be Light". Then there was a binary world with a Hero (God) and an Author—perhaps a demiurge—who found it a good place for creating the beginning of the World—of net.art. Thus, during the early 1990s, the so-called *heroic period* of net.art came about.[1]

This beginning of the present narrative mimics the layout of Mikhail Bakhtin's essay "Author and Hero in Aesthetic Activity",[2] which runs parallel with my aim. To encompass the full potential of Bakhtinian dialogism, it purports to cover nothing less than the entire world of words. I will be content with less however, and settle for an introduction and outline of the main characters in the (metaphorical) Universe of net.art and the rules they laid down for themselves. It should be noted that each and every time a breach against the rules in one specific part of this World also meant something special, and that breaking them seemed to be an intentional act.

Further, I will go on to make an analysis of the piece *Cunnilingus in North Korea*.[3]

So, at the beginning of time, net.art was made by a few artists around the globe, such as Heath Bunting, Vuk Cosic, Olia Lialina, Alexei Shulgin, sub-REAL, among others. Net.art was politically radical, anarchist and oppositional, and best of all—it was made to be *used* (in distinction to being *looked at*) from a home computer. First, for technical reasons, all net.art had to be made for fast and simple download. This privileged a certain strictness of design. If you had a 56K (kilo-bit) modem; you could be considered lucky.[4]

Having passed the stage of technological demands, the alphanumerical black-and-white pieces turned into a style and an aesthetic expression on its own that came to signify activism, strict norms and anti-capitalist regimes and a generally ascetic attitude. One thing these artists had in common was that they avoided using the Flash tool, since it made the producer (they preferred to avoid using the professional title "artist") dependent on a market brand—the firm Adobe. This decision limited expressions to digital, discrete, flat compositions. This preference brought them very close to the punk ethos of DIY (do it yourself). But it still worked best within the strict boundaries of the net.art-world, where arguments over *firstness* broke out regularly.

The work of Jodi.org (the duo Joan Heemskerk and Dirk Paesmans) and the 0100101110101101.org (pseudonym for Eva and Franco Mattes) probably made some newbie computer users think that their machines were crashed, as well as showing what they went for with the ".org", which should be interpreted as a statement against the commercial ".com". But not YHCHI.com. They ridiculed the interactivity of net.art, by comparing it with channel browsing. And their way of avoiding heavy pictures was omitting them altogether. They wanted streaming artworks in order to compete with TV, in terms of how fun it could be.

Now, they have obviously confronted all these "rules" for net.art head on—if not with their eschatological witty-dirty; "nether" as the Russian literary theorist Mikhail Bakhtin (1895–1975) calls it.[5] By crossing every literary border, Bakhtin would say, the piece gains its meanings through dialogism—in terms of genre, topics, subject perspective, etcetera. YHCHI.com, or YOUNG-HAE CHANG HEAVY INDUSTRIES, is the *nom-de-plume* of a duo that saw the light of day back in 1999, when Korean Young-Hae Chang and US-born Marc Voge started the company in Seoul. This commercial, dirty (in the sense that money and art should not be mentioned in the same sentence), aspect of their work is best understood as part of their series of value reversals; since it is not accepted to speak about "art" as just any other commodity. Yet they do it.

Enter Mikhail Bakhtin and the Burlesque

Here I am going to analyze one of their works of Net art—as they refer to their own products.[6] Most of these consist of videos produced as Flash-animations, united by their typeface, *Monaco*. The cultural producer behind this multiple-artwork(s) is, as I already said, YHCHI. The team often use a mix of a music and strictly alphanumeric signs, with figure-0s and letter-Os that look the same, with an oblique line within the "Ø". They also present themselves rather provocatively in an irreverent tone of folksy "laughter culture" that Bakhtin would have recognized.

LØNG LIVE NØRTH KØREAN CUNNILINGUS!

YHCHI enacts pieces of dramatized texts that I find interesting in view of the topic I will discuss here: *political humor*. In the end, I hope to have shown that what Bakhtin referred to as an analysis of grotesque realism offers an apt understanding of the frightening nuclear power and failing communist state of North Korea—and, of course, the so-called "comfort women" that Japan kept during the Second World War. But at the very least, the Dear Leader succeeded in keeping the North Korean citizens sexually satisfied—a national priority, privileging communist women over their bourgeois counterparts in the South.[7]

Political oppression is probably the most effective way to provoke any people to seek comical release. Humor and laughter have always been popular tools for dealing with threatening rulers by symbolically dethroning them. Mikhail Bakhtin analyzed this phenomenon as "grotesque" or "carnivalesque realism".[8] During Carnival, society returned to behavior associated with harvesting time in ancient Rome (Saturnalian feasts), and in Christian Latin terms bid meat (*carne*) farewell (*vale*) in time for Lent. This behavior implied the reversal of the official status of rulers and ruled: everything in the established hierarchies should be turned upside down. This socially sanctioned counter-order, where values were inversed, lasted for the duration of the festival according to a strict protocol. Then everything went back to normal. There is some overlapping between the Carnival in Bakhtin's sense, and the *carnivalesque discourse*.[9] This is, for example, the discourse of *grotesque realism*. As Muhammad A. Badarneh (2011) observes, political jokes "contain an element of *dialogism*" [Italics in original], which means not only that we interact with others' use of language, but we also express our own meanings through using linguistic turns that are "ideologically saturated".[10]

But also in present days, according to Badarneh, "the juxtaposition of the serious and the comic" retains an important symbolic meaning, allowing the people to have a good laugh behind the backs of their oppressors.[11] Under these conditions, jokes become authentic folk humor.[12] It is perhaps forbidden in the mass media, but it manages nevertheless to find its way into the public space without names or origins—it is just everywhere. Political jokes are of a less universal kind, according to Mulkay.[13] This means that they might not be shared by all, and it might even be a bit risqué to drop a joke in the public space. But in fact, opinion-wise, art worlds are tiny. And the genre of "Net art" is so narrow in its political and general outlook as to be predictable. (However, I believe it can safely be said that for obvious reasons no North Korean citizen will ever come to see the piece that I will analyze below.)

But on a more serious note, *Cunnilingus in North Korea* can also be understood as a recognition of all the Korean women who were forced to become prostitutes, or, to use Japanese euphemism ianfu (慰安婦), from *ian + fu/bu* adult female "who provided sexual services to 'comfort and entertain' (ian/wian) the warrior."[14]

Imagine a work of art called *Cunnilingus in North Korea* that shows no images of such activities—only verbal ones.[15] That which is withheld from sight can certainly be more enticing than overt pornographic imagery. So, what is the point? It is exactly to rub this image in, with pseudo-scientific and mock-theoretical language, playing the Bakhtinian game of grotesque realism in literature—and in action. In the 1930s and 40s, the Korean women did not have much choice when the Japanese forces came. It took a long time before they dared tell the world. But seen as if through a soft lens, *Cunnilingus in North Korea* could offer some comfort in a reversal of how they were mistreated, humiliated and raped. This time, even though there is no certain evidence, we can imagine them getting to enjoy a good, kind, and loving partner.

Cunnilingus in North Korea

The piece begins with a classical moving picture convention, counting down from 10 to 0. A drum sets off, its fast jazz-like beat filled in by the tones of a flute.[16] During the intro, in white letters on black strips, just like subtitles, the viewer sees the following words appearing on the screen:

            THE FØLLØWING IS A TEXT THAT NØRTH KØREA'S DEAR LEADER KIM
            JØNG-IL ASKED YØUNG-HAE CHANG HEAVY INDUSTRIES TØ PRESENT.

Why indeed should these two humble autonomous artists be trusted with a presentation by the leader of North Korea? In Bakhtin, high and low combine to form the most formidable *carnivalistic mésalliances*.¹⁷ However, the text continues:

> THANK YØU FOR INVITING ME TØ TALK TØ YØU ABOUT SEX AND GENDER IN NØRTH KØREA. DIALECTICAL SEX AND GENDER IS NØT JUST ØNE ØF MY INTELLECTUAL PASSIØNS. IT IS A TØP PRIØRITY FØR THE ENTIRE NATIØN: SEX AND GENDER.

Indeed, a *top priority* for the *entire nation*. So, this piece performs the same operation as Mikhail Bakhtin, who distils *popular laughter* through his analysis of works by the sixteenth-century author François Rabelais: it purports to be the Dear Leader, Kim Jong-Il, speaking about his "intellectual passion" in the rigorous distinction between "sex and gender". This proposition is mockingly made in perfectly contemporary academic language: "dialectical sex and gender" is hardly a phrase that resembles anything that would have been available to him.

> ... IT GØES WITHØUT SAYING
> THAT SEXISM IS LINKED TØ CAPITALISM.
> IT ALSØ GØES WITHØUT SAYING THAT
> SEXUAL EQUALITY IS INHERENT IN
> MARXISM. WHAT IS UNCLEAR IS
> WHETHER BY DEFINITIØN ALL CØMMUNIST
> NATIØNS HAVE SEXUAL EQUALITY.
> THE ANSWER,
> I'M SØRRY TØ SAY,
> IS NØ

As the words of the piece go on, one recognizes the voice of Nina Simone (or, to use her given name: Eunice Kathleen Waymon, the black American woman famous for performing civil rights songs) synching to the beat with rhythmically pulsating words, marking time with the music.¹⁸ So accompanied by Nina Simone's seductive voice, the lyrics she performs are as follows:

> Yeah. Yeah, yeah, yeah, yeah. All right, yeah.

This first line is sung to the accompaniment of the words below appearing on the screen:

> NØ. NØ, NØ, NØ, NØ.

Did someone mention dialectic? Well, here we have a straightforward case of dialectical aesthetics, a "yeah" mirrored back as a "no". And the black and white letters too, of course.

```
BUT HERE IN NØRTH KØREA,
WE HAVE SUCCEEDED IN
CREATING SEXUAL EQUALITY

[…

A CØNSTANT DIALECTIC HAS
REVEALED TØ THE MASSES, IN
THE MØST PRACTICAL AND
INTELLECTUAL FASHIØN, THAT
THE MØST IMPØRTANT MANIFES-
TATIØN ØF DIALECTICAL SEX
AND GENDER IS SEX ITSELF.

PURE,
UNADULTERED,
UNINHIBITED,
UTTERLY FREE SEX.
```

To be on the safe side, this last line is repeated three times. Then Ms Simone's voice again, on time with the piece: "yeah".

```
YEAH.
I REALIZE THAT
SØUTH KØREANS
BLUSH AT THE
MERE THØUGHT
ØF FREE SEX.
```

At this point, beginning with the word "blush", the screen progressively turns red.

```
…
YØU ARE, IN
FACT, SLAVES
TO BØURGEØIS
SEXUAL
INHIBITIØN.
…
```

By contrast, South Korea is a capitalist society, for sure. However, it does not matter, since as the Dear Leader muses,

```
MY INSTINCT IS TØ SAY
CØMMUNIST SEXUAL FREEDØM,
BUT, QUITE FRANKLY, SEX
TRANSCENDS, THRØUGH
DIALECTICAL MATERIALISM,
THE FRØNTIERS ØF ALL NATIØNS,
CØMMUNIST ØR CAPITALIST.
...
HERE THEN
ARE THE REAL
ISSUES IN
SEXUAL FREEDØM:
ALL RIGHT.
```

Here Ms Simone sings "all right", in synch.

```
ØRGASM,
ØR RATHER,
ITS RELATIVE
ABSENCE IN THE
BØURGEØIS FEMALE;
FEMALE
MULTIPLE ØRGASM
THRØUGH ØRAL SEX –
THAT IS,
CUNNILINGUS
[…]
GIVE IT TØ HER
IN AN EFFECTIVE
PRØLØNGED
AND LØVING MANNER;
```

Here *See-Line Woman* seriously begins:

>   See-line woman
>   She drink coffee
>   She drink tea
>   And then go home
>   See-line woman
>
>   See-line woman
>   Dressed in green
>
>   Wears silk stockings
>   With golden seams
>   See-line woman

At the word "green", the screen, as you have probably already guessed, turns green.

```
FEMALE MULIPLE
ØRGASM WITH
SEX TØYS

SUCH AS VIBRATØRS, AND
THE BØURGEØIS FEMALE'S
UNNATURAL INHIBITIØNS
```

Beginning with "such", the lines of this last screen are underlined with yellow.

```
…
IT WØULD BE IMPØSSIBLE,
IN THE CØNTEXT ØF THIS
ADDRESS, TØ DISCUSS
ALL THE FEMALE SEXUAL
INHIBITIØNS THAT ARE
MALE GENERATED

AND ENDEMIC
TØ CAPITALISM.
SUFFICE TØ
SAY THAT

WE NØRTH
KØREANS
PITY YØU
```

> See-line woman
> Dressed in red

By the word "red", the screen mockingly refers to the Dear Leader's pity for the "blushing" bourgeois South Korean citizens by turning red.

> Make a man lose his head
> See-line woman

So, "NØRTH KØREA'S DEAR LEADER", thanks for an invitation to lecture on the theme of female sexual pleasure in North Korea—equal to cunnilingus.

> See-line woman
> Black dress on
> For a thousand dollars
> She wail and she moan
> See-line woman

> Wiggle wiggle
> Turn like a cat
> Wink at a man
> And he wink back
> Now child
> See-line woman
>
> Empty his pockets
> And wreck his days
> Make him love her
> And she'll fly away
>
> See-line woman
> Take it on out now
> Empty his pockets
> And she wreck his days
> And she make him love her
> Then she sure fly away
> She got a black dress on
> For a thousand dollars
> She wail and she moan…

The beats also work as a measurement of sexual arousal, of a game with fertility that is played for the sheer pleasure of it. Burlesque laughter seeps in.

But the political joke gets even coarser on the scatological register. Thus, in speaking of the dialectics of sexual pleasure through oral sex, *Cunnilingus in North Korea* uses a highly unlikely gender-philosophical jargon. But there is no need to quote any psychoanalyst saying that sex (real, or in discourse) substitutes for power. Especially not with respect to a short and plump person such as the Dear Leader, who has access to nuclear arms. When we talk about power, we tend to express it as sex. Sex is power—and power is sexy.

South Koreans probably do not feel that way. We can only imagine what it must be like to live in South Korea under the constant threat of hostile actions from North Korea.[19] The Second World War that continued into the bitter struggle between the two Koreas has not officially ended—it is formally only a ceasefire. Since 2018, tourists have been allowed go there, but that does not erase the tragedy of all the people who have been shot and killed.[20]

By now, our "North Korea" in the universe of YHCHI.com has, however, become thoroughly genre-defined and properly sexualized. The current threat to strike the world with nuclear weapons is no news. The Dear Leader's (may he live in eternity!) grandson certainly watches his tongue, so that he cannot be held to any promise to downscale his arsenal of nuclear weapons on behalf of what he may or may not have said to the US president. On the contrary, he has made sure to starve his population to increase the reach of his nuclear missiles.

> HERE IN THE
> NØRTH, WHERE
> LIFE CAN BE
> DIFFICULT,
>
> WE SEE SEXUAL
> PLEASURE AS
> GETTING SØMETHING
> FØR NØTHING.
> …
> AND WE SEE PROLONGED
> SEXUAL PLEASURE
> AS GETTING A LØT
> AND GIVING A LØT,
> WITH ABSØLUTELY NØ
> CAPITALISTIC BARTERING.
> …
> IN NØRTH KØREA, ALL
> WØMEN KNØW THEY ARE
> THE EQUALS OF THEIR
> MALE PARTNERS.
>
> AND, JUST AS
> IMPORTANT, THEIR
> MALE PARTNERS
> KNØW IT, TØØ.

What a beautiful piece of Hegelian master-slave dialectic!

> …
> MOST NØRTH
> KØREAN WØMEN
> ESPECIALLY
> ENJØY UP TØ
> AN HØUR ØR MØRE
> ØF CUNNILINGUS.
>
> MØST NØRTH KØREAN MEN
> KNØW THIS, AND ENJØY
> GIVING PRØLØNGED
> CUNNILINGUS AS MUCH
> AS NØRTH KØREAN WØMEN
> ENJØY RECEIVING IT.

Another truth of teaching based on the sexual benefits of dialectic aesthesis.

> CUNNILINGUS IS AN ART,
> AND NØRTH KØREAN MEN
> KNØW ALL THE TRICKS
> ØF THE TRADE.
>
> THEY KNØW HØW TØ
> BLØW, LICK, NIBBLE,
> BITE AND SUCK
> WØMEN'S ERØGENØUS
> ZØNES,ARØUND AND
> INSIDE HER VAGINA.
>
> CUNNILINGUS
> IS A DIALECTIC
> LIKE ANY ØTHER.
> ...

Indeed, "CUNNILINGUS IS A DIALECTIC LIKE ANY ØTHER".

> AS NØRTH
> KØREA'S LEADER,
> I ACCEPT THE
> RESPØNSIBILITY FØR CERTAIN
> FAILURES IN
> ØUR CØUNTRY.
>
> BUT I TAKE GREAT PLEASURE,
> TØDAY, IN PRESENTING
> THIS TRIUMPH ØF
> NØRTH KØREAN CUMMUNISM —
> SØRRY,
> CØMMUNISM,
> IN SPITE ØF
> MY PEØPLE'S
> CØNTINUING
> HARDSHIPS
> AND THEIR
> ØPPRESSIØN
> FRØM WITHØUT.
>
> I CAN
> SAY WITH
> CØNFIDENCE
> THAT
> NØRTH KØREAN
> WØMEN ARE
> SEXUALLY

```
HAPPY WØMEN.

AND NØRTH
KØREAN MEN,
THANKS
TØ THEIR
SUPERIØR
KNØWLEDGE AND
PRACTICE ØF
CUNNILINGUS,
ARE PRØUD
TØ BRING
NØRTH KØREAN
WØMEN
TØ CLIMAX, AFTER CLIMAX
AFTER CLIMAX
AFTER CLIMAX
AFTER CLIMAX

THANK YØU,
FØR ALLØWING
ME TØ TALK
TØ YØU TØDAY
ABOUT WHAT
WE IN
NØRTH KØREA
CØNSIDER
A PARAMØUNT
ISSUE IN SEXUAL
EQUALITY AND
SØCIAL JUSTICE:
FEMALE
MULTIPLE ØRGASM
THROUGH
CUNNILINGUS.
```

The Borders in the World

The YHCHI.com-film/text continues in this carnivalizing tone, mocking and dethroning the ruler; talking about his interest in the "bodily material nether".[21] This interest takes me to another topic: foreign relations. Not, of course, that the Dear Leader is a stranger to women. I am certain that he is as experienced in this area as he is in, for example, golf.[22]

Post-Soviet international relations were characterized by a noticeable economic vacuum throughout the formerly communist world. All countries that had gotten used to a steady stream of Soviet economic support suddenly had no one to turn to. Still, no country probably felt it as harshly as North Korea. On October 3, 2017, the correspondent Margita Boström of Swedish Radio's P1 *Utrikeskrönika* (a news program that runs on Swedish National Broadcast Channel 1) reported that Cambodia seemed to be the only country volunteering to help North Korea in its hour of dire crisis and economic restrictions.[23] Even worse for North Korea, these constraints included China, since that country disapproved of North Korean attitudes toward nuclear arms tests.

Today, in Cambodian Siem Reap, where the temple Angkor Wat is located, we also find the Angkor Panorama Museum, built by Pyongyang Mansudae Art Studio, a North Korean art manufactory that has been described as "probably the greatest art group in the world".[24] Admittedly, it is hard not to jump to conclusions here, but US President Donald Trump may not be the first to have used that superlative. However, he actually was the first US president to meet with a North Korean prime minister.[25] Anyway, this studio has created almost all the monumental bronze statues of the two earlier Dear Leaders, Kim Il-Sung (may he live in eternity!) and Kim Jong-Il, his son. Thus, it is part of the Kim clan's propaganda machinery. You may wonder about size: did anyone mention using monuments to compensate for shortcomings in other areas? Jokes apart, I am certain that it did not affect the Dear Leader's capacity.

North Korean restaurants in Cambodia and standing commissions for public monuments in welded bronze testify to the warm relationship that once existed between the two countries under dictators Prince Norodom Sihanouk and Prime Minister Kim Jong-Il. They are said to have met in 1961, in Belgrade, and instantly took a liking to each other. In the 1970s, when Prince Sihanouk was forced into exile, he got a private palace next to Prime Minister Kim's.[26]

The end of YHCHI.com's piece runs, over and over, again:

```
LØNG LIVE NØRTH KØREAN SEXUAL EQUALITY!
LØNG LIVE NØRTH KØREAN CUNNILINGUS!
LØNG LIVE NØRTH KØREAN CØMMUNISM!
```

However, shouldn't each of these lines end in a question mark, instead of an exclamation point?

Conclusion

I started basically with sketching up a miniature aesthetic world of words. Even if you don't agree with me (or for that matter, my analysis), some things are more certain than others. For one, if you think that the people who are mentioned in this text have any faint resemblance to those existing (or who have existed), in the real world, you are absolutely right. In that sense, what seems like fiction is, alas, true.

[1] Cf. Mikhail Bakhtin, "Author and Hero in Aesthetic Activity," in *Art and Answerability. Early Philosophical Essays by M. M. Bakhtin*, ed. Michael Holquist and Vadim Liapunov, trans. Vadim Liapunov (Austin: University of Texas Press, 1990), 4–257.
[2] M. M. Bakhtin, Problema avtora, *Voprosy filosofii* (1977:7), pp. 149–160.
[3] In 2000, I saw the first version of this work, a video film-animation, that has not been shown since 2003. Recent versions are all text-based.
[4] But who remembers that today, when there are cable connections that allow downloads whose speed can be measured in units of TB (tera-bit)?
See also YOO Hyun-Joo. (2005), Intercultural medium literature digital. Interview with YOUNG-HAE CHANG HEAVY INDUSTRIES, 4. Connection to concrete poem. *Dichtung Digital*, #2, <www.dichtung-digital.de/2005/2/Yoo/index-engl.htm>, accessed 4 Oct 2017.
[5] Mikhail Bakhtin, *Rabelais and his World*, trans. Hélène Iwolsky (Bloomington: Indiana University Press, 1984).
[6] YOO Hyun-Joo. (2005), Intercultural medium literature digital. Interview with YOUNG-HAE CHANG HEAVY INDUSTRIES, 1. General Notes. *Dichtung Digital*, #2, <www.dichtung-digital.de/2005/2/Yoo/index-engl. htm>, accessed 4 Oct 2017. So, the duo stays aloof from messing with the privilege of being "first", preferring to be "cool"—as if watching how children fight from a distance.
[7] Of course, this piece of Net art that I will analyze was made before the ascent to power of Kim Jong-Un (b. 1983)—the grandson of the Dear Leader of North Korea Kim Il-Sung. The latter was born on 15 April 1912 in Mangyŏngdae, as Kim Seongju. As I already said, he became the Dear Leader (or dictator, if you insist) from 1948 until his death. Formally, he was the prime minister of North Korea until 1972 and since then its president (may he live in eternity!). I do not know if these conditions apply for his grandson, the son of Kim Jong-Il, born 16 Feb 1941 in Vyatskoe near Khabarovsk in Siberia (or, perhaps, he was born in 1942, near the mountain Paektu in what was then Japanese Korea). The latter succeeded his father as North Korea's leader/dictator from his father's death on 8 July 1994 in Pyongyang, until his own death on 17 December 2011, when he in his turn was succeeded by his own son.
[8] Bakhtin (1984). There are many researchers who hold the opinion that political jokes are a reaction to those in power in any particular society. However, opinions diverge as to whether this is a successful strategy. Some, like Charles Schutz, *Political Humor* (Cranbury, NJ: Associated University Press, 1977) and Avner Ziv, *Personality and Sense of Humor* (New York: Springer, 1984) say it helps people without any other means to fight back. Others, like Hans Speier, "Wit and politics: An essay on laughter and power", *American Journal of Sociology* (103 (1998):1352–1401) suggest it serves to paint a caricature of power rather than dethroning it. Michael Billig, *Laughter and Ridicule: Towards a Social Critique of Humour* (London: Sage, 2005) says that it actually works to uphold the *status quo*, and Christie Davies, "Humour and protest: Jokes under Communism", *International Review of Social History* (52 (2007), 291–305), proposes that this kind of political humor does not make any difference.
[9] Muhammad A. Badarneh, "Carnivalesque politics: A Bakhtinian case study of contemporary Arab political humor", *Humor*, 24:3 (2011), 308.
[10] Mikhail Bakhtin (1981), *The Dialogical Imagination*. (Austin: University of Texas Press), 272.

[11] Badarneh (2011), 305.
[12] Badarneh (2011), 306.
[13] Michael Mulkay, *On Humour: Its Nature and its Place in Modern Society* (London: Polity Press, 1988), 85–86.
[14] Sara Soh, The Comfort Women: Sexual Violence and Postcolonial Memory in Korea and Japan. *(University of Chicago Press,* 2009), 69. See also Erin Blakemore, "The Brutal History of Japan's 'Comfort Women'": Between 1932 and 1945, Japan forced women from Korea, China and other occupied countries to become military prostitutes", *History,* 20 Feb, 2018 https://www.history.com/news/comfort-women-japan-military-brothels-korea, accessed 15 Jan 2019. Kazuko Watanabe, "Trafficking in Women's Bodies, Then and Now: The Issue of Military 'Comfort Women", *Women's Studies Quarterly.* 27, 1–2 (1999), 19–30: It has been estimated that at least 80 percent of the "comfort women" were Korean. They were given to men in lower ranks of the army and navy, while Japanese and European women went to the officers. Korea and China were mainly Confucian countries where premarital sex was strongly disapproved of; thus they could be assumed to not have been exposed to venereal diseases.
[15] The piece itself can be found at <www.yhchang.com/CUNNILINGUS_IN_NORTH_KOREA.html>, and it is 6:19 minutes long. I strongly recommend the reader to look up the nearest computer and visit this website, because it is such an enjoyable and perfectly composed piece.
[16] *See-line Woman*, Remix, original by George Bass. From *Nina Simone*, Verve DZ 2217. Nina Simone (vocal), Rudy Stevenson (flute), Lisle Atkinson (bass), Bobby Hamilton (drums). Recorded probably 1964 in New York. <www.yhchang.com/CREDITS_V.html>, accessed 19 January 2019.
[17] Bakhtin (1984), 123
[18] YOO Hyun-Joo, (2005). Intercultural medium literature digital. Interview with YOUNG-HAE CHANG HEAVY INDUSTRIES, 1. General Notes. *Dichtung Digital,* #2, <www.dichtung-digital.de/2005/2/Yoo/index-engl. htm>, accessed 2 Oct 2017. The words, actually, are entirely random relative to the semantic meaning of the piece in Bakhtin's sense; it is more about the rhythm and pulse.
[19] There are many works on the website of the YHCHI.com on this subject, either mocking North Korea or showing its many strange faces.
[20] CNN, Visit Korean DMZ, https://edition.cnn.com/travel/article/visit-korean-dmz/index.html?gallery=11 (posted 3 May 2018) accessed 31 Jan 2019.
Wikipedia, List of border incidents involving North and South Korea, https://en.wikipedia.org/wiki/List_of_border_incidents_involving_North_and_South_Korea, accessed 31 Jan 2019.
[21] Bakhtin (1984), 123.
[22] "When the Dear Leader played his first (and only) round of golf at the country's sole club, the tricky 7,700-yard track at Pyongyang, it took him just 34 strokes to complete the 18 holes. And being a living deity, he did it with no less than five holes-in-ones on his way round, obviously." Tim Southwell, "The day Kim Jong IL became the world's best golfer, *GolfPunk,* http://www.golfpunkhq.com/golf-bedlam/article/the-day-kim-jong-il-became-worlds-best-golfer (published 24 May 2018) accessed 24 January 2019. This may sound

funny, but before laughing, see also this: "Unfamiliar with that scorekeeping shorthand, the North Korean state news agency covering the outing had read the five 1s on Kim's card as holes-in-one." Josh Sens, "Behind Kim Jong Il's Famous Round of Golf", *Golf.com*, https://www.golf.com/golf-plus/behind-kim-jong-ils-famous-round-golf (posted 1 June 2016) accessed 24 January 2019.

[23] Margita Boström, Kambodjas vänskap med Nordkorea. *Utrikeskrönika*, Sveriges Radio P1, https://sverigesradio.se/sida/avsnitt/970071?programid=4773 (posted 3 October 2017) accessed 24 January 2019.

[24] North Korean Art Gallery, https://www.dprk-art.com/index.php?option=com_content&view=frontpage&Itemid=54&lang=en, (without posting date, but no later than May 2007) accessed 31 January 2019.
See also Elsayed, Nadya. Behind Mansudae: Art from the Biggest Studio in North Korea. *VICE*, https://www.vice.com/en_us/article/7b7vj9/behind-mansudae-the-most-prominent-art-institution-in-north-korea (posted 29 Oct 2013) accessed 31 January 2019.

[25] Donald Trump assumed power on 20 January 2017 and is known, among other things, for his extensive use of tweeting as a technological platform – it allows messages of only 280 characters – for reaching his audiences.

[26] In any other case, this would have been enough to raise suspicions concerning the two leaders' sexual preferences. But of course this is an inappropriate and far-flung idea.

The Merry Widow and Socialist Realism

PER-ARNE BODIN

One musical genre that rather unexpectedly existed during almost the entire Soviet period was the Viennese operetta. Everything actually weighed against its presence in the Soviet context: fascination with capitalist or feudal luxury, the absence of any depiction of "the people," the alleged dearth of social criticism and political content. The Soviet operetta historian Moisei Iankovskii maintains in addition that most operetta singers joined the White side after the revolution.[1] The Viennese operetta was basically impossible in the Soviet Union, for its heroes and style were ill-suited to the concept of "Socialist Realism," which from 1934 on was the only permitted style in Soviet culture. Thus, my question concerns the strategies toward the Viennese operetta adopted by the authorities, the theaters, and individual directors. I want to focus my discussion on the perhaps best-known and beloved such operetta: Franz Lehár's *Merry Widow*, often called the "ultimate operetta," and its fate in the Soviet Union. I hope it will contribute to the somewhat neglected study of popular culture and its role after the revolution in 1917.

The cultural elite seems always to have viewed the operetta as an inferior genre intended for a middle-class or upper-class audience with bad taste. There has anyway been something shameful about liking it, although during almost the entire twentieth century it was a popular genre with much beloved and well attended performances throughout the world. Even Gustav and Alma Mahler were embarrassed to show that they liked *The Merry Widow*. Alma tells in her memoirs that after having attended one performance she and her husband danced the famous waltz at home, but when they failed to remember a certain passage they didn't dare to buy the piano score but peeked at one on the sly in a music store.[2] The philosopher Theodor Adorno was more openly positive, writing that *The Merry Widow* was one of the last operettas that had anything to do with art before the genre became mass-produced.[3] He also found the work to be characterized by a slight and tasteful South Slavic tonality and spoke about it appreciatively as sunken late Art Nouveau culture. Operettas after *The Merry Widow* he considered to be assembly-line products of inferior artistic quality.

Plot of the operetta

The Merry Widow premiered on New Year's Eve 1905 in Vienna. It is set in Paris and centers on the fictional Balkan principality of Pontevedro. Victor Léon and Leo Stein wrote the libretto, which is based on a French comedy by Henri Meilhac from 1861, *L'attaché d'ambassade: comédie en trois actes*. The librettists changed certain details, including the name of the country, which in Meilhac's play was a German principality called Birkenfeld.

Whereas the theme of the original comedy had to do with the unification of Germany, the new name Pontevedro alluded to great power politics, particularly the Balkan issue, and it becomes clear that Montenegro is the real country in question. Letijne, the capital city mentioned in the operetta, has almost the same name as the then Montenegrin capital Cetinje. In addition, several of the personal names, the pastiche folkloric elements, and the vaguely South Slavic tonality mentioned by Adorno point to Montenegro, which with Austrian support had become an independent state as early as 1878. Thus, the operetta hinted at the disastrous Austrian foreign policy that soon would lead to World War I.

The action takes place in Paris at the Embassy of Pontevedro, a country with a weak economy, terrible governance, and corrupt and lazy diplomats who furthermore regularly visit Maxim's, a local restaurant and night club frequented by prostitutes. The diplomatic legation is faced with a difficult problem. The immensely rich Pontevedrian widow Hanna Glawari is in town, and the diplomats are tasked with preventing her from marrying a foreigner, since Pontevedro would go bankrupt if she were to take her wealth out of the country. The person appointed by the ambassador to undertake the mission is the first secretary, Danilo, who had been in a relationship with Hanna before her first marriage but was spurned when he proposed to her. As the genre demands, *The Merry Widow* has a happy ending: love is born, Hanna and Danilo get each other, the Pontevedrian treasury is saved, and the diplomats can stay in Paris and carouse with the grisettes at Maxim's.

The premiere

The operetta landed right in the middle of what was then a political powder keg. The Montenegrins, Croats and Russians all objected to its portrayal of Pontevedro and organized a disruptive, joint Panslavic protest that forced one performance to abort. Danilo was the name of a real Montenegrin prince of dubious repute, which led to further opposition. The then ruler of Montenegro, Nicholas I, demanded in a letter to Emperor Franz Josef that the operetta be banned. The emperor did not comply, but he did attend a performance. When it was played in Constantinople several years after the premiere in Vienna, there were advanced plans among the local Slavic population to try to stop the production.[4] The uproar became a kind of dress rehearsal for what in 1914 would be the real assassination of heir presumptive to the Austrian throne Franz Ferdinand. *The Merry Widow* was prohibited in Montenegro until 2014, when the present pretender to the throne symbolically lifted the ban.[5] Montenegro was regarded in the early twentieth century as a "failed state," much as several other Balkan countries continue to be viewed by the global community. Permitting the operetta might be considered as a move designed to further Montenegro's current aspirations to join the EU.

Thus the operetta contained clear references to contemporary international politics. The Austrian censorship forbade the mention of Montenegro, as the librettists had originally called the country, although Pontevedro, as already noted, fooled no one. An allusion to the 1905 Revolution in Russia was also expunged.[6] In the original libretto, one of the guests at Maxim's, a Russian Grand Duke by the name of Kirill, lets drop that all Russians feel an inner turmoil, by which he means lovesickness. This translation of politics into eroticism, however, was translated back into politics by the censorship.

There are allusions in *The Merry Widow* to two more important issues in Austrian politics that were not banned by the censors. One was the alliance between Austria-Hungary and Germany (the "Zweibund") concluded in 1879, which was aimed at Russia. Later, in 1882, Italy also joined what became known as the Triple Alliance, which was one of the most significant factors leading to WWI. In the operetta it is used as a witty reference to extramarital affairs:

> Ein Zweibund sollte stets sie sein,
> Doch bald stellt sich ein Dreibund ein,
> Der zählt oft, der zählt oft
> Blos nach schwachen Stunden!
> Vom europäischen Gleichgewicht,
>
> Wenn Einer sich verehelicht,
> Von dem ist bald nichts mehr zu spüren.
> Der Grund liegt meistens nur darin:
> Es gibt Madam zu sehr sich hin
> Der Politik der off'nen Türen![7]

> A pact for two it should always be,
> But soon a pact for three will supervene,
> Which is often counted, often counted
> But only after weak moments!
> From the European balance of power
> When a person gets married,
>
> Of him, there is soon not a single trace.
> The reason lies mostly in this:
> Madam too readily gives in
> to the politics of open doors!

The second question that can be glimpsed briefly in the operetta is universal suffrage for men, which at the time was being introduced in Austria. In 1905 there was a large demonstration in Vienna for the right to vote. The political leadership supported the proposal, arguing that more democracy would lessen the power and influence of the various national movements. Women's suffrage was perhaps even more debated, and the voting issue was thus also of interest with respect to the burning national question in the Balkans. In the operetta it is framed in terms of Hanna's ability to choose among her many suitors:

> Es kämpfen die Damen schon lange
> Um das nämliche Recht mit dem Mann,
> Jetzt haben Madam' hier das Wahlrecht,
> Und fangen damit gar nichts an![8]
>
> The ladies have fought for a long time
> For the same rights as a man,
> Now has Madam' here the right to choose,
> And still makes no use at all of it.

Yet another allusion to a topical political question that we can see in the first quotation above is the "open door policy," which refers to an American proposal for free trade launched in 1899–1900 that is fully relevant even today.[9] In the operetta the reference suggests that Hanna is too generous toward her suitors. All three current political questions are reinterpreted as a romantic intrigue and whether Hanna will agree to marry Danilo. The audience was able to translate sex back into politics.

The operetta in the Soviet Union

Paradoxically enough, *The Merry Widow* survived the Russian Revolution and was staged as early as the early 1920s at the still private theaters that existed under the New Economic Policy.[10] Moisei Iankovskii notes that the old operettas were produced at the time as though nothing had happened.[11] The prerevolutionary political content of Lehár's work was now outdated and completely incomprehensible in the new Soviet context. Instead, it was the operetta as a genre that came to be a bone of contention in cultural policy. In a 1921 discussion of the mission of the theater in the new society Vladimir Maiakovskii referred scornfully to *The Merry Widow*. At issue was whether or not the theater should rise above daily life and whether art should be beautiful:

> А иначе говоря,—все красиво. Зависит только от того, как вы на это посмотрите. А «Веселая вдова»—тоже ведь красивая штука,—не угодно ли ее?[12]

The Merry Widow was evidently the most bourgeois and culturally worthless work he could think of.

The Russian Union of Proletarian Musicians (RAPM – Rossiskaia assotsiatsiia proletarskikh muzykantov), an influential cultural organization of the late 1920s whose views lay to the left of the Party's, wanted to ban Western European operettas, and in 1931 they succeeded in blocking some 200 of them, especially Viennese operettas, what they called "venshchina:" "Vienna trash." A special resolution published that year listed these works according to whether they could be staged in their original form, demanded more or less revision, or should be completely outlawed. The foreword to this extensive index also set forth a programmatic statement on the development of the operetta in the Soviet Union:

> В области музыкальной комедии ГРК (Главный репертуарный комитет) ведет решительную борьбу с "венщиной" т.е. с такой опереттой, в которой превалирует фарс, порнография, пошлость, «великосветская интрига» и т.п. (основы музыкально-репертуарьной политики ГРК).[13]

The Merry Widow would seem to fit all these deviations that the Soviet cultural bureaucrats felt must be combated in the operetta genre: farce, pornography, vulgarity, upper-class intrigues. It needed such extensive editing that it in fact became unperformable. Only a year later, in 1932, the Soviet regime liquidated RAPM, and as early as 1934 it once again became possible to stage

Viennese operettas.[14] The year before, in 1933, Anatolii Lunacharskii had argued that it was entirely possible to combine the operetta and Socialist Realism and put it to good use:

> Музыкальная драма, опера, музыкальная комедия и оперетта, феерии, включающие в себя монументальные картины,—все это полностью должно стоять к услугам театра социалистического реализма.[15]

Despite massive ideological pressure, the foreign operetta survived and even flourished at certain times in the Soviet Union. There were some successful efforts to create a revolutionary operetta, but the Viennese variety remained, and in 1935 the residents of Leningrad and many other cities could once again see *The Merry Widow*.[16]

Additional attempts were made later to abolish the genre in general and the Viennese operetta in particular.[17] Characters like Danilo were branded "tuxedo heroes," in contrast to the positive heroes of Socialist Realism. The final attack on the operetta occurred in 1948 in the wake of Andrei Zhdanov's 1947 assault on the writers Anna Akhmatova and Mikhail Zoshchenko. The denunciations were based on a Party resolution aimed at decadent formalism in music, directed among others against Dmitrii Shostakovich.[18] "Obraz i masky", a 1948 article in the journal *Teatr*, echoes RAPM language from the early 1930s to characterize a performance of *The Merry Widow* in Moscow by a troupe from Rostov:

> Болваны, идиоты, алкоголики все еще являются излюбленными персонажами западной оперетты.[19]

Lehár's operetta disappeared from the repertoire again for several years but returned during the Thaw under Khrushchev.[20]

The doctrine

The debate on the continued existence of the operetta and especially the Viennese operetta had recourse to a number of concepts to define the essence of correct Socialist Realism. The 1948 article cited above was central to the whole discussion; it distinguishes between the mask and the portrait, maintaining that the Soviet operetta is dominated by masks and clichés, two phenomena that must be combated. Masks and masking represent what is artificial and negative, false, and perhaps also politically incorrect: «Так рождаются маски, бессмысленные сцены вместо живого портрета.»[21] The opposite is realism. As Sheila Fitzpatrick shows in *Tear off the Masks!*

these are very fundamental concepts in Soviet ideology and Socialist Realism. Summarizing their political significance, she notes:

> Discussion of identity was closely linked with questions of disguise and concealment, since the Revolution had made certain social and political identities dangerous handicaps and thus fostered concealment. A disguised identity must be "unmasked" (razoblacheno), a very common term in early Soviet discourse.[22]

Katerina Clark shows in her book on the Fourth Rome that unmasking was also a basic concept in not only the show trials of high Stalinism but also in Stanislavskii's approach to acting, at least as he presented it himself in official contexts in the 1930s.[23] The article from 1948 referred to him as well. These notions were also used in the discussions about the right of the operetta to exist in the Soviet Union, so that references to masking had ominous connotations of anti-Soviet activity.

The word "masking" had been employed in a different and quite affirmative sense in the early 1920s. In 1923 the journal *LEF* featured Mikhail Levidov's article "Teatr: Ego litso i maski," which presents a very positive picture of Grigorii Iaron, perhaps the leading operetta director, singer and promoter in the country, and his interpretations of operetta characters.[24] Comparing him with Charlie Chaplin, Levidov notes that both artists use the method that the Formalists often referred to "laying bare the literary device as much as possible." Like Chaplin, Iaron merely plays himself, which confirms that operetta is not literature and not reality but something made up, like Charlie Chaplin in the movies. The concept of the mask is used in the article to define theatricality as such, that which distinguishes theater from literature. For the Socialist Realist critics it was tantamount to formalism in art, which became a fateful term of abuse during the Stalin era.

Iaron is mentioned in "Obrazy i maski" as one of the persons guilty of this development of masks in operetta. The entry on him in the Soviet encyclopedia of theater mentioned above presents a somewhat contradictory view of the notion of the mask. On the one hand, it is noted that he overcame the traditional mask in his art and created living characters:

> Как режиссёр Ярон отказался от воплощения традиционных образов-масок, от включения вставных номеров, ориентируя артистов на создание живых характеров.[25]

On the other, an added parenthesis seems to suggest that "masks" are on the contrary a rather positive phenomenon:

> Воспитанный в основном на неовенской оперетте, буффонно-эксцентрический актёр, Ярон создавал образы-маски (имел ярко индивидуальную внешность).

Iaron directed *The Merry Widow* in 1941 in Moscow. It was to have been presented at one of the city's summer theaters, but the war interfered.

Thus, much of the debate on the relationship between the operetta and Socialist Realism focused on different interpretations of the concept of the "mask" as either the essence of artistic quality or what is false and inauthentic in literature and was regarded by Soviet critics as the opposite of Socialist Realism.

The operetta was defended indirectly by reviewers who attempted to point out the aesthetic and political value of the genre. Moisei Iankovskii's book on the history of the Soviet operetta appeared in 1962 but was preceded by a more synoptic work as early as 1937.[26] He attempted in every way possible to embed the operetta in an acceptable Soviet context. He often wrote very critically about the Viennese operetta and spoke warmly of recently created Soviet productions, but in this manner he obliquely left room for the Western genre. He seems to have tried to rescue it by exploiting ideological divisions and setting it in a frame of acknowledged Soviet operettas.

The 1967 edition of the Soviet *Teatral'naia entsiklopedia* gives special emphasis to the view that Grigorii Iaron expresses optimism in his productions. This key defining notion in Socialist Realism lent his performances a form of legitimacy: "Его постановки отличались эмоциональностью, оптимизмом."[27] The happy endings so typical of both the operetta in general and Iaron's zestful productions were important factors contributing to the approval of the genre in Soviet culture. There were attempts to create an original Soviet operetta and show that there was a motif of class struggle in the French and Austrian prototypes. Much was also said, however, about their bourgeois and decadent elements. The Viennese operetta was on several occasions declared to be ideologically alien and a serious threat to Soviet youth. It remained as a kind of peculiar protest during the period of high Stalinism, however, and, except for a few years in the early 1930s and late 1940s, it never disappeared completely from the Soviet stage. The element of decadent late capitalist luxury in the operetta was in any case enticing enough to eclipse the Party's demands for Socialist Realism.

In "Obrazy i maski" Lehár's music for *The Merry Widow* is approved of, but his later operetta *The Blue Mazurka* is accused of "jazz rhythms" and "harmonic disorder" (bezoobrazitsa).[28] One major topic in the article concerns which operettas should be considered "classics," a term used by Soviet critics to evade criticism of older works for not keeping to the criteria of Socialist Realism.

The Soviet censorship

I. G. Iaron (a relative of Grigorii's) and Ia. Ia. Pal'mskii's translation of *The Merry Widow* appeared as early as 1906 and followed the original libretto closely. This was also the translation used during the Soviet period, albeit with significant changes and censorial interference.[29] An article in *Izvestiia* on 20 February 1940 noted of a staging of the operetta in Sverdlovsk that everything outdated, vulgar and crude had been expunged from the work, which resulted in a light, substantive and total theatrical experience:

> Классическая оперетта Легара «Веселая вдова» поставлена театром как цельный, легкий содержательный спектакль. В ней ценна работа театра над текстом, из которого убрано все устарелое, дешевое, грубое. Мастерское владение спецификой жанра и хороший вкус видны в этом спектакле.[30]

The production shows good taste, in other words. In the mid-1950s, a new translation by V. Mass and M. Chervinkii attempted to give the libretto what was called a genuinely literary quality.[31] This version confirms what appear to be already established censorial interventions and a levelling of the content that erased the erotic allusions. What specific changes were made to the text during the Soviet period? I will address this question on the basis of Danilo's aria and the "Song of the Vilja" and their performance in the Soviet Union.

"You'll Find Me at Maxim's" and "The Song of the Vilja"

In Danilo's opening aria he appears as an aristocratic bon vivant who is utterly unprofessional in the performance of his diplomatic duties. His thoughts center above all on Maxim's, a restaurant he visits every evening and from which he returns very late and very drunk. There he socializes with prostitutes, and it is obvious what he means when he says he is "sehr intim" with all the women at the place, with whom, as the prerevolutionary translation quite clearly and elegantly phrases it, he is "on an intimate footing": "Tam na noge korotkoi so vsiakoioi kokotkoi."

Beginning in the 1930s, when the operetta returned and the theaters were nationalized, the music was preserved, but, as the article in *Izvestiia* notes, the content was smoothed out and made less crude. The reference to Maxim's as a brothel disappeared, as did most of the girls and Danilo's abandonment of his country for the nightclub and then for Hanna, which of course in the end rescues Pontevedro. The provocative question at the beginning of the aria "Where is the Fatherland?"—since Danilo understands that it needs him—was also deleted, but it is present in the prerevolutionary translation: "Nu vot ia iavilsia. Gde zhe otechestvo?"[32]

In the Soviet productions Danilo continued to be a bon vivant dressed in a tuxedo (a "tuxedo hero"), and the luxurious milieu and his laziness and alcohol consumption remained as well. In the most bowdlerized version he doesn't even go to Maxim's but visits friends, which is perhaps somewhat surprising, considering his formal dress. Danilo's song becomes less erotic and more moral, although his drinking habits have not changed:

> иду тогда к друзьям –
> меня уже ждут там,
> /.../
> на сердце так легко
> и голову мне кружит
> веселье и вино.
> смеёмся без конца –
> от острого словца
> застольная беседа
> вином у нас согрета
> час утра недалёк –
> так пробки в потолок!
> до самого рассвета
> янтарный льёт поток.[33]

Thus, although the erotic content and Danilo's lack of patriotism disappeared, the upper-class motif remained as strong as ever despite the 1931 resolution, as did the element of farce and the questionable morality of the characters. It was stressed that the operetta ought to be understood as satire, but one recent Russian music scholar maintains that the survival of the operetta suggested to the audience the possible existence of a world different from their poor and colorless Soviet reality.[34]

"The Song of the Vilja" in the Soviet productions lost its suggestiveness. Gone is the erotic initiative of the Vilja/woman who entices the hunter into her dwelling, then seduces and abandons him:

> Als sie sich dann satt geküsst
> Verschwand sie zu derselben Frist!
>
> As soon as she was sated with kissing
> She disappeared at that moment!

In the Soviet recordings of the aria from the 1930s, this stanza is merely hummed by the singer.

The hunter instead becomes something of a poet who dreams of the Vilja, whom he has seen only once but never meets again. She becomes his muse, and he writes poems about her and is prepared to die for her. In one version of the song from the Soviet period we learn only that he dreamed about her. The female sexuality that is such an important theme in the operetta does not vanish completely in the Soviet version, but it is toned down, as is male desire. The prerevolutionary translation remained faithful to the original and preserves the eroticism, whereas the derivative Romanticism of the Soviet libretto is almost sexless. The hunter tries to convince himself that he only saw the girl in a dream, thus giving the song a pedagogical dimension and an urge to be normal:

> Красавицу Вилью однажды весной
> Увидел охотник за чащей лесной,
> И сердце его застучало сильней,
> Он, все позабыв, устремился за ней.
> Много дней прошло и лет.
> Ее давно простыл и след.
> Но влюблен, Вилью всюду ищет он.
>
> Вилья, о, Вилья, бродя по лесам,
> Я тебя, может быть, выдумал сам.
> Вилья, о , Вилья, наверно, ты мне
> Просто приснилась во сне..[35]

The Great Patriotic War

The Merry Widow during WWII is a special case. In 1941 Lehár's works were banned in the Soviet Union due to his close ties to the leaders of the Third Reich. The operetta was Adolf Hitler's favorite. The ban was not always observed, however.[36] It was staged by, among others, a Karelian theater troupe at the front outside besieged Leningrad. It became a demonstration against the war and an act of heroism to play it at a time when the area was under constant artillery bombardment. The work had such appeal, however, that Hitler overlooked and suppressed the fact that that the libretto had been written by two Jews, something that was not allowed to appear in the program notes. Stalin's censors were willing to ignore that Lehár was close to the Nazi leaders and that the plot exemplified bourgeois decadence.[37]

Dmitrii Shostakovich's *Seventh Symphony*, often called the "Leningrad Symphony," quotes "You'll Find Me at Maxim's," perhaps the best-known melody in the entire operetta. The most common explanation among music scholars is that it refers to Hitler's weakness for the work, and that the passage signifies the German attack on the Soviet Union. I would suggest instead that it is intended to demonstrate people's desperate desire to survive in the blockaded and starving city, or that, as one Soviet historian of the operetta claims, it belongs to the musical background shared by almost all, a part of their everyday life, or "byt." During the war, the banal becomes something essential.

The Socialist Realist element. Summary

The Viennese operetta and with it *The Merry Widow* survived in the Soviet Union also because it was eventually accorded the status of a classic. Some of the political content was by that time incomprehensible in the Soviet context and was not replaced with any other political subject, but the mere existence of the operetta on the Soviet stage had political implications. Danilo's contempt for his native land and the erotic theme were deleted. The satiric portrayal of Danilo as a decadent fop rather than a positive hero and the satire on stale bourgeois society in general is present in the texts and productions of the work, but greater emphasis is laid on the pleasurable aspect of this milieu. One very central element is the notion of masking, which as applied to the operetta implies for the Socialist Realist critics a scathing critique of everything inauthentic and false, in relation not only to the characters but also to the productions as such. *The Merry Widow* proved remarkably endurable, however, and perhaps more than anywhere else in the world, it was in the late Soviet Union that the operetta had its strongest foothold.

[1] Moisei Iankovskii, *Sovetskii teatr operetty: ocherk istorii* (Leningrad: Iskusstvo, 1962), 37.
[2] Stefan Frey, *Franz Lehár oder dass schlechte Gewissen der leichten Musik* (Tübingen: Niemeyer, 1995), 125.
[3] Theodor W. Adorno, *Gesammelte Schriften*. Bd 19, *Musikalische Schriften*, VI, 1. Aufl. (Frankfurt am Main: Suhrkamp, 1984), 249.
[4] Jelena Milojković-Djurić, "Franz Lehár's The Merry Widow: Revisiting Pontevedro," *Serbian Studies: Journal of the North American Society for Serbian Studies*, 25, 2 (2011), 259–72.
[5] Evening dedicated to the promotion of the operetta "The Merry Widow", accessed December 11, 2018. http://fondacija-njegos.org/en/crnogorsko-predstavljanje-vesele-udovice/.
[6] Barbara Denscher, *Der Operettenlibrettist Victor Léon: eine Werkbiografie*, (Bielefeld: transcript, 2017), 299.
[7] German text of the libretto at Die Lustige Witwe Libretto, Musik von Franz Lehár, http://www.opera-arias.com/léhar/die-lustige-witwe/libretto/. English translation by Lea Frey, accessed December 11, 2018. http://www.aria-database.com/translations/lustige_witwe.txt
[8] *Die Lustige Witwe*.
[9] Moritz Csáky, "Verschlüsselte Sprache der 'Lustigen Witwe'," in *Ideologie der Operette und Wiener Moderne*, (Wien: Böhlau, 1997), 97.
[10] Olesia Bobrik, "Venskaia operetta v Sovetskoi Rossii 1920–1940-kh godov: mezhdu 'santimentami' i tiuremnym iumorom," *Fioretti musicali. Materialy nauchnoi konferentsii v chesti Inny Alekseevny Barsovoi* (Moscow: Nauchno-izdatel'skii tsentr "Moskovskaia konservatoriia," 2011), 9.
[11] Iankovskii, *Sovetskii teatr operetty*, 37.
[12] Vladimir Maiakovskii, *Polnoe sobranie sochinenii: v trinadtsati tomakh*. T. 12, Stat'i, zametki i vystupleniia: noiabr' 1917–1930, (Moskva: Khudozhestvennaia literatura, 1959), 252.
[13] *Repertuarnyi ukazatel'. Tekst. Narkompros RSFSR, Sektor iskusstv, Gl. repertuarnyi kom*. T. 2, (Leningrad: Gos. izd-vo khudozhestvennoi lit., 1931), 77.
[14] Bobrik, "Venskaia operetta," 161.
[15] Antatolii Lunacharskii, Doklad na 2–m plenume Orgkomiteta Soiuza pisatelei SSSR 12 fevralia 1933 goda, accessed December 11, 2018. http://lunacharsky.newgod.su/lib/ss-tom-8/socialisticeskij-realizm-konspekt-doklada/
[16] Cf. the repertory list Aleksandr Gennad'evich Kolesnikov, *Problemy stsenicheskoi interpretatsii sochinenii Frantsa Legara na evropeiskoi i rossiiskoi scene vtoroi poloviny XX veka*, (Moskva: Dissertation: GITIS, 2001), 393–396.
[17] Iaron, chapter 14.
[18] "Postanovlenie Politbiuro CK VKP(b) Ob opere 'Velikaia druzhba'" V. Muradeli 10 fevralia 1948 g.http://www.hist.msu.ru/ER/Etext/USSR/music.htm, accessed December 11, 2018.
[19] E Grosheva, "Obrazy i maski. O stile sovetskogo teatra operetty", *Teatr*, Moskva 1948. № 11, 21–26., 21.

[20] Aleksandr Gennad'evich Kolesnikov, *Problemy stsenicheskoi interpretatsii sochinenii Frantsa Legara na evropeiskoi i rossiiskoi stsene vtoroi poloviny XX veka* (Moskva, 2016), 393–96.
[21] "Obrazy i maski. O stile sovetskogo teatra operetty", 21.
[22] Sheila Fitzpatrick, *Tear Off the Masks! Identity and Imposture in Twentieth-Century Russia*, (Princeton: Princeton University Press, 2005), 10.
[23] Katerina Clark, *Moscow, the Fourth Rome Stalinism, Cosmopolitanism, and the Evolution of Soviet Culture, 1931–1941* (Berlin: De Gruyter, 2011), 210–41.
[24] M. Levidov, "Teatr: ego litso i maski," *LEF: Zhurnal Levogo fronta iskusstv*, (Moskva, Petrograd: Gosudarstvennoe izdatel'stvo, 1923), № 4, 181.
[25] Grigorii Iaron, http://istoriya-teatra.ru/theatre/item/f00/s11/e0011305/index.shtml, accessed December 11, 2018.
[26] Grigorii Iaron, *Operetta: Vozniknovenie i razvitie zhanra na Zapade i v SSSR* (Leningrad Moskva : Iskusstvo, 1937).
[27] Iaron Grigorii, http://istoriya-teatra.ru/theatre/item/f00/s11/e0011305/index.shtml, accessed December 11, 2018. The verbatim report of the 1934 congress uses the word "optimism" many times to define the new literature, Vsesoiuznyi s″ezd sovetskikh pisatelei. Pervyi Vsesoiuznyi s″ezd sovetskikh pisatelei: 1934: stenograficheskii otchet. (Moskva: Sovetskii pisatel', 1990 [1934]).
[28] "Obrazy i maski. O stile sovetskogo teatra operetty", 22.
[29] Frants Legar, *Veselaia vdova : Operetta v 3-h d*.: Dlia fp. v 2 ruki s nadpis. rus. i nem. tekstom / Per. I. G. Iarona, L. L. Pal'mskogo. - SPb.: N. Davingof, b.g.
[30] *Izvestiia*. 20 februari 1940.
[31] L.L. Zhukova, "V mire operetty", (Moskva: Znanie, 1976), accessed December 11, 2018. http://istoriya-teatra.ru/books/item/f00/s00/z0000010/st007.shtml.
[32] Legar, 16.
[33] Ispolniaet Nikolai Ruban. Frants Legar. "Veselaia vdova". Vykhodnaia ariia Danilo, accessed December 11, 2018. https://rutube.ru/video/63262cb9430a02acb50b67613ebd18b1/.
[34] Bobrik, 149–66.
[35] "Pesnia o Vil'e (Veselaia vdova)" accessed December 11, 2018. https://vocal.land/catalog/other/2600/103163.
[36] Avgust v istorii Irkutskoi oblasti, accessed December 11, 2018. http://irkipedia.ru/date/irkutsk_reshitelno_vystupil_protiv_gkchp.
[37] A. V. Burleshin, "Kogda vstrecha ne raduet", *NLO* (2014:5), 129.

Rodimaia storonka?
A Ukrainian Director Films a Russian Poem in 1934

NATASCHA DRUBEK

To Irina, my favorite philosopher of (ne)Rodina and "Russian philologist"

Fig. 1 Still from the film *Garmon'* (1934)

> Гармонь, гармонь!
> Родимая сторонка!
> Поэзия российских деревень!

(Accordion, accordion! / My dearest motherland / Poetry of Russian villages!
Aleksandr Zharov (1926), used for the beginning of the film *Garmon'* (1934)

Igor' Savchenko's *Garmon'* (*The Accordion*, 1934) is a film based on poetry. It centers on a collectively empowered female body that puts an end to the ancient and unwanted bad habits of sexual pressure. This early Soviet sound film celebrates this empowered female collective as a delightful performance by a striding, singing, spitting, snorting, yawning, and beatboxing women's band. Together with his performers, many of them lay actors, Savchenko shaped an original and modern audiovisual image of changing gender relations in a rural setting embedded in a political plot.

Fig. 2 Tosklivyi from Siberia (played by Savchenko) and the local girls discussing who is a "kulak"

On the surface, the plot of this film comedy revolves around the political evaluation of old instruments in modern Soviet society. *Garmon'* has Timoshka using Marxist discourse when he plans to "liquidate the accordion as a class"—and with it, perhaps himself, as its player. This dilemma arises when he is given his new role as Komsomol leader due to his ability to accompany the women's songs and entertain as well as rouse the masses by playing the instrument. However, the popular accordion is not liquidated after all; rather, it is used to expel certain individual representatives of the kulak class. The film displays a liberal attitude towards so called "enemies of the people"—which was rather inappropriate in the USSR of 1934, when the country was preparing for the opposite.

Garmon' introduced the musical battle of the sexes which became popular in mainstream musical film comedies of the thirties directed by Grigorii

Aleksandrov and Ivan Pyr'ev. This also explains why *Garmon'*, which premiered in June 1934, finds itself today in the shadow of Aleksandrov's *Veselye rebiata* (*Moscow laughs / Jolly Fellows*), often incorrectly called the first Soviet musical, although it premiered half a year after *Garmon'*.¹

In its time, *Garmon'* was perceived as an attempt at an "Eastern" acculturation of the Western genre of the film musical.² The latter is related to the question of the (lack of) specificity of folklore in the film, which connects it with other, more avant-garde sound experiments of the day such as "voice-bands" using the human body instead of instruments. All of this might account for the film's later alienation from both the Russian and Ukrainian strands of (post-)Soviet film history and historiography. After the banning of *Garmon'* in 1936 and the criticism of his next film *Sluchainaia vstrecha* (*Chance Meeting*) for its "formalism",³ Savchenko was marginalized.⁴ It took him several years to overcome the ostracizing effect of his film experiments of 1934 and 1936. The end of his cooperation with the dissolving Moscow Mezhrabpom studio catalyzed his "return home" to Ukraine.

Poetic Cinema and Savchenko's Ukrainianess

> Ukrainian *Mykola Hohol* would become the great Russian writer *Nikolai Gogol*; *Davyd Burliuk* became the father of Russian futurism *David Burliuk*; *Oleksandr Dovzhenko* the Russian film director *Aleksandr Dovzhenko* and *Ihor Savchenko*—the Russian film director *Igor' Savchenko*.⁵

Savchenko can be called an understudied figure.⁶ Concentrating on Ukrainian language, folklore and themes, historians of Ukrainian film find it difficult to evaluate his contribution to Soviet Ukrainian cinema. Hardly any research has been conducted on the formal level of his early films. In his comprehensive 2009 article on "Ukrainian National Cinema and the Concept of the 'Poetic'", Joshua First does not mention Savchenko as a predecessor of the "poetic" Ukrainian school of the 1960s and 1970s (Paradzhanov, Osyka, Il'enko and others); he mentions his later work as being part of a "Stalinist folkloric mode of representing Ukraine, endemic not only of 1930s Dovzhenko but many of his contemporaries who worked in the republic: Ihor Savchenko, Ivan Pyr'ev, Ivan Kavaleridze".⁷

Excluding Savchenko from his Ukrainian patrimony would mean cutting ties with the younger generation of filmmakers, who clearly perceived him as connected to Ukrainian culture.⁸ After all, Savchenko was the teacher of Sergei Paradzhanov who after the war was able to make the key Ukrainian film, *Tini zabutykh predkiv* (*Shadows of Forgotten Ancestors*) (1964). It was based on a novella by Mykhailo Kotsiubyns'kyi (1912) and shot in Ukrainian. Ironically, it was not made by an ethnic Ukrainian but by one of Savchenko's most talented and controversial students, of Armenian descent, raised in Georgia. Savchenko's exercised his long-lasting pedagogical and national impact via the Soviet film school VGIK. His legacy was to become a teacher of a generation of film directors coming from both other backgrounds and other republics. He attracted the independent-minded, thereby considerably enhancing the diversity of Soviet post-war film and contributing to engendering some of the most daring, poetic and innovative oeuvres of the Thaw period as described by James Steffen:[9] besides Paradzhanov, his students included Marlen Khutsiev, Lev Kulidzhanov, Vladimir Naumov, Aleksandr Alov, Feliks Mironer or Latif Faiziev. Naumov remembers Savchenko calling his students a "conglomerate of insane individuals":

> Наш мастер во ВГИКе режиссер Игорь Савченко называл нас, своих учеников, "конгломератом безумствующих индивидуальностей". Ведь в нашей мастерской учились Саша Алов, Марлен Хуциев, Сережа Параджанов, Юра Озеров, Феликс Миронер, Латиф Файзиев, Гриша Мелик-Авакян… Саша Алов вскоре стал моим самым близким другом. Все мы работали друг у друга ассистентами. Первым ассистентом в моей жизни был Параджанов, а первым актером—Бондарчук, он снялся в моей курсовой работе "Юлиус Фучик. Репортаж с петлей на шее".[10]

Savchenko's Poetic Cinema and the Ukrainian School

Paradzhanov writes in his autobiography that his first contact with Savchenko was made via the idea of music in film which—alongside poetry—could be qualified as another major influence on Savchenko's cinema:

> [...] in Moscow I met straight away the excellent master Igor' Savchenko. He asked me "Why do you want to make films?" I said that I study at the conservatory but want to make music films and opera adaptations. He said: "This is interesting, come with me." They made me draw something, dance and sing something [...][11]

It seems that even after the war Savchenko was still interested in music as a counterpoint to narrative or prose-oriented cinema. Paradzhanov assisted Savchenko while shooting a film about the Ukrainian poet Taras Shevchenko in 1949, which was finished in 1951 by his students after his death in December 1950.[12] After Savchenko's death, Paradzhanov moved to Kyiv, where he devoted several of his films to Ukrainian biographies and topics: a film about the actress Nataliia Uzhvii (1957), wife of the Ukrainian futurist Mykhailo Semenko, *Ukrainskaia rapsodiia* (1961) and a film called *Dumka* (1957).[13]

The rareness of Ukrainian in films of the 1930s and especially the 1940s–1950s may point to the difficulty of the spoken language to establish itself in film during Stalin's rule—even for people like Dovzhenko, who in the 1930s was in excellent standing. This is why Savchenko may have inspired his students to create a film in Ukrainian, an idea that bore fruit with Paradzhanov's *Tini zabutykh predkiv,* which was not dubbed in Russian.[14]

Garmon' was made several years before Savchenko's "Stalinist folkloric mode of representing Ukraine"[15] set in. Although (post-)Soviet audiences have hardly had a chance to see *Garmon'* or Savchenko's next film, *Chance Meeting* (1936), we have to judge these films by themselves without extrapolating from the later costume picture *Bogdan Khmel'nitskii* (1941) on the brotherhood of Russia and Ukraine. The anti-Polish stance of this 1941 film demonstrates a resistance to the memory of an early republic, the Polish-Lithuanian Commonwealth, and with it, the idea of a modern European Republic on the territory of Soviet Ukraine. Khmel'nyts'kii was a Ukrainian Cossack leader who brought eastern Ukraine under Russian control by signing the Pereiaslav Agreement with Moscow. Mykhailo Sobuts'kyi calls Savchenko's late epic films *offitsioz*, and accurately describes the ambiguity of Ukrainian directors in the Stalinist era: They were the "most communist", and at the same time "dissidents". Sobuts'kyi pacifies the debate about Savchenko's later popularity when he notes: "It does not matter that he could please the authorities, but it does matter that he also was able not to please."[16] This is true not only concerning the censorship cuts in *Taras Shevchenko* but also with respect to *Garmon'*, which was not designed to please the tastes of the Kremlin.

A 1934 Film Adaption of a 1926 Poem

Die Poesie ist keine Form, sondern ein universales Vermögen, das im Volkslied erfahrbar wird. (Alexander Nebrig on J.G. Herder)[17]

In its use of verse *Garmon'* has a literally poetic aspect: after all, the script for the film was co-written by a poet. In 1977 the writer Aleksandr Zharov recalled that Savchenko had approached him with a script of a musical comedy inspired by his poem "Accordion". And that the director wanted to make a film "related to literature", in preparation for the forthcoming Soviet Writers' Congress.[18] Whether Zharov's memoir is accurate or not, most of Savchenko's films were adaptations of literary texts. Already his very first film *Nikita Ivanovich and Socialism* (*Nikita Ivanovich i sotsializm*, 1931, Azerfilm; lost) was based on an eccentric drama about a rich farmer, *Russia Perished* (*Pogibla Rossiia*), written by Savchenko who also played the negative role of the 'smart kulak', just as in *Garmon'*. The popular actor Mikhail Zharov in this film played another negative role.[19] His first film with a Ukrainian topic, *The Ballad of the Cossack Golota,* was based on a Russian novella.[20] The literary texts Savchenko used were mainly prosaic or dramatic, but in its dialogues *Garmon'* uses rhyming lines from a poem, partly in the form of a couplet or ditty (*chastushka*).

Zharov's conventionally crafted poem "Garmon'" (1926) was in its time a veritable hit that was read and discussed by a wide audience and turned into a stage play.[21] By 1934, however, it was already eight years old, its ideas and discourse dated. Some of the ideological concepts and also its pre-mechanical village seemed irrelevant references, since collectivization was already completed and the kulaks had been more or less "liquidated".[22] I would argue that the film's lack of modernity[23] is connected with Savchenko's attempt to avoid too narrow a party line. His previous film was first lauded, later rejected by the militant ARRK committee for its political concept. In *Nikita Ivanovich i sotsializm* Savchenko had already employed an "extravagant dance of tractors" ("feericheskaia pliaska traktorov"), as described by his collaborator Aleksandr Makovskii.[24] In *Garmon'*, however, there was no single tractor.

This "mistake" was criticized at the Kremlin screening in June 1934 by Stalin, who found it too jolly, since the film did not show the mechanical side of the collectivization; Kaganovich complained that there was not even a harvester (*lobogreika*).[25] A contemporary critic was of the opinion that the film's "political note" was its main deficiency.[26]

The positive reviews concentrated on the film's genre and poetics, saying that "the images of the poem are translated with great mastery into the language of cinema" ("Образы поэмы с большим мастерством переведены на кинематографический язык").[27]

The audience seems to have indulged Savchenko's choice of a timeless rural setting that perhaps harks back to a memory of the non-kolkhoz and pre-famine idyll as pictured in Kustodiev's painting of a circle dance in a prerevolutionary village:

Fig. 3 Painting: Boris Kustodiev: "Khorovod" (Circle Dance), 1912. https://commons.wikimedia.org/wiki/File:Кустодиев_Хоровод_1912.jpg

Garmon' was made at a time when literature was becoming increasingly important again among the arts—at least on the level of party discourse. As the norm of Socialist Realism started being implemented in 1934 in Soviet culture, literature was chosen to take the lead in prescribing what the doctrine was. And another thing happened: screenplays were promoted to the status of a leading Soviet literary genre. According to Anke Hennig, it was around 1934 that "the film script became a fourth genre on a par with epic, lyric and drama".[28] Of course, this all would not directly affect *Garmon'*, which already had premiered in June. Still, this film based on a poem suddenly proved not to be aligned with the new genre rules and their increasingly prosaic zeitgeist.[29] According to the new hierarchy of literary genres, *Garmon'* found itself somewhere between an inconspicuous mainstream film production and a marginal experiment: The script was an adaptation, but not of a novel, which now was the paragon for all other arts and media. Savchenko's subconscious flight into "verse cinema" just before the onset of Socialist Realism[30] might have been a retreat from political topics and genres which were exposed in the mid-thirties.

In Search of Soviet Poeticity and the Future Canon of Ukrainian Cinema

> A poet is the creator of the nation around him, he gives them a world to see and has their souls in his hand to lead them to that world. (J.G. Herder, *Auszug aus einem Briefwechsel über Ossian und die Lieder alter Völker*, 1773)

I would now like to ask whether there is a connection between *Garmon'* and what was later called the "lyrical" or "poetic" school of Ukraine. To answer this question, it is necessary to define what is meant by "poetic" and the "poetic Ukrainian cinema".

Joshua First initially grasps the "poetic" through Shklovsky's distinction between two cinematic genres, where "poetic" cinema is defined negatively, by the absence of the plot that is dominant in "prose" cinema:

> They are distinguished from one another not by rhythm, or not by rhythm alone, but by the prevalence in poetic cinema of technical and formal over semantic features, where formal features displace semantic and resolve the composition. Plotless cinema is "verse" cinema.[31]

First does not mention Savchenko's *Garmon'*, which in fact was criticized for "a prevalence [...] of technical and formal" features. However, this early sound film is a good example of "'verse' cinema" in the Shklovskian sense: the circular composition, the transposition of a *poema* into film, the variety of musical genres, the defamiliarizing (*ostranenie*) use of voices and noises as "attractions", and especially orally created sounds such as the beatboxing and lip-smacking produced by the women.

In the landscape of Soviet early sound films Savchenko's music-and-folk-poetry- driven film is a worthy counterpart to Pudovkin's contemporary sound experiment in his 1933 film *The Deserter* (*Dezertir*), which was another Mezhrabpom production. What is unique in *Garmon'* is its montage, which works with rhythmical structures of sound elements created by the body: noises, voices, sounds imitating instruments[32]—all in two types of music: symphonic, and folklore song and dance music. This audio-visual montage did not please the Kremlin audience, of course.

Garmon' could be called "verse cinema" if one studies the repetitive and circular patterns in the film connected with the dance element. If we follow First's other arguments about "poetic" films, we could say that by co-writing the script Savchenko pursued his "own authorial intentions"—but this would also be true of other Soviet directors-*auteurs*.³³ Many avant-garde directors had the urge to fill the position of the screenplay writer, especially after 1934, when the *stsenarist* was proclaimed to be the author (*avtor*) of the film and the director the mere manager of the shooting (*postanovshchik*).³⁴ Hennig argues that in 1934, script writing ("dramaturgiia kino") and adaptations of literary works were in competition, which would eventually lead to a "hegemony of scriptwriting inside the film industry".³⁵

First describes the (later) Ukrainian "poetic" director-as-author differently, stressing the attempt to free cinema from the dependence on literature:

> In engaging with official notions of national authorship, Ukrainian "poetic" filmmakers aimed to dissolve its literature-centered authority. Instead of the screenwriter, they believed that the director (along with the cinematographer) was more integral in constructing cinematic meaning. While certain screenwriters were associated with "poetic cinema," these were collaborations instigated by the director to accomplish his own authorial intentions.³⁶

This is certainly correct, but the tendency to reveal the specificity of the medium instead of relying on literary (pre)texts was already achieved by the Soviet avant-garde, not "poetic" cinema. "Poetic cinema" describes neither a certain aesthetical style nor a stable poetics; rather, it characterizes the "other" of mainstream Soviet cinema, a way to reveal "Ukrainian difference", even if it has not always been manifest.

We can agree that *Garmon'*—even if it came out in 1934—owed more to the aesthetics of the TRAM theater and the poetic spirit of the avant-garde than to what soon would be called Socialist Realism. However, how much of specifically Ukrainian poeticity can be found in *Garmon'*, and is it connected with the post-*Earth* cinematic strand of "otherness"? Savchenko was indeed one of those "filmmakers who [...] were all interested in modernist and avant-garde cinema in the Soviet Union and Western Europe—specifically, surrealism and expressionism, from an earlier period, and with the more open aesthetic system".³⁷ So why did he not continue where the tragedy *Earth* had stopped by choosing a Ukrainian setting for the comedy *Garmon'*, something that would have made everybody happy, including, it would seem, Ukrainian film historians today?

Firstly, the studio where *Earth* was produced in 1930 ceased to exist in the form of the formerly so vibrant VUFKU. Its "reorganization" into Ukrainfil'm meant a significant loss of autonomy, which also explains why it was easy for Pyr'ev to work there and arrange co-productions with the Soviet capital. Apart from Savchenko's ties to the Moscow Mezhrabpom studio, one could name a second reason: The real Ukrainian fields—just up until 1933 the scene of famines organized from Moscow—would have been an improper place for a filmmaker from Ukraine to stage a lighthearted comedy.

As long as Savchenko was part of the "other" of Soviet cinema, he made "poetic cinema" which continued explorations of the avant-garde in the USSR until the mid-thirties in sound film. One can observe a paradox here that is connected with the political situation: exactly in the moment when Savchenko started availing himself of Ukrainian history and filming in Ukraine, respectively, his ability to differentiate himself from mainstream Stalinist cinema declined.[38]

Garmon' boldly combines lyrical traits with avant-garde montage and cinematography that stress the technical aspects of film and display a pronounced auto-referentiality of the emerging sound cinema. Precisely this concentration on the new medium renders *Garmon'*, as an example of "verse' cinema", not only a poetic film but also an example of a film in which poeticity dominates over other functions.

Hence, I suggest applying to the concept of poetic cinema in the USSR a post-Formalist definition of poeticity, such as Roman Jakobson's. Clearly, neither Savchenko's sound film nor later Ukrainian poetic cinema can be fully measured by Formalist theory, which was more interested in cinematic narration. Jakobson, once part of the Russian Formalist School, was one of the experts on not only structural linguistics but also Slavic folk poetry. This is why the mature Jakobson's theory is a better fit than Shklovsky's poetry vs. prose opposition (which concentrates on the fabula). In his post-war "Linguistics and Poetics" Jakobson asked what artistic language can do, defining its "poetic function" in a rather technical formula which can be equally applied to cinema, especially "poetic cinema": "The poetic function projects the principle of equivalence from the axis of selection into the axis of combination. Equivalence is promoted to the constitutive device of the sequence."[39]

The linguist argued that language has different functions, yet only poetic language, namely, the versified type, displays the pure form of poeticity which is self-referential. The same goes for artistic or poetic films, where the (audio)visual medium is always being negotiated in front of the audience's eyes and ears instead of creating an immersive narrative with an invitation to identify with one of the protagonists. In works where the poetic function dominates, claims Jakobson, there is a pronounced self-referentiality. Savchenko's *Garmon'* is an example of a self-referential sound film production as well as "poetic cinema" based on folk material and using folklore's very own poetic methods, such as Russian folklore's favorite figures—parallelism, or repetitive form ("refrain"), or circular structures on which the macrostructure of the film is built.

The result is twofold: poeticity can be found in the early Soviet musical film *Garmon'*, which explores film poetics inspired by the repetitive structure and rhymes of folk songs rather than by linear narratives, thus allowing a self-referentiality of the medium. In addition, *Garmon'* was not filmed in a fake set in post-famine Ukraine with happy kolkhoz farmers—this dubious task was left to Savchenko's colleague from Siberia, Ivan Pyr'ev.

Precursors and Rivals of *Garmon'*

Garmon' looks for a positive expression of genuine folklore: Timoshka's return from scratching slogans to playing the accordion to everybody's delight. The crisis of this development is staged as a competition between choirs. Zharov's poem only hinted at such a possibility. In the film, the competition of the Old world with the New culminates in the singing of the female choir (led by the reformed accordionist Timoshka), which is directed against the male choir of drunken kulaks. When Timoshka understands that he cannot defeat the kulaks with political speeches or the posters he is inscribing while one of the rogues is molesting his girlfriend, he fetches the accordion from the haystack.

Fig. 4 Retrieving the instrument (*Garmon'*)

Only the jolly strains of the accordion are able to put the enemy to flight. The effect of the sound is visualized in the figure of a kulak holding his ears.

The soundtrack of this sequence bordering on cacophony is unique for a film musical of that time. Lahusen, LaPasha and McDonald interpret the choir contest politically, saying that the "class war had intensified, but Savchenko's film advocated a policy of appeasement, of the need for generational harmony and solutions, not with guns and force, but with music and fun. By 1934 and the film's release, such a luxury was itself a remnant of the past".[40] In 1933 when the film was started, such a situation was true in Ukraine but not yet in place in Moscow; one might consider this aspect for the year of 1936, when the film was shelved and the Great Terror was beginning. This means that the singers' dispute is not a dated pacifistic device. It is an exemplary mode of avoiding a fight in a musical.[41] A film musical could hardly show a Komsomol hero gunning down a kulak without losing its genre credibility. In the end it is Marusen'ka whose slap in the face of the *podkulachnik* resolves the situation:

Fig. 5 and 6 The defeated "podkulachnik" (*Garmon'*)

Fig. 7 and 8. Marusen'ka and her friends are laughing (*Garmon'*)

One wonders why it was exactly Savchenko who was the first Soviet director to attempt to turn verses into a feature film, something that confronted him with two problems at the same time—the musical and the literary aspects of film. Even if the music might help the verses when they join in their common rhythmic structures, *Garmon'* was still the only Soviet film daring to set out on this path. Transferring musical concepts and devices into film is rare in cinema.

Savchenko's cinematic poetics might have been inspired by an earlier sound film which combined folk music with rhythmic movement. I am talking about the film *Gopak* (also: *Dance* (*Plias*) by Mikhail Tsekhanovskii, 1931),[42] shot by cinematographer Andrei Moskvin, who shows the Ukrainian dance from unusual camera perspectives. Moskvin later worked with Eisenstein on *Ivan the Terrible* (*Ivan Groznyi*) (1944/1958), for which he shot the "interior scenes and effectively became what we call today the Director of Photography".[43] This is how Moskvin filmed the top shots in *Gopak*:

Fig. 9 and 10. The augmentation of the round ornament in Tsekhanovskii's Ukrainian *Gopak* (1931), shot from overhead

There are several elements which link *Garmon'* to *Gopak*. The movement of the dance is shown from above as a round form. In Tsekhanovskii's film the abstract round shape seems to move like a kaleidoscope—similar to the American films of Busby Berkeley, only not as rigidly regulated. Berkeley uses a top shot technique without a crane with a hole drilled in the ceiling to shoot the dance from above.

Both Berkeley and Tsekhanovskii were interested in filmic representation of the ornamental masses, and both revealed the dancers' bodies as abstract figures, rotating wheels or non-human wreaths. As Siegfried Kracauer wrote in *The Mass Ornament* (1927) on the "mathematics" of the dancing Tiller Girls:

> These products of American distraction factories are no longer individual girls, but indissoluble girl clusters whose movements are demonstrations of mathematics. As they condense into figures in the revues, performances of the same geometric precision are taking place in what is always the same packed stadium, be it in Australia or India, not to mention America. [...] The bearer of the ornaments is the *mass* and not the *people* (Volk), for whenever the people form figures, the latter do not hover in midair but arise out of a community.[44]

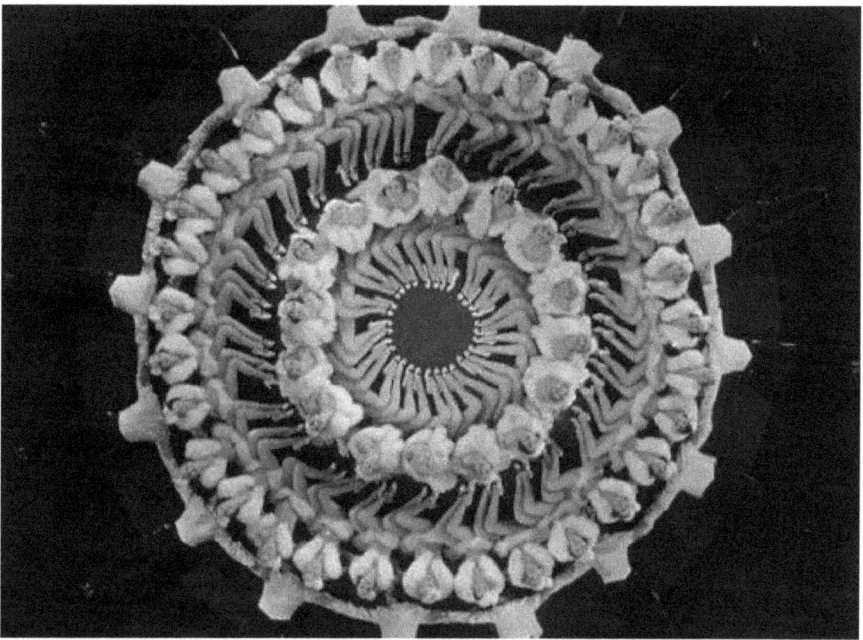

Fig. 11. Two rotating human wheels in the American film *42nd Street* (1933, Busby Berkeley)

We will hardly find mass ornamental effects of dance or play in *Garmon'*, where the ornamental is replaced by closeup or medium shots of women. In the director's script preserved in the RGALI archive, Savchenko planned to have the women striding with their elbows entwined ("Девушки идут 'сплетясь кренделькамиʼ"),[45] which in Russian connotes a form of winding. We see this in the very beginning of the film. In the final sequence there are different shots of the *khorovod* which can be translated as a circle dance (similar to the Greek *khora* or the Balkan *kolo*):

Fig. 12. Double circle dance in *Garmon'*

In *Garmon'* Savchenko and Evgenii Shneider, his cameraman, used a crane which enabled them to show the *gulian'e* from above but at an angle which looks more "epic"[46] and less abstractly ornamental compared to the Tsekhanovskii and Berkeley films; they filmed, among other things, the turnaround called "giant-strides" (*gigantskie shagi*), which produced a second circular image in the background. The rotating circles of people are plain and folklike, less contrived than the constantly changing patterns created by the professional dancers in Tsekhanovskii's[47] and Berkeley's films. In this sense Savchenko would agree with Kracauer's Marxist criticism of the ornament:

> The ornament is an end in itself. Ballet likewise used to yield ornaments, which arose in kaleidoscopic fashion. But even after discarding their ritual

meaning, these remained the plastic expression of erotic life, an erotic life that both gave rise to them and determined their traits.[48]

Even if Savchenko had the technical possibility to film the dancing bodies from above, he refrained from doing so. The bodies are not sexualized, nor do they turn into an abstract pattern, as in the parades of the 1930s.

One should mention that the *chechotka* in *Garmon'* is far from *gopak/ hopak* type dancing. This Ukrainian dance, originally called *kozak*, centered on male acrobatic dancing and jumping in the style of the Cossacks of the Zaporizhian Sich. The *g/hopak* was modified with collective circle dances including women who danced the *khorovod*, thus forming a synthesis of male and female dancing. This type of *gopak* was developed in the first decades of the twentieth century by the ethnographer of dance and choreographer Vasyl' Verkhovynets' (1880–1938), who published a book on the theory of Ukrainian folk dance in 1919. Verkhovynets' three-part *g/hopak* was exported abroad and presented at the First International Festival of Folk Dance in London 1936 as an example of a typical Ukrainian dance. In 1933 he worked in the Odessa film studio for Ivan Kavaleridze on the soundtrack of the Ukrainian film *Koliivshschina*. Nadezhda Kapel'gorodkaia, Kavaleridze's wife, was a member of the Ukrainian Women Choir Ensemble ZhinKhorAns, founded by Verkhovynets' and his wife Evdokia Verkhovynets-Kosteva in 1929/30 in Poltava as a new type of all-woman singing dance band which

> [...] represented a completely new genre of dramatized song, which immediately attracted a lot of attention. It was "ZhinKhorAns" that served as inspiration and was the beginning of all future Ukrainian folk and dance groups.[49]

Although *Garmon'* is not based on Ukrainian folk dance, it seems inspired by the idea of a non-professional female choir such as ZhinKhorAns. Moreover, "Garmon'" itself was performed by amateur collectives all over the USSR as late as 1936.[50] The structural connection between the ensemble from Poltava—"12 girls performing with sounds, action and dance"[51]—and these lay performances as well as those in the film *Garmon'* remains to be studied in greater detail.

Better documented are Dadaist and Poetist ensembles in neighboring Czechoslovakia, which performed collective recitations of texts without instrumental accompaniment.[52] Similar to E.F. Burian's "Voiceband" founded in 1927,[53] *Garmon'* built on the choral rendition of poetry, with one difference: *Garmon'* would not use syncopated jazz rhythms but Slavic folk tradition, as transformed by Mezhrabpomfil'm composer Sergei Pototskii into film music of the symphonic type alternating with accordion pieces. The original voicebands mostly performed *a capella* or with percussion. All voicebands of the 1920-1930s had in common a playful and democratic spirit; after all, voicebands rely solely on the body of the performer, thus eliminating class restrictions on music production, which could otherwise be either complicated to learn or require expensive instruments (such as the accordion, even if it is viewed as a popular choice). Until today the main "attractions" of voiceband performances are defamiliarized folk vocalizations.

This is another affirmation of Savchenko's interest in poetic experiments with folklore dancing and singing. *Garmon's* core is the song, whether the melancholic *romans* (associated with urbanity and so called *tsyganshchina*)[54] or jolly rural tunes; the structure of the film could also be described as a competition between the male song of the *kulaks* (the non-local "orphan" from Siberia, played by the director himself) and the song performed by a female choir (supported by a young *komsomolets* who is pictured as somebody who protects the girls' bodies from the lecherous *kulaks*).

If we look a bit closer it might even be read as a war of North vs. South. The women's mouth music in the film shows certain parallels to the performance of a ZhinKhorAns ensemble based on folk material as well as a renunciation of instruments medialized in film and accompanied by a film orchestra.

In both Soviet films—Tsekhanovskii's and Savchenko's—the dance scenes often do not show the heads of the dancers – the camera concentrates on bodily movements, as if not interested in the individuals. This contrasts with Berkeley's "parade of faces",[55] where the faces of the girls are shown individually in a closeup. Savchenko's and Shneider's interest in the dancing body is especially conspicuous in the slow-motion shots in the end of *Garmon'*, where we see the skirts and blouses of the women dancing by the camera in a closeup—the ones which Stalin found so appalling.[56]

Fig. 13. Women dance in slow motion in *Garmon'*

Stalin and, seconding him, the critic Aduev, did not approve of any cyclical structures in film, even if underpinned by authentic folk references. Aduev writes that the flight of the kulak would have been a dramaturgically better ending of the film, but "Savchenko preferred the obsolete figure of a rounding" ("Савченко предпочел фигуру закругления", "обветшалую")[57]. Neither was he willing to accept Savchenko's attempt to impregnate the first Soviet film musical with folk structures which are repetitive and not dramatically one-directional.[58] The "rounding figure" would imply that the prerevolutionary world might return at some point.

The dance as a collective movement in which single details are indiscernible is a plastic idea which was shared by Tsekhanovskii and Savchenko in the first half of the thirties. In *Garmon'*—after the headless *khorovod*—female faces are shown as well, but these shots are hardly comparable to the choreography of Berkeley's erotic "parade". The faces of the Soviet women are shown from below, not in a glamorizing way but moving into the frame bidirectionally in front of the camera, which does not allow the viewer's gaze to dwell on the bodies but rather conveys the experience of participation.

***

Verses and their poetics (rhythm and repetition) govern the "melodic lines" of *Garmon'* in a way that is unique in Soviet film history of the 1930s. Even drawing internationally on poetic structures is rare in film musicals or films with music of that time. The splendid isolation of Savchenko's film can be seen as an indirect attestation to his exploration of poetic cinema that would later engender alternative Soviet film aesthetics as well as the poetic film school of Ukraine. A lyrical strand was developed in Ukraine in the mid-1930s, as is manifest in the Ukrainfilm production *Strogii iunosha* (1936). However, it was precisely this ill-fated film which had to cope with the rather extreme case of the removal of its lead, the actor Dmitrii Konsovskii, that ended with his death in the GULAG. Even after his replacement the film ended up being "excised"—*iz"iatyi*, as Margolit and Shmyrev called their 1995 encyclopedia of censored films, *Iz"iatoe kino*.

Garmon' engages in a dialogue with other early sound films, specifically, a Soviet film from 1931 showing a dance performance of the Ukrainian *hopak* as an ornamental shape. Savchenko concentrates on amateur women's dancing and adds both a more human perspective and a comic element. The circular movement can be found in the musical structures, the rhymes and in the detail of the spinning flower which decides the fate of the lovers by the number of its petals: "He loves me, he loves me not".

In the beginning I spoke of *Garmon'*'s alienation among Russian language music films of its time; this cannot be considered a bad thing if we look at mainstream production, which often only copied foreign models and simplified earlier Soviet achievements. If *Garmon'*'s versified dialogues, the East European circular dance and the music inspired by traditional as well as contemporary folklore are the reasons for this isolation, one could indeed see the film as a predecessor of the poetic tradition of the Soviet (Ukrainian) cinema—not only following what Joshua First calls the "cultural trope"[59] of alterity, but in the sense of "poetic cinema" based on the principle of the song (*pesennoe nachalo*), a poeticity expressing itself not nationally as in the choice of a language, but rather structurally in the prevalence of the poetic function that governs the composition and rhythms of this musical comedy.

¹ Savchenko's film was based on a 1926 Russian poem (Aleksandr Zharov's "Garmon'"), written before the horrors of the collectivization which had an especially deadly effect on the director's homeland, Ukraine, where millions died of hunger in 1932 and 1933. From today's critical perspective the cinematic depiction of the prospering Soviet countryside dating from 1934 paints a surprisingly anachronistic picture and could even be perceived as a whitewashing of the Great Famine—especially, if the film had been set in Ukraine.

² This was noticed right after the premiere of the film in a Leningrad newspaper: "Звуковая картина 'Гармонь—едва ли не первый опыт создания музыкальной кино-комедии, жизнерадостной, чуждой всякому подражанию заграничным кино-опереттам, популярнейшей формы этого жанра за рубежом». (N.B., "Garmon", *Krasnaia gazeta*, 20 June 1934)

³ In *Kino* (№ 8, 11 February 1936). In the newspaper *Izvestiia* (17 November 1936) a feuilleton-review by the brothers Tur under the title "Record of Madness" ("Protokol breda") contained a biting critique of the film.

⁴ This film is about the pregnancy of a Soviet female athlete and the concept that modern Soviet fatherhood is non-biological. It deserves to be seen in the context of a film of the same year that discussed the question of monogamy under Soviet conditions: *Strogii iunosha / The Severe Young Man* (1936, Abram Room, based on a screenplay by Iurii Olesha). This surrealist hymn to a luxurious lifestyle, filmed in the Crimea, was doomed as well.

⁵ Yuri Shevchuk, "Linguistic Strategies of Imperial Appropriation: Why Ukraine is Absent from World Film History," in Larissa M. L. Zaleska Onyshkevych and Maria G. Rewakowic, eds., *Contemporary Ukraine on the Cultural Map of Europe* (Armonk, New York: M.E. Sharpe, 2009), 364.

⁶ Savchenko in Ukraine can be called an understudied figure. Since he allegedly had done nothing to advance Ukrainian cinema and did not use Ukrainian, Sergei Trymbach concluded that from the point of view of Ukrainian national cinema the director was marginal ("Dovzhenko, Savchenko, Parajanov: The Power of Art vs. the Power of the State." Quoted from a talk at the Savchenko conference in Cambridge 2011).

⁷ Joshua First, "Ukrainian National Cinema and the Concept of the 'Poetic'," http://www.kinokultura.com/specials/9/first.shtml 2009.

⁸ In the article called "The director as pedagogue" in the anthology edited by V. Sydorenko in 2006 Savchenko is not mentioned, which is peculiar since he was considered one of the most charismatic and influential professors at the film school VGIK of his time. Cf. the film by the daughter of one of his VGIK students, Nataliia Naumova, *The Short Life of I. Savchenko. Monologue on a Teacher* (2007).

⁹ James Steffen, *The Cinema of Sergei Parajanov* (Madison, Wis.: University of Wisconsin Press, 2012), 29.

¹⁰ Vladimir Naumov https://7days.ru/stars/privatelife/vladimir-naumov-svoim-otnosheniem-kzhene-yavozmutil-alenadelona.htm 19-1-2017, recorded by Elena Kostina. – As it seems, hardly any women had a chance to enter the directors' classes at that time, being taught by Eisenstein, Savchenko, and Romm.

¹¹ K.D. Tsereteli, ed., *Kollazh na fone avtoportreta. Zhizn'— igra* (Nizhnyi Novgorod, 2005)

¹² Ibid., 17.

[13] In 1965 he planned the film *Kiev Frescoes* which was never completed, and Aleksandr Antipenko, his cameraman, would not receive his VGIK diploma for shooting the film. In 1966 he left for Erevan (Ibid., 18).

[14] According to Ol'ha Briukhovets'ka, this is an exceptional case (e-Mail correspondence from December 2018).

[15] First, "Ukrainian National Cinema."

[16] Mihajlo Sobuts'kyi, 'Igor Andriiovich i sotsializm,' Dzerkalo tizhnia №39, 14 zhovtnja 2006. In Russian: 'Igor' Andreevich i sotsializm,' *Zerkalo nedeli*, № 39 (618), 2006, 14–20. http://dt.ua/CULTURE/igor_andriyovich_i_sotsializm-48066.html

[17] Alexander Nebrig, "Die Welt als Lied. Der globale Anspruch von Herders Stimmen der Völker in Liedern (1778/79)," in *Figuren des Globalen: Weltbezug und Welterzeugung in Literatur, Kunst und Medien*, Christian Moser und Linda Simonis, eds. (Göttingen: V & R, 2014), 315–325.

[18] A. Zharov, "'Kak poema stala fil'mom," *Iskusstvo kino* 1 (1977), 66.

[19] A. Makovskii, "Kino vverkh nogami."

[20] Savchenko chose the literary models for his films with care. In the instances when the script was not his own, he at least (co-)wrote it. Above I mentioned Joshua First's remark that the attempt to dominate the scenarist is a feature of directors of the "Ukrainian poetic cinema". The only exceptions to the rule are his films *Vsadniki* (*The Riders* 1938, based on the novel of Iurii Ianovskii; for more on this film cf. Sobuts'kyi. "Igor Andriiovich i sotsializm"), *Bogdan Khmel'nits'kii*, and *Tretii udar*.

[21] The 1927 dramatization for agit-brigades, theaters of the working youth (TRAM), and other amateur groups was executed by Zharov together with the poet Ivan Molchanov; cf. Aleksandr Zharov and Ivan Molchanov, "Timoshka-garmonist: Predstavlenie v 3 kart. S prologom: Instsenirovka poemy A. Zharova "Garmon"" (Moscow, Moskovskoe teatral'noe izdatel'stvo, 1927 and 1929). The 1929 edition
was accompanied by I. Dunaevskii's sheet music and had a print run of 9000, see Thomas Lahusen, Robin LaPasha and Tracy McDonald, *The Accordion, in two Parts* (undated manuscript), partially published in German as "Das Akkordeon" in T. Lipták & J. Murašov (eds.). *Schrift und Macht. Zur sowjetischen Literatur der 1920er und 30er Jahre* (Wien, Köln, Weimar: Böhlau, 2012), 221–258.

[22] However, the figure of the concealed kulak is a central motif as late as in Pyr'ev's 1936 film *The Party Ticket* (*Partiinyi bilet*) where a woman gives up her husband for the Communist Party when she learns about his kulak background. Cf. N. Drubek-Meyer, "Manuskript, Parteibuch, *trudoden'*, Fahrkarte. Geldsurrogate im sowjetischen Film 1936–39," in: Wolfgang Weitlaner (ed.), *Kultur/Sprache/Ökonomie* (*Wiener Slawistischer Almanach* Sonderbd. 54), 2001, 165–200. This article discusses equivalents of economic wealth as well as female empowerment in Soviet society of the 1930s.

[23] A. Zharov (1977) reiterates this argument: "— Хорошо ли, что в нашем фильме, посвященном первым победам колхозного строя, почти не видно машин, ну хотя бы трактора?"

[24] "Заключительный аттракцион – феерическая пляска тракторов, в которой, конечно же, не обошлось без полюбившихся Савченко кадров 'вверх ногами'". A. Makovskii, "Kino vverkh nogami," in: *Igor' Savchenko: Sbornik statei i vospominanii*, Kyiv: Mystetstvo,

75–81). It was in Baku where according to film director Makovskii the theater man Savchenko had invented the "Cinema Turned Upside Down" in a theater production called *Neft'/Oil*: "Так ведь это же сверхмирово! – обрадовался Савченко.. […] придет в кино вот такой Савченко и перевернет с ног на голову все наши представления о киноискусстве...".

[25] Aleksandr Troshin, "A drani podobno '*Garmoni*' bol'she ne stavite? Zapisi besed B. Z. Shumiatskogo s I.V. Stalinym posle kinoprosmotrov. 1934 g.," *Kinovedcheskie zapiski* 61, 296.

[26] N. Aduev, "Muzykal'naia ili liricheskaja epokha," *Kino*, 22/6 (1934).

[27] Lotar', *Leningradskaia Pravda*, 6 June 1934.

[28] Anke Hennig, *Sowjetische Kinodramaturgie. Konfliktlinien zwischen Literatur und Film in der Sowjetunion der 1930er Jahre* (Berlin: Vorwerk, 2010).

[29] Hennig (ibid., 192) sums up the demands of 1934: "Literaten sollen Szenarien schreiben und nicht Regisseure Literatur verfilmen."

[30] In this respect, *Garmon'* is not so different from *Veselye rebiata*, which marked the start of Aleksandrov's career as director of light entertainment with a political message: It contained mildly absurd couplets which were criticized for their inability to hold the film together—this was achieved by the patriotic songs. *Jolly Fellows* was based on an eccentric, secondary musical gesture: introducing "jazz" into Soviet mainstream film and Sovietizing American swing music.

[31] Viktor Shklovsky, "Poetry and Prose in Cinema," in Boris Eikhenbaum, ed., *Poetics of Cinema*, trans. Richard Taylor (Oxford: RPT Publications, 1982), 89.

[32] About "sound attractions" in this film cf. Natascha Drubek-Meyer, "'Zvukomontaž v fil'me *Garmon'* (1934) Igorja Savchenko, *Stumm oder vertont. Krisen und Neuanfänge in der Filmkunst um 1930*," in D. Zacharine, ed.: *Welt der Slaven*, Schwerpunkt: "Stumm oder vertont. Krisen und Neuanfänge in der Filmkunst um 1930", Vol. LIV, 2 (2009), 309–325.

[33] On "Der Szenarist ist Autor", cf. Hennig, *Sowjetische Kinodramaturgie*, 75.

[34] Ibid., 79. This, in fact, is a return to prerevolutionary film credits, which also privileged the writer over the director.

[35] Ibid., 194, 15.

[36] First, http://www.kinokultura.com/specials/9/first.shtml

[37] Ibid.

[38] As Sergei Kapterev pointed out at the Savchenko conference in Cambridge, *Bogdan Khmel'nitskii* exerted considerable influence on Eisenstein's *Ivan the Terrible*. Both directors with avant-garde roots became mainstream figures in Stalinist cinema after a period of disregard. Savchenko's film *The Third Strike* (1948) with Aleksei Dikii was highly valued by Stalin, who saw himself best represented by this Russian actorly persona.

[39] Roman Jakobson, "Linguistics and Poetics," in Thomas Sebeok, ed., *Style in Language* (Cambridge, Mass: MIT Press, 1960), 358.

[40] Thomas Lahusen, Robin LaPasha and Tracy McDonald, *The Accordion, in two Parts*, 2012. I am referring to the unpublished English original.

[41] Aleksandrov's film musicals by the way do not display any guns and rely wholly on "music and good clean fun". His first musical—differently from *Garmon'*—constructs the female star, never a collective body, a choir, a dance or voiceband.

⁴² Previously believed lost, the film was rediscovered in the Czech National Film Archive. Cf. Jana Rogoff's interview with Nikolai Izvolov, where the question of the genre of this short film is discussed (*kul'turfil'm* and *kino-pesnia*). (Jana Rogoff, "O nálezu v NFA, Michailu Cechanovském a filmové hrobařině. Rozhovor s Nikolajem Izvolovem a Sergejem Kaptěrevem," *Iluminace* 2 (2012)).
⁴³ Joan Neuberger, *Ivan the Terrible: The Film Companion* (London: I.B. Tauris, 2003), 19.
⁴⁴ Siegfried Kracauer, *The Mass Ornament. Weimar Essays*, trans., ed., and with an introduction by Thomas Y. Levin (Cambridge, Mass.: Harvard University Press, 1995), 75–76.
⁴⁵ RGALI, f. 1992, ed. khr. 476.
⁴⁶ Evgenii Margolit, "Zaklinanie eposom: *Garmon'* Igoria Savchenko i genezis sovetskoi muzykal'noi komedii," *Kinovedcheskie zapiski* 13 (1992), 120-133.
⁴⁷ N. Izvolov (cf. Rogoff, "O nálezu v NFA," 96) mentions that *Gopak* shows the dancers of the troupe of the Leningrad Gosudarstvennyi akademicheskii teatr opery i baleta (1920-92); before and after called the Mariinskii Theater. Izvolov describes his find of the film in the Prague: "HAPAK (1931, alternativní název PLJAS, česky Veselice) […] vyrobilo leningradské studio Sovkino, předchůdce Lenfilmu. Syžet filmu však nebyl znám – pouze to, že v něm byl natočen ukrajinský lidový tanec hapak v podání tanečního souboru Marijinského divadla (v té době se jmenovalo Státní akademické divadlo opery a baletu), v doprovodu orchestru tohoto divadla pod vedením Nikolaje Rabinoviče."). This theater was the home of classical ballet (for example the choreographer Marius Petipa).
⁴⁸ Kracauer, *The Mass Ornament*, 76–77.
⁴⁹ https://www.ukrainiandanceworld.com/single-post/2015/01/09/ПІСЕННОТАНЦЮВАЛЬНИЙ-АНСАМБЛЬ-«ПОЛТАВА»?fb_comment_id=10668393
⁵⁰ E.g., at the so-called Kolkhoz Olympics (Lahusen, LaPasha and McDonald, "The Accordion.")
⁵¹ "'Жінхоранс'—жіночий театралізований хоровий ансамбль у Полтаві. Створений в 1930 р. у складі 12 дівчат, які виконували пісні з відповідними музиці рухами, дією, хороводом чи танцем. Керували ансамблем подружжя: В. М. Верховинець (1880—1938) - диригент і художній керівник, композитор, фольклорист і хореограф та Є. І. Доля-Верховинець - режисер, у минулому артистка театру М. Садовського" http://histpol.pl.ua/ru/kultura/221-zhenkhorans
⁵² Jiří Hubička, "Voiceband Emila Františka Buriana", 18/4/2011, https://www.rozhlas.cz/archiv/zamikrofonem/_zprava/voiceband-emila-frantiska-buriana--880931(With historical audio examples).
⁵³ https://cs.wikipedia.org/wiki/Voice-band
⁵⁴ An analysis of the polemical discussion of the repoertoires of the accordion in the 1920s can be found in Lahusen, LaPasha and McDonald, "*The Accordion*".
⁵⁵ Jeffrey Spivak, *Buzz: The Life and Art of Busby Berkeley* (Lexington, Kentucky: The University Press of Kentucky, 2010), 73–76.
⁵⁶ Troshin, "A drani podobno '*Garmoni*,'" 295.
⁵⁷ Aduev, "Muzykal'naia ili liricheskaia epokha".
⁵⁸ Later, a similar song-like structure in the film *Lullaby* (Kolybel'naia, 1937, Dziga Vertov) was criticized.
⁵⁹ Joshua First, "Ukrainian National Cinema and the Concept of the 'Poetic'" http://www.kinokultura.com/specials/9/first.shtml 2009.

Cruel Romances of War:
Victimhood and Witnessing After Afghanistan

SERGUEI ALEX OUSHAKINE

We are the poets of songs nobody needs now.
We are still entrenched in those abandoned battle fields;
We are still lost in those unnecessary battles,
Where we left our souls.

V. Pustovitov, Over the River.
From the television program Songs Born in Afghanistan's Land, 1988.

"I did not send you to Afghanistan." This line became a meme in the Soviet Union in the late 1980s. Readers repeated it countless times in their letters to editors. Politicians quoted it in their speeches. Afghan war veterans cited it in their stories, songs, and poetry. Depending on the context, the phrase could mean an ultimate gesture of disrespect towards the ex-combatants or an expression of a fundamental disagreement with the Soviet invasion of Afghanistan (1979–89).

Surprisingly, the phrase was coined by *Pravda*, the main official outlet in the USSR. In 1987, it published an article by Piotr Studenikin, the chief military correspondent of the newspaper. Titled "The Time of Trial," it mostly described heroic deeds of Soviet soldiers in Afghanistan. To create a dramatic contrast to the heroism of the *afgantsy*, as veterans called themselves, Studenikin offered examples of "spiritual emptiness". A nameless group of heavy metal fans was quoted as saying: "What's so special about Afghanistan? People sign up to go there so that they could make big bucks (*chekov podzashibit'*), get some fancy rags (*triapkami pribarakhlit'sia*), and secure some medals to display on their chest, if they are lucky enough."[1] Against these "wily, cynical words", the *afgantsy* emerged as a moral counterbalance. The article emphasized its main point with bold font: "Having traveled the roads of Afghanistan, they came back home with a sharpened feeling of responsibility for the Motherland's concerns and plans." It was truly regretful, the article concluded, that sometimes "our sons who served in Afghanistan" had to face disrespect and indifference. As an example, Studenikin cites from a letter by a certain Yuri Vetokhin from Gurzuf:

For two years I was stationed in Afghanistan. At some point during my service, I got sick. Because of that, I was demobbed from the Soviet Army altogether. When at home, I started seeing doctors, and I was struck by their indifference. One of them told me directly: "I did not send you to Afghanistan."[2]

The article provoked a flood of angry letters, and four months later *Pravda* followed up with a lengthy review of readers' responses. This time, the remark of the nameless doctor in Vetokhin's letter was used as the title of the article. Generously quoting people's letters, Studenikin publicized a whole spectrum of critical issues associated with the Afghan war. *Pravda's* readers pointed to the silence in the Soviet mass media about military losses and described difficulties with local authorities. Most prominently, though, they voiced a clear sense of bewilderment about the discrepancy with which the military campaign was treated by the authorities. A letter from Anatoly Shevchenko (from Kovel), who lost his son in Afghanistan, vividly expressed this feeling. When requested to publish an obituary for his son in the local newspaper, Shevchenko was rebuked by a local party official:

"It is not appropriate to write about people like your son in our newspaper. Your son is not the first one who was killed there, and we cannot write about every death in the newspaper."

But if this is the case, I could not understand what my son has died for, then. The commander of our son's division wrote to us: "[...] Your son fulfilled his international duty with honor and dignity [...]" But if this is true, why did our local newspaper refuse to write just that? Instead, they expressed their condolences on the untimely passing of our son. But our son did not simply pass away. He died fighting... Our son's gravestone says nothing but the dates of his birth and death [...] Why could it not say that he died while performing his international duty in Afghanistan? What are we ashamed of?[3] (Fig.1–2)

The bewilderment and despair—*What are we ashamed of?*—would get only worse with time. In 1989, at the height of perestroika and glasnost, Andrei Sakharov, a famous Soviet dissident and nuclear physicist, emphatically stated during his speech at the Congress of People's Deputies of the USSR that "the war in Afghanistan was [...] a criminal gamble undertaken by unknown people, [...] and we ought to wash away this shame [...]"[4]

Multiplied in the media, Sakharov's speech in the Kremlin Palace produced a strong reaction. Not everyone shared his view; even fewer tried to follow his invitation to atone. Many ex-combatants took his speech as an insult. So, did parents of soldiers who died in Afghanistan. In the archive of the Altai Committee of Soldiers' Mothers in Barnaul (Russia), I found a letter sent in May 1991 from Minsk. A mother who lost her son in Afghanistan shared her feelings with the head of the Altai Committee, whose son also died there:

> I think the most important legacy that we could leave behind is the memory of our children. It is the memory of the glaring misdeed that they were subjected to. Maybe people will revisit this war again at some point in the future. But right now, there is nothing but dirt, and more dirt [...]⁵

Fig. 1–2. Graves of soldiers killed while "performing their international duty" and "official obligations" in Afghanistan. Barnaul, Russia, 2006. Photo by Serguei Oushakine.

In the 1990s, the situation seemed to be irreversible. High-profile contract killings among the *afgantsy* and their allegedly criminal business projects contributed to the formation of a stable sociocultural cliché that depicted the *afganets* as "a killing machine, with big fists, a weak head and no consciousness".⁶

The situation started changing around 2005, when the Russian film director Feodor Bondarchuk released *The 9th Company (Deviataia rota)*. Beautifully shot and well plotted, this war melodrama transformed the state's "criminal gamble" into a story about individual perseverance. "We were retreating from Afghanistan," the film's epilogue concluded, "We have won *our own* war." In 2007, Vyacheslav Nekrasov, an *afganets* and a spokesman for a veteran association, commented on the film, perceptively reflecting the ongoing change: "In the 1990s, we fell into one big hole. We are now climbing out of it."⁷ (Fig. 2)

Fig. 3. A poster for the US release of *The 9th Company*.

By the beginning of the new decade, things became very different. Indeed, the war was revisited and significantly revised. In 2010, the changing attitude culminated in the decision of the Russian parliament to create a new state holiday: "A Day of Remembrance of the Russians (*rossiane*) Who Fulfilled Their Service Duty beyond the Limits of the Fatherland".⁸ The awkwardly bureaucratic name of the new holiday revealed no direct link with the Afghan war, but its date—February 15—did. On that day in 1989, the last Soviet detachment finally left Afghanistan. *Afgantsy* had been celebrating February 15 as their major holiday since 1990. In 2010, it became a holiday for the whole nation.

When do the soldiers sing?

It took more than two decades to revisit the war in order to reframe it, and the celebration of the twenty-fifth anniversary of the withdrawal was quite illustrative for understanding the depth of this transformation. The ceremony was conducted on February 15, 2014 in the same Kremlin Palace where Andrei Sakharov had spoken twenty-five years earlier. This time, the framing of the war could not be more different. The event was opened by Nikolai Patrushev, the Secretary of the State Security Council, who reminded the audience that more than 620,000 officers "performed their military duty abroad" in Afghanistan. Among them, 92 were decorated with the highest Soviet award, the Star of Hero, but 14,453 ended up on "the list of mourning and consolation". He then proceeded to read a letter from President Putin, who praised "the unprecedented feat (*besprimernyi podvig*) of the Soviet troops in Afghanistan".[9]

This evolution of the Afghan campaign from a "criminal gamble" of the government to an "unprecedented feat" of the soldiers is striking. It would be wrong to assume that the transformation is universally supported, or that it is completed, or that it is irreversible. It would be just as wrong to reduce it to its propaganda effect only. The rewriting of the war did reflect the feelings and anticipations of many veterans and their relatives. Without dismissing the role of the state in this revision of the war, I want to look closely at a different force that I think also significantly contributed to altering the narrative about the Afghan war and its veterans. It is not accidental that the 2014 Remembrance Day ceremony in the Kremlin began and ended with extensive performances of songs written and delivered by *afgantsy*. Amateur war songs have been instrumental in modifying the popular perception of the invasion in general and of veterans in particular. I will use their performances to trace the evolution of the semantic and emotional valence of the Afghan war over the last three decades.

Some time ago, Irina Sandomirskaja analyzed the "rehabilitation" of bad poetry during the Stalinist period by looking at Nikolai Zabolotsky's poetic failures. The pressure of the censorship and Power, Sandomirskaja suggested, led to a particular poetic transformation from "*violence* as such to the *language of violence*". "Cruel language", as she calls it, became "the medium and instrument of violence".[10] In what follows, I continue this inquiry by exploring how cruel language was operationalized in the military chanson (*voennyi chanson*). Bad poetry of sorts, this genre was also a response to societal censorship. Less brutal than in Zabolotsky's case, perestroika's revelations forced amateur song writers to look harder for acceptable metaphors and devices. As a result, the experience of war violence was channeled through stylistic conventions of the cruel romance (*zhestokii romans*). With its emphasis on pain and grief, cruel romance offered veterans an affectively charged poetic framework to contain and popularize their narratives of war suffering.[11] Narrating its melodramatic stories on behalf of "the insulted and injured", the romance (and the war chanson) pleaded for justice, truth, and empathy.[12]

I realize that such songs are hardly the most informative medium for studying revisionist projects. The value of cruel romances of war is not in their documentary quality, and Sandomirskaja's reminder is still valid: "testimony is not information, and witnessing is not a speech act that produces knowledge".[13] It is the social and affective impact of these self-made poetic forms that I find important. Through their quasi-folkloric testimonies, *afgantsy* managed to achieve a set of crucial effects that the usual tools and formats could not. As performative acts, songs claim their part of a *public* space and *public* attention. Yet, as poetic constructions, they also gave the performer a certain degree of freedom in creating his own versions of the war. More crucially, songs belong to a *participatory* genre, which could be shared—emotionally or performatively—between the singer and his audience. It is this shared quality of the war song, I claim, that allows the singing soldier not simply to offer his musical number but also to insist on its authenticity in order to require respect for the experience that had inspired the production of the song in the first place. In this case, "every statement of witnessing [wa]s preceded by a vocative: "*You* have to believe me".[14] Cruel romances of the Afghan war, in other words, emerged as affective platforms that could precipitate negotiations of historical experience and enforce the recognition of historical actors (Fig.4). I am interested in approaching these songs and their performances as scripted social actions aimed at making active connections—between experience and expression, between expression and emotion, or between performers and their audience.

Fig. 4. A cover of *Military Brotherhood*, an edition of songs published by the Russian Social Movement of the Veterans of Local Wars and Military Conflicts.

Originally, the military chanson started as a quasi-underground phenomenon. Igor Morozov, who authored several major hits, explained that amateur war songs appeared immediately after the Soviet invasion in 1979. Within the army contingent in Afghanistan, the circulation of *magnitizdat* with songs was barely tolerated by the authorities; any attempt to bring recordings to the USSR could result in serious disciplinary consequences.[15] Perestroika changed the situation dramatically. Supported by the Communist Youth League (Komsomol), the military chanson evolved into a widespread movement, bringing amateur singers, poets, and musicians together. Many of them served in Afghanistan and used the medium of the song to organize the memory of their military experience. Others offered their creative talents, unburdened by the trauma of the war. In 1986, the main "Central" TV channel, available throughout the USSR, began a regular broadcasting of the song festival *When Soldiers Sing (Kogda poiut soldaty)*. Tellingly, the festival's name—itself a line from an old Soviet song ("When soldiers sing, children can sleep without worries"), – was quickly replaced with the more upbeat "Victory" ("Viktoriia").

This centralization of the genre was also its normalization. Song festivals provided the dispersed amateur movement with musical, poetic, and performative role models.[16] They also generated multiple local festivals and talent competitions throughout the Soviet Union. Within a few years there emerged a rather diverse niche centered on the production, distribution, and consumption of the military chanson.

This official romance with the military chanson did not last very long. Perestroika, with its criticism and openness, radically questioned the meaning and the purpose of "the Afghan affair". The collapse of the USSR brought a set of vastly different problems. Reports from Chechnya completely overshadowed the difficult memory of the Afghan war. Removed from television screens, soldiers' songs continued to exist in more democratic incarnations: until the genre went online, many street vendors in the country were offering cassettes and CDs with bootlegged compilations of songs.

The forty-year-old history of the Afghan war chanson gives us a chance to trace a striking poetic evolution of the warrior poet.[17] When the heroic tropes became unavailable for framing the experience and self-perception of the *afgantsy*, they activated two—emphatically non-heroic—narrative strategies. One of them was rather expected. Instead of depicting victories and acts of bravery, the songs drew attention to the victimization that soldiers were subjected to. The other strategy was less predictable but just as effective. By foregrounding war details and by appealing to the memory of soldiers fallen in Afghanistan, the singer of the military chanson positioned himself as a war chronicler of sorts. This dual self-repositioning produced a significant impact: the figure of the *afganets* evolved from "a killing machine with big fists, a weak head and no consciousness" into a radically different poetic subject: a man with a machine gun and a guitar, as a popular website dedicated to the military chanson defined it.

This transformation of the *afganets* into an armed victim and a witness of war was not unique. Boris Eikhenbaum, a leading Russian Formalist, studied a similar poetic phenomenon in 1933. Looking closely at the "battle scene theme" in Russian poetry of the nineteenth century, Eikhenbaum documented a certain paradox:

> Bards of the Age of Splendor associated with Catherine the Great came alive and began rhapsodizing about the feats of Russian military commanders: *The Thunder of Victory, Resound! Rejoice, oh brave Ross*! In real life, the "brave Ross" [i.e. Russian soldier] was far from rejoicing or yearning for a war. This military bravado was shared only by the top layer of the Court and the state bureaucratic elites.[18]

The patriotic saber-rattling ode would serve as a point of departure for literary experiments that approached the battle theme without the patriotic pathos.[19] Yet attempts by Konstantin Batiushkov and Evgeny Baratynskii to present war as "the beauty of horror" were hardly successful:

> There was a need for a different kind of poet. There was a demand for an individualized approach, for an individual tone and voice. Not a rhapsody about heroes, but a hero's own story told by himself. A detailed story full of concrete descriptions of daily life and behavior. The usual combination of "warrior" and "poet" [...] had to be configured in a different way—as a combination of *the professional warrior* for whom war is a natural order of things inseparably linked with his identity and biography, and *the amateur poet* (*diletant-poet*) who writes for his own brothers in arms.[20]

For Eikhenbaum, the poetry of Denis Davydov, a famous Russian warrior in the war against Napoleon, was a welcome solution to the dilemma of the "battle scene theme". In his hussar songs, Davydov did not just poetically transform his war experience into an everyday routine; he also "eroticized war by embodying it in a concrete figure of the hero and presenting it as a limitless outburst of emotions".[21]

Two centuries later, "Afghan songs" reproduced the same aesthetic and political collisions. Written originally by amateur poets with immediate war experience, these songs were also aimed at their brothers in arms, providing a symbolic alternative to the context that surrounded the invasion of Afghanistan. Devoid of epic scale and odic pathos, these songs did not glorify war participants but instead tried to articulate their emotional conditions.

In his recollections of the history of the war chanson, Morozov emphasized that amateur songs emerged in Afghanistan as a rejection of "the military-patriotic, victorious songs created by established Soviet composers". Recommended for performance among the soldiers deployed in Afghanistan, these—official—songs "were absolutely incompatible with the spirit and the character of the war."[22] New—vernacular, unofficial, alternative—songs written by "different kinds of poets", as Eikhenbaum would call them—were created to meet different demands. What they communicated was not patriotic fervor but a sense of dislocation, confusion, and rage.

Like the "naïve writing" described by Irina Sandomirskaja and Natalia Kozlova, these self-made cruel romances were also regulated mostly by the author's experience rather than by his knowledge of grammar and style. Produced from *below*, these forms of discursive creativity nonetheless position themselves *within* the existing system of power relations, trying to challenge its order of things.[23] Just like Davydov's hussar poetry, songs of local wars were military and militant at the same time, juxtaposing their own "truth from the trenches" to the "official and bureaucratic zeitgeist" of the army's leadership.[24] Speaking on behalf of the victim, these songs provided an acceptable framework for asking questions that otherwise would not be asked at all. Aleksei Kruzhalin, a warrior poet who served in Afghanistan in 1985–1986, expressed this function well in his song "Black Vulture" ("Chernyi grif"):

Who pushed the regiments into the meat grinder?	Кто бросал в мясорубку полки,
Who incinerated battalions in the flames of war?	Жег в огне той войны батальоны,
Who drowned our dignity and our laws	Кто в пучине кровавой войны
In the abyss of the river of blood?	Утопил нашу честь и законы? …
Our welfare is built on blood,	Наш собес заведен на крови,
On mothers' tears, on suffering.	На слезах матерей, на страданье.
In Afghanistan, we were called *Shuravi*,	Называл нас Афган «Шурави»,
Being sacrificed to Mars.	Марсу отдали нас на закланье.
Now, we are back home,	А сейчас мы вернулись домой,
Being strangers at this celebration of life.	И чужие на празднике жизни,
And our songs, like a midnight howl,	наши песни, как полночный вой,
Disturb the ear of the Fatherland that betrayed us.	

>Режут слух нас предавшей от-
>чизне.

"Black Vulture" is helpful for revealing a major difference between the two historical incarnations of the naïve song genre separated by almost two centuries. The "limitless outburst of emotions" is typical for both versions, but the directionality and the nature of affect in each case are different. The military poetry of the *afgantsy* does not attempt to eroticize the war. Instead, their songs of anger and distrust foreground issues of culpability, memory, and trauma. Their demands for responsibility would remain largely unanswered. Yet cruel romances of war would continue to "disturb the ear" of the state and society, forcing them to draw a meaningful distinction between the state's criminal gamble and those who were drawn into it.

Victimhood and witnessing

"Black Vulture" shows well how the experience of *subjection* ("being sacrificed to Mars") and the manifestation of *subjecthood* ("our songs disturb the ear of the Fatherland") are amalgamated in this poetic genre. Stories of (self-)sacrifice are often inseparable from disturbing accounts of the war experience. Victimhood and witnessing were two key discursive positions claimed by professional warriors who turned themselves into amateur poets. Authorial control over the song's *content* compensated for the unpredictability of the soldier's war *experience*. The veterans' ability to "disturb the ear of the Fatherland" was preconditioned on their status of "being sacrificed".

Although obliquely, "Black Vulture" also exposes the point where the narrative journey towards the position of the victim and/as witness begins. Namely, the growing frustration about the collapse of fundamental social conventions. In the stanza, the line "In Afghanistan, we were called *Shuravi*" is thematically opposed by the lines that lament about ex-combatants being estranged at home. The word *Shuravi* comes from the Persian "council," i.e. Soviet. What these lines depict, then, is a state of confusion in which soldiers' Sovietness is recognized and acknowledged—but only abroad, by foreigners. At home, they are recognized through various gestures of alienation. The return home is not a simple coming back. It is a re-location that produces disorientation.

Yuri Slatov's "The Password is 'Afghan'" can be read as a response to this increasingly problematic status of ex-combatants in the 1980s–1990s. Written after the army's withdrawal, the song encapsulated the basic affecttive and epistemological paradox of the *afgantsy's* experience:

Climbing mountainous passes, we suffocated from a lack of air.	Нам не хватало воздуха на горных перевалах,
In the Registan Desert, we dreamt of a sip of water.	Мечтали о воде мы в пустыне Регистан,
In medical battalion wards, we screamed from pain.	Кричали мы от боли на койках медсанбатов,
Yet, we cherish kindly the memory of our Afgan…	И всё-таки по-доброму мы помним наш Афган….
In the flow of people on a city street, I'd suddenly notice a familiar face – Tanned, with chapped lips.	В людском потоке улицы мелькнёт лицо знакомое – Обветренные губы, коричневый загар.
Perhaps, I've met him in Kabul, or Šindand, or Bagram. Or was it in Kandahar?	Быть может, был в Кабуле он, в Шинданде иль Баграме, А может сердце вздрогнет при слове Кандагар.
It does not really matter where exactly he came from. But it matters that he is from there; that he has been there. I won't pass him by unnoticed. Instead, I'll just say quietly The only word, the single password: Afgan.	Но мне не так уж важно, откуда этот парень, Мне важно, что оттуда, мне важно, что был там, И не пройду я мимо, а лишь скажу тихонько Единственное слово, пароль один: " "Афган".

Hardship, suffering, and deprivation associated with the participation in the Afghan war are emotionally neutralized here by a crucial affective attachment to the place of the invasion. "Pain" and "kind memory" crystalize around Afghanistan, generating a melodramatic biographic narrative and an emotional account of the military experience. It is instructive to see how the brotherhood of veterans is imagined here as a secret community of survivors united and symbolically protected by "Afgan". The war experience is both a form of security ("password") and an experience of injury ("pain"). Aleksander Khamov—another military officer who transformed himself into a professional singer—offered a striking metaphor for this "secret society" in his song "Forgotten Battalion": […] the gold of our medals got dull/ We are lost like needles in a haystack…/ Desperately looking for its fatherland/ There is a battalion/ Forgotten and left behind in the former life. Lost, marginalized, useless—these definitions of the "forgotten battalion" of *afgantsy* are just slightly less critical versions of the theme of societal betrayal already mentioned in Slatov's "Password". But the song highlights a paradigmatic socio-temporal contrast that became crucial for the military chanson: the shining gold of the heroes' medals in the "former life" would be linked with their current—dull and dusty—existence on the margin. Demobilization was presented as a state of progressive dispossession.

This paradox was historically conditioned. The political uncertainty of perestroika generated epistemological and moral uncertainties. The military invasion still constituted the identity of the *afgantsy*, yet the problematized status of the war resulted in identities that defied obvious classifications. "Was it All for Nothing?" by Slatov is a good example of this state of moral confusion and social displacement:

Was it all for nothing?	Ну разве это было зря
What are we blamed for?	Скажите в чем мы виноваты?
Ten years of war;	Десятилетняя война,
ten years of grief…	Десятилетняя беда.
And we are just ordinary soldiers…	А мы всего лишь в ней солдаты …
Was it really a lie?	Ну разве все это обман,
That a soldier came back crippled	Что возвратился он калекой
Leaving his leg to the dushmans;	Оставив ногу у душман,
Well, sorry, to the freedom fighters	Простите, щас у партизан,
Being marked forever by a trace of pain;	Навек отмечен боли меткой
a fearful trace.	Страшной меткой.

The British anthropologist Mary Douglas pointed out some time ago that confusion is a fertile ground for ritual: "In the disorder of the mind, in dreams, faints, and frenzy, ritual expects to find power and truth which cannot be reached by conscious effort."[25] As ritual performances, songs reflected and refracted societal confusion, offering veterans a tool for articulating their own—however naïve and amateur—version of order. Songs addressed and redressed soldiers' accounts of injustice by shaping them into a relatable story. Such ritualistic re-ordering is never innocent, of course. As René Girard reminds us, "the function of the ritual is to 'purify' violence".[26] The war chanson shows especially well how military violence becomes ritualized and thereby cleansed. Through a series of repeatable poetic formulas, violence is transformed into what, after Girard, could be seen as "good" or "beneficial" violence.[27] Cruel romances of war converted cruelty into tropes and metaphors that facilitated "the exploration, the modeling, the acceptance, and the social construction of the world".[28]

In "Was it All for Nothing?" we can glimpse a gradual (tropological) conversion of bad violence into good. A move from a macro-view of the war (*international duty*) to the soldier's point of view (*traces of pain*) modifies the contour of the war itself. In this and many other songs, the invasion of Afghanistan was rewritten as a sacrifice that was followed by a chain of betrayals. Preserving conventions of the cruel romance, the song unites lengthy complaints about wasted life and tragic fate with an emotional, albeit restrained, plea for compassion:

At some point, I will have a chance	Видно в жизни моей еще будет черед,
To pay all my dues.	за которым наступит расплата.
But this was a war for which	Это была война, за которую счет
the bill has to be paid by the innocent…	Представляется невиноватым…
This is our fate, but it is not our fault.	Это наша беда, но не наша вина,
This is a cruel truth we have to get used to.	Такова в том жестокая правда.
We will drink this bitter truth to the bottom.	Эту горькую правду мы выпьем до дна,
Just do not rush to add more to it.	Только к ней подливать нам не надо.
	Не за тем мы пришли, чтоб кого-то винить,
We are not here to blame anyone.	Дайте время во всем разобраться.
We need some time to get it sorted.	Мы ведь может понять,
Yes, we can understand.	Мы ведь можем простить.
Yes, we can forgive.	Но не трогайте раны «афганцев».
Just leave our wounds alone.	

Vladimir Mazur, "Ia v boiu ne pogib."

Guilt and blame projected onto the *afgantsy* externally are combined in these songs with their perception of being forced to atone for someone else's misdeeds. Indicatively, various attempts "to get it sorted" often lead in the songs to the same result—to a shift from the violence of war to the symbolic violence against the soldiers. Cruelty is not just verbalized; it is re-staged, subjecting the soldier to yet another form of suffering.

I wish my fate was different.	Быть бы доле иною,
It is all like bitter blood now.	Стала горькою кровью она.
What seemed to be war	Все, что было войной,
Turned out to be my fault.	Оказалась – вина.
Ruslan Baranovskii, "Chei ty syn?"	

I've already mentioned that various taxonomic confusions (e.g. war bills paid by the innocent) and semantic reversals (of war into guilt; *dushmans* into freedom fighters) largely stemmed from the basic sociopolitical disorientation of the time. The unrecognized war kept generating unrecognized identities: Soviets—abroad, strangers—at home. The *afgantsy*'s narratives offered multiple scenarios structured around tropes of misperception. Eventually they morphed into a stable plot: the veterans' social dislocation was depicted as acts of public humiliation in which the *afgantsy* are perceived by others as impostors. I will give only one emblematic example, but their list could be easily extended.

In the late 1980s, the group Golubye berety recorded "Awards Are not for Sale". Written by Slatov, the song became a major hit, often featured in CD compilations and anthologies. The story is a dialogue between an *afganets* and a "gray-haired granny." At a train station, "granny" accidentally bumps into a "tanned" young man with a medal on his jacket. She tries to shame him by insisting that it is unacceptable to buy awards in order to get the attention of girls at southern resorts: "You know nothing about wars; take the award off." In response, the soldier covers the medal with his hand—as if to protect it from being polluted by her smear—and drifts away into his memories, imagining a life where things were much clearer: "Suddenly, I recall the Afghan sky, our transparent sky":

I could have told this granny how mountains cried,	Я бы мог рассказать той старушке, как плакали горы,
How snow got red from the bright rubies of blood.	Как снега вдруг краснели от яркой рябиновой крови,
How quick rivers swallowed last screams.	И как быстрые реки топили последние крики,
How the sky threw MIGs in flames on the ground.	И как небо швыряло на землю горящие МИГи.
I could also tell her how grief settles in apartments.	А еще расскажу, как врывается горе в квартиры,
How distraught mothers could not be pulled away from graves.	Как безумную мать не могли оторвать от могилы,
Maybe then, you granny, would get it, without judging.	И тогда ты, старушка, поймёшь и меня не осудишь –
My rewards could not be bought on a market.	Ордена как у нас на базаре не встретишь, не купишь.

The metaphorical dichotomy underlying this dialogue is obvious: the polluted and polluting ("civil") society is contrasted with the clearly defined roles, duties and expectations of the battlefield. The immoral violence of misrecognition is neutralized by the memory of the morally justified violence of war. *Their* society of mistrust is circumscribed by the safe (protecting?) transparency of *our* Afghan sky. Again, the purification of the *war* violence, the transformation of the bad (imperial) war into the save haven of the soldiers is conducted retroactively—through the negative representation of the *post*-war condition. Having graduated from a "school of masculinity" in Afghanistan, the soldiers faced an opposite situation at home, and this discrepancy sometimes was reflected in a heavy politicization of the usually apolitical melodramas of the cruel romance. "Thank you, Mr. President", produced in 1994 by Kaskad, another very popular military band, was perhaps the boldest example of this approach:

Thank you, Mr President,	Спасибо, Господин Президент,
For the empty and dead eyes,	За мертвые пустые глаза,
For the fact that everything is possible now,	За то, что теперь можно все,
but it is impossible to live a life.	А жить нельзя…
For Rus' that was sold for dollars.	За проданную доллару Русь.
For the fear of tomorrow.	За страх перед завтрашним днем,
For our life at the bottom of a ditch	За то, что живем мы в канаве,
Filled with evil.	Наполненной злом.
It was a long, long journey.	Ехали, ехали, ехали долго мы
A long way from one misery to another;	Путь от беды до беды,
From one war to another.	От войны до войны.

This path—from one misery to another, from one war to another—coupled with the perception that "everything is possible now, but it is impossible to live a life" was interestingly translated into the iconography of memorials to the veterans of the Afghan war which started emerging in Russia in the 1990s. These ensembles similarly abstained from celebrating the heroism of the fallen soldiers, foregrounding instead the theme of sacrifice. Many monuments were inspired by "the black tulip", the vernacular name of the airplane that transported bodies of dead soldiers from Afghanistan to the USSR. (Fig. 10–11). The memorial complex in Barnaul—one of the very first Soviet memorials to the *afgantsy*—turned the tulip into a complex metaphor. The memorial's big stone bowl with the eternal flame was surrounded by a metal wreath of black tulips; however, a closer look could reveal another wreath enmeshed with the tulips—a wreath of thorns. The memorial to the fallen soldiers turns out to be a memorial to martyrs. (Fig. 7–8).

Fig. 5–6. *Black Tulip* in Ekaterinburg by Konstantin Griunberg. Photo by Serguei Oushakine, 2007.

Fig. 7–8. Thorns and tulips: a memorial to warriors-internationalists in Barnaul, Russia. Photo by Serguei Oushakine, 2006.

This idea of martyrdom would feed back into the military chanson, too: a special subgenre presents stories narrated by fallen soldiers. Neither ghosts nor spirits, they portrayed themselves as messengers who came back to share with their relatives and friends the story of their own demise. Predominantly though, cruel romances of war reframed victimhood as a form of suffering in the name of those who did not return. In his "I Did not Perish in a Battle", Vladimir Mazur, a warrior-poet with military experience in Afghanistan, linked together survival, death, and cruel romance:

I did not perish in a battle,	Я в бою не погиб, я вернулся живой,
I came back home alive.	мне судьбой предназначено было
I was chosen to sing on behalf of those	Спеть за тех, кто на этой войне был
Who shared that war with me,	со мной,
And who will stay in that war, forever.	и кого она не возвратила.
I will not be able to forget it.	Я об этом забыть не смогу никогда,
My children and grandchildren	будут помнить и дети, и внуки,
will remember this, too.	Потому что война – это то, что всегда
Because war always brings suffering.	нам приносит тяжёлые муки.

While being rather predictable in their metaphors and composition, such naïve romances nonetheless delineated an important narrative development. Being a veteran was not only about being a victim anymore. Also and importantly, it was about being a guardian of the memory of those who were not lucky enough to survive. War songs re-emerged as "notes of survivors".[29] Salvation for the forgotten battalion was discovered in memory and remembrance:

We won't perish; we won't vanish anymore.	А нам уже не сгинуть, не пропасть,
We've managed to escape that zone	А мы с тобою вырвались из зоны,
Where the abyss of the black tulip attempted	Где Чёрного тюльпана злая пасть
To swallow the banner of our battalion. …	Равняется на знамя батальона. …
	Теперь нам, усмехаясь, говорят,
Now, we are told condescendingly	Что мы с тобою призраки и тени.
That we are just shadows and ghosts.	А там десятилетие подряд
But I know where my generation	Отстреливали наше поколение,
Was being decimated for a decade.	Могилы за себя не постоят.
And those graves won't be able to defend themselves.	
	И если кто с упрёками вины
And if someone attempts to take us on a guilt trip	На нас наедет словом или тоном,
Through a word or even an intonation,	Пусть прозвучит у траурной стены:
Let the slogan of the Mourning Wall ring loudly:	«Равнение на знамя батальона,
"Follow the battalion's banner,	Равнение на память, пацаны».
Follow the memory of the fallen."	

Aleksandr Balev, "Ravnenie na znamia batal'ona".

This song by Balev usefully completes the poetico-political evolution of the *afgantsy's* self-perception: from the battalions "incinerated" by war (in Aleksei Kruzhilin's "Black Vulture") to the battalion "forgotten in the previous life" (in Aleksandr Khamov's song), to the battalion that "won't perish and won't vanish anymore", i.e. to the battalion ready to fight for the "decimated" generation (in Balev's song). Or, to phrase the same trajectory in a slightly different way: from war trauma to oblivion, and from oblivion to a new memory of the war and its losses.

As I've tried to show, the military chanson provided the warrior poets with an unusual discursive and affective instrument that helped to re-visit, re-evaluate, and re-order *publicly* their disorienting experience after the withdrawal from Afghanistan. Of course, this reframing of the military past was far from straightforward. And yet, as I suggested, the songs provide enough textual evidence to show how their authors managed to negotiate a contradictory experience by refashioning themselves as victims and witnesses of war. That is to say, by creating for themselves discursive positions from which they could be heard, acknowledged and accepted.

I want to finish with my last example, which succinctly reflects the overall trajectory that I have been unfolding in this essay. During perestroika, the song "We Are Leaving" became the *afgantsy's* anthem. Written in Afghanistan by Igor Morozov, whom I quoted earlier, the song was a symbolic epitaph for soldiers who perished there. Also, it was a dramatic admission of traumatic surrender and failure. It was a song of departure with no closure:

From subjugated mountain peaks,
we descend on earth, one charred step after another
Followed by shots of lie and slander,
We are leaving, leaving, leaving. …

Good bye, Afgan, an illusory world.
We are not supposed to think of you in good terms,
But our commander is wistful for some reason:
We are leaving, leaving, leaving.

Farewell, Mountains. You know better
About our pain and our glory
Would you ever be able, the land of Afghanistan,
To atone for mothers' tears? …

We are not to come here again.
So many of us fell here.
And so many things have not been finished. But:
We are leaving, leaving, leaving…

Current sociologists would be able
To squeeze our biographies in half a dozen lines
But can these scientists handle the East?
We are leaving the East, we are. We are leaving, leaving.

Farewell, Mountains. You know better
What price we've paid here
What enemy we've left unhurt,
Which friends we are leaving behind…
We are leaving the East.
We are…leaving…

С покоренных однажды небесных вершин
По ступеням обугленным на землю сходим,
Под прицельные залпы наветов и лжи
Мы уходим, уходим, уходим, уходим….

До свиданья, Афган, этот призрачный мир.
Не пристало добром поминать тебя вроде,
Но о чем-то грустит боевой командир:
Мы уходим, уходим, уходим, уходим.

Прощайте, горы, вам видней,
В чем наша боль и наша слава.
Чем ты, земля Афганистана,
Искупишь слезы матерей? …

Нам вернуться сюда больше не суждено
Сколько нас полегло в этом долгом походе,
И дела недоделаны полностью, но...
Мы уходим, уходим, уходим, уходим.

Биографии наши в полдюжины строк
Социологи втиснут, сейчас они в моде.
Только разве подвластен науке Восток?
Мы уходим с востока, уходим, уходим.

Прощайте, горы, вам видней,
Какую цену здесь платили,
Какие счеты с кем сводили,
Каких оставили друзей.
Мы уходим с востока,
Уходим...

As in many other songs, "We Are Leaving" interweaves the veterans' profound uncertainty about their role in the war with a deep emotional ambivalence about the significance of Afghanistan to their own identities. "Afgan" again emerges here as a heaven that had been conquered but that has to be surrendered. The *retreat* from the subjugated mountain peaks is a *descent* into a charred and polluting earthy hell. The marines are fallen angels here, mystified by their unexpected fall from grace.

Three YouTube versions of this song—from 1991, from the middle of the 1990s, and from 2013—represent well the evolution of the cruel romance of war during the last two decades. All versions were performed by the band Kaskad. In the earliest video from a concert studio, the story of withdrawal is presented as a combination of despair, bitterness, and barely tamed vocal hysteria. In military khaki, with medals on his chest, the band's intense lead vocalist turns the army's departure into an existential disaster, into his personal account of the unimaginable. Almost breaking into a shrill cry, the singers increase their pitch with each line to emphasize the main message: "We are leaving! We are leaving! We are leaving!" (Fig. 9.).

The second video (apparently from the mid. 1990s) offers a very different correlation between experience and expression. There are no singers in the video; their voices are completely disembodied. Instead, the toned-down soundtrack is visualized as a sequence of stills, photos, and videos that meticulously echo the lyrics. Appearing as objectivist and distanced, this version sent a strong "factographic" message, as if archiving the withdrawal for posterity (Fig. 10–11).

Fig.9. "We are leaving the East": a TV screenshot of Kaskad performing in 1991.

Fig.10–11. Documenting the withdrawal: screenshots from a music video *We are leaving*, mid. 1990s.

The latest video is from a performance by the band in the Kremlin on February 15, 2013. The most somber of all, this version is visually the most striking, but for a different reason. There is no documentary footage or intense vocal gestures. Performed by a combination of Kaskad's different cohorts, the song delivers a solemn yet wistful confirmation: We are *leaving*. Visibly aged and gray-haired, some of the veterans still wear uniforms with medals; one perched on his walking stick. In their performance, the story about the withdrawal from Afghanistan evolves into a rationalized and accepted disengagement: *We* are leaving. And not just the East. It appears that these worn-out veterans are also singing about their own gradual departure from this life: We *are* leaving. (Fig. 12–13)

Fig. 12–13. "We are leaving": a TV screenshot of Kaskad's performance in February 2013 in the Kremlin.

These three videos signpost the key stages in the development of the military chanson. The *afgantsy's* marginalization and oblivion gradually evolved into their ascendance to the stage of the Kremlin Palace, unimaginable a quarter of a century ago. As the despair of the early performance diminished, the social and political acceptability of the "lost war" and its "forgotten battalions" increased. Witnesses and victims of the Afghan war, the *afgantsy* also became slowly vanishing evidence of that war: professional warriors who traded their machine guns for guitars.

Of course, this story of downfall and ascendance was shaped by many more factors and forces. But the cruel romances of war helped to generate a particular symbolic and affective context, which, in turn, made possible much less poetic decisions. In November 2018, Vladimir Shamanov, the head of the Defense Committee of the Russian State Duma, chaired parliamentary hearings about the thirtieth anniversary of the withdrawal from Afghanistan. In his opening remarks, Shamanov basically repeated the formulas articulated three decades ago by Studenikin in *Pravda*. The *afgantsy* were presented again as "a moving force […] that is actively involved in the military and patriotic education of young people in a situation that is far from simple".[30]

The hearings did not produce much except for a decision to draft "a political assessment of the presence of Soviet troops" in Afghanistan. Clearly, such an "assessment of the presence" would be its reassessment. Nikolai

Kharitonov, another member of the Russian parliament, concisely outlined the direction of this upcoming re-evaluation: "It is necessary to state directly that the State Duma considers the moral and political condemnation of the decision to deploy Soviet troops in Afghanistan in December 1979 as inconsistent with the principles of historical justice."[31]

Most likely, this reassessment will complete several decades of ongoing efforts to transform the "criminal gamble undertaken by unknown people" into "the unprecedented feat of Soviet troops in Afghanistan". But it will hardly resolve the basic moral problem that was articulated so well by Anatoly Shevchenko more than thirty years ago in his letter to *Pravda*: If this *was* a feat, why were we ashamed of it for such a long time?

[1] *Pravda*, April 4, 1987.
[2] Ibid.
[3] *Pravda*, August 5, 1987.
[4] *Pravda,* June 5, 1989.
[5] The Archive of the Altai Regional Historical Museum, Barnaul. Fond of S. Pavluikova (not indexed).
[6] Svetlana Aleksievich, *Zinky Boys: Soviet Voices from the Afghanistan War* (New York: Norton, 1992), 94. For more detail about this cliché, see my book *The Patriotism of Despair: Nation, War, and Loss in Russia*. (Cornell University Press, 2009), 166–169, and Eliot Borenstein's *Overkill: Sex and Violence in Contemporary Russian Popular Culture*. (Ithaca: Cornell University Press, 2008), 167–173.
[7] Luke Harding, "It Shows Both Our War, And Not Our War," *The Guardian*, February 9, 2007, https://www.theguardian.com/world/2007/feb/02/russia
[8] Federal'nyi zakon ot 29 noiabria 2010, N-320-FZ. Available at http://www.garant.ru/products/ipo/prime/doc/55070017/#ixzz54UUshe7x
[9] "Kontsert k 25-letiiu vyvoda sovetskkh voisk iz Afghanistana," *Telekanal ORT*. February 15, 2014. Available at: https://www.youtube.com/watch?v=90qog9rHx4U
[10] Irina Sandomirskaja, "The Rehabilitation of Bad Poetry: Crickets, Children, and 'Cruel Language'", *Slavica Lundensia*, Vol. 21 (2001), 153, 165.
[11] Propp defined cruel romance as a form of urban folklore, close to ballads. Unlike folklore proper, it has a literary origin; yet like many folklore ballads, cruel romance also tends to limit itself to overdramatized narratives about tragic life circumstances. Vladimir Propp, *Poetika fol'klora* (Moscow: Labirint, 1998), 66.
[12] V. Smolitskii, N. Mikhailova, eds., *Russkii zhestokii romans*. (Moscow: Gos. Tsentr russkogo fol'klora, 1994), 6.
[13] Irina Sandomirskaja, "Derrida on the Poetics and Politics of Witnessing" in: *Rethinking Time: Essays on History, Memory, and Representation*, Hans Ruin and Andrus Ers, eds. (Huddinge: Södertörns högskola, 2011), 249.
[14] Sandomirskaja, ibid., 251.
[15] Interview with I. Morozov (http://avtomat2000.com/Morozov.html)
[16] Most songs from these festivals have been collected and transcribed on the web site *Avtomat i gitara: stikhi i pesni iz soldatskikh bloknotov*. Available at: http://avtomat2000.com/
[17] Elsewhere, I explored how songs of the Afghan and Chechen wars helped to reframe these imperial campaigns by linking their participants with the legacy of the Great Patriotic War. As a result, in the new millennium the veteran of the Chechen war emerged as "a son of a soldier who took Kabul, a grandson of a soldier who took Berlin", as one of the songs put it. See Serguei Alex. Oushakine, "Emotional Blueprints: War Songs as an Affective Medium" in *Interpreting Emotions in Russia and Eastern Europe*, Mark Steinberg and Valeria Sobol, eds. (DeKalb: Northern Illinois University Press, 2011), 248–276.
[18] Boris Eikhenbaum, "Ot voennoi ody k 'gusarskoi pesne'" in *Formal'nyi metod: Antologiia russkogo modernizma. Vol. 2. Materialy*, Serguei Oushakine, ed. (Ekaterinburg–Moscow: Kabinetnyi uchenyi, 2016), 582.
[19] Ibid., 591.
[20] Ibid., 597.

[21] Ibid., 598.
[22] Interview with I. Morozov (http://avtomat2000.com/Morozov.html)
[23] Natalia Kozlova and Irina Sandomirskaia, *"Ia tak khochu nazvat' kino"*. *"Naivnoe pis'mo": opytlingvo-sotsiologicheskogo chteniia*. (Moscow: Gnozis, 1996), 47–48. See also: Irina Sandomirskaja, "'Naivnoe pis'mo' piatnadtsat' let spustia, ili Na smert' soavtora" in *Neprikosnovennyi zapas* (82) 2012.
[24] Eikhenbaum, "Ot voennoi ody", 598.
[25] Mary Douglas, *Purity and Danger: An Analysis of Concepts of Pollution and Taboo* (London: Routledge, 2000), 95.
[26] René Girard, *Violence and the Sacred* (Baltimore: Johns Hopkins University Press, 1972), 36.
[27] Ibid., 37.
[28] Kozlova and Sandomirskaja, *Ia tak khochu nazvat' kino*, 37.
[29] Ibid., 69.
[30] "V GD proshli parlamentskie slushaniia k 30-letiiu vyvoda sovetskikh voisk iz Afganistana. November 21, 2018. http://duma.gov.ru/news/28893/
[31] Ibid.

Смерть во сне: нарратор и точка зрения в фильме Ларса фон Трира *Europa*

ALEKSEI SEMENENKO

Фильм Ларса фон Трира *Европа* (1991; *Zentropa* в американском прокате) неоднократно оказывался в центре внимания критиков и рассматривался с разных точек зрения. В этой статье мы обратимся к проблеме нарратора, которая имеет отношение не только к толкованию самого фильма, но и к теоретической проблеме повествования в аудиовизуальных текстах. Как мы собираемся показать, в визуальных текстах категория точки зрения (и намеренная игра с различными точками зрения) соотносится напрямую с адресатом и не обязательно связана с каким-либо типом нарратора, выдвигая на первый план дихотомию «зритель-текст».

Фигура недиегетического нарратора представляет собой одну из проблем в нарратологии. Разграничить диегетического и недиегетического нарратора, а иногда и просто вычленить нарратора из текста произведения зачастую весьма сложно. Эта сложность усиливается в аудиовизуальных текстах, где нарратор (особенно диегетический) довольно редко присутствует в повествовании и несет своего рода факультативную (например, жанровую) функцию. Такой визуальный текст, как фильм, в котором присутствует временное измерение, легко обходится без диегетического нарратора, а если он и появляется, то автоматически становится вторичным, а то и третичным по терминологии Шмида,[1] т.е. на самом деле – одним из героев повествования.

В нарратологических терминах основным приемом кинематографического повествования является так называемое изображение «от третьего лица» (Er-Erzählung). Однако подобное сопоставление не вполне правильно, потому что в визуальных текстах доминантой является именно не способ повествования, а *точка зрения*. В шмидовской же терминологии точка зрения безусловно связана с фигурой нарратора,[2] что нам как раз и представляется спорным. В кинофильме камера, которая обычно показывает зрителю происходящее «от третьего лица», – что обычно воспринимается как «безличное» повествование – в какой-то момент может перейти на позицию Ich-Erzählung (например, когда нужно подчеркнуть, что это видит именно какой-то из героев), а потом опять сменить ракурс. Иными словами, важно не кто показывает, а кто видит. Более того, из-за специфики съемки «от первого лица» (при этом часто ручной камерой), изображаемое может восприниматься как «документальное» повествование или же как маркированное субъективное восприятие некой реальности. Возможность одновременного изложения нескольких точек зрения в кинофильме (например, как в фильме Майка Фиггиса *Timecode*, 2000)³ практически сводит на нет функцию нарратора, выводя на первый план именно проблему точки зрения или *зрительной* позиции в терминологии Бориса Успенского.⁴

В этом эссе я хочу обратиться к еще более специфичному случаю наррации, а именно к повествованию «от второго лица», который представляет наибольшую сложность при разграничении типов нарратора. Шмид⁵ пишет, что «в зависимости от того, появляется ли нарратор только в экзегесисе или также в диегезисе, такой нарратор будет или диегетическим, или недиегетическим». Однако из примеров самого исследователя видно, что в конечном итоге эта проблема опять превращается в герменевтическую.

Рассмотрим повествовательную структуру фильма фон Трира *Европа*.

Нарратор в фильме представлен в виде незримого гипнотизера, который вроде бы обращается к главному герою фильма, Леопольду Кесслеру. В самом начале мы видим бегущие под светом фар рельсы под колесами поезда и слышим мерный голос Макса фон Сюдова:

> You will now listen to my voice. My voice will help you and guide you still deeper into Europa. Every time you hear my voice, with every word and every number, you will enter a still deeper layer, open, relaxed and receptive. I shall now count from one to ten. On the count of ten, you will be in Europa. I say one. And as you focus your attention entirely on my voice, you will slowly begin to relax. Two. Your hands and your fingers are getting warmer and heavier. Three. The warmth is spreading through your arms to your shoulders and your neck. Four. Your feet and your legs get heavier. Five. The warmth is spreading to the whole of your body. On six I want you to go deeper. I say six. And the whole of your relaxed body is slowly beginning to sink. Seven. You go deeper and deeper and deeper. Eight. On every breath you take you go deeper. Nine. You are floating. On the mental count of ten you will be in Europa. Be there at ten. I say ten.

К кому обращается повествователь: к зрителю, к главному герою или к ним обоим? Кажется, что это, судя по всему, недиегетический нарратор, потому что он сам полностью отсутствует в повествовании в качестве героя. Однако, как пишет Шмид, если фиктивный читатель тождествен нарратору, то перед нами диегетический нарратор.[6] Тем не менее, нам трудно поверить в то, что нарратор сам себя погружает в транс и отправляется в путешествие «в немецкой ночи», притворяясь «вторым лицом». Герой в фильме полностью подчиняется нарратору, как гипнотизер пациенту и как персонаж автору. Но здесь возникает еще одна неясность – ведь в этом случае нарратор становится идентичен (абстрактному) автору, а это противоречит теории Шмида,[7] который проблему различения абстрактного автора и нарратора также называет герменевтической. В любом случае, в самом начале фильма возникает неопределенность – идентичен ли зритель герою, тождествен ли автор нарратору, – которая, как мы потом увидим, является конструктивным принципом построения текста.

Лео Кесслер появляется в повествовании по воле нарратора. Все происходящее вполне может быть интерпретировано как сон зрителя, который мы видим под воздействием гипноза, и поэтому нам не удивительно, что нарратор полностью повелевает даже чувствами и мыслями Кесслера (а вместе с ним вроде бы и нашими):

> You are listening to the noise of rain beating against a large metal drum. Go closer. There's a fence and you have to stop. You are walking across the railyard, and you've been travelling by train from Bremerhaven, and before that on a ship from New York. You are in Germany. The year is 1945.
>
> […]
>
> You are in Germany just after the war. You are cold. You're covering yourself up with the clothes you have in your suitcase. You are to start your training as a sleeping car conductor. When you have rested you will be on your way to your new job. Get up. Get up and be on your way.

Можно, правда, интерпретировать это по-другому: есть гипнотизер-нарратор, пациент-герой и мы, зрители, которые наблюдают за этим сеансом. Эффект неоднозначности восприятия всего происходящего и постоянной смены точек зрения размывает границы между героем и зрителем, а также сном и реальностью.[8]

О похожем приеме пишет Успенский,[9] говоря о сдвиге точки зрения читателя (зрителя) как о принципе построения композиции текста. В фильме подобные сдвиги случаются периодически: например, нарратор не всегда напрямую «управляет» героем: его голос мы слышим лишь иногда, а все остальное время повествование разворачивается «обычным образом». Мы наблюдаем за всем с позиции безличной камеры и почти забываем про то, что это (наш) сон. Когда Кесслер объясняет мотивы своего приезда из Америки в Германию ("It's time someone showed this country a little kindness"), то мы воспринимаем это заявление как его собственные слова. Однако время от времени нарратор опять дает о себе знать и дает прямые указания герою: "Go forward one month in time. Be there on the count of three"; "Answer the call in the middle of the Berlin Frankfurt run"; "On the count of three you'll faint". Нарратор не только говорит герою, что делать, но и что чувствовать:

> You have enjoyed the tenderness of your wife, but now she is asleep and you are alone. For the first time you experience the fear of being on a train with no possibility of getting off, and no idea of where the journey may end.

В «обычном» фильме либо нарратор мог бы описать происходящее в душе героя, либо сам герой, либо это было бы показано выразительными средствами, однако здесь слова повествователя воспринимаются нами двояко: чувствует ли это сам герой, или все тот же гипнотизер-нарратор заставляет его чувствовать этот страх? В эти моменты наше зрительское восприятие резко меняется: повествование становится не безличным, а вновь приобретает некую точку отсчета, зритель чувствует бо́льшую вовлеченность в действие. Особенно явно эта двоякость выражена в кульминации фильма, когда шантажируемый герой закладывает бомбу под вагоном своего поезда. В конце концов, он же и останавливает часовой механизм, но мотивировка внезапного изменения его действий также дана в виде еще одного указания гипнотизера:

> You have carried out the orders. Now relax. I want you to sink down into the soft cool grass on the railbed. Look up. Look at the stars. See how the stars resemble illuminated cities on a map. Or maybe it is the fading lights of human lives. But you are here to help the lights burn brighter. Not to put them out. At any prize you must make this good again. Run for the bomb!

Жанровое клише (мятущийся герой смотрит на небо и испытывает нечто вроде катарсиса) вступает в резкое противоречие с происходящим. Наше зрительское восприятие опять нарушено: ожидаемая нами психологическая мотивировка подменяется императивом. Мы уже не можем однозначно сказать, почему Кесслер поступает так, а не иначе.

В сцене, где жена Кесслера, Катарина Хартманн, признается ему в том, что она – вервольф, черно-белое изображение вдруг меняется на цветное. На протяжении всего монолога Катарины, снятого традиционной «восьмеркой», мы видим только затылок Леопольда и лицо его жены, снятое крупным планом, и понимаем, что это «просветление» кадра означает распространенную метафору: у героя «открываются глаза». И опять же, в этой сцене нам совершенно не важно, кто нам это говорит / показывает, главное – кто это *видит*, чья это точка зрения. Иными словами, важен не адресант, а адресат.

Возвратимся к нарратору. Интересно, что в конце фильма, когда кафкианский абсурд достигает апогея, и Кесслер и пытается вырваться из него, нарратор «не вмешивается» в происходящее, давая действию идти согласно воле главного героя. Кесслер не выдерживает: "I've got this rotten feeling that everyone's been screwing me ever since I got here. That makes me mad. And now it's my turn to say something!" Он нажимает на стоп-кран, останавливая поезд: "Because I don't want this train to go to Munich, Bremen, Frankfurt or fucking Auschwitz! I want it to stay right here!" На короткое время именно он контролирует ситуацию, а это ему нужно лишь для того, чтобы «немного подумать». Тем не менее, вопреки воле героя поезд продолжает свое движение, и Кесслер не находит иного выхода для себя, кроме как взорвать бомбу. Вагон падает с моста в реку, и Кесслер безуспешно борется за свою жизнь в тонущем вагоне. Вновь мы слышим голос нарратора, который словно бы возвращает действие в привычное русло, давая нам понять, что этот короткий бунт главного героя был неким отклонением, которое и привело его к гибели:

> You are in a train in Germany. Now the train is sinking. You will drown. On the count of ten you will be dead. One. Two. Three. Four. Five. Six. Seven. Eight. Nine. Ten. In the morning the sleeper has found rest on the bottom of the river. The force of the stream has opened the door and is leading you on. Above your body, people are still alive. Follow the river as days go by. Head for the ocean that mirrors the sky. You want to wake up to free yourself of the image of Europa. But it is not possible.

Гипнотический сон обернулся кошмаром и смертью (заметим, что повествователь так и говорит: "the sleeper has found rest"). Зритель опять находится в замешательстве: ведь если это сон, то разве может он кончиться смертью, ведь в конце сна всегда наступает пробуждение, но повествователь запрещает это и главному герою, и нам, соответственно.

Мы смотрим на мертвого Кесслера, и в то же время не можем отделаться от мысли, что Кесслер – это мы, что это был наш и не наш сон одновременно. Инверсия точки зрения и постоянная игра на смене ракурсов и создает тот эффект, который нужен режиссеру: мы понимаем, что травма Европы неизбежна и неизлечима, и все попытки изменить детерминированность событий ведут только к еще большей травме. Метафора поезда, который никуда не может свернуть и идет по четко заданному пути, усиливает ощущение предопределенности и безнадежности происходящего.

¹ В.Шмид, *Нарратология* (Москва: Языки славянской культуры, 2003), 83.
² Там же, 109.
³ В этом фильме экран поделен на четыре части, и зритель на протяжении всего фильма следит за один и тем же сюжетом одновременно с четырех разных точек. Подобное изложение практически невозможно в письменном тексте, где «разноголосость» может быть изображена только последовательно.
⁴ Б. А. Успенский, *Поэтика композиции* (Москва: Искусство, 1970), 7. Ценным является указание Успенского на то, что даже в литературных текстах определенного рода (например, эпосе) вопрос о том, «кто это говорит» не является корректным в рамках этой системы (там же, 215). Думается, что кинематографическое повествование тяготеет именно к такому виду текстов.
⁵ Шмид, 86.
⁶ Там же.
⁷ Там же, 76.
⁸ Как справедливо пишет Хёстерей, "on the diegetic level, the mesmerizing sequence identifies the journey that Kessler and the audience are about to begin as an experience both real and unreal, one in which reality keeps slipping into surreality" (Ingeborg Hoesterey, *Pastiche: Cultural Memory in Art, Film, Literature*. (Bloomington & Indianapolis: Indiana University Press, 2001), 58). Таким образом, метанарратив в фильме несет функцию (пере)акцентуации разных точек зрения.
⁹ Успенский, 168.

The Representation of Public Memory in the Millennium Artistic Projects +2000/-2000, Even by Osvaldo Romberg, and General Reminder by János Sugár and Yuri Leiderman (edition 2)

ANNA KHARKINA

The representation of public memory became a popular exhibition practice after the collapse of the Soviet bloc as a reaction to the official ideological narratives, which previously gave no place to the people's own experience of historical events. Another lacuna of the historical narrative, which was also addressed in exhibitions, was the absence of East European art history in Western art history books. At the same time, these new narratives of public memory coexisted with smaller artistic endeavors which addressed the theme of memory in a way of their own that was not translatable into the logic of general post-Soviet historical discourse.

The proof-reader changed the meaning of the sentence in a way that it became wrong. To change it back to what I wanted to say: "Against the background of extensive international group exhibitions such as After the Wall and Aspects/Position, which sought to fill gaps in the representation both of more private memories and of art from the countries of the former Warsaw Pact, the solo/duo exhibitions +2000/-2000, even by Osvaldo Romberg and General Reminder by János Sugár and Yuri Leiderman tried to shift attention to different stories, thinking about history and our memory about it from the perspective not of a century, but a millennium." This text is an attempt to present a viewer reaction to what Romberg, Sugár and Leiderman tried to say with their millennial exhibitions. I am aware that I may be trying to read into them some meanings which were probably not there, but is this not the only way to relate to history spanning more than 1000 years?

Another purpose here is to ask how artists are testing the ability and right of museums/galleries to act as institutions of public memory. The contradiction between the bourgeois character of the art museum on the one hand and the artistic will-to-freedom on the other hand has been a much-discussed subject during recent decades. In his book *Conceptual Art*, the contemporary art historian Tony Godfrey describes as follows the changes that have occurred in this discourse:

An earlier generation of artists, from Henry Flynt to Robert Smithson, had hated the museum to the point of waging war on it; they saw it as dead—as corrupt as the commercial gallery system. But now artists use the museum. It has become not a site of unspecified evil, but a place to research and negotiate new meanings. If the museum was where things were made special, where meanings and values were discovered and preserved, then it had to be an ideal forum for the critical artist. By the mid-1990s the curating of shows in museums by the artists themselves had become almost a genre in its own right.[1]

Museum institutions and artists, therefore, tried to find a compromise or sometimes a symbiosis, a mutually beneficial way of coexisting. Both museums and artists strive for reconciliation. While artists experiment with the role of curators, museums/galleries are keen to offer their premises as an artistic laboratory space.

The Metaphorizing of History by Public Memory: Osvaldo Romberg's Installation +2000/-2000, even at the End of the Millennium

In many books, old or new, academic or popular, well-structured or written under the influence of transient inspiration, there exist hundreds of definitions of history. One of these belongs to Jorge Luis Borges: "perhaps universal history is nothing but the history of a few metaphors." The exhibition *+2000/-2000, Even* by Osvaldo Romberg, an Argentinian artist with Russian-Jewish roots, opened simultaneously on May 28, 1996 at 6:00 p.m. in different museums throughout the world. In my opinion, this exhibition of Romberg presented an expanded interpretation of Borges' aphorism.

Osvaldo Romberg, born in Buenos Aires in 1938, belongs to that group of the twentieth-century artists who chose the strategy of demystifying the European view on history and art. Commenting on Romberg's major works from the late seventies, Dominique Nahas points out in the preface to the catalogue of the exhibition *+2000/-2000, Even—Mythologies, from Altamira to Manet – An Emotional Analysis of Art History* that Romberg attacked the clichés of "art history and the myths of art-making."[2] The purpose of Romberg's effort was to undermine the monopoly of classical art history discourse by demonstrating that *"history doesn't exist, only artists exist."*[3] Continuing to develop this theme in the 1990s, Romberg experimented with the next question—whether history exists as a consistent story of the people in the universe. By his installation *+2000/-2000, Even*, he testifies that the history of the last 4000 years can be represented only as a set of short morals and separate images.

The techniques that Romberg uses in his installation are collages composed of pictures cut out from art books and journals and short texts from books on history with words singled out to make meaningful phrases. Each *text–collage* unit is scotch-taped to a glass rectangle hanging from the ceiling. Every composition has its own *negative*—a black silhouette reproduced in the mirror reflecting the figure formed by the collage's pictures. By creating this double image, Romberg accentuates the idea of positive/negative evaluation of the same historical event, time, or person, and the idea is also visible in the exhibition's title: *+2000/-2000, Even*. The word "even", as in the grammatical construction "even now/then", emphasizes the regularity of historical events. The back surfaces of the collages are painted in red, yellow or brown, "depending on the 'crisis' condition of the historical moments in each of the civilizations that is being commented upon."[4] Using these techniques, Romberg demands from his viewers that they try to compile all parts of the framed glass rectangles, and later understand the impossibility of this task.

This installation, organized at the end of the millennium in the galleries of fourteen cities—Philadelphia, Kassel, Vienna, Cologne, Saarbrucken, Buenos Aires, Budapest, Reykjavik, Tel Aviv, Santo Domingo, Barcelona, Chemnitz, Odessa, and Tokyo—attempts to introduce the universal history of humankind, and at the same time serves as a discourse on the possibility of the representation of such a history. To achieve the first aim, Romberg makes use of the function of human imagination. The way he joins the pictures and marks text sometimes seems obvious, as, for example, when he composes a collage from a photograph of Jackson Pollock, who was painting at the moment when the photo was taken, and a text drawn from an article on Syria's history—"language is possible without words." Sometimes it is difficult to guess what meaning unites the parts of a collage. By this method, Romberg preserves the viewers' right to invent their own interpretations of the collages. Nahas notes that Romberg's works "force us to reconstitute and recapitulate how we have assembled our interpretations of what we consider 'truthful' in history."[5] Romberg demonstrates that the truth of universal history is the result of our own imagination and the need to create meaningful connections between objects and events. That is why, to achieve his second aim, "the artist forces us to reconsider the traditional relation between text and illustration through time."[6] He problematizes both connections between them that are traditionally taken for granted and the possibility of history as a narrative.

One of Romberg's texts, derived from *Aleph* by Jorge Luis Borges, announces that "within text that is visible, it is possible to identify hidden texts where everything touches everything."[7] This is a formula which can be used to explain his work with texts. Romberg introduces the theme of universal history by claiming that "every image could be replaced with another image."[8] The elements of history are a collection of splinters of real events, a memory and a repetition. *Everything touches everything* in universal history, but the way we know it is by selecting fragments of our memory. "The divine powers of memory are used to remember certain places by means of images."[9] To remember, people need to find analogies, so the realm of history turns into a set of recognizable images and dictums, into metaphors of the events. The universal is represented as a mixture of scattered historical motives, like the collages on glass.

The exhibition itself follows the rules of people's memory of history. Organized in different places all around the world, it reveals and at the same time is subjected to the laws of scattering and repetition. Therefore, the metaphor for all parts of the installation is the Tower of Babel from Genesis, which describes the idea of universal history as such. The image of the Tower of Babel refers to the time when people had one language and one history. The story of their life was universal history. The real Tower is now lost and we refer to it as an ideal. Building the Tower, however, was excessive and contradicted the divine order of the world. God's solution, therefore, was to scatter people by separating their languages—the first in the history of subsequent separations of peoples, which also led to a change in the idea of historical narration. Separated people can have universal history only as a collection of splinters of real events, selected moments of memory.

Romberg accumulates analogies in his project to support the ideas of separation and repetition as the law of universal history as we perceive it today. From this point of view, the Tower of Babel and its destruction is our real history, which we try to grasp in the narration—or rather, multiple narrations—the unity that permanently exists yet at the same time is scattered through the multiplicity of languages which nevertheless seek to describe this history. Universal history is represented only in the form of slivers—memorized words and images. Public memory is the only way for scattered people to preserve universal history, by collecting the broken pieces of the past in the form of common metaphors.

Developing the Tower of Babel theme, Romberg organized the discussion of the Genesis (11: 1 – 9) fragment among contemporary intellectuals: "from a philosopher from Philadelphia to a Chinese critic. From a famous Korean video artist to art student attending the State University of New York."[10] He collected their reflections on the Biblical metaphor as excerpts from different languages. Because, as Marc Scheps, the director of Museum Ludwig, Cologne, puts it "the tower of Babel is in us and everywhere."[11] The Tower of Babel metaphor continues to challenge us. Still, questions remain. The critic Carlos Basualdo asks: "is it being suggested, from the beginning, that there is a relationship between babelic confusion and historical outcome? Is it being said… that there is history because there is confusion and that confusion is indeed the substance of history, of multiple, changing histories?"[12]

Nonetheless, this exhibition is not only about history. It is also about the place of an artist in history. "The world of art cannot function without inheritance,"[13] claims Romberg, because an artist needs images, materials, and cultures to form and represent. Nothing can emerge from nothing in the world of mortals. Yet the writing of history is itself a work of art. "Metaphor" in Greek means "to carry, to transport." Taken literally, this word explains Romberg's technique of singling out words and cutting out images. Carrying pictures and texts from different sources and contexts, he accomplishes a metaphorical act and creates his own context for the discussion. He takes pieces out of their historical environment using the artistic technique of cutting out, marking, and fastening together, similarly to how memory selects fragments from the past and assembles them by means of association, choice, and repetition. In this way, Romberg understands the possibility of contemporary universal history not as the pictures we see or the texts we read but as the act of metaphorizing the past in the public memory, as the sound of snipping scissors in the hand of an artist.

The Representation of Public Memory per se: The Exhibition General Reminder by János Sugár and Yuri Leiderman

The way in which János Sugár (Hungary) and Yuri Leiderman (Russia) use the museum space is different in comparison with Romberg. Their project *General Reminder* is a *nomadic* adventure rather than an installation. It was meant as a trip without any planned end or certain destination. Thus *General Reminder* cannot be completed because the project cannot be fulfilled in the space of a gallery. The realization of their idea is the *continuity* of artistic experiments. *General Reminder* is an exhibition that uses the museum primarily as a laboratory in which two artists try to invent the "catalysis"[14] that allows them to refer to public memory without presupposing the existence of the public itself.

General Reminder was initiated by Victor Misiano, a well-known Russian curator, as an attempt to create the concerted actions of two artists who had not known each other before. In the catalogue, Misiano tells the story of the origin of this project:

> The idea of this exhibition ... was born ... in Budapest in an absolutely private context. We were sitting in a cozy restaurant – János Sugár, Katalin Néray and me – and in the course of the conversation, I felt that Yuri Leiderman was missing. I felt that he would be interested in the subject we were discussing and that he would have a lot to add. I felt also that his personality fit perfectly with the intimate, confidential and intellectually tense atmosphere we had established. Motivated by this feeling of absence, I said that János and Yuri should meet, should be in dialogue and should in some way do a show together. In other words, this show appeared not as a professional project, but as a human fact.[15]

The artists' collaboration resulted in a series of exhibitions organized in five European cities: Budapest (1998), Gdansk (1999), Zagreb (1999), Moscow (2000), and Paris (2000). Each exhibition varied from the previous one, thus representing the development of the artists' cooperation. Sugár and Leiderman provided visitors with hand-drawn "informative sheets" for every exhibition that mapped the installed objects to make them easier to remember and understand. However, their initial idea to supply visitors with information was significantly different. They wanted to arrange a subscription for the catalogue (planned as "informative sheets"), which would be provided not earlier than a month after the exhibition ended. In this way, visitors would have some kind of explanation when they had already almost forgotten what they had seen. Although this idea existed only as a part of the preparatory plan, it characterizes the artists' intention not to help the viewers to comprehend the meaning of the exhibited objects but only to hint at the possibility of comprehension.

The idea of *General Reminder* as formulated by Sugár and Leiderman can be described by two interconnected themes. The first, which was proposed by Sugár, is the theme of "nonsense which has the structure of a meaning but can be understood only later ... which might have a meaning, but it is not obvious, or non-transparent."[16] The second was introduced by Leiderman:

THE REPRESENTATION OF PUBLIC MEMORY

> For me (and it seems for Janos as well) that show was mostly not about ... conceptualization of this or that kind of "communication" which is so trendy now, ... but about something more concrete and particular, about the appearance of stories, images somewhere in the nebulous zone between us.[17]

The artists seem to be speaking about different subjects: Leiderman tries to visualize the public memory of stories unconsciously accepted in the *past*, while Sugár thinks about a work of art that would carry *future* involvement into the sphere of public memory. Yet in the latter case, "future" is taken to be a future understanding of the objects' meaning, which stems from the present, the present of Sugár's artistic activity and its creative results. Leiderman proposes to refer to already existing meanings that unite the sphere of Western narration and, at the same time, remain as proto-verbalized ground for it. Sugár considers the time when the creation of objects defining the meaning, the sense of understanding, only just begins. Both interpret the situation of a visitor who according to their plan would "un-understand" rather than understand the meaning of their works, and this would simulate an ordinary situation of social interaction. Every person plunges into the stream of meanings preserved in public memory, but s/he can understand only a part of them. The rest exist as nonsense, as an un-understandable flood of stories. Leaving visitors' questions un-answered, and visitors themselves in a state of perplexity, the artists seek to represent the nature of public memory itself. Public memory is *something* (and uncertainty here is more correct than attempts at naming) that exists *between* narrations, *between* realized meanings. Yet according to Leiderman, this means not that nonsense has no order but that this order cannot be understood as information distributed by means of communication.

In consequence, to represent their ideas, Sugár and Leiderman had to find a means of their own that lay outside the road of narrative culture but made constant reference to it. The most obvious examples to describe their way of going beyond/between stories are two works by Leiderman: *Lobytangi* and the portraits of Eskimos with tattoos. In the preparatory correspondence Leiderman describes *Lobytangi* as a pack of paper dogs, each of which has its legs in a different position. The artist underlines that dogs should look like toys. He calls this object "Lobytangi," because this name, for him, hints at a "North Asian" word and can be compared with real Siberian city names such as "Neryungi" or "Khatanga."[18] Describing the Eskimo portraits, Leiderman gives an even more detailed explanation of his idea:

> There are images that interested me now that perhaps I'll use in our show. Some of them deal with Eskimos (kinds of hallucinogenic tattoos, which Eskimos might use if they used tattoos – they never do in fact). For me, they are trustworthy signs, the spectator will trust them as meaningful signs, even ethnographic, but having no links to reality—they are absolutely meaningless by themselves.[19]

Both objects can remind visitors of something with which they have already played (paper dogs), or that they have already studied (the culture of Eskimos), something from their almost forgotten past but with small changes. Leiderman's simulation of real things is so skillful that some viewers do not notice that they are looking at fakes. They can believe, for example, that Eskimos really have those tattoos, or that children really play with those dogs. Represented objects create a certain feeling of getting in touch with something already known. Nevertheless, being just pure references to past knowledge and experience, they refer not to certain things but to memory as such. This memory, which covers motives and subjects of common culture, is *public memory*, something that is partly realized but mostly unconsciously accepted in people's knowledge about a common past, about cultural, social, political, economic, and scientific history.

The success of *General Reminder* as an exhibition was at the same time its failure. It was successful because Sugár and Leiderman fulfilled their preliminary decision "from show to show … to investigate and establish some points of similarity and intersections between [their] works."[20] The artists' correspondence gives us many examples of how they managed to find the unity of their ideas in visual form.[21] However, this exhibition could be considered a failure from the point of view of the public, which was left with uncertainty as to the meaning of this event. Yet the artists envisaged a separation of the public from the observation of the entire progress of their actions. In a letter to Leiderman, Sugár proposes: "I see our future cooperation as a challenge, a confrontation of two artistic thinkings, which could eventually fit into a form of a gallery tour. A gesture first of all for ourselves, not primarily for the public."[22] Postponing the delivery of a catalogue, changing the location of the exhibition from one city to another, and hiding the ideas behind objects which just hint at them, *General Reminder* perfectly realized the intention of its authors. The paradox of this exhibition is that it exploits public memory to unify separated ideas, but at the same time, it illuminates the public's traditional activity of evaluating, interpreting, and criticizing. Nevertheless, the ability of the public to criticize is limited because the artists deliberately did not give the viewer all necessary information about the project. Thus, s/he cannot evaluate and interpret. Being totally confused, s/he ceases to be an active perceiver and meaning-maker and becomes a part of the project itself, a social being recalling his/her past in an effort to make sense of what s/he sees at the exhibition. Public memory, which comes to be actualized through the viewer's interpretative efforts, functions as a "catalyst." Un-understanding becomes a part of the meaning-making, though the subject of understanding remains un-defined. Some meaning is being produced in the *General Reminder*, we just do not know who owns it.

Leiderman claims that "we keep our project as a new kind of exhibition that leads somewhere outside of existing paradigms."[23] The public which *General Reminder* tries to tackle exists as an element of the museum institution. Thus, the project is defined by and possible only within the gallery space, which transforms a passerby into a spectator. This transformation asks the viewer to make sense of what s/he sees and to think that sense is somewhere in there to be found. Opposing themselves to the gallery organization and the public, the artists use this opposition as a part of their project. They develop the historical theme by means of their own methods and seek ways to involve visitors in their contemplation of the subject of public memory and cultural history.

[1] Tony Godfrey, *Conceptual Art* (London: Phaidon, 1998), 404.
[2] *+2000/-2000, Even: An Installation at the End of the Millenium by Osvaldo Romberg*, catalogue (New York: a +2000/-2000, Even Publication, 1996), 25.
[3] Ibid., 25.
[4] Ibid., 27.
[5] Ibid., 28.
[6] Ibid., 28.
[7] Ibid., 20.
[8] Ibid., 20.
[9] Ibid., 19.
[10] Ibid., 33.
[11] Ibid., 41.
[12] Ibid., 35.
[13] Ibid.,19.
[14] The concept "catalysis" appeared in the course of preparing the exhibition catalogue, which exists as an edited correspondence between Sugár and Leiderman and includes the notes and questions of the editor, Geneva Anderson. By using a chemical metaphor for aesthetic phenomena, Leiderman explains what he regards as the crucial difference between "mechanism" and "apparatuses." "For me," he writes, "apparatuses don't have commonly held associations to industrial machines, they are just structures or events which are affected by the influence of more than one force. And these forces can have different natures which are alien to each other." János Sugár and Yuri Leiderman, *General Reminder* (Budapest: the Ludwig Museum Budapest, 1999), 9. Each of Leiderman's objects in *General Reminder* is such an apparatus, and the speed of their work (the production of meaning) depends on different cultural catalyses inserted by the artist himself or by a viewer.
[15] Ibid., 3.
[16] János Sugár and Yuri Leiderman, *General Reminder* (Budapest: the Ludwig Museum Budapest, 1999), 7.
[17] Anna Kharkina, "Email interview with Yuri Leiderman." E-mail correspondence, Budapest, Hungary, January 13, 2002.
[18] János Sugár and Yuri Leiderman, *General Reminder* (Budapest: the Ludwig Museum Budapest, 1999), 17.
[19] Ibid., 11.
[20] Ibid., 18.
[21] For example, Leiderman's *Electrons' Names* object echoes the electrical lamps installed instead of one leg of a table in Sugár's installation *The Breakfast of Logos*, or Leiderman's *Skaldic Kennings* pictures, which display the idea of the "proto-boom of the universe right after the Big Bang" (ibid., 5), which refers to Sugár's contemplation of the beginning of the four-dimensional world after the Big Bang, visualized in his *Practical Transparency*.
[22] Ibid., 7.
[23] Ibid., 18.

The Three Great Stimulants

MAGNUS BÄRTÅS

Next spread: *The Three Great Stimulants*, ©Magnus Bärtås 2019

IV

Totalitarianism and the Experience of Experience

TORA LANE

The question of the total lies at the heart of the cultural critique of modern times, be it in terms of totality or totalitarianism. Adorno claimed in his famous 1949 statement about poetry after Auschwitz that the problem of the relation between culture and barbarism consists in society becoming more and more total, and it hardly needs to be mentioned that Hannah Arendt was able to subsume her analysis of the development of political culture in the 1930s under the term of totalitarianism. But the total was not only the object of critique—within the Hegelian Marxist tradition the notion was also considered to be the primary, if not the only tool for criticizing the fragmentation and alienation of society under capitalism, precisely because of the way in which it penetrated all aspects of society and private experience, as for instance in the thought of Georg Lukács or Mikhail Lifshitz. The total, of course, implies a dominance of the all, of everything, and what is at stake in the political and cultural question of the total in modern societies is not the total as such, but, as Arendt also shows in *The Origins of Totalitarianism*, the all/the total as an object of political and/or economic explanation and exploitation. If the notion of the total on the one hand poses the question of the forms and conditions of political and economic domination of the world, on the other, it also implores us to understand the breaking points and forms of opposition or escape. It is, however, precisely with regard to the latter that the notion of totality and totalitarianism poses a radical problem, because it implies the elimination of all forms of escape—indeed. the elimination of the very ground that would make an escape possible. As Arendt understands totalitarianism, it means the elimination of experience itself, because experience would be the ground where the total explanation ought to chafe or even go to the ground. In other words, what is indeed at stake in modernity is the possibility of experience. But then how is it possible to think about experience and its elimination in modernity? Arendt turns to experience as a point of seclusion, a space of intimate and inner reflection where the world speaks as the own, but she does not engage in a deeper discussion of this issue because her focus is the workings of political dictates. In order to further examine the question, I will therefore bring together her thought in dialogue with Bataille's more thorough treatment of the nature of experience in *Inner experience* (1943/54), where he inquires into the nature of experience and its threat in modernity. The question that appears in relation to both thinkers and the total movement of modernity is—can experience be understood as a given?

Arendt

Arendt's analysis of totalitarianism in the third part of *The Origins of Totalitarianism* is based on the role of the masses in the communist and fascist politics of the 1930s. Totalitarianism appealed to and was able to manipulate a "mob mentality"[1] typical of people in the period of early modern democracy, when they first appeared on the political scene. She describes totalitarianism less as a system or a structure than as a movement, or rather, a total movement, which at the same time is a movement of the masses and an atomized movement of individuals. In other words, it is a movement of the all, the masses, controlled by the one, the individual, and therefore it is a uniform movement of the masses, who are blind to their own singular experiences. In this movement, politics becomes only a tool, and all political assumptions must be framed in terms of the total, of "world rule".[2] In other words, politics and the political idea are secondary to the force of the movement. She distinguishes between the totalitarian ideologists (Lenin, Stalin) and the ideology from which they grew (Marxism) by insisting that Lenin and Stalin were more interested in the "logic of the idea" than they were in the idea itself, and she quotes Stalin, who had said that it was the "irresistible force of logic" that "overpowered Lenin's audience".[3] Ideology has a central role or is a central tool in this movement because of the way that it can explain *everything* "scientifically". To paraphrase Descartes, armed with an idea, politics could become the master and owner of history. The subject matter of ideology is, she writes, "history, to which the "idea" is applied; the result of its application is not a body of statements about something that *is*, but the unfolding of a process which is in constant change."[4] This movement instead appears as a movement of history that is conceived as an aim in itself, an idea that can be traced to Hegel. Thus, history is in the paradoxical position of being at once the ineluctable force that carries itself forward and the aim that must be achieved and implemented. In other words, history is a destiny that must be attained through political struggle. Her definition is not so far from that of progress—perhaps not progress as an ideology in itself, but almost and at least progress as refracted through the idea. The perfect totalitarian government is one where "all men have become One man, where all action aims at the acceleration of the movement of nature or history […]".[5] The total appears as the machinery, as a single movement that allows for no singularity, a constant change that allows for no change in its chain of changes, a *One* that is the total of what is in itself beyond and excludes any experience of it.

Thus the problem of mob mentality in the totalitarian societies of the twentieth century was not so much the ideological content of its politics as it was the idealist reading of history it proposed, which inoculated the fanatical members of the movement against both experience and argument, thereby erasing "the very capacity to experience, even if it be as extreme as torture or the fear of death."[6] This statement—that is, that the members of the totalitarian movement can be reached by neither "experience nor argument" does not imply, as the mainstream critique of the problem of totalitarianism holds, that they were impervious to reality, hard facts and real arguments. Arendt is not saying simply that ideology is de-realizing—because then totalitarianism would not hold total sway—but that totalitarianism sidesteps the very basis for any judgment: singular experience. Experience, she says, may well be fiction, which she calls the "reality of experience". Here there is an interesting parallel to Walter Benjamin, who argued in his essay "The Work of Art in the Age of Its Technological Reproduction" that the reproductive art of the cinema will no longer appeal to contemplation, but instead take viewers in its grip and infuse them with a vision of reality. This is the reason why art must become political.

Totalitarianism is built on governing the logic of the movement of the world as an exterior—an exterior and a movement that can be *one* movement and *one* exterior only as long as it excludes the inner. It does so by making people lonely yet incapable of bearing solitude. Solitude is a form of intimacy with the self, where the world, the other, begins to speak in the self, where man "trusts himself as the partner of his thoughts".[7] Loneliness, on the other hand, merely confirms the logic of totalitarianism with its laws of exclusion and isolation, telling man that he does not "belong to the world at all" thereby setting one person against the other in a situation of utter and therefore manipulable antagonism. In other words, experience happens in seclusion, but this seclusion opens for an experience of belonging—it is a form of speaking and acting with the world. Arendt quotes the image of the feast at noon in Nietzsche's *Zarathustra*, when "One became Two".[8] Here, the world or the self as a homogeny opens itself as heterogeny. This is not a nocturnal Dionysiac commune of the all, but a diurnal opening of the belonging to the world in the self. This is also the space of the beginning. And this is what is excluded in totalitarianism.

Bataille

Bataille's *Inner Experience* begins with the epigraph "Night is also a sun",[9] another quote from *Zarathustra,* and indeed the notion of the night and darkness is much more important for Bataille in his understanding of the inner. He emphasizes that *Inner Experience* is an essay in the sense of a sketch, an esquisse, or an attempt to understand the problem of experience in modernity. What is at stake for Bataille is experience as such, and more accurately, as experienced by him.[10] He understands this experience much like Arendt, following Nietzsche, as a form of intimacy with the self, where there is an experience of the common, the shared in the inner of the self, of transcendence, if you wish. However, Bataille approaches the problem of experience in modernity with a vocabulary based on notions of homogeneity and multitude. The inner experience that he seeks to depict is opposed to the alienating homogeneity of the modern world, which is not read in terms relative to totalitarian societies. Instead, he speaks of an experience which is "distanced" from "present-day man" because it is an experience from which present-day man distances himself. This experience is an experience of multitude and communication, but, he also adds, one of entirety and fusion. He seems to be looking for a state akin to the mystical experience that he both confirms and rejects throughout. It is an "inner experience, which is an experience which in itself must be "a sovereign authority". It is "an experience laid bare, free of ties, even of an origin, of any confession whatever",[11] and it is marked by the unknown. In his description of this experience, Bataille also turns to Nietzsche, but this Nietzsche is instead the Dionysiac Nietzsche and his ideas of nocturnal fusion. He writes:

> In experience, there is no longer a limited existence. There a man is not distinguished in any way from others: in him what is torrential is lost within others. The so simple statement "Be that ocean", linked to the *extreme* limit, at the same time makes of a man a multitude, a desert. It is an expression that resumes and makes precise the sense of a community. I know how to respond to the desire of Nietzsche speaking of a community having no object other than that of experience (but designating this community, I speak of a "desert").[12]

The inner experience that Bataille describes is "a voyage to the end of the possible of man",[13] a farewell to the authorities that determine the limits of the possible, but thereby also a restitution of individual sovereignty. And indeed, the question of limits becomes seminal for Bataille. By definition, the "inner" is a space delimited against the external world, and he also opposes the external and internal categorically when he writes that it is necessary to reject external means of dramatization. However, the confines of the inner are at the same time what protects man from his own limits and exposes him to them as the inner opens up for the possibility of an experience of limitless torrential existence and communication with others as outsiders. The inner is the possibility of the experience of the world in its entirety—this experience is ecstasy, a torrential existence, which at the same time is bliss, the "most sublime", the ocean that Nietzsche commands us to be, and at the same time, for Bataille, the desert as a desert of multitude. Why a desert? Allegedly because this place of utmost communication is also the place of utmost solitude. The biblical connotations take us to the hermit, who has left society and the world in order to open himself to God. For Bataille, therefore, the desert is the renunciation of the community communicated in society, the place of lost communication and revelation, because "[...] only revelation permits man to be everything".[14] In other words, the external community of society must be relinquished and renounced for the internal limitless society to take place.

The opposition between inner and outer community and communication is built on a distinction between inner and outer ecstasy. There is an ecstasy of the self in the external commitments of the world, and there is an internal ecstasy in the self, where the self can be regained as an authority and sovereign, and therefore as the place of a voice and communication. In the modern world, this inner life is threatened, because with the death of God, there is no locus for this experience. In other words, religion—and more specifically, Christianity—provided an idea of transcendence for which inner experience plays an important role, and modern society faces the task of thinking inner experience without God. Thus, the question that Bataille poses can be reframed as asking: how can there be an authority for inner experience (or experience as such) after the loss of God? And he poses it in the form of a quest for deliverance from his "prison" and his "tomb" as a desert and a death that he desires.

Although Bataille does not really engage in an analysis of society, he writes that the loss of God does not become a loss to "present-day man", because present-day man has resigned from raging against the dying of the light or of the night, to paraphrase Dylan Thomas, and thus turned himself into "a mouse in the cat's paws: you wanted to be everything, the fraud discovered, you will serve as a toy for us".[15] Present-day man becomes a toy because of his refusal to begin to approach experience and to face the "anguish" of experience. In other words, there remain consequences of the loss of God for society because society has lost the cultural locus where transcendence in and through the self is thought. Bataille, that is, suggests that there is a form of individualized, if not internalized totalitarianism as an internal rejection of the inner. And perhaps, inversely, Bataille's desire for inner experience, for the desert and death, also stems from his contempt for present-day man and the way that his homogeneity takes over language. He writes:

> this reign of words
> continuity
> without dread, such that dread
> be desirable[16]

Moreover, what Bataille sees is present-day man speaking with "poetic facility, diffuse style, verbal project, ostentation and the fall into the worst: commonness, literature."[17] In other words, what Bataille desires is communication, a community without commonness, without literature and the reign of words.

In relation to his description of inner experience, Bataille thus uncovers the processes or movements of experience in relation to the anguish and horror felt before inner experience in the homogeneity of "present-day man". In his view, the rejection of inner experience stems from a preoccupation with "projects". Life is projected in the form of projects, and projects mean "the putting off of existence to a later point". The world of "project" is also the world of "progress", the world in which we find ourselves that follows its own movement and thereby resists becoming ours as experience. And here there is a similarity to the resistance to experience that Arendt finds in totalitarian societies. Namely, both argue that the loss of experience results from a preoccupation with history, time in terms of a project as a total aim in itself. What experience does, and why it gives rise to such anguish, is that it breaks the project, and the refusal to face experience is the refusal to postpone projection to existence to a later point and to face it in its now: "Now experience is the opposite of project: I attain experience opposite to the project of having it."[18]

Yet in the midst of his desire for ecstasy, which appears at the same time as ecstasy in and beyond the world, Bataille also describes experience as "a fissure/ my fissure/ in order to be broken". Here, perhaps, there is another image of experience, or of the experience of experience, not of how the outer world breaks in the inner, divides, multiplies, but simply of how the projection of the world breaks. Thus, experience, or the experience of experience, appears as a fall out of time which nevertheless preserves the "experience" of this time. And Bataille finds a beautiful quote from Proust to describe experience, namely "time made tangible to the heart",[19] which is not a movement into, but an experience of ecstasy in the self. Therefore, what Bataille can perhaps tell us with regard to the study of totalitarianism and the expression of those who have experienced it, is that although totalitarianism can effectuate such an erasure of the very ability to experience, perhaps we can look for points where experience breaks, where the loss of experience is experienced as in the forgotten words of Mandelstam:

> And men can love, men can know,
> even sound pours itself into their fingers,
> but I forgot what I want to say
> and the unbodied thought goes back to the palace of ghosts.
>
> That transparent thought keeps repeating the wrong thing,
> Keeps fluttering like a swallow, my friend, Antigoné…
> And echoes of Stygian ringing
> burn on her lips, black like ice.[20]

[1] Hannah Arendt, *Totalitarianism. Part Three of the Origins of Totalitarianism* (New York: Harcourt, Brace and World, Inc., 1968), 5.
[2] Ibid., 22.
[3] Ibid., 170.
[4] Ibid., 167.
[5] Ibid., 165.
[6] Ibid., 6.
[7] Ibid., 175.
[8] Ibid., 477.
[9] Georges Bataille, *Inner Experience,* trans. Leslie Anne Boldt (Albany: State University of New York Press, 1988) Ibid., xxx.
[10] In the "Psychological structure of Fascism" (1933), Bataille had made a rather opposite reading of fascism than that of Arendt, where homogeneity is accorded to the democratic state and heterogeneity to the abject and the sovereign supreme in the face of fascism. The question of fascism is not a central issue in *Inner Experience*, but the question of homogeneity is.
[11] Bataille, *Inner Experience*, 3.
[12] Ibid., 27.
[13] Ibid., 7.
[14] Ibid., 25.
[15] Ibid., 25.
[16] Ibid., 57.
[17] Ibid., 49.
[18] Ibid., 54.
[19] Ibid., 137.
[20] Osip Mandelstam, *Complete Poetry of Osip Emilevich Mandelstam*, trans. Burton Raffel and Alla Burago (Albany: State University of New York Press, 1973), 110.

On Grammatical Meanings

JOHN SWEDENMARK

The ideal of simplicity in linguistic descriptions (or "grammar") parallels that of mathematics, but it also has a phenomenological foundation, each language being itself a notation, optimised through the ages for the usage of learners and speakers/writers. That is to say, economy is already present in the synchronic system of any human language, and this fact must be borne in mind by anyone who is constructing a description or a notation: it must be adapted to the semiotic repertoire at work; otherwise it cannot be but a foreign intruder.

Consider, for instance, the stranglehold Latin grammatical categories had on modern languages as criticised by Otto Jespersen in his *The Philosophy of Grammar*. Much of the logical enterprise pursued by "generative grammar", including the promise that all languages can be fit into one description ("Universal Grammar") goes back to a similar categorial mistake: a notation that in the end only can represent itself—an empty formalism. (Although it must be said that the continuous defence of Chomsky's general assumptions has brought forth several important insights, such as the role of the determiner as head of the noun phrase in modern languages.)

It is in this perspective that Markedness Theory, as developed by participants of the Prague School in the 1930s, remains a convincing example of what could be achieved—even though the project was largely abandoned after World War II due to new requirements on linguistics, especially those imposed by cybernetics and in general by scientism.

Jakobson's work on Russian cases and Trubeckoj's phonology applied semiotics—the description of differences—to systems that were already semiotic. This might seem tautological, but was in fact a discovery within logic, and helped develop the notion of a "system".[1]

For Markedness Theory, asymmetry is the condition for signification. The unmarked alternative (generally but not exclusively the zero form of a word or word order) contrasts with the exception, typically an ending or an aberration in word order. A good example is the general tendency (with numerous exceptions that have to be explained individually) of third-person verb forms "expressed" by the zero form: no ending.

I put "expressed" within quotation marks because the word coincides with the fallacy that Markedness Theory first and foremost challenges: the assumption that the grammatical category is a semantic content. This is a view that permeated American linguistics from Bloomfield onwards, characteristically by talking about "morphemes" rather than differences. Instead, if asymmetry is chosen as the starting point, language contains "only differences, with no positive terms", to quote Ferdinand de Saussure, whose insights, mediated by Sergei Karcevski, came to fruition in Markedness Theory. When the linguist describes the differences, taking them as her starting point, she comes close to an understanding of the actual functioning of language as it operates in the unconscious mind of the subject—or in the apt expression of the Dutch phenomenologist and philosopher of the Prague School Hendrik Pos: "la conscience originaire".[2]

This "originary consciousness" can be exemplified with the case systems of Indo-European languages. The child learns the basic differences of the case endings and their correct usage. The adult gradually comes to master the more sophisticated, secondary functions of the cases. But for the adult who is intent upon learning a new language with case endings, originary consciousness is not available, so she is doomed to grind away at grammatical categories that are often brought in from a distant, dominant language, until maybe one day they become unconscious enough for the speaker to feel she is fluent.

Many other examples could of course be given. But the lesson to be learned—not least in connection with language teaching—is that grammatical meanings are of another kind than semantic meanings, since they are founded on asymmetry. Grammatical meanings function systematically in a way that is not optimally represented in a table or a pigeon-hole paradigm. And their functioning is unconscious—that is, not open to reflection except by way of linguistic description.

Therefore, the ideal of economy in description (to quote my favourite thinker on graphic design, Edward Tufte "as little ink as possible") coincides with the unconscious knowledge of the subject, her originary consciousness.[3] Markedness Theory began this effort brilliantly, but it did not persevere, or did so rather marginally, in, for instance, the "A-morphous morphology" of Stephen Anderson.[4] It is regrettable that the heyday of semiotics, and especially the insights of Jacques Derrida, gave so little inspiration to the study of the most basic systems of signification, those of grammar, and instead found a home in fields of cultural studies.[5] There semiotics has made very important contributions. It is my hope, however, that linguistics—in cooperation with developments in neurology—will soon return to Prague and pick up the work again. Or rather—I left linguistics twenty years ago to become a writer—this is hopefully already the case somewhere in the world.

I would like to end this complaint with a few clarifications that might make it easier to understand my aim.

Firstly, I understand a language to be a system of systems, each with its own design, some of which function on the basis of asymmetry, whereas others are more nominalist. These systems and their interdependence must be investigated individually for the sake of contrastive linguistics and pedagogy, but they must also allow for a description of the history of systems (or constructions) and their diffusion in time and space. Trubeckoj's last article on the Indo-German problem is a good starting point, as is of course current work outside Markedness Theory on linguistic typology and grammaticalisation.[6]

Secondly, in connection with the foregoing, I would like to stress that binarism is a dead end for linguistic research and for an understanding of the contribution of the Prague school. Grammatical meaning (or originary linguistic consciousness) cannot be captured with plusses and minuses on the basis of a logic of presence and absence. Another kind of logic is possible which (with as little ink as possible) describes the differences in themselves, on their own terms, and is open to an understanding of the many different kinds of difference that cooperate within even a single language. In a speech given at the Free Seminar in Literary Criticism (Fria seminariet för litterär kritik) in Stockholm, I suggested Grothendieck's work with the description of topological aberrations as a good starting point.[7] As a symbol, I used a fresh bouquet consisting of all kinds of flowers, none of which could represent the entire multitude of forms.

Lastly, I cannot but marvel at my own primitive use of the word "description" in this essay. It seems as though I am wishing for a science that represents the facts of the world. And yes, I must confess to a dream that progress lies ahead: that originary linguistic consciousness might be represented in a way that is accessible even to speakers, and above all to learners.

[1] Roman Jakobson, "Notes on the Russian Case System", *On Language* (Cambridge, Mass.: Harvard University Press, 1934/1990).
[2] Hendrik Pos, "Phénoménologie et linguistique", *Écrits sur le langage* (Genève/Lausanne: Sdvig Press, 2013).
[3] Edward Tufte, *The Visual Display of Quantitative Information* (Cheshire, Conn.: Graphic Press, 1983).
[4] Stephen Anderson, *A-Morphous Morphology* (Cambridge, Mass.: Cambridge University Press, 1992).
[5] Jacques Derrida, *De la grammatologie* (Paris: Éditions de Minuit, 1967).
[6] See Nikolaj Trubeckoj, "Grundzüge der Phonologie" and "Gedanken über das Indogermanenproblem", in *Readings in Modern Linguistics*, Bertil Malmberg, ed. (Stockholm: Läromedelsförlaget, 1972).
[7] John Swedenmark, "Skillnad och återkoppling," in *Språk och oförnuft*, Magnus William-Olsson, ed. (Linderöd: Ariel, 2015).

How Lenin's Language Was Made: Russian Formalists on the Material of History and Technique of Ideology

ILYA KALININ

> Lenin spoke his piece with elemental force, rolling his thought like an enormous cobblestone. When he spoke of how simple it was to build a Socialist Revolution, he swept all doubts before him like a wild boar trampling through the reeds.
>
> Viktor Shklovsky (1919)[1]

I will start with a short introduction to the theory of Russian Formalism, stressing its revolutionary social and anthropological pathos.

The theoretical and revolutionary project announced by Viktor Shklovsky in 1914 aimed at much more than to renew philological knowledge, or even the arts as such. In his first manifesto "Resurrection of the Word" (1914) Shklovsky assesses the everyday context of his time as follows: "Nowadays, old art has already died, new art has not been born, and things have died—we have lost our awareness of the world [...] we have ceased being artists in everyday life, we do not love our houses and our clothes, we easily part with life, for we do not feel life".[2] And he conceives of the "new artistic forms" as the means for reviving the lost sensibility towards the material aspect of the world. Thus "the resurrection of words" calls for the resurrection of things.

By putting forward the device of "estrangement" ("defamiliarization") as the key principle that regulates the relationship between art and life, Shklovsky distances himself from the law of "economy of creative forces", the governing principle of positivist aesthetics. It is precisely on the negation of this law of economy that Shklovsky develops the device of "estrangement", which distinguishes between, on the one hand, the sphere of practical ordinary language and "practical" perception of the material world and, on the other hand, the sphere of poetic language and renewed, refreshed perception based on its own "law of expenditure of energy".[3] Such is the general logic of this distinction. Customary actions—from small body movements to prosaic ordinary speech—become automatized due to their repetitiveness. This automatization, during which the perception of words and things does not affect their material and sensual basis, maximizes the economy of effort. In such a way, everydayness—existential and discursive alike—overlaps in Shklovsky with the field of unconscious automatism, which is responsible for the promptness of reaction and reducing the loss of energy. At this point the law of economy encounters a certain boundary, an obstacle, but it does so on its own territory. By falling into an absolute automatism, the quotidian slips away not only from the field of interpretation, but from the field of perception as well. It becomes the sphere of unconscious practices which are absent from the realm of consciousness. Thus, automatized or habitualized perception eats not only things, but human relationships and basic, existential affects as well. By making our use of material objects easier, automatization deprives us of access to their sensual, perceptual materiality; by accelerating social communication, it terminates the sense of community. Automatization dematerializes things and reifies human beings.[4] Automatism (of both perception and action) yields specific mediators in the face of abstract categories and unconscious motoric, habitual and repetitive movements which deprive us of an immediate, sensual, intimate perception of the world. So the Formalists' critique of automatized effects of ordinary life and practical language could be compared to the Marxist critique of alienating and reifying *false consciousness* (ideology).

In Shklovsky's view, art has the task of compensating for the loss of life experience caused by the instrumentalization of perception. Art not only brings back what was lost, but also creates a certain sensual and meaningful surplus. That surplus relates not to the economy of effort, but, on the contrary, to the necessity of spending additional energy on overcoming "the complication of the form, which increases the duration and complexity of perception".[5] Art rehabilitates perception, makes it last longer and transfers the accent from its instrumental function to the intensity of perception *per se*. And if automatization only preserves rather than creates energy, then art, on the contrary, requires additional expenditures of energy in order to perceive the form that has been made more difficult, but it also releases enough energy which is demanded to bring habitual perception out of the sphere of the unconscious.

The Formalists described literature as the destruction of the habits of perception and interpretation formed by everyday life,[6] routine cognitive schemes and ideological habits. In this sense, the mechanisms of literature (or poetic language) and history (in its revolutionary extremum) turned out to be isomorphous with each other. The concept of defamiliarization formulated by Shklovsky becomes, then, not only the universal mechanism of art but also the immanent law of history. While the Formalists tended to bare the poetic device—the "literariness" of literature, the revolution (history *par excellence*) was seen by them as "baring" the historical device of history (historicity) itself.[7] Russian Formalists understood history as a force capable of seizing literature's prerogative to drastically modify traditional patterns of reception. Whereas estrangement was usually achieved in the literary field by revealing and renovating an already "naturalized" literary device, in the fields of history and biography the same effect was created by means of an existential upheaval and social revolution which estranged an already "naturalized" ideological vision. With the declaration in his manifesto "Art as Device" that "automatism eats away at things, at clothes, at furniture, at our wives, and at our fear of war",[8] Shklovsky associated the possibility of recovering the freshness of perception and social life through various forms of excess—including a shocking disintegration of ordinary life.[9] As a result, history and literature subjected each other to deforming reflections.

In this regard, the affirmation of a homology between the mechanisms of form- and meaning-formation that are simultaneously foundational for both art and history did not signify the aestheticization of history and its extreme forms as found in revolution and war. The movements of history and poetic language were identified with one another not via the category of the *beautiful* (as in the case of Filippo Marinetti's poetics), nor via the psychological factor of vitality and communion with the existential basis of reality (Ernst Jünger's autobiographical war experience), nor by means of a manifestation of ethical amorality. In the case of Shklovsky and Russian Formalism as a whole, the basis for this identification lay in comparable models for the production and reception of forms and meanings founded on mechanisms of shift, break, rupture, deformation, irony and parody.

Poetic language, according to Shklovsky, differs from practical language in its ability to renew perception of the world and to support the mechanism of literary evolution. For this reason, the revolutionary leader's language, called upon to renew social reality itself, necessarily possessed not only persuasive force but also the estranging, performative and transgressive power of poetic language.

As I already mentioned, the Formalists' first principles were the opposition of poetic and practical languages and the conceptualization of historical movement as an expression of the work of estrangement. As a result, poetic language, broadly understood, became one of the most powerful engines of historical dynamism. This immediately either cast doubt on the original thesis that practical language (for example, the political language of revolutionary leaders) is purely the sphere of the entropic laws of automatization, or it demanded that the poetic mechanisms of estrangement and deautomatization be attributed to certain cases of the use of practical language. Lenin's language was the clearest example of such a revolutionary (poetic) deployment of practical language.

A special issue of the journal *LEF* published in 1924 under the title "Lenin's Language" was devoted to a study of the political language of the revolutionary subject. Participants in this special issue included representatives of *OPOIAZ* (*Obshchestvo izucheniia poeticheskogo iazyka*, "Society for the Study of Poetic Language") and the Moscow Linguistic Circle—Viktor Shklovsky, Boris Eikhenbaum, Boris Tomashevsky, Yuri Tynianov, Boris Kazansky, and Lev Yakubinsky.

To assess this issue of *LEF* as merely an expression of prudent political servility would be to completely misapprehend both Formalist theory and its intellectual ambitions, which extended far beyond philological knowledge. Description of Lenin's language as implementing the laws of poetic language that had been "discovered by the Formalists" was for them an official opportunity to extend their theory of literary evolution into the sphere of social and political history as a whole. The very concept of the "device" that bares the "made-ness" of a literary work found its application in the critical analysis of ideology (bourgeois ideology) to which the Formalists turned, following Lenin's example. In this manner, ideology (false consciousness in Marxist terms) is revealed as opposed to history (and revolution) in precisely the same manner as automatized practical language is opposed to poetic language. The language of Lenin is transformed into an agent of a poetic, revolutionary disavowal of ideology, the durability of which relies on the ideological automatization of false consciousness and everyday habits of perception (and by the way, in his own critique of bourgeois consciousness and the alienating reification that it produces, Georg Lukács also writes on the "depersonalizing effect of automatization in bourgeois life").[10] In order to reveal the revolutionary, estranging power of Lenin's language, it was necessary to subject it to the same formal-poetic analysis that the Formalists had applied to their literary objects of study.

Boris Eikhenbaum, for instance, had laid bare the autonomous *skaz* nature of Gogol's language in his classic essay "How Gogol's 'Overcoat' Was Made", demonstrating that the aesthetic effect of the novella is founded neither on a mimetic illusion of realism nor on the humanistic utterances of the "little man", but rather on the articulatory texture of poetic language itself, on "the articulatory gesture" as he defines its mechanisms. In precisely the same manner, in their collective analysis of Lenin's language, the Formalists attempted to discover its revolutionary potential not in the content of Lenin's arguments, but rather in the formal "poetic" principles (or technique) he employed.

From the analysis (included in this issue), it follows that for Lenin, the fundamental means for disavowing an opponent's utterances was precisely to bare the device that undergirds their rhetorical constructions (as Shklovsky states: "Lenin's disputes with his opponents, whether with enemies or party comrades, usually begin with a dispute 'about words',—with the declaration that 'the words have changed'".)[11] Here, the orientation toward expressivity, which "resurrects the word," coincides with an orientation toward ideological efficacy. The formal requirements that poetic language must satisfy in order to fulfill its artistic function turn out to be identical with the formal requirements of political language. And, in the language of political polemics and agitation, the formal method itself discovers material that corresponds completely to its conceptions of the laws of artistic language.

To the alien, automatized rhetoric that belongs to an elevated and sophisticated oratorical tradition Lenin opposes his own "lively" or vivid poetics that relies on a shift of perception, a disappointment of expectations, by introducing speech elements from low, everyday language. Strikingly, it is the language of Lev Tolstoy, whose innovation consists in the estrangement of dominating literary conventions and in the baring of the conventional nature of social relationships, that turns out to be the closest stylistic analog to Lenin's political language. Moreover, papers represented in this *LEF* collection insist that the method used by Lenin in the struggle with his political opponents over the consciousness of the masses is none other than the formal method, which reveals the automatization of alien political discourse that replaces the rude material of history with pure ideological *phrase-mongering* (as Eikhenbaum writes: "Lenin's attention is brought to bear […] on everything that has the character of an automatic usage of the word that deprives it of its real meaning".)[12] Instead of deforming the material itself—that is, by making history—such automatized political language glides on the surface of abstract categories and schemes of ideology and compensates for its historical and poetical weakness with rhetorical superfluity ("revolutionary jabbering";[13] in Lenin's terms, *revolutsionnoe krasnobaistvo*). So, Lenin turns out to be one of the most famous Russian Formalists; he bares the device of revolutionary or counterrevolutionary ideologies—which in this case are similar. And just like the Formalists, Lenin—according to their interpretation—equates historical and poetical mechanisms (as Boris Kazansky writes: "For Lenin, a speech, an article, or a book were 'art'—the very art that, according to Marx, was a rebellion").[14]

In Shklovsky's article "Lenin as a Decanonizer", the leader's language is systematically described as poetic language that performs a shift, breaking both habitual contextual linkages and automatized connections between concepts and meanings. "Lenin was called the 'cleaver,' and truly, he sought to cut phenomena apart, to disaggregate them. [...] The better a new term fits, the less useful it is. [...] As soon as a word grows attached to a thing, it ceases to be felt and loses its emotional tone".[15] According to Shklovsky, instead of using an already established conceptual apparatus, time and again Lenin carries out the task of demonstrating the living connection and disconnection between sign and meaning, between word and concept: "Every speech and essay seemingly begins once again from the start. Terms are lacking—they appear only in the middle of the matter at hand, as a concrete result of the work of disaggregation".[16]

In his essay "The Lexicon of Lenin as Polemicist", Yuri Tynianov implements his own stylistic method as developed in his book *Problems of Poetic Language* (1924). He unwinds a dense semantic and stylistic (and even phonetic) analysis of the superior agitational features of Lenin's call to "steal the stolen goods!" (*Grab' nagrablennoe!*) by comparison with the older slogan "expropriate the expropriators!" (*Ekspropriiruite ekspropriatorov!*). According to Tynianov, the "dynamic imperative" effect, which is present in a greater degree in Lenin's version of the call than in the earlier one, is achieved thanks to lexical and etymological richness and a stylistic orientation adequate to the situation. Poetic saturation (including even the phonetic expressiveness of the alliterative unit "gr") is in fact a factor in political efficacy (which here corresponds to poetic features).[17] An orientation toward expressivity coincides with an orientation toward political effectiveness and historical effect.

Polemical in relation to his opponents and persuasive relative to the masses, Lenin's speech parodies the rhetorical devices of the "past historical tradition", bares vanishing relationships between words and things or between words in their own right—the specificity of idiomatic lexical constructions. In other words, Lenin demonstrates that an out-of-date political language has lost its connection to reality and correspondingly, lost the ability to transform that reality (thus Lenin's poetic language follows Marx's Eleventh Thesis on Feuerbach). Here we see the emergence of a circular construction that is typical of Formalist poetics and interpretative techniques: born in revolutionary struggle, Lenin's language becomes a revolution in "the field of declamatory and journalistic language",[18] and for this reason turns out to be capable of intensifying the revolutionary struggle—that is to say, History. So, Lenin's language works not only as a weapon of revolutionary struggle but also as its subject.

Ideology is understood here as a vanishing device, as automatized speech, as a substitution of a "revolutionary jabbering" for a revolutionary and poetic gesture, when a "living word" that renovates the world is replaced by a petrified idiom. The device stops deforming material, the word stops affecting reality, the historical process congeals in an ideological construction. Tynianov depicts this relationship between historical motion and its linguistic representation as follows:

> Every word is the encapsulation of a process, and for this reason it either runs ahead, preceding the process itself, or it lags behind, becoming attached to some particular phase of the process. To prevent the process from congealing in consciousness, to prevent reality from becoming monotone in the prism of the word, one must test the words, baring their relationship with the thing.[19]

This is historical labor connected both with Formalist literary critique and with the critique of ideology that takes place in Lenin's language. But the very study of Lenin's language undertaken by the Formalists bares their own device, explicates their own political message—the declaration of their metalanguage as the language possessed with dynamic historical power.

Here I will turn to a digression of both a theoretical and a historical nature. The post-Marxist currents in Western cultural theory that arose following the Second World War have been associated primarily with the neo-Marxism of the Frankfurt School and in particular with the works of Antonio Gramsci. The early Roland Barthes, of the *Writing Degree Zero* (1953) and *Mythologies* (1957) era, as well as Louis Althusser's classic essay "Ideology and Ideological State Apparatuses" (1970), and finally the works of Frederic Jameson and Terry Eagleton, all figured as pioneering studies that revealed the political dimension in poetic language and in the language of culture in general. In addition to the critical theory of the Frankfurt School and Gramsci's concept of hegemony, these works relied on the ideas of Berthold Brecht and Walter Benjamin. Somewhat later, Valentin Voloshinov's book *Marxism and the Philosophy of Language* (1929) also assumed the role of predecessor in this regard.

Characteristically, the concepts of Russian Formalism that began to penetrate the West at about the same time were almost never read in this neo- or post-Marxist vein (with the rather idiosyncratic exception of Jameson's somewhat imperfect and poorly understood study of Formalism). Barthes himself, who relied at the outset on Brecht and his idea of the "alienation effect" (*Verfremdungseffekt*), had little conception of the genealogy of this notion, which reaches back through *LEF* theoretician Sergei Tretiakov to Viktor Shklovsky.

An analysis of the Formalist description of Lenin's language in comparison with Benjamin's ideas, in particular as expressed in his essay "The Author as Producer", allows us to specify more fully and correctly the origin and subsequent trajectory of these conceptions concerning poetic (or artistic) techniques as a means of production that corresponds to the interests of one or another social class.

Benjamin's ideas as expressed in this essay would later become a commonplace of post-Marxist critique, which identifies the dominant forms of culture as an apparatus (means of production) that reproduces the ideological hegemony of the ruling class. Yet Benjamin himself relied not only on Brecht's work but also on the example of Sergei Tretiakov. In a concise form, we may present his ideas as follows. Intellectuals must realize that the cultural forms that they use (literary techniques, the system of genres, habitual notions concerning nature and the role of creative work) are themselves nothing more than a means of production that is literally owned by the bourgeoisie. For this reason, even when intellectuals attempt to transcend the limits of the class that gave them birth, in an attempt to turn the technical mechanisms that they have acquired through education and acculturation back against the bourgeoisie itself, they continue to reproduce the given relations of cultural hegemony and social domination and subordination that give shape to this technical apparatus. Thus, intellectuals and the proletariat are separated not only by a class identity or distinct political positions, but rather by a cultural heritage and methods of cultural reproduction, which intellectuals attempt in vain to put into the service of the proletariat.

The way out of this vicious circle of reproducing past forms of cultural hegemony— inevitable even when these forms are subjected to criticism, as long as this critique is articulated in the hegemonic language—was envisioned by Benjamin, in the wake of both Brecht and Tretiakov, as consisting in the deconstruction of the bourgeois cultural apparatus—the very means of bourgeois cultural production itself. In this manner, the problem of new techniques (new devices in poetic language) coincides entirely with the problem of finding a truly critical political and social position that allows bourgeois intellectuals to stand on the side of the proletariat. Specific means for this deconstruction and readaptation of the cultural apparatus to the novel task of proletarian cultural construction are found: 1) in the method of montage, which introduces a rupture in representational systems that pretend to organic unity and are characteristic of the bourgeois cultural and everyday mythology (in Roland Barthes's terms); 2) in the interruption of action (as in the theater of Brecht), a device that evokes critical reflection rather than psychological identification, as in Stanislavsky's mimetic, cathartic and bourgeois theater; 3) in the device of collage, applied to quotations of foreign (bourgeois) speech in order to reveal its class motivations; 4) in the transition from pseudo-organic forms of individual creativity to collective, analytical and technologized form, such as a newspaper or the cinema; and finally 5) in the direct involvement of the writer-intellectual in processes of social construction (Benjamin cites the example of the practices of the LEF authors, and above all of Tretiakov, who went out to collective farms and factories where they not only described labor processes but participated in their organization).[20]

It was precisely these elements of Lenin's speech that were subjected to Formalist analysis in the *LEF* collection under discussion here. According to this analysis, Lenin was an exemplary "author–producer" who demonstrated that an intellectual of bourgeois origins who had received a classical bourgeois education and who was linked, thanks to this, to the bourgeois cultural apparatus and its characteristic means of cultural production, might nonetheless deform these very means, adapting them to the needs of the proletariat.

1) Lenin's language continuously employs the device of "the retardation of action", thereby revealing the abyss between the object or concept and the word and rendering it impossible simply to proceed in a purely reflexive manner according to the familiar names of things. "Each time, he establishes a new relationship between word and object, never just naming the thing and never just establishing a new name".[21]

2) Lenin continuously turns to the device of cited speech, which would later become the basis for Brecht's "alienation effect": Lenin's critique of his opponents' political positions is staged as a critique of the language on which they are based. In other words, Lenin demonstrates his understanding of the fact that political tendencies are always founded on specific discursive mechanisms, on specific systems of cultural means of production, as Brecht or Benjamin would say. "Lenin reacts in a definite manner to the style of others and, arguing with his opponents and enemies, frequently pays attention to

the stylistic features of their speech. Each party for him is equivalent not only to a certain worldview, but also to a certain stylistic system of speech" (Eikhenbaum).[22]

3) Lenin (as has already been mentioned in connection with the Formalist emphasis on deautomatization) struggled against the rhetorical apparatus that was characteristic of culturally sophisticated bourgeois writing. Lenin "ironizes regarding the technique […] of concealing a theoretical lack of principle beneath 'streams of language'",[23] as Eikhenbaum writes, and he continues: "Everything that bears the mark of 'poetry' or philosophical elevation evokes anger and mockery in Lenin. In this he is as ascetic and severe as Tolstoy".[24] As a true "author–producer", Lenin sets the cultural apparatus of developed bourgeois rhetoric in opposition to the immediate praxis of social problems and relations: "Fewer pompous phrases, more simple, everyday actions and concern about a pood of bread and a pood of coal" (Lenin).[25]

4) Lenin seeks to bring his linguistic apparatus, his means of production, the subject of which would no longer be the bourgeoisie, but rather the proletariat, into correspondence with the ordinary oral speech of the oppressed: "Lenin, unlike many other political authors and orators, does not prize literary speech, but instead values simple conversational language, introducing the most common, often even vulgar words and expressions into his articles and addresses".[26] And once again: "The 'spirit' of everyday words and expressions […] is a distinctive feature of his style. In this respect he enters into close historical correspondence with the destruction of traditional 'poetic qualities' that was characteristic of Tolstoy and which in a radical new form appears again with the Futurists—in particular with Maiakovskii" (Eikhenbaum).[27] So Lenin, who in his aesthetic taste was a kind of classicist, is interpreted by the Formalists as a follower of the avant-garde movement.

5) Finally, (following Benjamin and Formalist's analyses) we should stress that Lenin's conception of the role of the newspaper as a collective means of production that empowers the worker with his or her own voice requires a separate consideration that exceeds the boundaries of the present paper.

In conclusion, we must affirm that in the Formalist description of Lenin's language we can discern critical intuitions that reveal culture as an ideological apparatus of the ruling class. This critical intuition would go on to become an important part of *LEF* theory regarding new modes of cultural production.[28] Later, through the *LEF* member Sergei Tretiakov, these same conceptions would serve to fertilize the critical thought of both Bertolt Brecht and Walter Benjamin. Finally, they would in turn become an important theoretical basis for post-Marxist cultural critique in the latter half of the twentieth century.

[1] Viktor Shklovsky, *Sentimental Journey*, trans. Richard Sheldon (Dalkey Archive Press, 2004), 24.
[2] Viktor Shklovskii, "Voskreshenie slova", in *Sobranie sochinenii. Vol. 1. Revoliutsia*, Ilya Kalinin, ed. (Moskva: Novoe literaturnoe obozrenie, 2018), 201–211. [Viktor Shklovsky, "Resurrection of the Word," in Alexandra Berlina, ed. and trans., *Viktor Shklovsky. A Reader* (New York: Bloomsbury Academic, 2017), 70.]
[3] See Viktor Shklovskii, "Iskusstvo kak priem," in *Sobranie sochinenii. Vol. 1*, 250–269. ["Art as Device," *Viktor Shklovsky. A Reader*, 73–97.]
[4] See further Ilya Kalinin, "Vernut': veshchi, plat'e, mebel', zhenu i strakh voiny. Viktor Shklovskii mezhdu novym bytom i teoriei ostranenia," *Wiener Slawistischer Almanach*, Sonderband 62 (2005), 351–387.
[5] Shklovsky, "Art as Device," 80.
[6] Gary Saul Morson, *The Boundaries of Genre. Dostoevsky's "Diary of a Writer" and the Tradition of Literary Utopia* (Austin: University of Texas Press, 1981), 352.
[7] Shklovsky's *Sentimental Journey* can serve as a brilliant example of this optics.
[8] Shklovskii, "Iskusstvo kak priem," 256. ["Art as Device," 5.]
[9] Ilya Kalinin, "History as the Art of Articulation (The Historical Experience and Metaliterary Practice of Russian Formalism)," *Social Sciences*. 37. 1 (2006), 43–60.
[10] Georg Lukach, "Roman kak burzhuaznaia epopeia," in *Literaturnaia entsiklopediia*, vol. 9 (Moskva: OGIZ, RSFSR, 1935), 795–832.
[11] Viktor Shklovskii "Lenin kak dekanonizator," in *LEF*, 1 (1924), 55.
[12] Boris Eikhenbaum, "Osnovnye stilevye tendentsii v iazyke Lenina," in *LEF*. 1 (1924), 61.
[13] Ibid., 62.
[14] Boris Kazanskii, "Rech' Lenina (Opyt ritoricheskogo analiza)," *LEF*. 1 (1924), 112.
[15] Shklovskii, "Lenin kak dekanonizator," 53–54.
[16] Ibid., 55.
[17] Iurii Tynianov, "Slovar' Lenina-polemista," *LEF*. 1 (1924), 89–90.
[18] Ibid., 92.
[19] Ibid., 104.
[20] Walter Benjamin, "The Author as Producer," in *Selected Writings*, vol. 2, part 2, trans. Rodney Livingstone and others (Cambridge, Mass.: Belknap Press, 1999), 768–783.
[21] Shklovskii, "Lenin kak dekanonizator," 56.
[22] Eikhenbaum, "Osnovnye stilevye tendentsii v iazyke Lenina," 58.
[23] Ibid., 59.
[24] Ibid., 62.
[25] Quoted in Eikhenbaum, "Osnovnye stilevye tendentsii v iazyke Lenina," 60.
[26] Ibid., 59.
[27] Ibid., 70.
[28] See: Ilya Kalinin, "Ugnetennye *dolzhny* govorit' (massovyi prizyv v literaturu i formirovanie sovetskogo sub'ekta, 1920-e – nachalo 1930-kh godov)," in *Tam, vnutri: Praktiki vnutrennei kolonizatsii v kulturnoi istorii Rossii*, Alexander Etkind, Dirk Ufel'man, Ilya Kukulin, eds. (Moskva: Novoe literaturnoe obozrenie, 2012), 587–664.

"We Have Turned into Wild Beasts. Why Are We Here?": Russians, Assyrians and Kurds in Northern Persia during World War I

DAVID GAUNT

I don't want to weep alone, so I'll say something else too painful to hide.[1]

In late 1917, Russian literary critic, revolutionary, and future founder of Formalism Viktor Shklovsky began a tour of duty as a commissar for Kerensky's Provisional Government sent out to withdraw Russian troops that were occupying northern Iran. His previous experiences of brutality in war-torn Ukraine should conceivably have hardened him, but he was stunned by the total horror that he met. As he wrote in his war memoirs: "I had seen a lot of destruction. I saw incinerated villages of Galicia and houses reduced to pulp, but I wasn't prepared for the sight of the Persian ruins."[2]

Trying to end their "Great Game" imperialist rivalry in Asia, in a convention of 1907 Russia and Britain divided Iran into zones of influence. Russia's sphere was in northern Iran, and Russia quickly built up its diplomatic, religious and military presence along one side of the Persian-Ottoman border. The Shah's government was in debt to the Russians for having put down rebels demanding a constitution. Russia desired northwestern Iran (a province called Azerbaijan) as an extension of its penetration through the Caucasus and as a place from which to get supplies and workforce for the nearby oilfields of Baku. Russia built a series of railroads to enable economic exchange. Through its diplomatic corps, Russia became the de facto ruler of the area, while the Persian political appointees felt free to act with criminal impunity. Many of the Russian diplomats were very pro-Kurdish, while the military officers saw the Kurds as the prime enemy.[3]

Russia was not the only neighboring power aspiring to grab land from Iran. The Ottoman Empire also had its eyes set on annexing the same part of northern Iran and had moved its army across a large swath (varying from 50 to 100 kilometers) of the borderlands. The Ottomans controlled this territory from 1905 until 1912, when their soldiers went off to fight in the Balkan Wars. It was expected that the Turks would soon return. Among the pro-Turkish elements in northern Iran were many Turkic-speaking Azeris and Afshars, and there were also Kurdish tribes that adhered to Sunni Islam and were in opposition to Iran's official Shia version. The democratic revolutionaries despised Russian political interference and were also pro-Turkish and pro-German. The Young Turks, who came to power in 1908, continued the occupation strategy and encouraged these groups to support Turkish claims.

By the time that World War I came to the Caucasus in November 1914, the Russians and the Ottomans had had a long experience of skirmishes along the Turkish-Iranian border. Both also sent spies and gathered intelligence in preparation for an awaited larger conflict.[4] Although the Ottomans withdrew their soldiers from the occupied territories in 1912, they kept up agitation for annexation and in the process made considerable use of jihadist anti-Christian rhetoric to fire up hatred of Russian influence. The Russians sought support among the economically important Armenian and Assyrian Christian minorities, something for which they were later to pay dearly. The centuries-old imperialist Russo-Turkish struggles turned into an interfaith, interethnic powder keg. As Florence Hellot-Bellier observes, the many atrocities and massacres committed during the World War had been announced years earlier, creating a climate of chronic desperation, anxiety, panic and fear among the non-Muslims.[5]

When Shklovsky arrived in Persia in late 1917, World War I had been going on for three years, and Russian-Ottoman friction had exploded into full-scale war in the borderlands with catastrophic consequences for native Muslims and Christians alike. He settled in the city of Urmia, a place that before the war was a booming economic center that sent supplies and laborers to workplaces throughout the southern Caucasus. Once the war between Russia and the Ottoman Empire officially broke out, Iran declared itself neutral, but the imperialist ambitions of the belligerents resulted nevertheless in many battles and a succession of occupations. In northern Iran, Urmia and other towns filled up with refugees from both sides of the border. Harvests were poor, often no crops could be sown in abandoned fields, and even the seed and draught animals had been eaten. Knowing they were to go home, Russian soldiers confiscated, plundered and stole anything they came across that could be eaten or sold. The result was a horrible famine that lasted for years, and in its wake followed epidemic disease.[6] Starving families and orphans flowed into Urmia hoping to find help. Shklovsky realized that the Russian soldiers under his responsibility had become disillusioned, demoralized savages brutalized by the conditions of warfare in this corner of the world. "I knew how cruel the Kurds are," he writes, "but the East in general is cruel."[7] He continues: the Assyrians were no less cruel—for instance, they had skinned several Englishmen alive simply for being interested in ancient monuments. And the Kurds had slaughtered Persians, "cutting off the enemy's genitals and stuffing them into his mouth." When they captured Vice-Consul Alexander Iyas at Sawj-Bulaq, he was beheaded and his head was placed on a spear and paraded as a trophy.

All sides in the conflict committed unspeakably brutal and atrocious acts of inhumanity. The chaos he observed led him to conclude that Russia's military made matters worse. He writes:

> ... in all the hundreds of thousands of soldiers in our army, couldn't there have just possibly been something good, something worthwhile? There was. But the condition of our army – the total disillusionment, the deep despondency, the willingness to resort to sabotage if only to end the war – all this brought out the worst, not the best, side of men.[8]

Russian soldiers waiting to be evacuated plundered the bazaars, stealing anything they could sell or exchange for rubles. No bazaar was too small to be looted and destroyed. Women were raped, houses burned. Even before 1917, the Russian diplomats in the occupied territories criticized their own army for its brutal and disproportionately murderous reprisal raids on Muslim communities.[9] Confronting soldiers making yet another pogrom, Shklovsky was faced down by one of the soldiers who rationalized his comrades' behavior, telling him: "Wild beasts have lived here since time immemorial. We were brought here – and we have turned into wild beasts. Why are we here?"[10] Lacking a better response, Shklovsky urged his government to hasten the army's evacuation "in the name of revolution and humanity."

The violence that Shklovsky observed against the native Christian population of the Ottoman-Iranian borderlands has recently been crystalized in memory into an important part of the narrative of the Assyrian Genocide, on which there is now a considerable body of research. At present there is some international recognition that a genocide was perpetrated during World War I on "Assyrians" (used as an umbrella term for many separate Christian groups calling themselves Assyrians, Syriacs, Syrians, Chaldeans or Arameans) in the shadow of the much more systematic Armenian Genocide. Scholarly research on this topic is, however, limited and diversified.[11] One major issue is that the Assyrians, hardened by centuries of tribal war, were fierce in their resistance and prone to bloody retribution. All sides heroized their warlords, no matter how despicable, and neglected or denied the suffering of other ethnic groups. For activities in northern Iran the Armenians glorified the guerrilla leader Antranik Ozanian, the Assyrians did the same for their generalissimo Agha Petros ("whose name became a terror to the Moslems"), and the Kurds had Simko of the Shekak tribe.[12] Represented as patriotic freedom fighters, their cruelty in battle was downplayed. In the Assyrian case, heroization of their warriors opened the way to accusations by pro-Turkish scholars that the Assyrians deserved punishment.[13] The fact that there was continual violence on all opposing sides also makes it difficult to separate out just who were the perpetrators and who the victims. Can victims become perpetrators? With respect to the Turkish-Iranian border zone, it may be more helpful to speak of a society of extreme violence in which the various enemies become trapped and have no other alternative than to terrorize their neighbours. One scholar speaks of a "zone of genocide" in this part of the Middle East.[14]

In late Ottoman times several hundred thousand Assyrian Christians were split east-west following the twists of the Tigris River, which led to essential differences in churches, dialects and history. Because of geography and conflicts over religion, the various Aramaic-speaking peoples usually had little or nothing to do with each other. Most of the western group belong to the Syriac Orthodox Church, which up to recently populated the farm villages of Tur Abdin in the province of Mardin.

This article, however, deals exclusively with the eastern group that up until World War I lived in the Hakkari Mountains and in the Urmia district of northwestern Iran. They belong either to the Church of the East (traditionally termed Nestorians by historians of religion) or its breakaway Chaldean Uniate Catholic rival. These were the first to accept the term Assyrian and have made it the internationally recognized designation in English, but particularly in France it takes the hybrid form of Assyro-Chaldeans, while the translator of Shklovsky's Sentimental Journey uses the name Aissor/Aissors—a transliteration of the name used in Russian and Armenian—to denote the Assyrians.

A modern memory of terrible atrocities under Ottoman rule unites the various Assyrian groups, but the telling of events differs greatly. Between 500,000 and 600,000 Assyrian, Syriac and Chaldean Christians lived inside the Ottoman and Persian Empires. After World War I a combined delegation of some of the major groups to the Paris Peace Treaty negotiations presented the total figure of 250,000 deaths, which was purported to have been half of the prewar population. Some 40,000 of the victims were stated to have originated in Iran (mostly the districts of Urmia and Salmas), 80,000 came from the province of Van (basically the Hakkari Mountains and surrounding areas). Thus, the number of war-related deaths in the Ottoman-Iranian border zone was estimated at 120,000 persons.[15] This statistic has proven impossible to check, and how the figures were gathered in the chaotic power vacuum between the armistice ending the hostilities in November 1918 and the publication of the Assyro-Chaldean claims in July 1919 is a mystery; the data are most likely based on informed guesswork. Given that the delegation aimed at winning an independent state by claiming severe victimization, the figure is probably somewhat inflated. However, despite exaggerated claims, contemporary sources agree that the number of deaths from fighting, famine and disease must have been very large.

The form that the violence took varied due to local factors and resulted in different outcomes. Some, like the Assyrians of the Hakkari Mountains, managed to save a large part of the people despite huge losses, but finally they lost their homes and lands. Their story is basically one of a militarily organized ethnic cleansing leading to permanent exile.

The "Urmia" memory of genocide concerns the prosperous mixed Armenian, Assyrian and Chaldean population living in the northwestern districts of Urmia and Salmas, both of which bordered Turkey. As already mentioned, this region benefitted from the economic boom caused by the discovery of oil at nearby Baku and the construction of railroads and new cities in Georgia and Armenia. Given the weakness of the Shah's rule, this border region witnessed great tension and conflict between the Ottoman and Russian Empires in the prewar period. Both had ambitions to grab the area and stationed military and intelligence officers there. The Ottomans tried to woo the local Muslims to side with them and even resorted to holy war propaganda. Meanwhile, the Russians sought allies from among the local Christians. Russia kept a small military presence—basically guards for its many consulates. It was not enough to withstand an Ottoman invasion. In the escalation up to the outbreak of war Russian military commanders decided to arm a defence force militia of Assyrian and Armenian villagers living along the border. This was done against the advice of Russian diplomats, who warned that arming the Christian minority would cause a backlash among the Muslim majority and inflame anti-Christian sentiments which were already at the boiling point. Russian officers gave instructions and supplied rifles. In the months leading to the outbreak of war the Assyrian militias fought many skirmishes with Ottoman forces crossing the border.[16]

However, on New Year's Day 1915 Russia pulled out of Iran because it needed its troops more for the ongoing battle of Sarikamish farther to the west. At the same time, the Christian militias were also withdrawn. Suddenly the Christian communities were left unprotected, and thousands fled in panic northwards through the snow, following the retreating troops. From the Ottoman side a makeshift army under the command of Van's governor Jevdet (a close relative of Minister of War Enver Pasha) immediately occupied the Urmia and Salmas districts. The Turks remained in control from January until May 1915. During this time the remaining Armenians and Assyrians were abused—villages were assaulted, and captured villagers were massacred, many women were taken captive, raped, and forced to convert to Islam. Thousands of people sought asylum in French and American mission compounds but were harassed anyway. On several occasions people given asylum were taken out by occupation authorities and hanged or shot.

A large massacre took place in the village of Haftevan (in the Salmas district) at the end of February 1915, when seven hundred adult male Armenians and Assyrians were murdered and dismembered in a humiliating manner. The locals pointed to Governor Jevdet and the Van gendarmerie under his command as the perpetrators, aided by local Kurdish tribes. In what was a premeditated atrocity, the Christians had been summoned to this village under the pretence that they would get ration cards, thus guaranteeing near complete attendance. Vice Commander K. Matikyan of Russia's First Caucasus Army counted 707 corpses. He reported:

> ... with my own eyes [I saw] hundreds of mangled corpses in pits, stinking from infection, lying in the open. I saw headless corpses, chopped off by axes, hands, legs, piles of heads, corpses crushed under rocks from fallen walls.[17]

The official Turkish history of the Caucasian campaign referred to this event as an "unfortunate incident" and put the blame on undisciplined soldiers and local volunteers.[18] Russian Vice Consul at Urmia Pavel Vvedensky reported finding fifteen wells stuffed with beheaded bodies and several barns filled with corpses. Horrified, he could not hinder the Christian militiamen who had relatives among the murdered from taking bloody revenge upon their Muslim neighbours.[19]

Within a few weeks, reports by Russian authorities and foreign missionaries about these and other massacres of Armenians and Assyrians came to the attention of the international media.[20] The Iranian government, weak though it was, registered a strong protest over the behaviour of the Turks. Iranian officials had been forced to witness repeated acts of

> ... violence committed by your soldiers, who in the course of battle have pillaged many villages, torched many others, and reduced all of the inhabitants to a state of misery. This violence is most noted in the areas where there are

many villages inhabited by Christians, where the population has been violated and mercilessly massacred.[21]

Thus, according to the Urmia genocide narrative, in 1915 an ill-prepared Ottoman military occupation unleashed local hostility, which in turn set the local Armenians and Assyrians on a campaign of punitive reprisals.

At the Paris Peace Conference, the Assyro-Chaldean delegation estimated the number of deaths among the Assyrian and Chaldean communities for the entire period 1914–1918 in northern Iran as 40,000. There is no estimate of how many Muslims were killed, though they must have numbered in the tens of thousands. Lacking statistics, Kurdish losses were expressed in the form of destroyed villages and disappeared families: fifty-two of eighty-one Baradost tribe villages destroyed and its 1,080 families reduced to 157; the small Kuwaruk tribe reduced to seven families from an original 150; of the 2,000 houses of Rawanduz, only 60 remained. This ruination was attributed to both Russians and Ottomans.[22]

A second and independent narrative is that of the Assyrian tribesmen originating in the Hakkari Mountains, which lie on the Turkish side of the border. These mountaineers had a semi-feudal society divided into tribes, each led by a chief. A figure called the Mar Shimun ruled over all the tribes. As the patriarch of the Church of the East, the incumbent Mar Shimun Benjamin XXI was not just the religious leader but also a secular power and the tribal military commander. The tribes had the Ottoman legal status of *aşiret*, which meant that they were self-governing, so members could carry weapons despite being non-Muslims. Very fierce in their ways, they were well accustomed to Kurdish tribal warfare, cattle theft and clan feuds.[23] Although they seem to have been able to defend themselves before, by the late nineteenth century the Assyrians were obviously on the losing end of intertribal warfare, and Ottoman officials ignored their grievances. In this new situation the Assyrians began secret dealings with Russian agents and received promises of arms and even support for an independent state.[24] The Ottomans became aware of these negotiations, and shortly before war with Russia was declared, Interior Minister Talaat ordered that the Assyrians be punished for conspiring with the enemy—starting with those closest to the border with Iran—to be deported to central Anatolia and dispersed so that there would be few of them in any one village.[25] This order could not be implemented due to the outbreak of war. Instead, tribal militias attacked Assyrian villages, killing some inhabitants and forcing the others to flee. The Assyrian tribes agreed to co-operate with Russian detachments that were advancing in May 1915 to relieve the Armenians besieged in Van. The Assyrians were assigned the task of stopping an Ottoman force on its way towards Van. The tribes succeeded, but in revenge the defeated soldiers went on a rampage, slaying Christians of all faiths in the towns and surroundings of Bashkala, Siirt and Bitlis. Infuriated, Talaat ordered that the Assyrians be pushed out of Hakkari, never to return.[26] The ethnic cleansing of the Assyrians was accomplished during the summer of 1915 through a massive invasion of regular troops together with neighbouring Kurdish tribes. Although the Christian tribesmen fought back fiercely, they were outnumbered and outgunned, which forced them to flee first up to the highest peaks and finally to make a mass exodus to Iran, losing many lives on the way. They were at first welcomed in Iran and got support from foreign philanthropic organizations. However, as the refugees resumed collaboration with the Russians and were favoured by them, the attitude of the local Muslims changed into animosity. As one observer later put it: "they were as welcome as the children of Israel to Balak on the plain of Moab."[27]

After September 1915 the Assyrian Urmia and Hakkari genocidal narratives merge and become intertwined until the end of the war. Inside Iran the tribesmen volunteered to co-operate with the Russian army. The existing Christian militia and the Assyrian warriors combined into battalions commanded by mountaineer chiefs and fought side by side with the Russians in many campaigns throughout the border zone. The Assyrians were only used to tribal warfare and they had no idea of military discipline and were out of control once a battle had begun.[28] The civilian Christians of Urmia and Salmas were in a very insecure position as attacks on villages, shooting, plundering, kidnapping, and massacres continued. The situation degenerated as the Russian revolutions of 1917 caused its army to disintegrate, for the soldiers only wanted to go home. This was the moment that Viktor Shklovsky arrived on the scene. To keep the peace after the Russian withdrawal, the Assyrian and Armenian brigades were assigned to carry on alone with leftover Russian supplies.[29] They had some limited aid from a few Russian officers who remained as advisers, and the various foreign missionaries plus the French sent a military advisor Nicolas Gasfield and an ambulance corps to set up a hospital.[30]

As the Russians pulled out, the insecure Christian militias behaved very badly in their policing function, killing Muslims in and around Urmia. Totally unorganized Assyrian brigands usually referred to as "Assyrians from Caucasus" (presumably meaning not locals) roamed the countryside pillaging and massacring Muslim villages. In Urmia, the townsmen were in turmoil. Civilians were kept awake by gunshots, and the governor as well as Muslim leaders plotted to annihilate the non-Muslims. Paul Caujole, the head medical doctor working at the French hospital set up in the Muslim sector, thought that he was witnessing a "horror that exceeds all of the visions that could be imagined by Baudelaire… Persia is the paradise for assassins."[31] Inspired by the governor, an alliance of Persian revolutionaries and Muslim clerics conspired to wipe out Urmia's Assyrians and Armenians and set a date for an uprising. On 22 February 1918 a force of Persian Cossacks invaded the town and everyone who could ran for their rifles and began shooting. From 22 to 24 February there were fierce house-to-house street battles between Christian militias and armed Muslims. In the end the Assyrians won, but hundreds, perhaps thousands of people had been killed. According to Caujole, most of the victims were Muslim, and even pro-Assyrian accounts agree that few Assyrians died in these battles. French military advisor to the Assyrians, Gasfield, called it an "orgy of bestial cruelty". The main conspirators went in procession to the American mission and asked for and got asylum.

A peace agreement was negotiated between Urmia's Muslims and the Mar Shimun representing the Christians on 25 February. This did not stop the violence. The official newspapers printed incendiary anti-Assyrian editorials, the gist of which was that the Assyrians had been ungrateful to Iran for giving them asylum and now had begun killing innocent Iranian civilians. These outlaws must be taught a lesson.[32] On 16 March the Mar Shimun and his guards had been murdered in an ambush by Simko, the chief of the Shekak tribe. The assassination was probably instigated by agents of the Persian government. This led the Assyrians to go on a vicious rampage to avenge the killing of their leader. In the course of the following weeks the Christians killed many leading Persian politicians, officials and clerics. Gasfield reported of a "veritable anti-kurdish pogrom".[33] Throughout northern Persia a state of anarchy reigned from which it would never recover. The Kurds retaliated with massacres of Christians in Salmas (15 June) and Urmia (31 July). Eyewitness Mary Shedd, wife of the leader of the American mission, summarized: "The situation was so complex, so chaotic, so barbarous and full of change, that it is difficult to make it comprehensible to those who did not live through it."[34]

In July 1918 an Ottoman army invaded the region, and local Muslims joined it to surround Urmia. In complete panic, tens of thousands of desperate Assyrian and Armenian civilians fled southwards hoping to get to safety behind British lines. During this long march the defenceless refugees were under constant attack both from Turks and Persian Kurds which only ceased after they met up with the British. Most of the survivors were put in sprawling tent camps at Baquba in Iraq. Placed there were an estimated 25,000 Assyrians from Hakkari, 10,000 Assyrians from Iran and 15,000 Armenians.[35] Conditions were dire, with a reported 7,000 Assyrians dying there. The very first monument to Assyrian victims of the war was established by Agha Petros and dedicated to the memory of suffering in the camp. Many of the men were recruited as soldiers into the British Levy (Local Enlisted Volunteer Yeomanry) to brutally supress Kurdish and Arab rebellions. Armed and supported by the British, a serious attempt by Agha Petros and Assyrian warriors to return to Hakkari and Urmia was averted by the Turkish military. The final remaining Assyrians were forced out of Hakkari.[36]

Collaborating with the British had dire consequences, for when the British left Iraq the Assyrians were attacked by the new Iraqi army. The Assyrian village of Simile was the scene of a bloody siege from 7 to 11 August 1933, and 7 August has now become the official day of Assyrian martyrdom. These attacks were particularly outrageous, as they had been predicted years in advance, and the British and the League of Nations had promised the Assyrians relocation to a safer homeland, but nothing came of these plans.

To begin with, exiled Hakkari and Urmia Assyrians seldom used a rhetoric of "victimization"; instead, they created a discourse about a heroic war that they, despite great bravery, had lost. Often their main protagonist at the Paris Peace Treaty, Joel Werda, referred to them as a "belligerent people" fighting on the side of the allies.[37] They had won many battles but lost the war. They now had their modern martyrs and warrior heroes. They took pride in their military prowess, calling themselves the "smallest ally," but they complained bitterly that they had gone unrewarded in the peace talks. They repeatedly insisted that they had been betrayed by the British and the League of Nations.[38]

For a scholar of genocide, the story of the Assyrians during World War I is a challenge. The United Nations' definition of genocide implies that it is an intentional action taken by a government to destroy a minority characterized by racial, religious or ethnic difference from the majority. It should also be possible to indicate the perpetrators and organizers and their ideologies. The black-and-white popular image pits an evil butcher against innocent victims. There have not been many genocides in modern times, so comparison with the Assyrian case is difficult. However, looking at the Assyrian experience, it is possible to single out some phases that are clearly genocidal.

The ethnic cleansing of Hakkari ordered by the Young Turk Minister of the Interior Pasha is quite definite. He commanded the provincial governors and military to clear out the Assyrians and never let them return. The question of Iran, which was in a state of anarchy during the Russian withdrawal, is complex. The desire of local tribes and even the collusion of Persian officials and politicians to wipe out the Christians can probably be proven. However, it is equally clear that Assyrian militias and brigades collaborated with the Russian occupation and took disproportionately bloody revenge on Muslims. Does such aggression on the part of a victimized people negate a previous legitimate claim to have been the victim of a genocide? Can a condition of anarchy make it impossible to identify the aims of the perpetrators? And can victims also become perpetrators when they overreact to defend themselves? "Nowhere was the inner lining of war, its predatory essence, so clear as in the crevices of Persia."[39]

[1] Viktor Shklovsky, *A Sentimental Journey: Memoirs 1917–1922*, transl. by Richard Sheldon (Ithaca: Cornell University Press, 1970), 100.
[2] Ibid., 99.
[3] Vice Consul in Urmia Vladimir Minorsky (1877–1966) became a leading world scholar on the Kurds, and wrote many articles on them for the *Encyclopedia of Islam*; Vice Consul Basile Nikitine (1885–1960) became an expert on the Middle East and wrote extensively on the relations between Kurds and Christians; Vice Consul in Sawj-Bulaq Alexander Iyas (1869–1914) took unique photographs of Kurdish tribes, now in the Finnish Museum of Photography.
[4] For Russian activity see M. S. Lazarev, *Kurdistan i kurdskaia problema (90-e gody XIX veka – 1917 g.)* (Moscow: Nauka, 1964); V. T. Maevskii, *Voenno-statisticheskoe opisanie vanskogo i bitlisskogo vilaetov'* (Tiflis: Shtab Kavkazkogo Voennago Okruga, 1904); Vladimir Genis, *Vitse-konsul Vvedenskii: sluzhba v Persii i bukharskom khanstve (1906–1920gg.)* (Moscow: Sotsial'no-politicheskaia mysl', 2003), John Tchalenko, *Images From the Endgame: Persia through a Russian Lens 1901–1914* (London: Saqi, 2006); for Turkish infiltration see Fethi Tevetoğlu, *Ömer Naci* (Ankara: Kültür ve Turizm Bakanlığı Yayınları, 1987).
[5] Florence Hellot-Bellier, *Chroniques de massacres annoncés: Les Assyro-Chaldéens d'Iran et du Hakkari face aux ambitions des empires 1896–1920* (Paris: Geuthner, 2014).
[6] Mohammad Gholi Majd, *The Great Famine and Genocide in Persia, 1917–1919* (Lanham, Md: University Press of America, 2003).
[7] Shklovsky, *Sentimental Journey*, 87.
[8] Ibid., 113.
[9] Peter Holquist, "Forms of Violence during the Russian Occupation of Ottoman Territory and in Northern Persia (Urmia and Astrabad) October 1914–December 1917," in *Shatterzone of Empires: Coexistence and Violence in the German, Habsburg, Russian and Ottoman Borderlands*, Omer Bartov & Eric D. Weitz, eds. (Bloomington: Indiana University Press, 2013), 334–361.
[10] Shklovsky, *Sentimental Journey*, 101.
[11] David Gaunt, "The Complexities of the Assyrian Genocide", *Genocide Studies International*, 9 (2015), 83–103.
[12] Andranig Chalabian, *General Andranig and the Armenian Revolutionary Movement* (Southfield, Michigan: author 1988); Joel E. Werda, *The Flickering Light of Asia or the Assyrian Nation and Church* (No place: author 1924) gives him the attribution "terror to the Moslems" on page 131; Martin van Bruinessen, "Kurdish Tribes and the State in Iran: the Case of Simko's Revolt", in *The Conflict of State and Tribe in Iran and Afghanistan*, Richard Tapper, ed. (London: Croom Helm, 1983), 364–400.
[13] Salahi Sönyel, *The Assyrians of Turkey: Victims of Major Power Policy* (Ankara: Turkish Historical Society, 2001).
[14] Christian Gerlach, "Extremely Violent Society – an Alternative to the Concept of Genocide", *Journal of Genocide Research* (2006), 455–471; Mark Levene, "Creating a Modern 'Zone of Genocide': The Impact of Nations and States on Eastern Anatolia 1878–1923", *Holocaust and Genocide Studies* 12 (1998), 93–133; David Gaunt, "Sayfo Genocide: The Culmination of an Anatolian Culture of Violence" in *Let Them Not Return: Sayfo – the*

Genocide against the Assyrian, Syriac and Chaldean Christians in the Ottoman Empire, David Gaunt, Naures Atto & Soner Barthoma, eds. (New York: Berghahn, 2017), 54–69.

[15] Said Namik & Rustem Nedjib, *La Question Assyro-Chaldéene devant la conférance de la paix*, (Paris, 1919).

[16] K. P. Matveev & I.I. Mar-Yukhanna, *Assiriiskii vopros vo vremya i posle pervoi mirovoi voiny* (Moscow: Nauka, 1968).

[17] Letter of 24 February/ 9 March 1915 in *Genotsid armian v osmanskoi imperii: Sbornik dokumentov i materialov*, M. G. Nersisiyan, ed. (Yerevan: Izdatel'stvo Aiastan, 1982), 276–77.

[18] Genelkurmay Başkanlığı, *Birinci Dünya Harbi'nde Türk Harbi Kafkas Cephesi 3 ncü Ordu Harekâti*, vol 2:1 (Ankara: General Staff, 1993), 582.

[19] Genis, *Vvedenskii*, 44.

[20] *The Treatment of the Armenians in the Ottoman Empire 1915–1916*, James Bryce & Arnold Toynbee, eds., in the Parliamentary Blue Book series (London: Government Press, 1916) 139, 146, 153, 197; see also the Iranian collection of official protests concerning Ottoman army atrocities committed on Iranian territory: Empire de Perse, *Neutralité Persane: Documents diplomatiques* (Paris: Georges Cadet, 1919) 139, 153, 155.

[21] Minister of Foreign Affairs Moaven od-Dowleh to Turkish Ambassador Tehran 5 March 1915, *Neutralité Persane*, document 266.

[22] Wadie Jwaideh, *The Kurdish National Movement: Its Origins and Development* (Syracuse: Syracuse University Press, 2006), 126–127.

[23] David Gaunt, "Too Close for Comfort: Relations between Kurds and Syriacs and Assyrians in Late Ottoman Times", *Wiener Jahrbuch für kurdische Studien*, 3 (2015), 45–66.

[24] Matveev & Mar-Yukhana, *Assiriiskii vopros*, 44–45; Lazarev, *Kurdistan*, 301.

[25] Telegram, Minister of Interior to Governor of Van, 26 October 1914 in Ottoman Archives, Istanbul DH 46:78.

[26] Telegram, Minister of Interior to Governors of Van and Mosul 30 June 1915, Ottoman Archives, Istanbul DH 54/240.

[27] Report of missionary Edward McDowell, Urmia August 1916, in Hellot-Bellier, *Chroniques de massacres*, 601.

[28] Eva Haddad (pseudonym), *The Assyrian, the Rod of My Anger* (Australia: E. Haddad, 1996), Malik Yaqu Ismael, *Aturaye oo tre plashe tiwilaye* (Tehran: Cultural Commission of the Young Assyrians, 1964) in German translation in Rudolf Macuch, *Geschichte der Spät- und Neusyrischen Literatur* (Berlin: Walter de Gryter, 1976); Werda, *Flickering Light*, 8–27. An exception that does use the victim concept is Basil Nikitine, "Une petite nation victim de la guerre: Les Chaldéens", *La revue des sciences politiques* (1921), 602–625.

[29] Peter Holquist, "The World Turned Upside Down: Refugee Crisis and Militia Massacres in Occupied Northern Persia" in *Le genocide des Arméniens* (Paris: Armand Colin, 2015), 130–54.

[30] Paul Caujole, *Les tribulations d'une ambulance française en Perse* (Paris: Les Gémeaux, 1922); Nicolas Gasfield, "Au Front de Perse pendant la Grande Guerre Souvenir d'un officier français", *Revue d'histoire de la guerre mondiale* 2:3 (1924, 120–151); for the efforts of the American mission see Mary Lewis Shedd, *The Measure of a Man: The Life of William Ambrose Shedd Missionary to Persia* (New York: George H. Doran, 1922);

Daniel Méthy, L'action des grandes puissances dans la region D'Ourmia (Iran) et les Assyro-Chaldéens: 1917–1918", *Studia Kurdica* 1:5 (1988), 77–100.

[31] Caujole, *Les tribulations*, 76.
[32] Hellot-Bellier, *Chroniques de massacres*, 531.
[33] Méthy, L'action des grandes puissances", 93.
[34] Shedd, *Measure of a Man*, 231–38.
[35] Claire Weibel-Yacoob, *Surma l'Assyro-Chaldéene (1883–1975): Dans la turmente de Mésopotamie* (Paris, 2007).
[36] Racho Donef, *Massacres and Deportation of Assyrians in Northern Mesopotamia: Ethnic Cleansing by Turkey 1924–1925* (Stockholm: Nisibin, 2009).
[37] Werda, *Flickering Light*, 219.
[38] Yusuf Malek, *The British Betrayal of the Assyrians* (New Jersey: Kimball Press, 1935); Mar Shimun Eshai, *The Assyrian Tragedy* (no place: 1934).
[39] *Sentimental Journey*, 78.

Kropotkin on Violence:
Memoirs of a Revolutionist

KARIN GRELZ

When Peter Kropotkin's autobiography *Memoirs of a Revolutionist* was first published in book form in 1899, it included a preface by the Danish critic and literary historian Georg Brandes.[1] In his introduction Brandes emphasized that the prince was a peaceful man, not intending to sacrifice anyone but himself on the altar of revolution. The reception of the book was overshadowed, however, by another wave of terrorist acts in Russia at the turn of the century and later also by the riots and revolutions of 1905 and 1917. Relating to and interpreting Kropotkin's attitude to terrorism and revolutionary violence thus became a central issue not only for his readers, but also for the subsequent publishers of his memories.

In the following I will give some examples of how this aspect of his thought has been presented and commentated upon in various editions of his memoirs.

Calling himself a revolutionary was for Kropotkin primarily a scientific standpoint that meant looking at and interpreting human society from an evolutionary point of view. He regarded evolution not as a uniform movement, but as a transformational process that sometimes went slowly and sometimes developed more rapidly. Occasionally this would lead to radical societal changes, but it would still be the result of an evolutionary process – "a chance combination of accidental circumstances"[2] – rather than a planned, organized action. The transformation that he envisions in the concluding passage of his memoirs is therefore a comparatively peaceful event:

> [...] and I am convinced that whatever character such a movement may take in different countries, there will be displayed everywhere a far deeper comprehension of the required changes than has ever been displayed within the last six centuries, while the resistance which the movement will meet in the privileged classes will hardly have the obtuse obstinacy which made the revolutions past so violent.[3]

In his memoirs Kropotkin describes the development of the revolutionary movement in Russia during the second half of the nineteenth century. He explains the insurgencies and outbreaks of revolutionary violence among workers and peasant serfs as righteous forms of self-defense in response to the excessive violence and brutality exerted by landlords and the tsarist regime. He also describes how the protests calmed down as soon as promises were given that the system of serfdom would be abolished.[4]

After the abolition manifesto had been signed, reactionary forces began exploiting the fears of Alexander II in order to postpone and block the planned reforms. Rumors were spread about revolutionary conspiracies and death threats against the tsar that provoked the despotic side of his personality. When reaction struck back, and the elder revolutionaries were imprisoned or resigned in the face of an invincible adversary, the younger generation was radicalized, Kropotkin explains: "Sheer exasperation took hold of our young people."[5]

Kropotkin's private experience of the reaction under Alexander II made it impossible for him during these years to see a constitution as the best solution to Russia's problems. His aim was to increase the awareness of the poor and enslaved, who he thought would be left to be dominated by the wealthy landowners under a democratic constitution as well. He found his ideal among the independent and assiduously studying Swiss anarchists in the Jura Mountains and in the populist movement in Russia, where the young generation refused to take advantage of their inherited riches and became socialists by sharing the lives of workers and peasants. Both phenomena he obviously regarded as contributions to the evolutionary development of mankind.

Kropotkin shared the concepts of Darwinism but did not embrace the interpretation it was given by Thomas Huxley.[6] He accepted mutual struggle as a basic condition for evolution, but he also anticipated a principle of mutual aid as a complementary law of nature, necessary for a progressive evolution of the species. The problem with the latter was, according to him, that it is so natural and self-evident that it has gone unnoticed by scientists. Inspired by colleagues who approached the same question from the point of view of zoology, he looked for occurrences of mutual aid in historical documents and chronicles that would support this idea. One of his favorite examples was the Paris Commune, where central societal functions had continued to work even without a government, thanks to separate individuals' ability to cooperate and take responsibility for communal affairs.[7]

Kropotkin's private experience also showed that the two mechanisms – mutual struggle and mutual aid – often existed side by side. One example brought up in his memoirs is the complex personality of Alexander II, who alternated between a sympathetic and a hateful element or side. Another example is the terrorist next to the bleeding Alexander II, who, still with a bomb under his arm, rushed to help the wounded emperor after the attack.

Kropotkin's own revolt was primarily against what he regarded as a misinterpretation of the facts of nature: the "war cry" – "Woe to the Weak" – that came out of Huxley's reading of Darwin.[8] In line with this perception, the most central concern and the driving force behind Kropotkin's autobiographical project thus seems to have been an ambition to explain, from his position as an eyewitness, the psychological mechanisms behind violence as such – peasant insurgencies as well as individual violence and terrorist acts. To this he then added, as a counterbalance, his private observations of the progressive force of mutual aid.

The principle of mutual aid has challenged the two dominating political ideologies of the twentieth century, which both in different ways built upon the law of mutual struggle. The Marxist utopia was to be reached through a dynamic struggle between classes, while the market-liberal vision is based on a milder form of concurrence between free economic subjects. In both cases the refining process is hampered by individuals who collaborate with those who are to be defeated or outcompeted. Within both ideological systems the mechanism of mutual aid appears to be either naïve or an obstacle to progress. There has thus been a tendency – although for diametrically different reasons – to amplify Kropotkin's consent to violence, while his own thought developed in the opposite direction. The posthumous editions of Kropotkin's memoirs bear witness to this conflict.

The Russian and English versions of Kropotkin's memoirs have never been fully aligned with each other. The first chapter was written in Russian, but after he got the opportunity to publish his memoirs as a series of articles in *The Atlantic Monthly* he began writing them directly in English. In 1899 an extended version of the English text came out in book form in London and Boston. Kropotkin did not have time to rewrite or translate the book into Russian; this was done instead by his colleague Isaak Shklovsky under the pseudonym Dineo. His translation, *Zapiski revoliutsionera,* was published in 1902 by an émigré Russian publishing house in London.[9] Attempts were made to produce two slightly amended versions in St. Petersburg in 1906, but both were confiscated, and it was not until 1918 that Kropotkin's memoirs could be printed in Russia.

After his return from exile in June 1917, Kropotkin planned to make a revised and extended version by merging his original Russian manuscript with Dineo's translation, but he died in 1921 without having realized the project. The task was carried out instead by the administrator of his archive, Nikolai Lebedev. In the first two posthumous editions, 1924 and 1929, Lebedev marked the new material with square brackets and inserted Kropotkin's explanatory comments in footnotes. The 1929 edition included, moreover, a supplement consisting of two chapters that originally had been written in Russian: thirty-seven pages about the Chaikovsky Circle and almost as many about his stay in Western Europe.[10]

Lebedev also prepared a special edition of *Zapiski revoliutsionera* for the series *Russkie memoary, dnevniki, pis'ma i materialy* ("Russian Memoirs, Diaries, Letters and Materials"). It was published in 1933, and in an introductory note Lebedev referred to a Russian manuscript from Kropotkin's archive in London, upon which this edition was based.[11] Yet the difference between this and the 1929 version is not as big as one might have expected. The lion's share of the text is identical with Lebedev's previous redaction, and only a few new passages have been added that cannot be found in any of the earlier Russian and English versions. Both the brackets and the supplementary chapters seem conspicuous by their absence, but possibly this was Lebedev's way of finalizing an "original" Russian text. All subsequent editions in Russian have consequently been based on this version, while the English publishers have made abridged editions by reproducing the 1899 English text and adding some of the new material in the notes.[12]

Lebedev's 1933 volume included a longer preface written by Piotr Paradizov, a party official who criticized Kropotkin for voluntarism and idealistic deviation and described anarchism as "a dying current in social thought".[13] By then, anarchism was indeed beyond the end of its life in Russia. In April 1933 Lebedev was sentenced by OGPU to three years of deportation to Vologda for anarchistic propaganda, and he disappeared before the sentence was carried out.[14] Both Paradizov and the main editor of the series, Vladimir Nevsky, were accused of anti-Soviet conspiracy and shot in 1937, and the series was closed down.[15]

In the original preface from 1899 Georg Brandes emphasized Kropotkin's peaceful mission. Paradizov, for his part, opposed Kropotkin's "mutual aid" to the Marxist class struggle, but still gave a rather fair picture of Kropotkin's anarchist ideas, albeit in negative terms: Marxism demands the elimination of classes, anarchism wants to equate them. Marxism speaks of class struggle, anarchism of 'mutual aid'.[16] In the 1971 reprint of the first English version, the editor Nicolas Walter made the opposite move when he stated in his preface that "Kropotkin's testimony should be treated with caution":

It is important to realize that Kropotkin was a much more aggressive character than one might guess from his Memoirs and from his later reputation.[17]

Although Walter went on to assure the reader that the world needs more people like the prince, and that "a Kropotkin in Russia today would rebel against an even crueler regime", the supplements added by Lebedev in 1929 and 1933 suggest that Walter was right in his suspicions about Kropotkin's aggressive character. The Russian versions of the memoirs actually disclose a more violent side than do the English ones.

Summing up the chapter on the Chaikovsky Circle that Lebedev added to the 1929 edition, Kropotkin elaborates on the principle of revenge, and openly defends the terrorist acts accomplished by Vera Zasulich and Sergei Kravchinsky (Stepniak):

> Права была Вера, мстя за Боголюбова, прав был Сергей, мстя за всех жертв Мезенцева из III отделения, вообще прав был бы тот барин или мужик, который так глубоко почувствовал бы обиду мужика, что пошёл бы мстить за неё.
>
> Придёт время, когда такая месть не будет нужна. Обиды не будут такие, как теперь. Но пока сознание обидчика, что месть и про него найдётся и на него может нагрянуть,—пока только *это* сознание и способно удержать всесильного обидчика. И самый факт такой мести будит в людях сознание, что не следует давать себя в обиду даже *меньшую*, чем та, за которую отомстили, и тем самым ограничивает круг обид.
>
> Так идёт прогресс в человечестве.
>
> Явись такие мстители за крестьянскую обиду—и через десять лет сами крестьяне перестанут сносить те обиды, которые они теперь сносят—не безропотно: этого никогда не бывает, – но без явной мести обидчику. Уровень самоуважения поднимется в крестьянстве. Вырастет *личность*, и вырастает лучше, чем если бы то же самоуважение начало вырабатываться в крестьянине легальным путём, посредством законодательства и суда.[18]

[Vera was right to avenge Bogoliubov, Sergei was right to avenge all the victims of Mezentsev from the Third Department, and in general, any master or serf who might feel the injury done to a serf that deeply would be right in taking revenge for it.

The time will come when such revenge will not be necessary. Injuries will not be as they are today. But for now, the offender's awareness that revenge can descend upon him as well – for now, only *this* awareness is capable of restraining an all-powerful wrongdoer. And the very fact of such revenge makes people aware that they should not permit themselves to be injured even by a *lesser* wrong than the one that has been avenged, and this will limit the scope of injuries.

Such is the course of human progress.

If such avengers of wrongs to the peasantry appear, in ten years the peasants themselves will cease enduring the wrongs they endure now – not meekly: that never happens – but without openly taking revenge on the offender. The level of self-respect will rise among the peasantry. The *individual* will grow, and it will do so better than if this self-respect had begun to be developed in the peasant by legal means, through legislation and the courts.]

One of the added passages in the 1933 edition also turns in a programmatic, violent direction. In the chapter about Kropotkin's life in St. Petersburg, where he recalls the time after his return from Siberia, a declaration is inserted that actually undercuts Paradizov's critical statement in the preface about anarchism's mild equation of classes:

> Чтение социалистических и анархических газет было для меня настоящим откровением. И из чтения я вынес убеждение, что примирения между будущим социалистическим строем, который уже рисуется в глазах рабочих, и нынешным буржуазным быть не может. Первый должен уничтожить второй.[19]

[Reading the socialist and anarchist newspapers was for me a real revelation. And I came away from my reading with the conviction that there can be no reconciliation between the future socialist order that is already looming before the workers and the current, bourgeois system. The former must destroy the latter.]

The violent associations of the verb *unichtozhit'* (destroy) rhyme badly with Kropotkin's own vision of a relatively peaceful change in the concluding chapter of his memoirs. The formula about a coming socialist "order" that will exterminate the bourgeois system is probably representative of the young Kropotkin, but one can wonder whether this is a passage that the elder anarchist, with his stubborn aversion to governmental structures, would have included. In the political reality that prevailed after October 1917 this sounds more Marxist than anarchist, if it is read as a political program.

Although the above excerpts seem to be Kropotkin's own words, they were in fact not included in the editions that he edited and authorized. Whatever motive guided Lebedev and Kropotkin's wife in their editorial work on the posthumously published volumes – loyalty to the deceased, text-critical accuracy, or strategic considerations for publication – they had to cope with the fact that Kropotkin's formulas now echoed the violent expressions and practices of the Bolsheviks.

What happens, then, if we read Kropotkin more loyally, and accept mutual struggle and mutual aid as mechanisms which are prerequisites for life and development, but neither good nor bad as such? The power of his memoirs and the dimension that will continue to intrigue future readers derive from his personal reflections on the explicit violence he encountered in his childhood and his subsequent attempts to grasp and conceptualize this scientifically as an adult. By his own example, Kropotkin demonstrates that the instinct for mutual aid can lead to the exercise of violence as well as to compensation for it. The central point he makes in his memoirs is that any civilizational process worthy of the name is about conceptualizing explicit violence as an anomaly, rather than as a fundamental state – in individuals as well as in society as a whole.

[1] Peter Kropotkin, *Memoirs of a Revolutionist* (Boston and New York: Houghton, Mifflin & Company, 1899); Peter Kropotkin, *Memoirs of a Revolutionist* (London: Smith, Elder & Co, 1899): https://archive.org/details/memoirsofrevolut02kropuoft/page/n7.

[2] Peter Kropotkin, *Memoirs of a Revolutionist*. With a New Introduction and Notes by Nicolas Walter (New York: Dover Publications, Inc., 1972), 502.

[3] Ibid.

[4] Ibid., 135–136.

[5] Ibid., 427.

[6] Ibid., 498–499.

[7] Ibid., 486.

[8] Ibid., 499.

[9] P.A. Kropotkin, *Zapiski revoliutsionera* (London: Fond vol'noi russkoi pressy, 1902), http://books.e-heritage.ru/book/10090034.

[10] P.A. Kropotkin, *Zapiski revoliutsionera* (Moskva: Politkatorzhan, 1929) vol. II, 198–266.

[11] P.A. Kropotkin, *Zapiski revoliutsionera* (Moskva—Leningrad: Academia, 1933), XV.

[12] Peter Kropotkin *Memoirs of a Revolutionist*, Edited by James Allen Rogers (New York: Doubleday & Company, Inc., 1962).

[13] Kropotkin 1933, VII–XIV.

[14] International Memorial, *Zhertvy politicheskogo terrora v SSSR*, accessed March 15, 2019: http://lists.memo.ru/d19/f484.htm (Lebedev, Nikolai Konstantinovich).

[15] Ibid. http://lists.memo.ru/index16.htm (Paradizov, Petr Pavlovich); http://lists.memo.ru/index14.htm (Nevskii, Vladimir Ivanovich).

[16] Kropotkin 1933, X.

[17] Kropotkin 1971, XX.

[18] Kropotkin 1929, 233–234.

[19] Kropotkin 1933, 170.

Taking Over Gallows Hill

ANDREAS GEDIN

On a small rock ledge facing the forest and sea beyond, lies a text written in paving stones. They are rocks that have been disciplined into blocks and here also forced into words: TAKING OVER.

Living and dying is of course the obvious task of nature. But to punish one's fellows is the privilege of man. As such, the death penalty is the height of culture, setting us apart from the naturalness of nature. To the north of Visby lies Gallows Hill, where there is a gallows construction dating from the 13th century. It stands on the highest point of the mountain so that the dead bodies would be visible from the sea, like the light from a beacon. But this did not forebode a safe harbor, instead it signaled the ultimate punishment. The limp bodies swaying slowly in the wind spoke a clear language.

På en liten klipphylla som vetter mot skogen och havet längre bort, ligger en text skriven med gatstenar. De är urberg som tuktats till kuber och här också tvingats till ord: TAKING OVER.

Att leva och dö är givetvis naturens självklara uppgift. Men att straffa sina likar, det är människans privilegium. På så vis är dödsstraffet en kulturens höjdpunkt som skiljer oss från den naturliga naturligheten. Strax norr om Visby ligger Galgberget med en galgkonstruktion, som ursprungligen är från 1200-talet. Den är placerad på bergets högsta punkt så att de döda kropparna skulle synas från havet, likt ljuset från en fyrbåk. Men här varslades det inte om en trygg hamn utan i stället signalerades om det yttersta straffet. De lealösa kropparna som vajade stilla i vinden talade ett tydligt språk.

Next spread: *Taking Over Gallows Hill*, ©Andreas Gedin 2019

V

Bringing back space to the historiography of Russia

KARL SCHLÖGEL

The eminent Russian contemporary of Friedrich Ratzel and Karl Lamprecht, the founders of the Leipzig school of cultural studies, was Vasily Ossipovitch Klyuchevsky, the master of pre-revolutionary Russian historiography[1]. In Klyuchevsky's work, space and time are always interrelated in a perfect way. His history of Russia is systematically a history of the ways of transferring culture, of expansion, colonization, retreat, regression etc. His history of the formation of empire is always one of creating the trans-ethnic, trans-national imperial space and of its reconstruction, both in a literary and in a more general sense. Klyuchevsky's historiography had no chance of surviving after the upheavals in Russia and his school disappeared for a long time, in order to give space to other interpretations and methods that were in the spirit of the time: the histories of the relations of production and of class struggle.[2]

We have not yet reconstructed the failure of the impressive schools stemming from the Russian Silver Age. It seems to me, that Russian scholars like Ivan Grevs and Nikolai Antsiferov are still waiting to be redisovered: Antsiferov as a scholar who elaborated a strict methodology of "ekskursiia", of *flânerie,* in both Franz Hessels and Walter Benjamin's terms[3]. It needs more research to bring back the innovations of the Russian Silver Age in the historiographic field: the blossoming of local history, the intensive research done on the ground – in the factories, in the estates, in the villages, in the big and small cities; the discovery of the periphery and the mental reconstruction of the imperial space. Even in the early Soviet form – as in the projects of *Zemlia i fabrika* in the 1920s – the spirit of these new ways of doing historiography survived, including early forms of *Oral History avant la lettre.*

Today in Post-Soviet Russia we can observe a powerful comeback of the spatial dimension of Russian culture and history. There are fascinating works – in the form of meta-theoretical reflections as well as in detailed localized studies, i.e. area studies.[4] There is a booming industry of "geohistory", "geo-culture", and primarily, "geo-politics" in post-Soviet Russia today, including speculative and ideological pseudo-scholarship like Aleksandr Dugin and others,[5] who fill the vacuum left by Soviet culture: The brutal neglect of natural conditions, the ignorance of the "spirit of the Russian landscape", the violent economic exploitation and destruction of landscapes, above all of the Russian countryside, will take its revenge. There was always a discourse on geography in the search for Russian identity: the "Russian soul" and the broad and endless horizon of Russian space, "geography as fate," in the words of Petr Chaadaev. Space was always a topos of Russian identity. But space has been ignored to a large extent by Soviet Marxism and by Soviet leaders. The Soviet Marxist-Leninist discourse was about economic and class relations, physical and geographic nature figured not as an objective condition for social life and for economic and cultural progress, but as an enemy. To build communism was to overcome the resistance of "objective factors" as natural conditions, conservative mentality etc.

I am convinced that Western scholarship on Russia – including the 20th century history – has to take up this issue again. I cannot go into details, but it is obvious for me, that there cannot be a history of the late Russian Empire without the dimension of creating "imperial space" through reforms, industrialization, transport revolution, railway construction, telegraph and others means of communication, in short: without the production of the imperial space. It is for me obvious that there cannot be a history of Russian Revolution and Civil War excluding the fragmentation of the empire, the disruption and degradation of the networks of communication, the transformation of the mental maps etc. And there is no history of "Stalinism" beyond the violent transformation of the spaces of pre-revolutionary Russia and the production of spaces of "Stalinism as civilization" (Stephen Kotkin)[6]. How can we continue our discourse on "totalitarianism" without knowing how distances within this immense and large territory have been mastered? How can we discuss total power without taking into account that this power, theoretically unlimited, was in fact very limited, to the borders of a city or county, limited to the local NKVD, so that people could escape into the world beyond any control of state institutions. There is no history of "total power" without raising the question of where this power was based or executed. That is: without placing and spacing Russian history[7]. To reflect on space is a claim for complexity and for escaping simplifications. Historiography on Russia has to include or to develop a kind of spatial hermeneutics.

[1] Vasilii O. Kliuchevskii, *Kurs russkoi istorii v piati chastiakh*, Sankt Petersburg 1904–1922.
[2] My reflections on space and the narratological consequences are in Karl Schlögel and Elisabeth Müller-Luckner, eds., *Mastering Russian Spaces. Raum und Raumbewältigung als Probleme der russischen Geschichte* (München: R.Oldenbourg Verlag 2011); Karl Schlögel, *To Read Time in Space* (New York: Bard Graduate College, 2016).
[3] Nikolai Antsyferov, *Dusha Peterburga* (Petrograd: Izdatel'stvo Brokgauz i Efron, 1922).
[4] Most essays in Vladimir Kagansky, *Kulturnyi landshaft i sovetskoe obitaemoe prostranstvo* (Moskva: Novoe literaturnoe obozrenie, 2001)
[5] Aleksandr Dugin, *Osnovy geopolitiki: geopoliticheskoe budushchee Rossii* (Moskva: Arktogeia, 1997).
[6] Stephen Kotkin, *Magnetic Mountain: Stalinism as a Civilization* (Berkeley: University of California Press, 1995).
[7] Emma Widdis, *Visions of a New Land: Soviet Film from the Revolution to the Second World War* (New Haven: Yale University Press, 2003).

Stalin's Two Bodies?
A Socio-Political Dimension[1]

KIRILL POSTOUTENKO

1

In 1957, a starkly original Italian novelist and an equally outstanding German–American scholar simultaneously—but independently from one another—put on paper their respective reflections upon the dual nature of kingship. The novel, set in the shadow of Giuseppe Garibaldi's unstoppable progress in Sicily, features an imagined conversation between Don Fabrizio Corbera, the Prince of Salina—a proud but clearheaded holdover of the crumbling order—and his brother-in-law, Ciccio Màlvica—a self-appointed spokesman of the mainstream Sicilian nobility. Notwithstanding the disastrous performance of the last two Bourbons on the island—Ferdinand II and Francis II—Màlvica is said to believe that the idea of monarchy always remains the same—ostensibly perfect and free from any personal influence (*svincolata dalle persone*).[2] This, however, is the opposite of what Don Fabrizio has in mind: as long as a king embodies a certain idea, his performance cannot fall below a certain threshold without compromising it.

Turning to the pages of Ernst Kantorowicz's seminal monograph on medieval political theology reveals the same dichotomy between "ideal" and "real" kingship, neatly (or sometimes less neatly) arranged into clusters. As is the case with the opening of Lampedusa's novel, the relationship between the King's two bodies soon appears, depending on the source quoted, pure and simple—or exceedingly complex. The voices stressing the apartness of the two refer to the discrepancy between the person and his or her office known since antiquity but not clearly conceptualized until the thirteenth century in legal and theological discourse.[3] Here the standard distinction is between the incumbent of a Dignity, corruptible in all possible ways, and the Dignity itself, stainless and lasting forever.[4] Generally speaking, this clearcut division is not far from the textbook sociological differentiation between an individual and his or her social role.[5] However, in my opinion, reading *The King's Two Bodies* as a case study of social role theory might be a bit simplistic: unlike a teacher or a doctor, the typical king or queen never ever "takes a break" and remains the only human being performing the task in a given kingdom for the whole duration of his or her tenure. The connection between the person and the role is great indeed, and it would probably not be wise to squeeze it into a dated sociological straightjacket.[6]

In fact, in a large number of cases the connection between the "two bodies" appears to be much more intricate than the typical relation outlined above between an idea and a person: for example, whereas the king/queen might be dead (mortal) and alive (immortal) at the same time (*Le roi est mort! Vive le roi!*), all past, present and future kings/queens may live on in the same "mystical person".[7] Furthermore, the natural body of the sovereign should be protected with the utmost zeal—but it is still possible to indict him (or her) in the name of the Crown![8] The list of complexities goes on and on, but even the small sample presented here points to the deliberate confusion between the two royal bodies as perhaps the most interesting aspect of Kantorowicz's study.[9] But what was the specific point of breaking up the kingly *individuum* into a couple of loosely defined and intricately connected bodies in the Late Middle Ages? And why does this apparently clumsy and muddled arrangement pop up in all kinds of epochs and cultures? Unless at least a tentative answer is given, "Stalin's two bodies" will remain a flashy slogan with limited explanatory force.

Combined with the later analyses of other scholars, Kantorowicz's scattered remarks point to the protection of the crown from its bearer's incapacity or malpractice as the main reason for splitting the king's body into two.[10] Along with the notorious complexity of succession rules in dynasties, human fallibility—particularly in the largely non-competitive system of hereditary monarchy—presents challenges to both the functioning and the prestige of the crown:[11] an immature, senile, avaricious or negligent sovereign could seriously damage the office which he or she not just represents but embodies for an unspecified, sometimes very long period of time. In such a situation, it is only practical that one of the ruler's hypostases should be insured against subjective risks by its halo of eternity, perfection and omnipresence. On the other hand, the deliberately blurred boundaries between the bodies prevent kingship from being banalized: devoid of its transcendent attributes, the natural body of the king would lose its majestic beauty and mystical power, turning the sovereign into an executive officer at his or her own court. All in all, while the protection of the crown required the two bodies of a king (or a queen) to be separate, the successful functioning of the current monarch demanded some smokescreen in front of the split. This must be the main reason why Kantorowicz's theory is not as straightforward as some would want it to be.

While some scholars (including Irina Sandomirskaja) have tested the possibility of the "leader's two bodies" on the Soviet material,[12] coming to definite conclusions requires both a cross-evaluation of existing arguments and an analysis of some previously unconsidered material.

2

Six days after Vladimir Lenin's death, the two bodies (or, rather "faces") of the deceased Soviet leader were quite explicitly compared and contrasted on the second page of the Bolshevik party daily *Pravda*.[13] Whereas one, referred to by Vladimir Ulianov's most popular party pseudonym (Lenin), was directed towards all peoples of all times, another, more casually denoted by the leader's patronymic (Ilyich), faced the mourners attending his funeral on Red Square in Moscow. Nevertheless, Lenin's memorial cult has little to do with the simultaneous functioning of the ruler's "two bodies" described by Kantorowicz. So, one has to pass over the numerous refrains of Sosnovsky's dychotomy in the Soviet press and instead survey the body duplication of the first Soviet *vozhd* before January 21, 1924.

Lenin's aversion to the personality cult is a commonplace of both research literature and Soviet propaganda,[14] but for all his indignation and protests, he neither stopped the placement of his serialized bust across Russia (in 1919–20), nor prevented the appearance of the cities Leninsk or Ulyanovka on the Soviet map (in 1919 and 1922, respectively).[15] Even before that, in 1918, the birth house of the future revolutionary leader in Simbirsk was adorned with a memorial plaque, and the agitational train "Lenin" began crisscrossing the country.[16] Around the same time, in 1920, when Lenin's activity in the government and Bolshevik Party was at its highest, the Ninth Congress of the Bolshevik Party decided to continue with the publication of Lenin's complete works, seeking to provide *the* guidance for party leaders and ordinary members alike.[17] All in all, less than a year after the revolution, the work of producing the "second" eternal, infallible, fixed and standardized Lenin next to the one toiling at Sovnarkom was well underway.

However, it was with the first signs of Lenin's deteriorating health in the summer of 1921 that the parallel development of the ruler's two identities gained momentum. The image of Lenin projected onto the general population was a contradiction in itself, seeking as it did to combine governmental business as usual with post-historical sanctity. The news of the leader's medical problems began reaching general audiences with a one-year delay:[18] even in July 1923, half-paralyzed, speech-impaired and confined to the suburban

Gorki residence, Lenin was reelected Head of the Council of People's Commissars.[19] At the same time, Lenin's oeuvre and image were styled as though set in stone for the ages: founded in 1923, the Lenin Institute, symptomatically enough subordinated to the Lenin Museum, was entrusted to collect all manuscripts and artefacts pertaining to the life of the first Soviet leader.[20] In the background of this unstoppable monumentalization, the "real" Lenin, ailing but active, was desperately fighting a losing battle to partake in the political process, taking full advantage of his formal and informal authority in order to make his voice heard, texts read and opinion respected.[21] But the political committee (Politburo) of the Bolshevik Party was determined to keep Lenin out of politics under the pretext of his poor health (entrusted to enforce this isolation, Iosif Stalin also had a personal stake in this issue, as Lenin was wary of his voracious political appetite).[22] Hence "Lenin" was destined to become a collection of prefabricated opportune quotes and giant portraits well before his actual demise.[23]

In this brief survey, Vladimir Ulyanov-Lenin seems to fit into the pattern sketched out by Kantorowicz: the increasingly static and uniform image, projected towards eternity and universally adored, makes up for the increasingly incapacitated natural person lurking in the background.[24] However, appearances in politics are often deceiving. On the surface of it, there is an attempt to shield the crucial post in the state government from the harm inflicted by the progressing illness of its holder. In practical terms, however, in 1924 nobody cared too much about the main executive office of postrevolutionary Russia—the Head of the Council of People's Commissars: after Lenin's death, it quickly faded into insignificance in the hands of Aleksander Rykov—a trusted technocrat with little political clout. A year and a half before that, in April 1922, Iosif Stalin was elected to a different position in a different branch of government, becoming the first ever Secretary General of the Russian Communist Party of Bolsheviks. Post factum, Stalin was massively hailed as Lenin's successor,[25] and, indeed, the first step in the new leader's access to absolute power owed less to his own talents than to the *vozhd's* reluctant last-minute endorsement.[26] However, having assumed the newly created office, Stalin promptly bent it to his will in ways unforeseen or even unimaginable before.[27] All in all, the first Bolshevik passage of executive power largely followed the Russian blueprint of treating succession rules lightly and emphasizing the personal right of the current ruler to freely select his or her successor more or less on a whim.[28] Under such circumstances, there was, in my opinion, little rationale for creating and sustaining the complex fiction entertained by medieval thinkers. But how should we answer the same question in regard to Stalin's much longer reign?

3

As with Lenin, the most general argument in favor of Stalin's two bodies à la Kanotorowicz is the sheer number of his heavily standardized, tightly policed and mass-produced visual and verbal representations: already in 1933, long before the apogee of Stalin's personality cult, there were over a hundred Stalin posters and busts on Moscow's Gorky street alone and 16,5 million of his books in print; in a few years, each third issue of Pravda featured Stalin's portrait, and each column mentioned him at least a dozen times.[29] More specific evidence concerns the co-presence of the "human" and the "superhuman" leader within public discourse: whereas some posters portray grotesquely oversized, semi-divine, monumentally staid images, others present Stalin marching along with workers and other "normal people."[30] The same contrast is somewhat differently employed in the cinematic depictions of Stalin, where the fictional, surreal, abstract leader slowly but steadily replaces the everyday human being: noticeably averse to documentaries and naturalistic painting which could lay bare his physical imperfections, Stalin on screen and canvas was increasingly detached from the frail, inept, thick-accented prototype. In any case, the isolated attempts to sculpt and paint Stalin from life were, for the most part, aborted at early stages.[31] Particularly after the Great Patriotic War, when boosting Russian nationalism was supposed to divert attention from the less than stellar military record of the commander in chief,[32] the secretary general sanctioned the replacement of his chief movie impersonator—the Georgian Mikhail Gelovani – by Alexei Dikii, who bore little resemblance to the real-life Stalin but boasted a track record of playing Russian military heroes instead.[33] Last but not least, the alleged trace of "two bodies" was noticeable in Stalin's peculiar habit of addressing himself in the third person in his own letters, articles and speeches.[34] To demonstrate Stalin's awareness of his bodily duplicity, a number of scholars refer to the story about his reprimand of his unruly son Vasily, who happened to claim that he was "Stalin," too. In response to this statement, the Secretary General, having denied that either Vasily or his father (!) was "Stalin," pointed at the only "true" Stalin in the room—the leader's official portrait hanging on the wall.[35] What should we make of all this?

To begin with, the "conversation" referred to in the previous paragraph is most likely a product of the popular imagination: although it is quoted almost verbatim in representative collections of Soviet anecdotes,[36] Artyom Sergeev, Stalin's stepchild and an alleged source of the legend, never mentions it in his memoirs.[37] Then again, there had been neither discernible reason nor even opportunity for Stalin to acquire and sustain "two bodies" in Kantorowicz's sense. First, in the vein of Russian secular autocracy, Stalin's reign was largely a personal rule with some bureaucratic elements only loosely related to past tradition. Whenever the Soviet people had a need to express their admiration of Stalin, they addressed a person rather than an office, being (or pretending to be) happy in his presence, professing love, seeking fatherly protection and paying relatively little attention to his words or functions.[38] If we place Stalin in the context of leaders with a strong record of veneration, his ruling personality seems to be no more divided than that of a French king (for whom,, the passage of the crown did matter a great deal).[39] Second, even if there were an office to be protected from the ruler's incapacity, no such condition obtained: unlike his predecessor, Stalin was relatively healthy until the end, and, aside from the fear-induced negligence of his entourage after the fatal stroke, there were no attempts to silence him or replace the actual "private" ruler with a convenient "public" proxy.[40]

Does this all mean that the search for the "Stalin's two bodies" was a waste of time? Probably and hopefully not. Even if Kantorowicz's model did not quite work on the Soviet material, there must be some other reason for the pairs of Stalins to be so laboriously constructed and maintained. To be sure, some of Stalin's well-documented bifurcation techniques—for example, massive visual self-propaganda or the split of official image into the popular and the transcendental facets —were popular with autocracies regardless of time or region: in the context of some ancient Roman emperors, modern European kings and twentieth-century dictators (including Lenin), Stalin's visual self-replication looks fairly mainstream.[41] Other doublings, however, could be interpreted with greater precision. Thus Stalin's much-cited illeism—his self-references in the third person—might warrant specific attention, despite a long and varied history of the device itself.[42] On the one hand, the significance of Stalin's illeisms should not be exaggerated: his *Collected Works* contain just over 150 references to "Stalin," as opposed to many thousands of deictic self-references in his texts.[43] Furthermore, within this relatively insignificant group, no more than a third of references stress the canonic character of Stalin's works, referring to "Stalin" as an author. Still, although Stalin's discourse contains no really stable, universal and transhistorical, canonic "second body," the rupture within his name, in Irina Sandomirskaja's words, is used to produce a mobile canon in which the unswerving connotation of absolute rightness was instantly adjustable to personal political objectives.[44] This becomes evident in the juxtaposition of two early writings that blatantly contradict each other: whereas in one the secretary general claims for "Stalin" the right to "change" and "clarify" his position according to changed circumstances,[45] in another, he snaps: "Stalin's formulations do not need clarifications."[46] Admittedly, Stalin was not the only leader capable of managing his own image,[47] but few of his peers could hide so well behind the constantly changing—and yet seemingly unchangeable—pseudo-canonic Self.[48]

Another possible lead for further inquiry is the changing dynamics in the use of Stalin's verbal and visual replicas. There is some evidence of an increasing monumentalization of Stalin's second body after WWII: whereas Stalin's portraiture of this period in art and print media is increasingly dominated by non-interactive, stand-alone, immobile images,[49] his texts make use of the word combination "Stalin's formula."[50] The leader's abstract, timeless, universal body seems to eclipse the personal, local and historical one once and for all. Stalin's increasing tolerance towards simultaneous displays of his first and second bodies appears to confirm this hypothesis. During and after the Great Patriotic War, the secretary general publicly spoke against the backdrop of his own portraits at least three times—(1) at the official ceremony devoted to the twenty-fourth anniversary of the October Revolution (November 6, 1941), (2) at the meeting with voters of the Stalin electoral district (February 9, 1946), and (3) at the public celebration of his seventieth birthday at the Bolshoi Theatre (December 22, 1949). However, the pictures documenting the co-presence of the leader's two bodies at the events of 1941 and 1946[51] have not, to my knowledge, made it into print: in any case, *Pravda*, *Izvestiia* and (in the first case) the invited official painters pointedly ignored the second body altogether.[52] In contrast, the pictures of Stalin's seventieth birthday featuring his gigantic youngish photo behind and above its actively applauding (and aged) prototype duly made it to the first pages of both the state and the party dailies.[53] It might be interesting to compare this development with the analogous double-body displays in different cultural and socio-political contexts such as late socialist Romania (Nicolae Ceaușescu addressing the Congress of Political Education and Socialist Culture in June 1976)[54] or modern Bavaria (Prime Minister Markus Söder promoting technological progress in the Free State).[55]

Figures 1 and 2

Figure 3

STALIN'S TWO BODIES?

Figure 4

Figure 5

Figure 6

Figure 7

Figure 8

Figure 9

Figure 10

[1] I am most grateful to Irina Valkova for her advice and support. The part of this essay devoted to the rhetoric of comparisons between the kings' and leaders' bodies was funded by the German Research Society (Special Research Area 1288 *Practices of Comparisons*).
[2] Giuseppe Tomasi di Lampedusa. *Il Gattopardo* [1957] (Milano: Feltrinelli, 2002), 14. In the popular English translation of the novel, the words quoted are mysteriously missing (Giuseppe Di Lampedusa, *The Leopard*, transl. Archibald Colquhoum (London: Collins, 1960), 15).
[3] Bernhard Jussen, "The King's Two Bodies Today," *Representations* 106 (2009:1), 106; Ernst H. Kantorowicz, *The King's Two Bodies: a Study in Mediaeval Political Theology*, Princeton, N.J.: Princeton University Press, 1957, 497.
[4] Kantorowicz, *The King's Two Bodies*, 386, 418, 435 etc.
[5] Here are just a few examples: Ralph Linton. *The Study of Man* (New York: Appleton Century Crofts, 1936), 255; Michael Argyle, Adrian Furnham, and Jean Ann Graham, *Social Situations* (Cambridge, Cambridge University Press, 1981), 177; Ralf Dahrendorf, *Homo Sociologicus: Ein Versuch zur Geschichte, Bedeutung und Kritik der Kategorie der sozialen Rolle* [Homo sociologicus: A critical study of history and meaning of the category of social role] (Opladen: Westdeutscher Verlag, 1971), 30, 33.
[6] For the insightful discussion of this matter (based on different materials) see: Erving Goffman, *Encounters. Two Studies in the Sociology of Interaction* (Indianapolis, IN: Bobbs-Merrill, 1961), 88. See also: Ralph H. Turner, "The Role and the Person," *American Journal of Sociology* 84/1 (1978), 1–23. On the obstacles to role exchange in totalitarian politics and communication see: Kirill Postoutenko, "Prolegomena to the Study of Totalitarian Communication," in *Totalitarian Communication: Hierarchies, Codes and Messages*, ed. Kirill Postoutenko (Bielefeld: transcript, 2010), 17.
[7] Kantorowicz, *The King's Two Bodies*, 4–5, 31, 46, 143, 171, 312, 372, 400–401, 409, 497. See also: Ralph Giesey, "The Two Bodies of the French King," in *Ernst Kantorowicz*, Robert L. Benson and Johannes Fried, eds. (Stuttgart: Franz Steiner, 1997), 227, 230.
[8] Kantorowicz, *The King's Two Bodies*, 7; Kirill P. Kobrin, "Ernst Kantorovich nad istoriei: drobiashchiesia tela vlasti [Ernst Kantorowicz over and above History: the bodies of power break apart]," *Neprikosnovennyi zapas*, 3/95 (2014), 138.
[9] This view is persuasively advocated in the following article: Michael P. Rogin, "The King's Two Bodies: Abraham Lincoln, Richard Nixon and Presidential Self-Sacrifice," *Massachusetts Review*, 20/3 (1979), 554–56.
[10] Kantorowicz, *The King's Two Bodies*, 360, 370; Marie Axton. *The Queen's Two Bodies. Drama and the Elizabethan Succession* (London: Royal Historical Society, 1977), X, 12–14; Kobrin, "Ernst Kantorovich nad istoriei: drobiashchiesia tela vlasti", 124; Giesey, "The Two Bodies of the French King," 225–26.
[11] See Kay Junge, "Zepter und Kerbholz, Macht und Geld. Der Vertrag zu Gunsten Dritter und die Institutionalisierung symbolisch generalisierter Kommunikationsmedien [Scepter and tally stick, power and money: A third beneficiary party contract and the institutionalization of symbolically generalized media of communication], in *Soziale Differenzierung: Handlungstheoretische Zugänge in der Diskussion*, Thomas Schwinn, Clemens Kroneberg, and Jens Greve, eds. (Wiesbaden: VS Verlag für Sozialwissenschaft, 2011)," 226. See also some recent data: Timothy Besley, Marta Reynal-Querol, "The logic of hereditary rule: theory and evidence," *Journal of Economic Growth* 22 (2017), 123–44.

[12] Victoria E. Bonnell, *Iconography of Power: Soviet Political Posters under Lenin and Stalin* (Berkeley: University of California Press, 1997); Alexei Yurchak, "Bodies of Lenin: The Hidden Science of Communist Sovereignty", *Representations* 129 (2015:); Irina Sandomirskaia, "Iazyk-Stalin: 'Marksizm i voprosy iazykoznaniia' kak lingvisticheskii povorot vo vselennoi SSSR [Stalin as a language: 'Marxism and the Questions of Language' as a linguistic revolution in the Soviet galaxy]," in *Landslide of the Norm: Language Culture in Post-Soviet Russia*, Ingunn Lunde & Tine Roesen, eds. (Bergen: Slavica Bergensia, 2006).

[13] Lev [S.] Sosnovsky, "Ilyich-Lenin," *Pravda*, № 22/2, January 27, 1924, 2. Benno Ennker should be credited with rescuing this remarkable text from oblivion (see: Benno Ennker, "Die Anfänge des Leninkultes [The beginnings of the Lenin cult]," *Jahrbücher für Geschichte Osteuropas* 35/4, (1987), 548).

[14] Bonnell, *Iconography of Power*, 139; Hans Maier, "Political Religions and their Images: Soviet Communism, Italian Fascism and German National Socialism," *Totalitarian Movements & Political Religions* 7/3, (2006), 268; Ennker, "Die Anfänge des Leninkultes," 543; G. Alekseev, "Kolichestvennye parametry kul'ta lichnosti [The quantitative parameters of the personality cult],"*SSSR: Vnutrennie Protivorechiia* 6 (1982), 7–8.

[15] Here I follow Victoria Bonnell, *Iconography of Power*, 142. See also: François-Xavier Coquin, " "L'image de Lenine dans l'iconographie revolutionnaire et postrevolutionnaire [The Image of Lenin in revolutionary and postrevolutionary iconography]," *Annales: Economies, Societes, Civilisations* 44/2 (1989), 227–228.

[16] Coquin, "L'image de Lenine," 225–226.

[17] Coquin, "L'image de Lenine," 230.

[18] Ennker, "Die Anfänge des Leninkultes, 545.

[19] Ennker, "Die Anfänge des Leninkultes, " 546.

[20] See: Nikolay S. Komarov, "K istorii Instituta Lenina i Tsentral'nogo partiinogo arkhiva (1919–1931 gg.) [Towards the history of the Lenin Institute and the Central Party Archive (1919–1931)]," *Voprosy istorii* 10 (1956), 181–191; Ennker, "Die Anfänge des Leninkultes," 547.

[21] For a fascinating account of this struggle, see: Benno Ennker, "Das lange Sterben des Vladimir I. Lenin. Politik und Kult im Angesicht des Todes [The long dying of Vladimir I. Lenin: Politics and cult from the standpoint of death]," in *Der Tod des Diktators*, Thomas Großbolting and Rüdiger Schmidt, eds. (Göttingen: Vandenhoeck & Ruprecht, 2011), 35–57. See also Bonnell, *Iconography of Power*, 147.

[22] Ennker, "Das lange Sterben des Vladimir I. Lenin," 43.

[23] Yurchak, "Bodies of Lenin," 154, 156.

[24] Yurchak, "Bodies of Lenin," 122, 124–125.

[25] On the popularity of the slogan "Stalin is Lenin today," see Matthew Cullerne Bown, *Art under Stalin* (Oxford: Phaidon, 1991), 97. The formula itself was coined by an obliging outsider (Henri Barbusse, *Staline: un monde nouveau vu à travers un homme* [Stalin: A new world seen through one man] (Paris: Ernest Flammarion, 1935), 312, but its mass use began only after Stalin's sixtieth birthday. For other verbal and visual succession narrratives, see Victoria E. Bonnell. *Iconography of Power*, 156–157, 161–162; Anita Pisch, *The Personality Cult of Stalin in Soviet Posters, 1929–1953* (Acton: ANU Press,

2016), 188; Chonghoon Lee, "Visual Stalinism from the Perspective of Heroisation: Posters, Paintings and Illustrations in the 1930s," *Totalitarian Movements and Political Religions* 8/3-4 (2007), 506; Nicola Hille, "Der Führerkult im Bild. Dir Darstellung von Hitler, Stalin und Mussolini in der politichen Sichtagitation der 1920er bis 1940er Jahre [The leader cult in images: The representation of Hitler, Stalin and Mussolini in the visual political propaganda of 1920s-1940s]," in *Der Führer in Europa des 20. Jahrhunderts*, Benno Ennker and Heidi Hein-Kirchner, eds. (Marburg: Verlag Herder-Institut, 2010), 46. In the last article Stalin's case is put in the context of the suprisingly similar "invented genealogies" of other totalitarian leaders.

[26] Boris I. Nikolaevskii, *Tainye stranitsy istorii* [The secret pages of history] (Moskva: Izdatel'stvo gumanitarnoi literatury, 1995), 170.

[27] Nikolaevskii, *Tainye stranitsy istorii*, 166; Robbins Burling, *The Passage of Power* (New York: Academic Press, 1974) 214. For a general perspective, see Amos Perlmutter, *Modern Authoritarianism: A Comparative Institutional Analysis* (New Haven, CT: Yale University Press, 1981), 1-2; Roger B. Myerson, "The Autocrat's Credibility Problem and Foundations of the Constitutional State," *American Political Science Review* 102 (2008), 135.

[28] Michael Cherniavsky, *Tsar and People: Studies in Russian Myths* (New York: Random House, 1969), 89; Richard Wortman, "The Representation of Dynasty and 'Fundamental Laws' in the Evolution of Russian Monarchy," *Kritika*, 13/2 (2012), 265; Yurchak, "Bodies of Lenin," 132. In fact, many dictatorial regimes used a similar arrangement, so the Lenin-Stalin succession might be a cross between the tradition and the political environment (see: Gordon Tullock, *Autocracy* (Dordrecht: Kluwer Academic Publishers, 1987), 151).

[29] See Maier, "Political Religions and their Images," 268; Sarah Davies, *Popular Opinion in Stalin's Russia: Terror, Propaganda and Dissent, 1934-1941* (Cambridge: Cambridge University Press, 1997), 114, 118; David L. Brandenberger, "Sostavlenie i publikatsiia ofitsial'noi biographii vozhdia-katekhizisa stalinisma [The composition and publication of the leader's official biography – Stalinism's catechesis]," *Voprosy istorii* 12 (1997), 142; Bonnell, *Iconography of Power*, 160; Alekseev, "Kolichestvennze parametry kul'ta lichnosti," 8-9; Robert Tucker, "The Rise of Stalin's Personality Cult," *American Historical Review* 84/2 (1979), 366; Jan Plamper, *The Stalin Cult: A Study in the Alchemy of Power* (New Haven, CT: Yale University Press, 2012), 228. Even Stalin's sympathizers were shocked by the ubiquity of his kitchy doubles (see Henri Barbusse, *Staline*, 6-7; Lion Feuchtwanger, *Moskau 1937. Ein Reisebericht für meine Freunde* (Amsterdam: Querido Verlag, 1937), 73.

[30] See Bonnell, *Iconography of Power*, 142; Nicola Hille, "Der Führerkult im Bild", 120; Eike Hennig, "Hitler-Porträts abseits des Regierungsalltags [Hitler's portraits outside of the governmental routine]," in *Führerbilder. Hitler, Mussolini, Roosevelt, Stalin in Fotografie und Film*, Martin Loiperdinger, Rudolf Herz, and Ulrich Pohlmann, eds., (München: Piper, 1995), 27-49. The contrast is particularly vivid in the two posters produced by Gustav Klutsis within a year's time (1930-1931)—see FIGURES 1 and 2.

[31] See Plamper, *The Stalin Cult*, 141; Bown, *Art under Stalin*, 99.

[32] For detailed and thoughtful analysis of this period, see David Brandenberger, *National Bolshevism: Stalinist Mass Culture and the Formation of Modern Russian National Identity, 1931-1956* (Cambridge, MA: Harvard University Press, 2002), 183-96.

³³ See Oksana Bulgakowa, "Herr der Bilder – Stalin und der Film, Stalin im Film [The ruler of images—Stalin and cinema, Stalin in the cinema]," in *Agitation zum Glück: sowjetische Kunst der Stalinzeit*, Alisa Ljubimova and Hubertus Gassner, eds. (Bremen: Edition Temmen, 1994), 67; Nikolas Hülbusch,"Džugašvili der Zweite: Das Stalin-Bild im sowjetischen Spielfilm (1934–1953) [Dzhugashvili the Second: The Image of Stalin in Soviet feature films]," in *Personality Cults in Stalinism—Personenkulte im Stalinismus*, Klaus Heller and Jan Plamper, eds. (Göttingen: Vandenhoeck & Ruprecht, 2004), 214, 237; Judith Devlin, "Visualizing Political Language in the Stalin Cult: The Georgian Art Exhibition at the Tretyakov Gallery," in *Political Languages in the Age of Extremes*, ed. Willibald Steinmetz (Oxford: Oxford University Press, 2011), 102.

³⁴ Konstantin M. Simonov, *Soldatami ne rozhdaiutsia* [Nobody's born a soldier] (Moskva: Veche, [1964] 2012), 168 (quoting Marshal Ivan Konev); Svetlana I. Allilueva, *Tol'ko odin god* [Just one year] (New York: Harper & Row, 1969), 340; Abdurakhman A. Avtorkhanov, *Zagadka smerti Stalina* [The riddle of Stalin's death] (Frankfurt am Main: Posev, 1976), 313–14; Konstantin M. Simonov, *Glazami cheloveka moego pokolenia* [In the eyes of my generation], (Moskva: Kniga, [1979] 1990), 357; Evgenii A. Dobrenko, "Mezhdu istoriei i proshlym: pisatel' Stalin i literaturnye istoki sovetskogo istoricheskogo diskursa [Between history and the past: Stalin the writer and the roots of the Soviet historical discourse]," in *Sotsrealisticheskii kanon*, Hans Günther, Evgeny Dobrenko´, eds. (Sankt-Peterburg: Akademicheskii proekt, 2000), 951; Mikhail I. Vaiskopf, *Pisatel Stalin* [Stalin the writer] (Moskva: Novoe literaturnoe obozrenie, 2001), 167; Sandomirskaia, "Iazyk-Stalin: "Marksizm i voprosy iazykoznaniia kak lingvisticheskii povorot vo vselennoi SSSR", 275–277; Georgii A. Kumanev, *Govoriat Stalinskie narkomy* [Stalin's People's Comissars are speaking] (Smolensk: Rusich, 2005), 56 (quoting Stalin's longtime comrade-in arms Anastas Mikoyan).

³⁵ Dobrenko, "Mezhdu istoriei i proshlym," 651; Plamper, *The Stalin Cult*, XIII; Rosemary Sullivan, *Stalin's Daughter. The Extraordinary and Tumultuous Life of Svetlana Allilueva* (New York: Harper, 2015), 140; Simon Sebag Montefiore, *Stalin: The Court of the Red Tsar* (New York: W&N, 2004), 6.

³⁶ See, for instance Evgeny V. Anisimov, *Istoriia Rossii ot Riurika do Putina. Liudi. Sobytiia. Daty* [Russian history from Riutik to Putin: People, Events, Dates] (Moskva: Piter, 2013), 484.

³⁷ Artem F. Sergeev, Ekaterina F. Glushik, *Besedy o Staline* [Conversations about Stalin] (Moskva: Krymskii most-9D, 2006); Artem F. Sergeev, Ekaterina F. Glushik, *Kak zhil, rabotal i vospityval detei I. V. Stalin. Svidetel'stva ochevidtsa* [How I. V. Stalin lived, worked and brought up chidlren: An eyewitness account] (Moskva: Krymskii most-9D, 2011).

³⁸ Rosalinde Sartorti, "Großer Führer, Lehrer, Freund und Vater'. Stalin in der Fotografie ['Great leader, teacher, friend and father'. Stalin in photography]," in *Führerbilder*, 189–209; Sarah Davies, "The Cult of the Vozhd': Representations in Letters, 1934–1941," *Russian History/Histoire Russe* 24/1–2 (1997), 136; Hans Günther, "Wise Father Stalin and his Family in Soviet Cinema," in *Socialist Realism Without Shores*, Thomas Lahusen and Evgeny Dobrenko, eds. (Durham, NC: Duke University Press, 1997), 178–90; Jan S. Behrends, "Freundschaft und Sowjetunion, Liebe zu Stalin: Zur Anthropomorphisierung des Politischen im Stalinismus [Friendship and Soviet Union, Love to Stalin: On

anthropomporphization of the political in Stalinism]," in *Die Massen bewegen: Medien und Emotionen in der Moderne*, Frank Bösch and Manuel Boruta, eds. (Frankfurt am Main: Campus Verlag, 2006), 172–92; Nelli Romanovich, "K voprosy o personifikatsii vlasti v Rossii [On the question of personification of power in Russia]," *Vlast'* 9 (2009), 13–16; Graeme Gill, *Symbols and Legitimacy in Soviet Politics* (Cambridge: Cambridge University Press, 2011), 121; Dmitry. Iu. Astashkin, "Obraz I. V. Stalina v poslevoennoi sovetskoi propaganda 1945–1956 gg. (na primere Novgorodskoi oblasti) [The image of Stalin in the Soviet postwar propaganda of 1945–1956: the example of the Novgorod district]," *Vestnik Novgorodskogo Gosudarstvennogo Universiteta* 69 (2012), 6; Oleg V. Khlevniuk, "Stalin as Dictator: The Personalization of Power," in *Stalin. A New History*, Sarah Davies and James Harris, eds. (Cambridge: Cambridge University Press, 2005), 108–20; Katerina Clark, "Stalinskii mif o velikoi sem'e [The Stalin myth of the Great Family]," in *Sotsrealisticheskii kanon*, 785–96. See also some empirical data: Kirill Postoutenko, "Listening to Comrade Stalin: Multimodality and Code-Switching in Public Response to the Leaders," *Russian Journal of Communication* 8/2 (2016), 142; Kirill Postoutenko, "Anschlußverhalten in totalitärer Gesellschaft zwischen Pathos und Ethos: Zur Rezeptionsanalyse der Rede von Joseph Stalin auf dem VIII Sowjetkongress der UdSSR am 8. November 1936 [The connecting behavior in totalitarian society between pathos and ethos: The analysis of the reception of Joseph Stalin's speech at the 8th Congress of Soviets on November 8, 1936]" (unpublished manuscript).

[39] See Giesey, "The Two Bodies of the French King," 226, 239; Tadami Chizuka, "L'idée de deux corps du roi dans le procès de Louis XVI [The idea of the king's two bodies at the trial of Louis XVI]. *Annales historiques de la Révolution française 310* (1997), 643–50. For other examples of princely or presidential reliance on personal traits (or, to be precise, their medially constructed simulations), see Ulrich Keller, "Franklin D. Roosevelts Bildpropaganda im historischen und systematischen Vergleich [Franklin D. Roosevelt's visual propaganda in the historical and systemic context]," *Führerbilder*, 148–49; Sergio Bertelli, *The King's Body* (University Park, PA: Penn State University Press, 2001), 9.

[40] See Oleg V. Khlevniuk, *Khoziain. Stalin i utverzhdenie stalinskoi diktatury* [The master: Stalin and the formation of Stalinist dictatorship] (Moskva: ROSSPEN, 2010), 458. Again, the relation between health and fitness for office is not a given: the case of Franklin D. Roosevelt attests to the fact that even a fairly irrelevant handicap (FDR's physical immobility caused by polio) of the executive could in principle lead to a major cover-up involving both politics and media (see Sally Stein, "The President's Two Bodies: Stagings and Restagings of FDR and the New Deal Body Politic," *American Art* 18/1 (2004), 32–57).

[41] See Peter Burke, *The Fabrication of Louis XIV* (New Haven, CT: Yale University Press, 1992), 16, 17, 85, 91, 93, 113, 184; Igor N. Golomshtok, *Totalitarnoe iskusstvo* [Totalitarian art] (Moskva: Galart, 1994), 212; Jean-Charles Balty, "Ateliers de sculpture et diffusion de l'image impériale. L'exemple des provinces de la Méditerranée occidentale [The sculptors' studios and the dissemination of the imperial image: the example of provinces]," in *La transmission de l'idéologie impériale dans l'Occident romain*, Milagros Navarro Caballero and Jean-Michel Roddaz, eds. (Bordeaux: Ausonius, 2006), 221–46; John Ma, "Le roi en ses images: essai sur les représentations du pouvoir monarchique dans le monde hellénistique [The king and his images: essay on the representation of the

monarchic power in the Hellenic world]," *Pratiques du pouvoir monarchique dans l'Orient hellénistique et romain (IVe siècle avant J.-C. - IIe siècle après J.-C.)*, Ivana Savalli-Lestrade and Isabelle Cogitore, eds. (Grenoble: UGA Éditions, 2010), 148–64; Michael Schindhelm, "Die toten Augen sehen alles – Führer-Monumente im Sozialismus [Dead eyes see everything: leader monuments in socialism]," in *Oh Du, geliebter Führer: Personenkult im 20. und 21. Jahrhundert*, Thomas Kunze and Thomas Vogel, eds. (Berlin: Ch. Links, 2013), 296–303; Daniel Leese, "The Cult of Personality and Symbolic Politics," in *The History of Communism*, ed. Stephen A. Smith (Oxford: Oxford University Press, 2014), 351.

[42] Rod Elledge, *Use of the Third Person for Self-Reference by Jesus and Yahweh. A Study of Illeism in the Bible and Ancient Near Eastern Texts and Its Implications for Christology* (New York: Bloomsbury, 2017).

[43] The variance is particularly telling given Stalin's nearly universal avoidance of the first-person personal pronoun singular—я—in his political speeches and articles (see: Kirill Postoutenko, "Performance and Management of Political Leadership in Totalitarian and Democratic Societies: The Soviet Union, Germany and the United States in 1936," in *Totalitarian Communication: Hierarchies, Codes and Messages*, 96, 109.

[44] Sandomirskaia, "Iazyk-Stalin," 275–77. See also Vaiskopf, *Pisatel' Stalin*, 369–70. The sorry state in the 1930s of the Solvychegodsk museum of Stalin's prerevolutionary exile shows how little the second Bolshevik leader cared about the long-term canonization of his actual historical past (see Ekaterina Studentsova, "K istorii sozdaniia muzeia Stalina (1934–1935) v Sol'vychegodske [On the history of the establishment of the Stalin museum (1934–1935) in Solvychegodsk]," in *Kul'turnoe nasledie Russkogo Severa: pamiat' i interpretatsii*, ed. Zinaida Mekhren'gina (Sankt-Peterburg: Pushkinskii Dom, 2009), 160–72).

[45] Iosif V. Stalin, "VII rasshirennyi plenum IKKI. Zakliuchitel'noe slovo [Concluding remarks at the 7th extended RKKI plenum, December 13, 1926]," in Iosif V. Stalin, *Sobranie sochinenii* 9 (Moskva: Gosudarstvenno izdatel'stvo politicheskoi literatury, 1951), 43.

[46] Iosif V. Stalin, "Tovarishchu M. I. Ulianovoi. Otvet tovarishchu L. Mikhelsonu [A letter to comrade M. I Ulianova. A response to comrade L. Mikhelson, September 16, 1927]," in Iosif V. Stalin. *Sobranie sochinenii* 10 (Moskva: Gosudarstvenno izdatel"stvo politicheskoi literatury, 1951), 65. Overall, beginning in the late 1920s, Stalin and other prominent Bolsheviks openly discouraged ordinary party members from substantially discussing (let alone amending) the leaders' texts; see: Kirill Postoutenko, "Canonization and random signaling between followers and leaders in Soviet Union, Nazi Germany and 'New Deal'-USA," in *Ruler Personality Cults from Empires to Nation-States and Beyond: Symbolic Patterns and Interactional Dynamics*, Kirill Postoutenko and Darin Stephanov, eds. (forthcoming)). It should be noted that the same strategy was employed by Hitler and his associates during their early public appearances (see Siegfried Kracauer. *Totalitäre Propaganda* [Totalitarian propaganda] (Frankfurt am Main: Suhrkamp, [1939] 2013), 86–87.

[47] See, for instance, Sergio Luzzatto. *L'immagine del duce. Mussolini nelle fotografie dell'Istituto Luce* [The images of the leader: Mussolini on the photographs of the Luce Institute] (Roma: Editori riuniti, 2001), 51–74.

[48] See Lilly Marcou, "Staline entre le mythe et la légende," *Politix* 5/18 (1992), 101; Oksana Bulgakowa, "Herr der Bilder," 66; Vaiskopf, *Pisatel' Stalin*, 12. It is not without interest that, unlike Lenin who often signed his articles and decrees after the Revolution with his private surname plus his party nickname—*В. Ульянов (Ленин)* (see details in Vil'iam V. Pokhlebkin. *Velikii psevdonym* [The great pseudonym] (Moskva: Iudit, 1996), 29), Stalin normally avoided such a conflation, apparently cherishing the freedom to divide and unite his discursive "body" according to circumstances.

[49] See Bown, *Art under Stalin*, 176; Kirill Postoutenko, "Towards a conceptual history of canonization in totalitarian societies," *Ariadna histórica. Lenguajes, conceptos, metáforas* 5 (2016), 199.

[50] Iosif V. Stalin, "Tovarishchu A. Kholopovu [A letter to the comrade A. Kholopov, July 28, 1950]," in Iosif V. Stalin. *Sobranie sochinenii* 16 (Moskva: Rychenkov, 1997), 64. The fact that the private letter was promptly published in *Pravda* (№ 214/11686 [August 2, 1950], 2) shows that its author had few misgivings about his formulation.

[51] Preserved at the Russian State Archive of Cinema and Photo Documentation (Krasnogorsk, Russia). The signatures are respectively РГАКФД-2311 ч/6 (FIGURE 3) and РГАКФД А-5794 ч/6 (FIGURE 4).

[52] See: *Izvestiia*, № 264/7640, November 7, 1941, 1, 2 (FIGURES 5, 6); *Pravda*, № 35/10117, February 10, 1946, 1 (FIGURE 7). I have reproduced just one newspaper's coverage for each event because in each case *Pravda* and *Izvestia* used the same set of pictures. In step with the official media, Iraklii Toidze's painting *Comrade Stalin's Performance at the Official Ceremony devoted to the Twenty-Fourth Anniversary of the Great October Socialist Revolution* (1948) ignores Stalin's background portrait. Apparently the artists's sensitivity to the configuration of the leader's political body was one of the factors that earned him the Stalin Prize of the First Degree (see: Vladimir Svin'in, Konstantin Oseev, *Stalinskie premii. Dve storony odnoi medali* [Stalin's Prize: Two sides of the same coin] (Novosibirsk: Svin'in i synovia, 2007), 300). Subsequently, copies of the painting found wide circulation as both a poster and a book insert (see: *Za Rodinu! Za Stalina! Komsomoltsy i molodezh vooruzhennykh sil SSSR v Velikoi Otechestvennoi Voine. 1941–1942 gg.* [For the homeland! For Stalin! Komsomol members and youth of the Soviet Armed Forces in the Great Patriotic War, 1941–1942], ed. Sergei S. Smirnov (Moskva: Voenizdat, 1951), unpaginated).

[53] Compare, for example, the archival photo (РГАКФД, А-8988-6 ч/6—see FIGURE 8) with the nearly identical one published in *Pravda* on December 22, 1949 (№ 354 (11463), 1—see FIGURE 9). As expected, *Izvestiia* ran a similar picture on the same day (№ 301 (10141), c. 1).

[54] The picture is reproduced in Vladimir Tismaneanu, "Ceaușescu's Socialism," *Problems of Communism* 34/1 (1985), 62.

[55] See Söder's posting on Twitter on October 2, 2018 (FIGURE 10): <https://twitter.com/Markus_Soeder/status/1047141595907264513?s=20>

«Следующей почтой вышлю все». Переписка советских сотрудниц секретариата Международной Демократической Федерации Женщин с «Москвой» в первые послевоенные десятилетия

YULIA GRADSKOVA

Первая книга Ирины Сандомирской, которую я прочитала, – *Я так хочу назвать кино* (вместе с Натальей Козловой) – произвела на меня большое впечатление вниманием к деталям и глубиной интерпретаций.[1] Это был анализ советской женской автобиографии, показывающий в частности, как конструкции советского «казенного» языка используются автором для описания пережитого. Возвращаясь к своей героине 15 лет спустя, Сандомирская отмечала, что автор автобиографии, озаглавленной «Я так хочу назвать кино», начинает писать свою биографию, так как она «узнает и не узнает себя» и свое прошлое в официальных версиях советской истории, транслируемых по радио и телевидению.[2] Очевидно, что за прошедшие годы советская женская повседневность и способы ее описания получили дальнейшее осмысление в публикациях исследователей советской культуры и гендерной истории, однако проблемы распознавания личного и женского, выраженного с помощью официального советского языка, продолжает оставаться дискуссионной.

Данная статья посвящена советской гендерной истории и анализирует деловую переписку между советскими сотрудницами, работающими в международной организации, одной из основных задач которой провозглашалась именно защита прав и интересов женщин. Статья предполагает внести вклад в дискуссию о деятельности крупной транснациональной женской организации периода Холодной войны – Международной Демократической Федерации женщин (МДФЖ), которая уже привлекла внимание историков[3]. Однако, в центре этой статьи – переписка между советскими представительницами этой организации, а именно, между сотрудницами Секретариата МДФЖ в Париже (а потом в Берлине) и руководством Антифашистского Комитета советских женщин в Москве.[4] Несмотря на официальный характер этой переписки[5], она представляет собой особый интерес для историка – в отличие от преимущественно мужского состава сотрудников других организаций, представлявших СССР за границей, МДФЖ организовывала свою работу с помощью женских кадров. И хотя переписка носила в основном официальный и нередко секретный характер, анализ писем позволяет не только лучше понять внутреннюю жизнь организации и основные направления ее деятельности, но и жизнь ее сотрудниц.

Статья использует архивные документы Комитета Советских женщин (ГАРФ) а также документы международного отдела ЦК КПСС (РГАСПИ). В первой части статьи я коротко представлю историю МДФЖ и меняющийся контекст, в котором осуществлялась переписка, а ее основная часть посвящена анализу самой корреспонденции.[6]

Международная Демократическая Федерация Женщин была создана в 1945 в Париже; ее официально объявленной целью было привлечение международного внимания послевоенной Европы и мира к правам женщин, антифашистское единство и борьба женщин-матерей за предотвращение новой войны. Федерация в целом следовала советской интерпретации «женских прав» – женщины должны были иметь равные с мужчинами права, но их «особое предназначение» – материнство – одновременно превращало их в «особый» субъект прав и предполагало их особую функцию. Материнство, рассматриваемое как естественная функция любой женщины, предполагало также и особые психологические качества, в частности, миролюбие. В то время как многие другие национальные и международные организации (например, Women's League for Peace and Freedom) также следовали идее о большей предрасположенности женщин к миролюбию, а значительное количество католических женских организаций выступали от имени женщин-матерей, заявленная миссия новой организации удачно вписывалась в послевоенный контекст общественных транснациональных организаций и связывала воедино идеи равенства, защиты материнства, счастья детей и мира.

Ведущая роль в подготовке учредительного съезда Федерации принадлежала коммунисткам и участницам движения сопротивления на юге Европы – Франции, Италии, Югославии[7]. Однако с самого начала СССР играл особенно важную роль в этой организации, а положение женщин в «странах социализма» преподносилось как пример наиболее удачного решения женского вопроса в официальном журнале Федерации *Женщины мира*.[8] С развитием Холодной войны и усилением противостояния между Советским блоком и «Западом», Федерация все чаще рассматривается последним как «коммунистическая» (см. рассекреченные документы ЦРУ), в 1949 США запрещают деятельность американского члена Федерации – Конгресса американских женщин, в 1954 году Федерация лишается статуса наблюдателя (статуса В) в ООН, а в 1951 штаб-квартира Федерации оказывается вынуждена отказаться от своей резиденции в Париже переехать в Восточный Берлин. Таким образом, основной орган практической работы организации, Секретариат, с 1951 по 1990 г. находился в Берлине, а организация обычно рассматривалась на «Западе» как просоветская и прокоммунистическая. Международный престиж организации вновь возрос в 1960–70-е гг.; в частности, ООН объявил 1975 год Международным годом женщин, поддержав инициативу Федерации. Также МДФЖ стала одном из активных сторонников разработки Конвенции по отмене всех форм дискриминации в отношении женщин (CEDAW), принятой ООН в 1979 г.[9].

Таким образом, в течение многих лет Федерация играла довольно важную роль как в советской внешней политике, так и в международном движении за права женщин. Удивительно однако, что в то время, как транснациональная деятельность организации оказалась во многом забыта по причине ее слишком тесной связи с СССР и «коммунизмом»[10], российские историки, в том числе гендерные историки, также не обратили на нее особого внимания. Однако в том случае, когда эта организация упоминалась в контексте женской истории России, ее советские участницы описывались с помощью советского официального языка. Так одна из работниц Секретариата МДФЖ в Берлине, Валерия Калмык, «зарекомендовала себя компетентным и инициативным работником»[11], другая, Ксения Проскурникова, «снискала глубокое уважение и заслуженный авторитет советской и международной общественности»[12]. Сходным образом описывается и жизнь главы Советского Антифашистского комитета и одного из вице-президентов МДФЖ, Нины Поповой, в недавно опубликованной биографии Григорьевой.[13]

Именно поэтому историческая контекстуализация переписки советских сотрудниц (прежде всего в отношении политики холодной войны и сталинизма) и внимание к советским языковым клише представляется особенно важным для изучения деятельности МДФЖ. Например, интересно было бы узнать, что думали о своей работе женщины, которые в 1950-е годы были направлены на работу в Берлин. Как чувствовали они себя в городе, с одной стороны связанном с воспоминаниями о недавней войне и преступлениях нацизма, а с другой – до постройки берлинской стены в 1961 году – приоткрытом «Западу»? Как они относились к женщинам-активисткам и феминисткам из Западной Европы, Африки, Азии и Латинской Америки, с которым они встречались на мероприятиях Федерации, а также индивидуально? Влияли ли эти встречи и их работа в Федерации на их взгляды и оценку положения женщины в СССР? Представляется, что анализ содержания и языка советской официальной переписки позволяет получить ответы на некоторые из этих вопросов. Среди строчек рапортов и отчетов иногда можно обнаружить строки, имеющие непосредственное отношение к повседневной работе в Секретариате, взаимоотношениям между советскими представительницами и женщинами из других стран, а также проблемам, с которыми сталкивались советские представительницы в МДФЖ.

Социально-политический контекст, в котором были написаны эти письма, менялся от первоначальной радости победы над нацизмом к тяжестям послевоенного быта, началу холодной войны и новому витку политических репрессий. После смерти Сталина и XX съезда КПСС, напротив, наступил период пусть и ограниченных, но дискуссий о «культе личности», а также нового открытия страны. Поэтому интересно узнать, как эти события повлияли на характер переписки.

В первой части статьи я анализирую положение сотрудниц Секретариата в отношении женского комитета в Москве, вторая посвящена работе Секретариата в Берлине в переломный момент советской истории – смерти Сталина и XX съезда КПСС, а в последней части я обращаюсь к проблеме «женского» в официальной переписке.

«Лучше сначала посоветоваться, а потом высказывать свою точку зрения» – советские сотрудницы Секретариата и контроль Москвы

Документы первых лет работы МДФЖ показывают, что работа этой организации рассматривалась как важный механизм для распространения знаний об СССР и «странах социализма» и увеличения советского влияния за рубежом. В эти годы Сотрудницы Антифашистского Комитета Советских Женщин отправляли значительную часть корреспонденции на русском с пометкой «секретно», и архивные файлы содержат немало комментариев к биографиям и деятельности иностранных участников. Так, например, материалы архива содержат краткие характеристики некоторых иностранных и советских участниц учредительного съезда МДФЖ в Париже. Многие потенциальные участницы конгресса описывались не только с точки зрения их общественных позиций, но и влиятельности. Так, например, Генриетта Букмастер характеризовалась как «[и]звестная американская писательница. Произведения преимущественно о неграх»[14]. Еще одна участница характеризовалась следующим образом:

> Миссис Элеонор Воган (Нью-Йорк). Представительница школы нянь, Ассоциации родителей. Ассоциация насчитывает 5000 членов. Миссис Воган – редактор журнала «Современная промышленность» с 75000 тиражом. Является одним из самых распространенных в США журналов по вопросам промышленности. Цель журнала – наладить отношения между дирекцией и рабочими на предприятиях.[15]

Документы, присланные сотрудницами Секретариата в Москву, сначала поступали в Антифашистский Комитет Советских Женщин. Затем руководитель комитета, Нина Попова, составляла на основе полученной информации краткие рапорты и запросы, которые нередко направлялись непосредственно на имя одного из секретарей ЦК, Георгия Маленкова, или других сотрудников аппарата ЦК ВКПб с пометкой «секретно». Решения ЦК по важным вопросам деятельности Федерации направлялись затем обратно в Антифашистский комитет, а уже оттуда инструкции посылалась в Секретариат.

> В секретариат т. Маленкова Г. И.
>
> На номер 136415 от 22 февраля 1952 года
>
> Решение ЦК ВКПб по вопросу об участии советской делегации на международной конференции в защиту детей состоялась 21 марта 1952 года. Просьбы Антифашистского Комитета Советских Женщин, изложенные в информации о состоянии подготовки к вышеупомянутой конференции, положительно разрешены в оперативном порядке.
>
> Завотделом внешнеполитической комиссии ЦК ВКПб В. Терешкин
>
> 27.03.1952 [16]

Анализ писем показывает, что в случаях, когда имидж СССР оказывался особенно уязвимым для критики в результате советской экспансионистской политики или попыток диктовать свои условия тем или иным странам и политическим деятелям (например, вторжение советских войск в Венгрию 1956 года или война в Корее 1950–1953), сотрудницам Секретариата в Берлине предписывались особые тактики поведения. Так, например, реагируя на попытки некоторых международных организаций в 1957 году эвакуировать часть венгерских детей на Запад через территорию Австрии, Комитет Советских Женщин советовал своим представительницам в Берлине следующий порядок действий для подготовки очередного заседания Бюро МДФЖ:

> Какие же вопросы можно было обсудить на Бюро? Учитывая, что борьба за смягчение международной напряженности, обострившаяся в последнее время, является одной из важнейших задач, Бюро должно призвать к борьбе за смягчение этой напряженности, за решение всех международных вопросов путем мирных переговоров.
>
> В этой связи желательно заслушать сообщение делегации [МДФЖ], посетившей Египет, и принять решение по вопросу о Ближнем и Среднем Востоке (призвать женщин к выступлениям с требованием вывода израильских войск из Египта, компенсации нанесенного Египту ущерба, регулирования всех спорных вопросов Ближнего и Среднего Востока мирным путем). […]
>
> Следовало бы несколько затянуть посылку делегации [МДФЖ] в Венгрию.
>
> Наряду с этим, может быть, было бы целесообразно пригласить на Бюро делегацию Совета Венгерских Женщин, заслушать их и принять письмо к венгерским женщинам, а также ко всем женщинам мира, с призывом помочь вернуть венгерских детей на родину. (Из письма председателя комитета советских женщин Н. Поповой и ответственного секретаря комитета советских женщин Л. Петровой в Берлин, Зое Ивановой от 18.02.1957).[17]

В свою очередь некоторые материалы переписки показывают, что подобное дирижирование работой организации со стороны Москвы нередко вызывало недовольство других сотрудниц Секретариата, в том числе коммунисток из других европейских стран, а в 1960-е гг. – и представительниц многих развивающихся стран. Так, одна из активных итальянских лидеров МДФЖ в 1950е годы, член парламента Италии и председатель крупнейшей женской организации страны – Союз Итальянских Женщин (UDI), Мария Маддалена Росси, по словам советской представительницы в Берлине, в частном разговоре сказала, что

МДФЖ – «это маховик партии». Росси также настаивала на необоснованном исключении организации югославских женщин из МДФЖ в 1949 г. во время советско-югославского конфликта[18].

Режим секретности требовал постоянного внимания сотрудниц Секретариата, а нарушение предписанного порядка работы с документами вызывало замечания со стороны Москвы:

> Дорогая Зоя Петровна!
>
> 28 декабря мы получили вашу почту, в которой имелись письма на имя Н.В. Поповой, запись беседы с Левон и письмо Лили Вехтер, а также отдельные вырезки из газет. Все эти материалы носят секретный характер, однако оформлены они были простой почтой.
>
> В дальнейшем просим Вас обращать внимание на оформление почты, чтобы оно соответствовало содержанию.[19]

В тоже время анализ документов показывает, что попытки тотального контроля со стороны Москвы никогда не могли быть реализованы полностью. Советские сотрудницы секретариата в Берлине ежедневно должны были взаимодействовать с политическими активистками разных стран и нередко должны были принимать быстрые и самостоятельные решения в отношении тех или иных предложений, идей или событий. Учитывая длительное время, которого требовала пересылка корреспонденции в Москву и получение новых инструкций, становится очевидно, что нередко решения принимаемые советскими сотрудницами, явно противоречили ожиданиям их руководства. Это подтверждает, например, следующее письмо от Галины Горошковой из Берлина, отправленное в разгар войны в Корее. Оно свидетельствует, что несмотря на призыв автора «воспитывать ее» и объяснять ей, что нужно делать, Горошкова, по-видимому, имела свой собственный взгляд на происходящие события и действия, которые должны были быть предприняты в интересах МДФЖ и Советского Союза.

> Секретно. Антифашистский Комитет Советских женщин.
>
> Тов. Поповой Н. В.
>
> Тов. Парфеноввой Н. М.
>
> Дорогие товарищи!
>
> Поскольку я здесь оторвана от ряда источников информации, которые доступны вам, мне труднее бывает решать вопросы, имеющие большое

политическое значение, к которым я отношу вопрос опубликования ответа Рузвельт[20] в советской печати. Вот почему в подобных случаях я очень прошу писать поподробнее, почему лучше именно так, а не иначе. Это будет помогать мне в решении других вопросов, поднимать мой политический кругозор, воспитывать меня. 28.10.1952)[21]

Однако в следующей части письма Горошкова продолжала выражать несогласие, на этот раз с другим требованием Москвы:

> Ваши замечания по брошюре о правах женщин очень трудно реализовать полностью. Я уже вам писала, что это должна быть брошюра, рассчитанная на широкие массы, а не учебник или теоретический труд. Вот почему в рамках массовой популярной брошюры невозможно втиснуть все, что нам хотелось бы сказать по этому вопросу и даже в связи с ним. (с. 193)

В ответном письме из Москвы, подписанным Ниной Поповой, Горошковой предлагалось точнее следовать правилам и инструкциям и чаще советоваться с Москвой:

> Для нас вопрос ясен. Следует выполнять принятые решения. Ваша задача в этом и состоит, чтобы, руководствуясь принятыми решениями и полученными здесь указаниями, добиться, чтобы Секретариат занимался не «исканиями», а действовал. [...]
>
> ...
>
> Хочется дать Вам один совет: когда решаются такие большие принципиальные вопросы, как выставка, как отношение Секретариата к движению в США и др. – лучше сначала посоветоваться, а потом высказывать свою точку зрения. Когда Вы высказываете на Секретариате свою точку зрения, а потом запрашиваете нас, вы ставите и себя и нас в затруднительное положение. При обсуждении таких острых принципиальных вопросов Вы можете внести предложение, отложить решение вопроса под каким-либо предлогом, скажем, под предлогом необходимости изучить вопрос, подумать.[22]

«Как теперь будет, если Сталин – деспот, тиран, как говорит западная пресса?» Советские сотрудницы Секретариата в Берлине и разоблачение «культа личности» Сталина

Пожалуй, одним из наиболее сложных моментов в работе советских сотрудниц МДФЖ в Берлине в первые десятилетия деятельности организации стали события XX съезда КПСС. Представляется, что в этот момент Москва потеряла прежний контроль за деятельностью сотрудниц, инструкции запаздывали, и все решения должны были приниматься на месте и индивидуально. Именно события первых дней и месяцев после XX съезда позволяют понять степень самостоятельности/зависимости советских представительниц в их повседневной работе:

> Ставлю вас в известность, что наше положение в Секретариате МДФЖ осложнилось тем, что наши друзья на основе различных сообщений по радио и в прессе обращаются к нам с вопросами относительно культа личности и в частности, о роли Сталина в истории нашей партии, государства и международного рабочего движения. Много толков вызвало выступление Микояна на XXм съезде, а затем выступление Вальтера Ульбрихта от 4.03 и 18.03, когда он заявил, что Сталин не является классиком марксизма-ленинизма, а в другой статье он изложил часть из неопубликованного доклада Хрущева на XXм съезде о культе личности. Эти статьи вызвали много толкований самого различного характера, но в большинстве случаев друзья приходили к нам и с возмущением говорили, что Ульбрихт не имеет права так говорить о Сталине, и как бы высказывали нам свое сочувствие. (письмо Зои Ивановой Н. Поповой, , 24.03.1956)[23]

Так как сотрудницам Секретариата задавали много вопросов, Зоя Иванова и, видимо, другие советские сотрудницы в конце концов вынуждены быть давать какие-то пояснения. Однако, как свидетельствуют архивные документы, их собственные знания были весьма ограничены, особенно в первые дни после XX съезда:

> Что касается самой личности, тов. Сталина и других, я ответила на этот вопрос, чтобы не дать повода для неправильных толкований. К тому же тогда я абсолютно ничего не знала, что я узнала позже из доклада Хрущева.[24]

Представляется, что Иванова была особенно обеспокоена престижем женской организации и Советского Союза:

> сейчас нам отмалчиваться нельзя, это может отдалить наших друзей от нас и повредит нашей работе здесь. Нам кажется , что нужно внести ясность о роли Сталина в истории советского общества. Нельзя допустить, чтобы наши друзья ориентировались на западную вредную прессу и был повод для неправильных толкований, выгодных нашим врагам. (с.66)

Однако она испытывает разочарование, так как не получает нужных ей инструкций и объяснений у других советских работников в Берлине:

> Мы обратились за советом в партком и посольство, но они наотрез отказались нам что-нибудь советовать.
>
> Еще раз выражаем сожаление, что по таким принципиальным и важным вопросам для международного фронта, мы, работники (хотя и маленькие) этого фронта, находящиеся далеко от страны, информируемся в последнюю очередь и оказываемся в очень затруднительном положении. (с.67)

Таким образом, можно заключить, что советские сотрудницы секретариата в Берлине ощущали себя прежде всего ответственными за соблюдение международных интересов Советского Союза, а не защитницами прав женщин. Внезапное изменение дискурса в 1956 году привело к временному кризису устоявшегося нарратива о советском и, следовательно, к существенным проблемам в исполнении рабочих функций. При этом, многие «работники этого фронта», как сотрудницы определяли себя, старались исполнить свою задачу как можно лучше и поэтому готовы были принимать собственные решения и даже спорить со своим московским руководством.

«И время занято так, что нет ни минуты даже для работы над собой». Общественное и личное в жизни советских сотрудниц Секретариата

Как уже говорилось, официальные письма и документы, сохранившиеся в архиве, практически не дают возможности понимания того, что думали советские сотрудницы Секретариата о Федерации и ее руководстве, насколько важными представлялись им интересы и права женщин и как они оценивали работу сотрудниц Секретариата из других стран. Как уже говорилось, не удалось найти никаких сведений о биографиях этих сотрудниц, их семейной жизни и внерабочих интересах. Однако, часть документов предоставляет нам возможность «заглянуть» в повседневную жизнь сотрудниц Секретариата и, в том числе, обратиться к «специфически женским» аспектам их опыта советской работы за рубежом.

Представляется, что работа в секретариате была довольно напряженной эмоциональной работой, которая требовала хорошего психологического и физического здоровья. Действительно, взаимоотношения с другими сотрудницами были в центре внимания советских представительниц – весь успех их работы зависел от установления и поддержания хороших отношений с коллегами и умения убеждать и аргументировать. Именно поэтому вопросы здоровья и эмоционального климата нередко оказывались в центре секретной переписки; по всей видимости, каждая сотрудница должна была информировать Москву о существующих или возможных проблемах. Например, в письме от 29 июня 1956 года Зоя Иванова описывает проблемы взаимоотношений и рабочей этики другой советской сотрудницы, Дрыниной.

Секретно. Поповой

> Должна вам сообщить, что у т. Дрыниной сложились не очень хорошие взаимоотношения с друзьями из комиссии журнала. [...]. Зам. Редактора сказала мне, что Нина непозволительно грубо с ними разговаривает, не принимает совершенно замечаний на ее предложения. Но она не знает условий пропаганды и условий работы женских организаций в странах и не прислушивается к нам.

[Далее автор письма сообщает, каким образом она пыталась изменить ситуацию]:

> Я попытаюсь с ней еще раз поговорить, узнать в чем дело, что ей мешает, кроме того, что ее работа не интересует. Чем ее можно заинтересовать. Но, Нина Васильевна, она ведь взрослый человек, ей 35 лет, работала в обкоме, и я считаю неудобным с ней разговаривать в таком плане. Может, я и не права в этом?[25]

В то время, как образ женщины-матери, как уже отмечалось, занимал большое место в пропаганде МДФЖ, сотрудницы Секретариата в своих письмах в Москву практически никогда не выражали собственную женскую и материнскую позицию и не аргументировали свое мнение с помощью собственного опыта материнства или материнской позиции. Однако мне удалось найти два документа, которые позволяют понять, что по меньшей мере некоторые сотрудницы Секретариата были матерями, совмещали материнство с работой в Секретариате или были эмоционально связаны с детьми на расстоянии. Оба этих документа упоминают материнство вскользь, как «частное» и не имеющее прямого отношения к «работе» дело.

В первом случае, многостраничное письмо из Москвы лишь в самом начале содержит краткое и написанное «казенным» языком поздравление сотруднице в Берлине (Кошелевой) по случаю рождения ребенка. Остальная часть письма – это обычная рабочая информация:

> Дорогая Татьяна Кирилловна!
>
> Получили твое письмо. С величайшей радостью поздравляю тебя со счастливым материнством и благополучным исходом родов. Приятно слышать о том, что малый вполне здоров и растет не по дням, а по часам. Сердечно поздравляю и С.И. – молодого отца. Желаю ему вместе с тобой воспитать здоровую смену.
>
> Т.К.! Мы внимательно ознакомились со всеми письмами, присланными нам. Нужно сказать, что содержание писем Жаннет и Мари-Клод, а особенно твоего, удивило нас. Главный вопрос – созыв заседания исполкома. Нам кажется, что аргументы, изложенные Ж. и М.-К. – неубедительны. (8–08–1946)[26]

Таким образом, можно заключить, что, несмотря на использование образа женщины-матери в пропагандистских материалах Федерации, рождение ребенка у одной из сотрудниц организации не становится поводом для выражения личных эмоций. Напротив, советское идеологическое клише «здоровая смена» призывает адресата письма рассматривать это событие не с эмоционально-телесной, а с государственно-идеологической точки зрения.

Другое письмо (от Л. Петровой) – вероятно, ответ на письмо сотрудницы (Горошковой) в Берлине, где она с беспокойством спрашивала о самочувствии своей дочери-студентки:

> Галина Николаевна!

С Иночкой говорила. Откуда Вы взяли, что она грустит? Наоборот, она очень жизнерадостна, ходит в университет. Занимается после университета. Правда, ее трудно застать дома, потому что не хватает учебников, она вынуждена заниматься у подруг. Вы не беспокойтесь, дома все благополучно.[27]

Письма из Москвы также информируют о перечисленных зарплатах и переводах.

> Зинаида Алексеевна!
>
> Деньги на 1950й год оформили только в начале января и перевели вам телеграфом 20 января (задержка была из-за оформления образцов подписей). Внешторгбанк заверил, что деньги будут у вас не позднее 21 числа. [....]
>
> Что касается 1949 года, то все наши кредиты за тот год исчерпаны, так как ваши командировочные расходы отнесены валютным управлением за счет лимита зарплаты, а в 1950м году могут быть покрыты только за счет экономии, потому что никаких дополнительных средств ни в коем случае на дают.
>
> С уважением,
>
> С. Ильин [28]

Наконец, письма свидетельствуют о том, что работа советских представительниц в Секретариате было довольно напряженной, что иногда превращало служебную иерархию в подобие семейной:

> Я очень виновата перед Вами, дорогая Лидия Ивановна, опять не смогла перепечатать замечания. Не ругайте меня. Каждый день ложусь в 1–2 часа и встаю в 7 утра и время занято так, что нет ни минуты даже для работы над собой.
>
> *Сделаю обязательно. Следующей почтой вышлю все!* (из письма Горошковой в Москву Лидии Петровой, 1.12.1952).[29]

Заключение

Анализ переписки, и тем более деловой и секретной, конечно, не позволяет нам узнать о взглядах авторов на их работу непосредственно. Однако переписка, пусть официальная и секретная, тем не менее позволяет нам немного лучше представить общую атмосферу принятия решений в Федерации и то место, которое отводилось советским представительницам Москвой. В то же время, несмотря на все ограничения накладываемые характером переписки, мы также можем узнать чуть больше о том, как описывали свою работу женщины, чья основная деятельность состояла в защите прав женщин на международном уровне. В частности, переписка показывает, что работницам Секретариата вполне удалось овладеть деловым языком организаторов международных встреч, поддерживать отношения с московским начальством и налаживать непростые отношения с представительницами других женских организаций. В то время, как главной задачей советских сотрудниц в Секретариате явилось исполнение предписаний Москвы, в условиях МДФЖ это означало умение использовать гибкую тактику, показывать дружелюбие и скрывать свои чувства. С другой стороны, ни один из найденных мною документов не дает основания предполагать, что сотрудницы Секретариата испытывали личную потребность (помимо функций делегированных им государством) в выражении какой-либо позиции в защиту интересов той или иной группы женщин. В отличие от представительниц женских организаций других стран, в том числе коммунисток, на многочисленные дискуссии и мнения которых советские представительницы постоянно ссылаются в своих документах, они сами по большей части лишь транслировали те идеи, которые требовало московское руководство МДФЖ. Наконец, они продолжали выполнение своих «материнских функций», которые рассматривались руководством как «естественные», но которые они, как и большинство советских женщин, выполняли в свободное от работы время, не имея возможности выбора.

[1] Наталья Козлова, Ирина Сандомирская, *"Я так хочу назвать кино". "Наивное письмо": опыт лингво-социологического чтения* (Москва: Гнозис, 1996).
[2] Ирина Сандомирская, "Наивное письмо 15 лет спустя или на смерть соавтора." *Неприкосновенный запас* (2012), 2 http://magazines.russ.ru/nz/2012/2/s14-pr.html
[3] См. Francisca De Haan, "Continuing Cold War Paradigms in Western Historiography of Transnational Women's Organizations: The Case of the Women's International Democratic Federation (WIDF), Women's History Review" (2010) 19(4), 547–573; Melanie Ilic, "Soviet Women, Cultural Exchange and the Women's international Democratic Federation," in *Reassessing Cold War Europe,* ed. Autio-Sarasmo, S. & K. Miklossy (London: Routledge, 2011), 157–174; Chiara Bonfiglioli, *Revolutionary Networks. Women's Political and Social Activism in Cold war Italy and Yugoslavia (1945-1957),* PhD Dissertation, (Utrecht: Utrecht University, 2012) https://dspace.library.uu.nl/bitstream/handle/1874/254104/Bonfiglioli.pdf?sequence
[4] Антифашистский Комитет Советских Женщин был создан в Москве в 1941 по приказу Сталина, вскоре после официального вступления СССР во Вторую Мировую Войну. Впоследствии комитет был переименован в Комитет Советских Женщин. Нина Попова была первым председателем комитета (Ilic, "Soviet Women; Р.А. Григорьева, *Голубь мира Нины Поповой. К 65-летию победы в Великой Отечественной войне, создания МДФЖ и 45-летию присвоения Москве звания города-героя.* (Москва: Тончу, 2010).
[5] Все цитаты приводятся с сохранением орфографии и пунктуации оригинала.
[6] Государственный архив Российской Федерации (ГАРФ), фонд 7928, Антифашистский Комитет Советских Женщин; Российский Государственный Архив Социальной и Политической Истории (РГАСПИ). Фонд 17 137 818.
[7] Chiara Bonfiglioli, *Revolutionary Networks.*
[8] Журнал издавался на английском, французском, немецком, испанском, русском, а с 1970-х годов – на арабском языке.
[9] Francisca de Haan, "The Global Left-Feminist 1960s. From Copenhagen to Moscow and New York", in *The Routledge Handbook of the Global Sixties,* Chen Jian, Martin Klimke et al., eds. (London& New York: Routledge, 2018), 230-242.
[10] Ibid. См. также Jadwiga Pieper-Mooney, "Fighting Fascism and Forging New Political Activism: The Women's International Democratic Federation in the Cold War," in *Decentering Cold War History,* ed. J. Pieper-Mooney & F. Lanza (London: Routledge 2013), 52–73; Celia Donert, "Whose Utopia? Gender, Ideology and Human Rights at the 1975 World Congress in East Berlin", in *The Breakthrough. Human Rights in the 1970s,* Jan Eckel & Samuel Moyn, eds. (Philadelphia: University of Pennsylvania, 2014), 68–87.
[11] Елена Тончу, *Россия – женская судьба. Век XX–XXI.* (Санкт-Петербург: Тончу, 2004), 199.
[12] Ibid., 263.
[13] Григорьева, *Голубь мира Нины Поповой.*
[14] ГАРФ 7928 1 4, 1.
[15] ГАРФ 7928 1 4, 3.
[16] РГАСПИ 17 137 818, 37.
[17] ГАРФ 7928 4 115, 10.

¹⁸ "*Маддалена мне сказала, что о работе у нее нет желания даже говорить. Все бесполезно, т.к. даже советские не понимают их позицию. Но пройдет время и все поймут, что они правы, также как поняли ошибку с Югославией. Она имеет в виду: характер массовой организации должен быть иной, чем сейчас, и что автономия сейчас только на словах, а на деле 'МДФЖ это маховик партии'".* (В ЦК КПСС. Комитет советских женщин направляет информацию советского представителя в МДФЖ т. Ивановой З. П., 2.04.1957. ГАРФ 7928 4 115, 79) Подробнее об этом см. Bonfiglioli, *Revolutionary Networks*.

¹⁹ ГАРФ 7928 4 106, 1956, 6.

²⁰ Элеонор Рузвельт (Eleanor Roosevelt) в 1945–1952 являлась послом США в ООН, она также была главой Комиссии ООН по правам человека. В письме, адресованном генеральному секретарю МДФЖ, Мари-Клод Вайян-Кутурье от 1952 г., одним из авторов которого была Рузвельт, категорически отвергается советская версия о применении американскими войсками в Корее бактериологического оружия (РГАСПИ, 17 5 818, 146).

²¹ РГАСПИ, 17 137 818, 192.

²² РГАСПИ 17 137 818, 4.11.52, 118–119.

²³ ГАРФ 7928 4 106, 64.

²⁴ Там же, 64.

²⁵ ГАРФ 7928 4 115, 75–76.

²⁶ ГАРФ 7928 4 5, 20–21.

²⁷ ГАРФ 7928 4 66, 1952, 157.

²⁸ ГАРФ 7928 4 45, 1950, 11.

²⁹ ГАРФ 7928 4 66, 155–156.

Politics and Talk:
the Final Debate in the 2018 Swedish Elections

JAAKKO TURUNEN & INGA BRANDELL

Politics does not always contain talk. Demonstrating in the streets with banners, slogans or songs is a political act which itself does not include talk. The same goes for repression by the police of demonstrations considered unlawful. Nor does the political act of *exit*, such as for example refusing to pay taxes or simply emigrating and leaving the polity to which one belonged necessarily include talk. And, of course, in the case of using those "other means" of politics, as war was defined by Clausewitz, talk is mainly absent. In an ordered, peaceful democratic parliamentary setting, however, politics is very much about public talk.

Now, talk in a democracy includes many different conditions and contexts, from being part of a social chat outside any formal setting to very organized debates in elected assemblies. It can be difficult to draw a line between talk and exchange by means of texts posted on internet chat sites or Twitter or sent out for comments to any of the many institutional and bureaucratic settings that constitute the structure of a modern polity. Central among these places where talk takes place is the parliament. With the rise of parliamentarism, free and unhindered talk became in fact institutionalized and has formed thereafter the bedrock of democratic politics. Institutionalized talk in the parliament has a number of connected aspects. It is the primary medium for debating and forging laws that come to legislate daily life in the polity. Talk has a deliberative function in the legislative process. However, talk in the parliament is also the medium of sovereignty to the extent that it materializes the link between the members of the parliament and their constituencies. Further, talk in the parliament also informs and enlightens the public and thus takes part in the ongoing discussions in the public sphere. Talk has thus a perlocutionary function.

Public talk during election time is yet another context, which, within the structure of both ancient and contemporary democracy, constitutes the linchpin of rule by the people. It is here that both its basic values and its practical functioning are unfolded: the freedom of speech and assembly as fundamental values, and the possibility for voters to make an *informed* and hence, based on their ideological or other preferences, *rational* choice of a political party or politician when casting their ballots. The final televised debate, whether between the two candidates for the presidency, as in France or the United States or between party leaders during parliamentary elections in other countries, is often the climax of public political talk. It engenders popular and mass media comments and is sometimes also considered to be decisive for the results of the election.

The dramaturgical and aesthetic aspects are also relevant in face-to-face debates involving several participants. So is the role of the mediator(s), i.e., the journalists who steer the debate. Scholars invested in mass media research have of course investigated both the content and the impact of the format on political talk. Here we will dive into such an exchange, the televised final debate in the 2018 Swedish parliamentary election, in particular one sequence of it. Our purpose is a bit different. We will discuss and test some contemporary approaches to public talk, thereby at the same time contributing to the analysis of current politics.

The final debate in the 2018 elections

The leaders of the eight political parties represented in the Swedish parliament gathered on September 7, 2018 for a "Final Debate", organized by the state-funded Channel 2. Sweden, with its long history of Social Democratic dominance, had since 2014 been ruled by a minority government led by this party. With good reason, the coming election was considered unpredictable, and forming a government was expected to be difficult. The party leaders' view of this coming process was one of the five selected topics for the debate. The others were the crisis in the health care system, climate politics, integration politics and the economy.

The question concerning government coalitions had become pressing as the election campaign progressed. The traditional "blocs" in Swedish politics—the Alliance on the right, which included the Moderates and three small parties (the Centre, the Liberals and the Christian Democrats), and the Red-Greens on the left, which formally included the Social Democrats and the Greens and informally also the Left, were both undermined by the rise of the populist Sweden Democrats, who were predicted to score anything between 15 and 25 percent of the vote. The opinion polls indicated that neither bloc would be able to form the government alone and would need to gain support from the other bloc, as both blocs had renounced the SD as a potential coalition partner. In addition, polls indicated that the small parties from both blocs—the Greens, Liberals and Christian Democrats—were all on the verge of falling below the electoral threshold and thereby out of the parliament, something that rendered the election outcome unstable and unpredictable. This created a double dynamic in the debate. On the one hand, the blocs had to show their unity. On the other hand, the smaller parties had to point out their distinctiveness within the blocs. In principle, then, the conditions for a great deliberative performance were set: pressure to forge a common will, willingness to argue for different courses of action, a common enemy, and an audience waiting to learn about the formation of a common will, possible future courses of action, and to make up their minds as to which party they would vote for.

One of the five topics, climate politics, is particularly interesting, and we will focus on an extract from it. Being in a sense the "least" political of the topics, it offers good ground for digging into the nature of deliberation in Swedish politics. Climate policy is not only a technocratic question for the experts and politicians, but involves broad public opinion building. This double bind—decision-making inside institutions and public opinion formation in society—captures the nature of deliberation as the complex idea developed by Jürgen Habermas in his book *Between Facts and Norms*, to which we will return below. On the one hand, deliberation in this understanding is a desired mode of talk within the representative institutions; on the other hand, it is a way to form public opinion that can also to be used against those in power. A TV debate like the one discussed here captures both aspects of deliberation. It is a showcase of politicians talking to one another. At the same time, the real audience of the debate sits at the other end of the TV signal and is tuned to make an informed opinion on the basis of the different political views presented on the matter.

Ways to analyze political talk

Given the centrality of talk to democratic politics, political science has actively worked on the question of how talk takes place or should take place in politics. Each of the aspects of talk described above—deliberative, representative, and perlocutionary—has its own traditions of inquiry.

In most studies of deliberation, political scientists more or less versed in Habermas's work often make two claims. Deliberation is seen as a way of debating that adjusts and coordinates conflicting interests so that a consensus based on the facts may emerge. The other claim is that deliberation, being rational by nature, always brings about a better solution to concrete problems. Both claims rest on the argument that deliberation is about the truth that is transmitted in talk. Perhaps the best example of this tradition comes from the study of the Discourse Quality Index, a tool designed to assess the deliberative quality of argumentation in politics.[1] The Index is designed to construct the truth value of an argument as the proxy of its deliberativeness. In other words, the most deliberative talk is supposed to be that which proceeds logically from true premises to true conclusions.

The researchers behind the DQI hold that this assumption is derived from Habermas's communicative action and the validity claims—the claims for truth, normative rightness and truthfulness—he held to be universal to any adult interaction. Such a clinical view of deliberation is, however, questionable if we look at Habermas's work as a whole. In his habilitation thesis, *The Structural Transformation of the Public Sphere*, Habermas traces the history of how the exchange of information through speech was able to establish a general public opinion that challenged the position of the monarch and paved the way for social emancipation.[2] A different view on deliberation emerges in his *The Theory of Communicative Action*, which puts more emphasis on the mode of talk than on its power in society.[3] However, these two ideas find one another in his later work *Between Facts and Norms*,[4] where the transformatory critique developed in *The Structural Transformation* finds its place in autonomous civil society, and the discursive rationality as a critique of public communication developed in *The Theory of Communicative Action* is placed within the institutions of democratic governance. In this sense, Habermas's view on deliberation is grounded in the ability to build public opinion on facts and to use that power against both the authority of the *ancien regime* and any attempts to use power to steer individuals. Hence rationality for Habermas was never reduced to an apt description of reality, but is a communicative property for questioning power and coercion in society.

Political talk understood as rhetoric

Thus, Habermas's view on deliberation did not lack considerations of power relations in society. However, his examples, especially in his earlier works, still very much relied on debates that are best characterized as concerning factual questions. Such debates rarely take place in real politics, not even in Sweden. Instead, political talk is rhetorical, understood in a broad sense. For Christian Kock, rhetoric is concerned with the domain of deciding between different courses of action.[5] Politics in his view then appears as debate or deliberation over new courses of action, where different participants deliberate over them, represent different sides of the polity and try to persuade their listeners—the three aspects identified earlier in talk in politics.

Deciding on different possible courses of action is different from the epistemic concern about the truth value of the argument developed, for instance, in the DQI, as well as from the common view that rhetoric is just about persuasion everywhere and always.[6] For Kock, rhetoric is not about resolving conflicts by retracting or modifying opinions. Nor is it about establishing the validity of different positions. It is about discussing different options. And that which belongs to the domain of talk—choices to be made in politics, economics, education—affects the kind of rhetoric that is used. Politics as legislative business, or, more generally, matters concerned with the prevailing order in polity, is about legislating how the world should be; it is rarely just about telling how it is. Indeed, more rhetorically oriented political scientists commonly speak about the future orientation of political actions emanating from the conflicts that characterize politics.

To follow Kock's reading of Aristotle, rhetoric was not a universal art of persuasion, but was limited to a specific domain of debate (*bouleuometha*) where we—and he quotes *Nicomachean Ethics*—"deliberate, take counsel or make a decision".[7] Aristotle, Kock further points out, limited deliberation to the practical and political capacity of the people concerned. Consequently, it was not for the Athenians to deliberate on matters having to do with India or how to square a circle, "for the first are not in *our* power, the second is wholly beyond the power of action".[8] Kock argues that deliberation is limited to the practical concerns of polity, where different choices can legitimately exist, but which nevertheless fall under the power of human action and the sovereignty of the polity. On matters relating to a good life, many possibilities can coexist. It is here that deliberation is needed. Practical reasoning that aims at deciding on the preferable course of action proceeds from the good value *backwards* to different actions that can help bring about that good. This contrasts sharply to an epistemic logic that proceeds from a true proposition and attempts to *maintain* the truth conveyed by the proposition. Deliberation in this sense does not necessarily bring about consensus, but it forges a will to which one either freely consents or under the prevailing circumstances acquiesces. From this view, rhetoric—and deliberation as its crowning jewel—should be understood as actions carried out in the public sphere.

Back to the final debate

Let us now return to the debate and scrutinize an excerpt of it. The sequence below is introduced by an exchange of opinions between the Centre – "the greenest in the Alliance" – and the Sweden Democrats, whose climate consciousness had been questioned many times during the election campaign. The Centre Party begins by stating that climate change is the fateful question of our time. In contrast, the leader of the Sweden Democrats (SD), Jimmie Åkesson, begins with a confession: "I am convinced that climate change is a fact. I am convinced that humans affect climate change." He thus places himself within the discursive consensus on climate change in Swedish politics. He continues less placidly by pointing out that Sweden stands for one per mille of the world's CO_2 emissions and therefore the SD, Åkesson argues, will financially invest elsewhere, where emissions are higher than in Sweden. The reporter asks the Centre leader, Annie Lööf, if "it is more effective to diminish [emissions] abroad?" to which Lööf replies that "[n]aturally we will invest abroad, [...] but how can we assume the responsibility if we do not go first ourselves? The Sweden Democrats want in addition to leave international cooperation. You have declined the climate law, you have turned down zero emissions, [said] no to the Paris Agreement [...]. Jimmie Åkesson, you say no to the Paris Agreement, that global agreement that many countries have concluded in order to diminish emissions. You call yourselves Sweden democrats but in reality you are "somewhere-else-democrats", that is, someone else should fix it. We have to assume the leadership..." Once Annie Lööf finishes, the mediators turn back to Åkesson with the question: "Can one do it somewhere else than in Sweden, Jimmie Åkesson?" to which Åkesson replies "No, and our politics is not about... it is about, we will in fact increase Swedish food production..." The fateful question of the world has thus effectively become a question of Swedish leadership and local food production. Åkesson does recognize in the end of his reply that this is not really the question that was originally put on the table, but it is too late now, for the argument about "climate leadership" is continued by the following speakers, the leaders of the Greens, the Moderates, and the Social Democrats.

The sequence is typical of televised political debate, where two (or more) politicians engage in an exchange with the TV reporters mediating it. In the quoted sequence, the politicians present their "good" and desired course of action. It is, as Kock pointed out when there are many desired courses of actions that deliberation can and does take place. The sequence is also typical in that it creates a catchy phrase that is used to reproduce an image of the political position of the opponent. In this case, Annie Lööf turns the party name "Sweden Democrats" into a trope of "somewhere-else-democrats" to characterize the climate policy of the SD. This trope neatly plays into the hands of Lööf, whose argument was that Sweden should show "leadership" in the climate question, irrespective of the counterargument that the material effect of Swedish climate policy globally is negligible. The two different courses of action: leadership and reputation (or what Åkesson calls "symbolic") in Lööf's argument contrast with the material results in Åkesson's argument. In fact, they never really meet because the trope of "somewhere else" is used to mediate the turns in the exchange. Perhaps this is persuasion. The mediators, at least, were persuaded by the vibe and sound of the trope and used it to steer the debate further.

Kock's focus on rhetoric as belonging to a certain domain is relevant here, and his argument that its logic proceeds from the goal to the means to achieve it describes the reality of political talk more aptly than the logical exercise mapped in the DQI. But his approach is unable to capture the drastic reduction of complexity and contingency prevalent in the beginning of the debate, when climate change is presented as the Big Question, a wicked problem of the world necessitating action as well as awe, and Åkesson's tactical but rational maneuvering between Sweden and somewhere-else. During a couple of turns of argument, the problem and the different positions proposed become a matter of territorially delineated "leadership". There is a magnificent reduction of complexity achieved here.

How did the two party leaders end up there? Neither position as such could be considered wrong. Rather, as Kock argues, in the case of action, multiple different courses can be equally legitimate and reasonable. Nor can it be argued that Åkesson gave his "adherence freely", as Kock describes the result of persuasion taking place in practical matters. It is equally problematic to argue that Lööf, with the wit of "ethos and pathos, topical selectivity, audience adaptation, presentational devices, and more,"[9] persuaded him. Rather, Åkesson got trapped, but he did not give up his position or change his course of action, and the complex issue became a simple one. On a more serious level, it is the reduction of a complex question into something simple and manageable that poses the greatest threat to deliberation. On multiple occasions, Kock underlines the Aristotelian insight that a choice cannot be true or false; with choices there is always a plurality of actions and ideas. It is this plurality that has gone missing in the example from the televised election debate. There are at least two possible explanations of this reduction.

One lies within "discourse", the other addresses the turn-taking as controlled by the mediators and the rhetoric of it. We will now look more closely at both.

The above excerpt showed how both discourse and certain catchy phrases can steer the debate. Coming from outside the mainstream of Swedish politics, Åkesson felt it necessary first to indicate his sympathy with the hegemonic discourse on climate change; his criticism could only take place within this constellation. Yet this is not all there is to it. As is revealed here, the interactive dynamic within the turn-taking cannot be subordinated to the discourse. The moderators were instrumental in hooking on to Lööf's phrase "somewhere else" and turning it to support her argument on leadership. The concept of "leadership" had appeared in the debate for the first time in connection with the need for health care reform. It emerged when the leader of the Moderate Party contrasted the presence of resources and of political will: resources alone are not enough, there must also be political will. Annie Lööf from the Centre Party continued the Moderate leader's reasoning: by not tackling the problems in the health care system, the Red-Green government was showing disrespect towards the citizens. Better management, that is leadership, is both possible and necessary. Annie Lööf used the term "leadership" to distinguish between the political blocs, where the government in charge was accused of lacking political will, and thereby leadership, and where the Alliance "must show leadership". It is clear that the use of the term "leadership" was extended from the question of implementing specific policy measures to the general ability to steer the country. Political will and leadership, however, are not quite the same thing. Political will accompanies questions of power, representation and even sovereignty, but leadership is an administrative and technocratic term. Political will articulates a connection between the people and the politicians, whereas leadership articulates a self-subsistent elite. Political will is about decisions and directions in politics; leadership is about the stamina to implement and manage issues. Thus "leadership" in this debate became a standard rhetorical weapon with which the Alliance could attack the Red-Greens as lacking leadership, as being incapable of it and perhaps not understanding its importance. Leadership is connected with the main election promise of the Alliance to change the government, which is itself, of course, a political ambition but is presented as a technical question of leadership.

From rhetorics to semiotics

The fact that the same concept came to organize several different political domains constitutes a problem within the idea of deliberation that Kock entertains. His main argument against epistemic reasoning on deliberation is that, because deliberation concerns choices, it cannot be driven to any one true position. On the contrary, a legitimate pluralism should prevail. The excerpt above shows how the legitimate pluralism that existed in the beginning of the debate on climate policy was reduced to a question of leadership by the moderators of the debate. But it also shows how the term "leadership" itself was already a contextual reduction of a more complex question about political will and vision which tended to become technical and subject to measures of management. Further, the fact that "leadership" was the proposed solution to problems ranging from health care to climate policy also indicates that politics in this understanding is expected to yield to standardized responses with little or no contextual consideration. This is not deliberation in the sense understood by Kock.

To pursue further our analysis of the final debate and the study of talk in politics, we turn to cultural semiotics in the mode developed by Yuri Lotman. In the beginning we pointed out that final debates before general elections tend to "condense" the political situation at hand. Lotman approached culture as a process of turning entropy into information.[10] In our case, this approach leads us to ask how certain ways of understanding performed in the debate came to provide organization both to it and also to contemporary Swedish politics in more general terms.

In the excerpt we have used to discuss deliberation, a powerful reduction of choices seems to take place. This is concretized in the way that the catchy phrase "somewhere-else-democrats" is able to disparage the Sweden Democrats and exclude Åkesson's arguments from the realm of Swedish politics. Why just this phrase turns out to be so central is due to both institutional and semiotic conditions. On the institutional plane, the debate reflects the political blocs, where the Sweden Democrats are ostracized while the Centre remains in the neoliberal mainstream. The same division is further reflected in the fact that it is Åkesson, who feels the need to affirm his position within the common discourse on climate change, and it is Annie Lööf's phrase that is used by the moderators to question Åkesson. In other words, the phrase "somewhere-else-democrats" not only reflects the institutional balance of power and political discourse, but was also used effectively by the logics of a

TV debate to create tension, contrast positions and drive home an easily digestible position that would somehow sum up what the debate was all about. On a semiotic level, putting the Sweden Democrats "somewhere else" is also an exclusion in a cultural sense. It is the text of "somewhere-else-democrats" that calls for a semiotic analysis: where does it come from? What is the information that is generated by the text? How does that information evolve? In other words, what kind of semiotic space is constructed by the phrase?

"Somewhere-else-democrats" is used to level criticism for not showing "leadership". As we saw, leadership evolved in turn out of political will, the political capacity that was used to explain the lack of results despite the alleged abundance of resources. "If it were only money and tax increases there would be no problems in Sweden", the Moderate leader criticized the Social Democrats. "You took away that special political will that was there to cut the health care queues", he continued. The Centre leader soon after adds that "showing leadership" explains the differences in access to health care in the country. This leadership then travels into climate politics, where the Centre continues "we also have to take leadership". Leadership thus appears to play out at two different levels. On the one hand, it is clearly an elite project that unfolds in the international arena, where Sweden performs as an exemplary country and declares that it will become the first fossil fuel-free country in the world. On the other hand, leadership is the leverage of the arguments directed against the still incumbent government: it is the lack of leadership that has thwarted policies to cut the health care queues, set the schools back on track, improve the infrastructure. The link between these two levels, as well as the phrase "somewhere-else-democrats", create a semiotic universe where taking responsibility and showing respect, both globally in the face of climate change and locally by tackling the health care queues, become condensed in the idea of leadership.

During the following autumn, the 2018 election was often described as the election where ideas and commitment came to occupy the foreground. The eventual good performance of the Centre party and the Christian Democrats—the latter of which initially feared losing its place in the parliament—was, for instance, explained by the argumentative skill of their leaders and the fact that these two parties showed a strong commitment to their central values. In the debate after the election, analysts generally claimed that this mirrors a new divide alongside the old left–right one, adding to politics a conservative-nationalist versus a progressive or "alternative" global value dimension. However, even this cursory analysis of "somewhere-else-democrats" puts many questions marks on this interpretation.

In the guise of a conclusion

More importantly, and in contrast to this mirror vision of the results of the election, we submit that the political talk itself in this debate can tell more about what is underway in Swedish politics. By way of conclusion, we thus put forward two tentative theses informed by Lotman's cultural semiotics on this debate and Swedish politics. These theses build upon the way in which the term leadership emerged to provide structure in and for the debate.

To begin with, both leadership and its semiotic origin in this debate, political will, have territorial boundaries. Hence leadership can only be shown within the Swedish jurisdiction. "Somewhere else" than in Sweden does not make sense in this context. Leadership thus requires that a link between the global and the local be institutionalized as bearing responsibility, putting forward an example, making a point. It is difficult to deny the rational potential in Åkesson's argument that climate change is best fought where emissions are highest, but this undeniably does not make a point in global politics, nor does it set a target worth aspiring to in domestic affairs. To apply the prism of Sweden to global problems is as such nothing new to Swedish politics, but reflects the longer tradition of Swedish exceptionalist thinking manifested perhaps most outspokenly in assuming the moral—and now also green—voice of the world. This voice, here conveyed as leadership, excludes the rationality and feasibility of focusing on concrete technical solutions to climate change unless they take the form of territorially bound Swedish leadership.

Secondly, leadership as an elite project posits the importance of values, but it ascribes these values to the elites and detaches them from the citizens' concrete interests. To organize politics only around values marks a definite rupture from Social Democratic society, where economy and interests were closely linked to values. Values can be serviced by identification, but interests often call forth action and therefore might have a closer bond with rights. In this closing debate, the rights of the citizens are evoked only in connection with immigrants. Climate leadership—and other areas of leadership promoted during the debate—were not about everyone's right to clean air or the relationship between the citizen and the state, but about self-referential talk whose main purpose was to provide a structure for politics that can claim progress and that everyone can admire but with which no interaction, no engagement, is necessary. This, perhaps unintentionally, was also the outcome of the moderators' actions during the debate. By structuring the exchange on catchy phrases initially designed to exclude, they contributed to reducing the possible courses of action present in the debate and advanced politics relying on symbolic values with no concrete and active bond between the citizen and the state.

Instead of making an "informed choice" on the basis of information about the different parties' proposed solutions to the problems and issues discussed, voters were left to themselves. Thus, in the condensed setting of the final debate, the information received was not much about proposed actions and solutions, while the meaning generated—once again—told us "who we are".

[1] Marco M. Steenbergen et al., "Measuring Political Deliberation: A Discourse Quality Index", *Comparative European Politics*, 2003(1): 21–48; Jürg Steiner et al., *Deliberative Politics in Action: Analyzing Parliamentary Discourse* (Cambridge: Cambridge UP, 2004); Jürg Steiner, *The Foundations of Deliberative Democracy: Empirical Research and Normative Implications* (Cambridge: Cambridge UP, 2012).
[2] Jürgen Habermas, *The Structural Transformation of the Public Sphere* (Cambridge MA.: The MIT Press, 1991).
[3] Jürgen Habermas, *The Theory of Communicative Action. Vols. 1 and 2* (Cambridge MA: The MIT Press, 1984 and 1987).
[4] Jürgen Habermas, *Between Facts and Norms* (Cambridge MA: The MIT Press, 1996).
[5] Christian Kock, "Choice is Not True or False: The Domain of Rhetorical Argumentation," *Argumentation* 23 (2009): 61–81.
[6] Christian Kock, "Aristotle on Deliberation: Its place in ethics, politics and rhetoric", in *Let's Talk Politics*, eds Hilde van Belle et al. (Amsterdam: John Benjamins, 2014).
[7] Kock, "Choice is not True or False," 67.
[8] Eudemian Ethics, 1226a, quoted in Kock, "Aristotle on Deliberation," 14.
[9] Kock, "Choice is not True or False," 77.
[10] Yuri Lotman, "On the Semiosphere," *Sign Systems Studies* 33.1 (2005): 205–229.

Reforms, Guns, and Soft Power
– Reflections on Russian Military Thinking

GUDRUN PERSSON

Dmitrii Alekseevich Miliutin, the Russian War Minister, attends a meeting with four members of the royal family: Tsar Alexander II, the heir apparent, Grand Dukes Mikhail Nikolaevich and Nikolai Nikolaevich. It is 24 March 1873. A lot is at stake.[1]

A few days before, Miliutin had been attacked personally—as had the military reforms he had been conducting since 1861. During the past twelve years, military education has been modernized, the military organization has been reformed, military districts had been introduced, and the War Ministry had taken control of the planning. Yet to be taken now is the main decision to pave the way for the introduction of universal conscription in Russia. In order to secure financing and broad political support for this major reform, the entire political and military elite has gathered for a strategic conference in the Winter Palace in St. Petersburg.

As is apparent from the seniority of the participants—which included five grand dukes, two field marshals, a number of senior ministers, and the Tsar as chairman—the issues discussed were of overriding importance.

A serious conflict broke out 10 March, the fourth day of the conference. The conservative opposition launched an alternative reform proposal. In practice, this plan would have undermined all of Miliutin's reforms, since it aimed at resurrecting the military organization that had been in place before the Crimean War (1853–1856)—an organization which had been condemned after the Russian defeat as rigid and ineffective. "A monstrous project", Miliutin wrote later. Field Marshal Fedor Fedorovich Berg, supported by Grand Dukes Mikhail Nikolaevich and Nikolai Nikolaevich, were among those who supported the alternative proposal. The meeting on 24 March took place separately from the conference.

Miliutin threatened to resign. Alexander II, who initially supported the plan, tried to calm him by explaining that it was not a question of changing the military administration (*voennoe upravlenie*) but only the organization of the troops. Miliutin was baffled:

> But is not the organization of the troops an essential part of the military organization (*voennoe ustroistvo*) of the State. The organization of the troops is

> linked to all the instructions of the War Ministry in every detail. Especially now, when we are about to introduce a new law on military service…

He wanted to create an organization in peacetime that resembled the structure during war, not least since the railways had drastically shortened mobilization time. Miliutin had tried to build a system that would adapt more readily to the requirements of contemporary warfare. With the growing size of wartime armies, military administration and organization had grown more complex. This required centralization. The troops needed weapons and supplies on an unprecedented scale. The shortened mobilization times required that plans were made in peacetime for the mobilization and the concentration of the troops. At the same time, flexibility was needed to allow each district to be responsible for the battle preparedness of the units within its jurisdiction. This required decentralization. The balance was delicate, but Miliutin believed he had achieved it through a unified War Ministry and the military districts. What he feared most was a return to the old, pre-Crimean army organization. Unity would be lost. Looking at Prussian efficiency in military organization and the requirements of contemporary warfare, Miliutin concluded that a step backwards would be detrimental to Russia's ability to defend herself.

His opponents wanted to create several independent armies, which would have undermined not only the War Ministry but also the military leadership of the military districts.

Tsar Alexander II eventually sided with his War Minister, against the will of his relatives. It was decided not to make any substantial changes to army organization.

Miliutin won the battle with the support of Alexander II, but he was disappointed. Apart from the larger political issues of the policy of reform, the conflict also had some ideological overtones concerning privileges and a resurrection of the pre-1856 Russian army organization. His opponents represented privilege and birth, whereas Miliutin represented merit and competence and the "self-made" man. He wrote in the diary that he started to keep after the conference at the age of 57:

> The dark clouds had passed by; apparently things had become quiet. The latest reports [by me] to the Tsar have reassured me. But I have no illusions. I know that the intrigue against me does not go away easily; after a defeat [the enemies] do not lay down their weapons, but will await new opportunities to renew the attacks, openly and behind the scenes.[2]

However, in spite of several attempts later, no dramatic changes were made to Miliutin's reforms in the coming years. The events in connection with the military reform in 1873 touch on vital questions such as military thinking, learning from foreign wars, and 'consequently' reform and reaction.

Rapid change

This article will focus on Russian military thinking during a few periods of rapid change. First, some of the contentious debates of the mid-nineteenth century will be discussed. Then, the contemporary issues will be outlined against the backdrop of the dissolution of the Soviet Union. This is not only a vastly understudied topic, but is also a subject that is closely connected to the larger issue at hand—the balance between strategy and political choices, and ultimately political reform in both Imperial and contemporary Russia.

In the mid-nineteenth century, the armed forces were affected by technological and scientific advances in conjunction with political, economic, and social change. Industrialization and technological development led to specialization and division of labour. New machinery in the factories, steam engine trains, and new production methods increasingly required specialists. The armies were no different, being, as one historian put it "not an independent section of the social system, but an aspect of it in its totality".[3]

A number of technical innovations—rifled weapons, railways, the electric telegraph—were introduced, and they affected the way wars were fought and armies were trained. Large standing armies grew smaller as the use of reserves and the introduction of universal conscription after the Prussian example spread across Europe. At the same time, nationalism gained in strength as Germany and Italy became unified nation states. The Austrian Empire was shaken to its foundations, and in 1867, the Austro-Hungarian dual-monarchy was created. In a mere twelve years, France had lost its position as the leading military power in Europe to Prussia.

The use of rifles, which made it possible to shoot with more speed and accuracy than with the old muskets, raised questions about tactics and the education of both soldiers and officers. Speed became a crucial factor in mobilization, which led to higher demands on advance war planning. The new military technology, while important, was only one aspect of change and—although expensive—was not the most difficult issue. Technology, after all, could be bought from abroad or copied at home. The creation of a large reserve force that could be called up in case of war required educated soldiers and officers who could train civilians in a relatively short period of time.

Consequently, the questions of military education, organization, and advance war planning (involving strategy, transportation, and supply) posed a greater challenge to the Russian army. The social and military implications were far-reaching. Soldiers as well as officers needed to be educated, and officers needed skills to quickly instruct civilians. The implications for the battlefield were also extensive in view of increased firepower.

The impact of firepower

In fact, one of the most topical questions discussed by military thinkers in Miliutin's time was the consequences of increased firepower. The development raised many questions: about possible changes in the tactical formations and entrenchment tactics, about ways to boost morale and to prepare the troops for the storm of bullets and shells on the battlefield of the future. Ultimately, how could the soldiers be trained to survive in the coming storm of steel?

Mikhail Dragomirov (1830–1905), an internationally renowned military thinker and member of, for instance, the Swedish Academy of War Sciences, was sent as a military observer to the battle of Königgrätz (1866), one of the deadliest battles of the period, which resulted in an Austrian defeat. It is worth briefly examining his writing in order to put into context one of the major debates in the 1870s—the impact of firepower.

Dragomirov's insistence on the moral element in warfare, which led him to talk more about the traditional bayonet attack than firepower, has given him a bad reputation in view of the Russian defeats in 1904–05 and in the First World War. As a consequence, his ideas and the rationale for his conclusions have been somewhat obscured. What did he say that made such an impression on contemporaries? His basic ideas can be summarized in three principles:

- to teach the soldier only what was necessary in war;
- to treat the soldier with respect;
- to emphasize the bayonet attack in training, not because firing was not important but because the bayonet attack required more psychological strength, which was more difficult to train and took longer to acquire.

These thoughts stood in sharp contrast to the traditional view in Russia on how to create an effective army. The first point was one of Suvorov's principles, but after the Crimean War, it also encompassed an indirect criticism of the army of Nicholas I, where the emphasis on training lay on the parade ground. The second point related to the efforts to create a more humane environment for the soldier, which was linked to a more restrictive use of corporal punishment. The third point essentially subscribed to the Napoleonic principle that war was largely a moral exercise.

It was L. M. Baikov, a young General Staff graduate, who started the debate in 1872 with an article in *Voennyi sbornik*,[4] a military journal founded in 1858, initially with Nikolai Chernyshevskii as the editor for a brief period.

Baikov claimed that the lessons of the battle of Königgrätz had not been properly appreciated. He acknowledged—in accordance with Dragomirov and others—that Königgrätz had shown the need to create a national (*narodnaia*) army and had demonstrated the need for national education and universal military service. However, he challenged Dragomirov in the tactical field by claiming that the traditional infantry attack in closed-order column had become almost impossible. He questioned the validity of Dragomirov's oft-repeated Suvorov dictum "The bullet is a fool, but the bayonet is a fine fellow". Königgrätz had led to a new age in tactics—the 'tactics of fire' as opposed to the 'tactics of the bayonet'. This meant that many small units should be the formation for attack, not the closed-order mass column. Baikov claimed that the infantry was by far the most important unit on the field, whereas artillery and cavalry had been assigned to support infantry. Fire was now the dominant factor on the battlefield.

An observer with the Prussian army in 1870–1871, L. L. Zeddeler, expressed similar views in an article where he summarized his impressions from the war.[5] More cautiously than Baikov, he noted the growing importance of fire on the battlefield and wondered whether Suvorov, had he been alive, would have trained his troops to attack in closed formation. He pointed out that the war had shown that the frontal attack had become very difficult to conduct and led to enormous losses. He argued that firearms had gained strength on the battlefield to the degree that "at least in this war, they have replaced the bayonet attack".

Dragomirov replied to both articles.[6] He accused Baikov of being incapable of an objective analysis and of being a "knight of the bullet". Dragomirov did not see anything that changed the established truth that fire prepared the way for the bayonet attack. He stressed that the bullet and the bayonet did not exclude, but rather complemented each other; consequently, the dispersed order was a complement to the closed order. The purpose in war was not to kill and wound as many as possible, but "to force the enemy to surrender to us". The morale of the troops (that is, the bayonet attack) is the determining factor on the battlefield, and it made little sense to talk about "tactics of fire" and "tactics of the bayonet", since the only tactics worth the name was "sound tactics".

In response to Zeddeler's doubts about Suvorov's training methods had he been alive, Dragomirov coldly replied that this issue was irrelevant:

> A change of weapons might lead to a change in training methods in how to handle this weapon, but it hardly has anything to do with the moral strength of people.

Why were Dragomirov and others so reluctant to diminish the emphasis on the bayonet in favour of fire? It was not, as sometimes believed, that the Russian tactical thinkers were unaware of, or underestimated, the increased importance of fire on the battlefield. One reason was the conviction that diminishing the emphasis on the bayonet would negatively affect the soldier's will to fight. It could potentially lead the soldier to be more concerned for his own safety than to concentrate on the task, which was to move forward in spite of the rain of bullets. In other words, firepower was seen as something that potentially could paralyze the troops.

There was also the fear that the soldiers would use all of their ammunition at an early stage and then would have to fight without any bullets. This was important, since there were several kinds of rifles in the Russian army, and the majority of them were effective only at close range.

Another reason for concern was that dispersed order meant less control of the troops. The closed column symbolized order. As armies had grown larger, so had the battlefield, and choosing dispersed order for the main formation could lead to complete chaos.

Finally, the 1870–1871 war could be seen as an eloquent confirmation of the opinion that technology alone is not sufficient to win wars. In this war, the Prussian needle gun was technically inferior to the French *chassepot*, yet Prussia had won.

The rediscovery of Miliutin

Miliutin resigned in 1881 after twenty years in office. Alexander II was killed and Alexander III did not ask for Miliutin's services. However, his thoughts and accomplishments are increasingly being rediscovered in contemporary Russia—almost a hundred years after his death. During the current military reform of the Russian Armed Forces, Nikolai Makarov has found inspiration from Miliutin. Makarov was Chief of the General Staff between 2008 and 2012, and he is one of the masters behind the military reform introduced in 2008. In his memoirs, *Na sluzhbe Rossii* (2017), Makarov clearly expresses his appreciation of Alexander II's War Minister.

Nikolai Makarov's career is closely tied to a period of rapid change. He had been approved to the prestigious General Staff Academy in Moscow on 30 August 1991—just briefly after the fatal coup attempt that would precipitate the dissolution of the Soviet Union. In 1992, the Armed Forces of the newly created Russian Federation were facing enormous challenges: to complete the troop withdrawal from Eastern Europe and to create armed forces that would correspond to the new political and military situation. The Soviet Union had ended, the Soviet Armed Forces of about 3.5 million men were disbanded, and Russia was the *de jure* successor state. It was a turbulent time, but Makarov thought about the future and wrote his thesis about the consequences of potential NATO membership for Estonia, Latvia, and Lithuania. "The buffer would disappear", he noted.

Makarov clearly identifies with Miliutin's view of meritocracy and competence, and underlines that nobody in his family had chosen the military path. The memoirs contain an excerpt of Miliutin's last article from 1912 (the year of his death), and Makarov claims that it could have been written today. In the article, Miliutin touches on the need for improved military materiel for specialized branches of weapon. He also notes that war now (1912) breaks out suddenly and unpredictably in spite of international agreements, and he worries about the great technological gap between Russia and Europe.

Makarov's memoirs are obviously a tendentious source, but they nevertheless give some valuable insights into his thinking about military reform in Russia. And in fact, the main parts of the reform were introduced during his time as Chief of the General Staff. Not only did the troops become adapted to today's realities, but financing of the reform was also secured when the State Armament Programme 2011 was approved. It was this massive emphasis on the military—against the wishes of the Finance Ministry—that forced Finance Minister Aleksei Kudrin to resign.

Makarov's career is deeply rooted in the Soviet Armed Forces. Early on he joined the Communist Party, since a career without a member card was unthinkable. He served in East Germany in the 1970s, then in the Far East and Kaliningrad in the 1990s, and he finally reached Moscow in 2001.

He is deeply critical of the military reforms of the 1990s. According to him, the only thing that was done was to cut the number of soldiers, without a cohesive idea. The Russian Federation could afford comprehensive reform, and even the West provided additional funds for it, but, Makarov claims, the reformers did not understand what was needed.

Nine steps of reform

So if his predecessors had no comprehensive approach to reform, what is Makarov's recipe? He provides a list of nine steps—incidentally a list that could be used in any reorganization not only within the defence sector, and not only in Russia.

- A conceptual view of the problems to be solved
- Create a group of likeminded colleagues
- A clear vision of the end result
- Detailed planning, calculations, and reasons
- Control of all the steps and their connections
- Ability to act quickly in case of disagreements and conflicts
- Strong but just demands
- Decisiveness, courage and boldness in performance
- Information support

Regarding military reforms, Makarov writes, one has to be patient. Nothing happens quickly, and the results come after many years—and then the key to success is in exercises. "Without exercises there is no army", he writes. Consequently, he was a major proponent of re-establishing strategic exercises, of which Zapad 99 was the first.

Naturally, Makarov has not been alone in reforming the Armed Forces. Many of the reform foundations can be found in the early 2000s, when Sergei Ivanov was Minister of Defence. President Putin clearly supported these efforts. Makarov writes, cautiously, about his problems, and competitors, for instance, about his conflict with then Chief of the General Staff Anatolii Kvashnin. At one point, Kvashnin tried to transfer Makarov from the Armed Forces to the Interior Troops. When Makarov served in Samara, he discovered extensive embezzlement of defence resources, and he was almost charged with the crime himself—a story that could easily be found in the Russian classics.

Apart from exercises, another major factor of success was the integration of the General Staff into the Ministry of Defence. This provided the unified decision-making process that Makarov—and before him, Miliutin—had wanted. He is also cautious about the future of his reform and underlines the need for a continued reform process. New features are not always applied, he complains. "Stereotypes, created during decades, a sloppiness of thought, a resistance to going with the times and to learning from peacetime experience, still characterize, unfortunately, some of the generals, admirals and officers of the Armed Forces," he points out, and ends with an appeal to continue. "It's hard, often unrewarding. But there is no other way…"

The impact of soft power, colour revolutions and controlled chaos

This brings us to some of the most discussed questions in the contemporary debate. In the mid-nineteenth century, the issues in focus were (1) the appearance of conscript armies and trained reserves, (2) the growing importance of officer education and the rise of general staffs, and (3) the impact of technological development and firepower, including the military application of the steam railway, the electromagnetic telegraph, and the rifling of muskets and cannons. Currently, the debate revolves around questions like (1) whether the character of war has changed fundamentally, (2) the relations between military and non-military means, (3) the importance of non-nuclear deterrence in relation to nuclear deterrence, (4) the role of 'colour revolutions' in contemporary warfare.

First, it should be noted that contemporary Russian military thinking has been studying the impact of both the technological development of the Western powers and the political, economic, and social changes in Russia and the outside world. The military theoretical debate has reflected these fundamental changes: the dissolution of the Soviet Union, the reduced Russian territory (particularly in the Western parts), and globalization. The search for a national identity, in later years becoming a policy of patriotism, has had its equivalent in the military strategic debate, and thus the search for a new Russian military strategy. International developments have also affected Russian military thinking, which constantly discusses the impact of Operation Desert Storm 1991, and the US and NATO interventions in Serbia

(1999), Afghanistan (2001), Iraq (2003) and Libya (2011). Russia's own experiences from the wars in Chechnya, Georgia (2008), Ukraine, and Syria are also constantly discussed.

In so doing, many of the Soviet theorists and military thinkers of the past are being re-discovered. Russian military thinking has impressive traditions both from tsarist times and the Soviet period, with names such as Dmitrii Miliutin, Mikhail Dragomirov, Genrikh Leer, Aleksandr Svechin, Mikhail Tukhachevskii, Georgii Isserson, and Nikolai Ogarkov, to mention but a few. Throughout, a debate has been described between two main schools of thought—one that emphasizes the need for modern technology, and the other that stresses the qualities of the soldier. The traditionalists warn against exaggerating the importance of high technology to win future wars. This is something of an oversimplification, to be sure, and in fact the different schools often go hand-in-hand and overlap each other.

A particularly topical subject in Russian military strategic thinking in recent years concerns the view on soft power, so-called "controlled chaos" or "manageable chaos" (*upravliaemyi khaos*), and colour revolutions. It is essential to examine this topic more thoroughly, since it is central to an understanding of how the Russian view of modern conflicts has evolved. The views of soft power and 'controlled chaos' as distinct features of contemporary and future wars are clearly expressed in the Russian military theoretical debate.

According to the Concept of Foreign Policy in 2013, the use of soft power is a factor in international politics. As the 2016 Foreign Policy Concept describes it: "In addition to traditional methods of diplomacy, 'soft power' has become an integral part of efforts to achieve foreign policy objectives".

On the one hand, soft power can be used as a complement to classic diplomacy. On the other, there is a risk of soft power being used as a tool to intrude into the domestic affairs of states, through "among other things, to finance humanitarian projects and projects relating to human rights abroad", according to the Foreign Policy Concept. Vladimir Putin defines it as "instruments and methods to achieve foreign policy objectives without the use of weapons—information and other levers of influence". In 2018, Vice Minister of Defence Aleksandr Fomin stated that "[…] it is clear that hiding behind the term 'soft power' are activities such as meddling in domestic affairs by organizing colour revolutions, which in turn leads to a violation of the balance of power with catastrophic consequences for regions and the entire world".

In the military theoretical debate soft power is seen as one weapon among others. Makhmut Gareev, an influential military theorist and a veteran of the

Second World War, links the annexation of Crimea to soft power and strategic deterrence.[7] According to him, it is necessary to learn from Crimea in order to "perfect our soft power, political and diplomatic means and information tools, and thus increase effectiveness in the system for strategic deterrence".

It is noteworthy that soft power, in this line of thinking, is put at the same level as strategic deterrence—a level usually associated with nuclear weapons and high-precision long-range conventional weapons. In fact, the Russian interpretation of "soft power" is quite different from the conventional view of increasing a country's power of attraction.[8] This reflects a militarized standpoint where soft power is seen as an instrument of statecraft.

Another term used in the Russian military theoretical debate is "controlled chaos" (*upravliaemyi khaos*). Putin used the term "controlled chaos" in his pre-election article on defence in 2012. It means that Russia was under attack from the West, which by various methods—political as well as economic—was destabilizing and undermining Russia's neighbours and ultimately Russia itself. It is sometimes used in connection with a discussion of soft power. Gareev equates the two. In recent years, several articles in military theoretical journals have been devoted to controlled chaos and to colour revolutions. Aleksandr Bartosh, a corresponding member of the General Staff Academy, traces the concept of "controlled chaos" to the US, claiming that it was this "technology" that led to the dissolution of the Soviet Union.[9]

In a talk at the General Staff Academy in 2017, Foreign Minister Sergei Lavrov described controlled chaos as an American tool to "strengthen the influence of the USA". In Iraq, Syria, and Libya the concept of chaos was used deliberately, according to Lavrov, whereas in Afghanistan during the NATO-led operation it was applied involuntarily.

The term "colour revolution" was included in the National Security Strategy for the first time in 2015, where it is described as a threat to Russia's state security. It is indicative that the General Staff is paying close attention to "colour revolutions" and that in recent years has been thinking about developing a concept to counteract "hybrid" wars against Russia and her allies.[10] In addition, since 2017 a new course has been introduced at the General Staff Academy: "Army and Society". One of the purposes of the course, according to Defence Minister Sergei Shoigu, is to study countermeasures for "colour revolutions". Among the subjects studied are information war, information security, and cultural policy, not least to counteract the "falsification of history".

According to Valerii Gerasimov, Chief of the General Staff, contemporary warfare includes such various means as official history writing, diplomacy, economy, information operations, as well as science, sports, and culture.

Igor Popov and Musa Khamzatov argue in their book *Voina budushchego* (2016) that recent conflicts demonstrate that "peaceful demonstrations, anti-regime demonstrations, and in some cases foreign military intervention which throw entire countries and regions into a state of controlled chaos can now be called a new type of contemporary warfare". Such a war, they argue, goes far beyond the framework of the traditional understanding of these wars. They include political intrigues, struggles for resources and financial flows, and irreconcilable civilizational conflicts. On the battlefield in these wars regular forces act alongside a number of new actors—irregular forces of rebels and fighters, criminal gangs, international terrorist networks, private military companies, legions of foreign mercenaries, units of *spetsnaz* and intelligence formations from different countries, military contingents of peacekeepers from international organizations, and even non-governmental and humanitarian organizations and structures, representatives of the printed and electronic mass media, volunteers, and activists from civil society.

Furthermore, it is important to note that the discussion about colour revolutions is not new, and aspects of it featured in Russian military thinking long before any perceived contemporary colour revolutions occurred. Worth mentioning here is the thinking about wars of rebellion (*miatezhevoiny*). Evgenii Messner (1891–1974), is seen by many Russian theorists as an early insightful theoretician in this school. A former officer in the tsarist army, he later joined the White side during the Soviet civil war and was forced into emigration. Now all is forgiven, and some of his writings, including parts of "Rebellion—the name of the Third World War," is freely available on the Internet.[11]

These thoughts on colour revolutions could be seen as a consequence of the fact that the dissolution of the Soviet Union is regarded as incomprehensible to the current political leadership in Russia, and that it therefore must have been orchestrated from abroad.

It is clear that colour revolutions and controlled chaos are seen as Western concepts created by the US and NATO and used to destabilize Russia. It is to meet these alleged threats that Russian military theorists are developing new theories and doctrine.

There is clearly an underlying longing for an ideology in many of the current writings. General Aleksandr Vladimirov, for instance, notes that Russia needs to rally the country around "nationally vital resources": religion (the

Russian Orthodox Church), the (Russian/russkii) people, the state (Russia), the idea (Russian culture), and the language (Russian).[12] This echoes the past, albeit not as eloquently formulated as it was by Sergei Uvarov (1786–1855), Minister of Education under Nicholas I: "Autocracy, Orthodoxy, Nationality".

Finding the balance

The modernization of the Russian Armed Forces over the past ten years is producing results. Military capability has clearly increased. At the same time, the challenges are substantial. Then—and now—it is about more than technological innovations and new weapon systems. In the mid-nineteenth century, universal conscription was considered necessary, and the soldiers needed education in order to act more independently on the battlefield. Today, the boundaries between war and peace and offensive and defensive operations are becoming increasingly blurred. From a Russian perspective, fundamental questions are raised about how to motivate future generations to fight—and for what.

Whether technical or organizational, and in any time period or indeed in any large organization, innovations always entail risk, and their consequences are not always easy to predict. Introducing an innovation, which may seem innocent enough, is a large undertaking which is not easy to correct. Therefore, one can expect large organizations such as armies to show a certain reluctance to jump too quickly to adjust to change. On the other hand, a general "wait and see" attitude is potentially dangerous and can lead to devastating results. Much of the problem consists in finding a balance in peacetime between adapting to change and determining the actual value of innovations for war. There is a balance to be found here between novelty and tradition, between leaping to conclusions and resisting change. The fact that its position is directly linked to the security of the state does not make the army's situation an easy one. It is hardly surprising, therefore, that armies are often described as being marked by a curious contradiction. On the one hand, they are oriented toward the present and future in their efforts to make the most rational use of their means and to be as efficient as possible. On the other hand, they are often perceived by both insiders and outsiders as the bearers of traditional values represented by ceremonies that should be preserved at all cost. This balancing act between future and past becomes more evident in times of rapid change.

A balance needs to be found between technology and morale. The pre-1914 European armies were later accused of disregarding technology and of putting too much emphasis on morale. The experience of the First World War certainly seems to vindicate this criticism. Nevertheless, many wars of the twentieth century have demonstrated time and time again that an army with poor morale, regardless of its technological superiority, does not win wars.

In the beginning of the twentieth century, Russian military thinkers worried about the technological gap between Russia and Europe. Today, the gap is still there, and Russia has far to go to "catch up". But, as we have seen, Russian military thinkers of the twenty-first century are developing concepts involving other means of force, the so-called non-military resources. As a consequence, almost every part of society is increasingly seen as a battlefield that spans everything from nuclear weapons to history and culture.

Thoughts and doctrines on future war need to find a balance between perceived threats and the resources available to meet those threats. Therefore, political support is essential—in any country and in any time. At the moment, the West is seen as the main threat to Russian national security, and the response has been to label domestic NGOs "foreign agents", to circumscribe the ability of any dissenting voice to act. The authoritarian political system, with a strong figure head at the top, is described as "the right one" for Russia, feeding into the tradition of Russian great powerness. The current political leadership often quotes words ascribed to Alexander III: "Russia has only two allies: its army and its fleet".

In the long-term perspective, an historical experience is perhaps valuable. In the late nineteenth century two incompatible features resulted in a mismatch between Russia's strategy and policy: on one hand, the strategy was characterized by an excessive sense of military inferiority, and on the other, a reluctance to accept any diminution in Russia's international standing and prestige. It led to an avoidable overextension.[13] But rather than recognize this, Russia overstretched, with disastrous consequences. This is a poignant lesson from the past.

[1] For details on the conference, see Gudrun Persson, *Learning from Foreign Wars: Russian Military Thinking 1859-1873* (Solihull: Helion, 2010), 134-44.
[2] D. A. Miliutin, *Dnevnik D. A. Miliutina* 4 vols. (Moscow: Gosudarstvennaia ordena Lenina Biblioteka SSSR imeni V. I. Lenina. Otdel rukopisei., 1947-50), vol. 1: 78.
[3] Michael Howard, *The Franco-Prussian War: the German Invasion of France, 18701871*. Reprint of 1961, ed. (London: Routledge, 1991), 1.
[4] L. Baikov, "Vliianie srazheniia pod Keniggretsom na taktiku," *Voennyi sbornik* (6, 1872), 303-352.
[5] L. L. Zeddeler, "Pekhota, artilleriia i kavaleriia v boiu i vne boia, v Germano-Frantsuzskoi voine 1870-1871 godov," *Voennyi sbornik* (7, 1872): 33-114.
[6] M. I. Dragomirov, "Po povodu nekotorykh statei vyzvannykh poslednimi dvumia kampaniiami," *Voennyi sbornik* (12, 1872), 253-274; (1, 1873, 89-106).
[7] Makhmut Gareev, "Velikaia pobeda i sobytiia na Ukraine," *Vestnik Akademii voennykh nauk*, 2 (47), 2017, 4-10.
[8] Joseph Nye, *Soft power: The means to success in world politics* (New York, Public Affairs, 2004).
[9] A. A. Bartosh, "Model upravliaemogo khaosa v sfere voennoi bezopasnosti," *Vestnik Akademii voennych nauk*, 1, (46), 2014, 69-77.
[10] Valerii Gerasimov, "Sovremennye voiny i aktualnye voprosy oborony strany," *Vestnik Akademii voennykh nauk*, 2 (59), 2017, 13.
[11] Rossiiskii voennyi sbornik, *Khochesh mira, pobedi miatezhevoinu! Tvorcheskoe nasledie E. Messnera*, http://militera.lib.ru/science/0/pdf/messner_ea01.pdf
[12] Aleksandr I. Vladimirov, *Osnovy obshchei teorii voiny, Chast I. Osnovy teorii voiny*, (Moscow: Universitet Sinergiia, 2013), 477-94.
[13] William C. Fuller, C., Jr. *Strategy and Power in Russia 1600-1914*, (New York: Free Press, 1992), 462-63.

Exchanging Trade for Recognition.
A Russian Mission to Sweden

HELENE CARLBÄCK

The Russian Question

This is a story from the early 1920s, when the new state of Soviet Russia was struggling to be recognized by the rest of the world. The story focuses on Russia's relations with Sweden—how could Sweden become a platform for the Bolshevik regime from which to reach out to the West and win diplomatic recognition, and who were the mediators to fulfill these aspirations? How were they received in Sweden during the first years of full-fledged parliamentary democracy, when the government changed annually and the view of Bolshevik Russia also fluctuated in step with the revised political frameworks?[1]

When we turn the spotlight on Europe in the early 1920s we see unpredictability and unclear developmental trends. The political map of the continent had been redrawn. The catastrophic war, the Great War, La grand catastrophe, had recently been fought. Empires had collapsed, revolutions had demolished established regimes, new states had arisen out of former territories. In Russia, the left wing of the Social Democratic Party, the Bolsheviks, had made a coup and seized power with slogans such as "All power to the soviets!" and "Down with the Provisional Government!" Implemented in practice, these slogans meant that the political parties in the popularly elected parliament—conservatives, liberals, agrarian socialists (Socialist Revolutionaries) and Mensheviks—were eliminated. Another slogan of the Bolshevik revolutionaries—"Peace now!"—was realized when Russian left the Entente military alliance and withdrew its troops from the war, whereupon the Central Powers Germany and Austria-Hungary were able to turn their full attention to the war against the Entente.

The Bolsheviks socialized the industries and banks of the country, confiscated foreign property, and annulled foreign loans to the state. They appropriated the estates of the Russian landowners to distribute it to landless peasants. A social upheaval had taken place on a scale not seen since the French Revolution.

Thus the Bolsheviks had crushed their domestic rivals, appropriated the property of the upper class and foreign entrepreneurs, and turned a cold shoulder to states that had invested in railroads, mines and loans. And they had enabled the Central Powers to concentrate their forces on attacking the British and French armies in the still ongoing world war. The reaction was not long in coming. With financial and military support from the Entente, a Russian resistance movement soon took to arms. France and Great Britain, and following them, small countries such as Sweden, declared a blockade against Soviet Russia. A civil war broke out between Reds and Whites. The Bolsheviks—the Reds—won, and by 1921 they had control of the new state of Soviet Russia. Its territory had been decimated, since regions in the western border areas had broken away as independent states, but it was still the largest country in the world.

Peace after the civil war, however, did not, as the Bolshevik government believed it would, mean a continuation of centrally managed economic policy, an approach that the Bolsheviks imagined would lead the country to communism much more quickly than Marxist theorists had predicted. Instead, demonstrations and riots broke out everywhere in the winter and spring of 1921. In the countryside the peasants demonstrated against the state's forced requisition of grain and other agricultural products; during the civil war the agrarian surplus had been taken from the peasants to feed the army and the workers in the cities. The government yielded and allowed the peasants to keep and sell a certain surplus. In the cities, the population protested against the scarcity of goods in the stores. The government ended food rationing and again allowed merchants to trade and businessmen to open stores and cafes. State control of the larger firms, industries and banks, however, remained in the hands of the Bolsheviks. As did control of the political arena; the country became a one-party state, although rival factions lived on in the 1920s, only to be completely silenced a decade later. These groups demanded increased party democracy, more power to the workers, less top-down control by the party. One of the Bolshevik representatives in Sweden with whom we will become acquainted below, Valerian Osinsky, took part in factional strife and would later pay with his life for such activities.

How, then, did the rest of the world view the new country of Soviet Russia? With disgust and wonder, amazement and admiration, curiosity and fear, depending on the viewer. A key factor in the Bolsheviks' subversive policies was the conviction that the revolution would spread to other countries. The Bolsheviks would not remain alone. But the world revolution failed to materialize. The Bolsheviks were the only ones to have carried out a revolution. Soviet Russia would for a long time be the only country under communist rule. The Bolsheviks did, of course, work together with communists and left-wing socialists in the West and anticolonial movements in the East to promote revolution on a global scale, but the fact that Soviet Russia stood alone forced the country to adopt a more traditional foreign policy. The goal was to become recognized as the legitimate government in Russia. That would reduce the risk of a counterrevolution and counterattack on the part of political rivals who wanted to topple the Bolshevik regime, and it would allow Russia to re-enter world commerce with exports of grain and imports of input products needed to build up its own industries.

Europe's reaction to Soviet Russia's aspirations was reflected in the 1920s in discussions of the so called "Russian question" at major European conferences in Versailles, Genoa, Cannes, and Rapallo. Different approaches became apparent there, both among and even within countries. In the case of France, it was compensation for lost property and annulled government loans that was crucial if the Soviet Russian regime was to be recognized. Great Britain placed high priority on the cessation of communist-supported propaganda in the British Empire. The British prime minister Lloyd George was at the same time working on a political unification and economic development of Europe in which the reintegration of Russia was a natural component.

With respect to the smaller European countries, demands that Soviet Russia compensate foreign citizens for seized property were an important factor, at the same time that voices were heard from entrepreneurs who had not lost property there but advocated that ties be regulated in order to enable commercial exchange. There was also a dividing line between the left and the liberals, on the one hand, who wanted to have normalized relations in order to avoid a new military rearmament, and the right, which above all feared the "communist contagion".

So what were Sweden's interests vis-à-vis the new Russia? Swedish companies in Russia were mostly concentrated in the metalworking and engineering industries, branches in which Sweden, relative to its population, had the largest share of the Russian market before the revolution. Several major Swedish transnational firms involved with industrial production had become established in Russia during the decades before the revolution, including L. M. Ericsson, ASEA, and SKF. Others had sales offices there, and around the time of the revolution there were some twenty Swedish trading houses that imported and sold machines, engines, tools, steel, and household goods. With the 1917 revolution and the following civil war, Swedish exports largely died out, and the importation of Russian raw materials ended completely. Because unemployment in Swedish manufacturing had now reached historic highs, both the engineering industry and the labor movement were interested in kick-starting exports to the East.

After the great powers had lifted their blockade of Soviet Russia, in 1920 the Russian cooperative movement Tsentrosoyuz and the Swedish General Export Association (Svenska Allmänna Exportföreningen) signed a contract on the supply of Swedish industrial goods. The agreement was between two non-governmental organizations, but it included a state element—the parties would be entitled to make use of coded telegrams and courier bags in the other country to communicate with the homeland. Sweden was the first to conclude such an agreement, and it aroused criticism in the French press and elsewhere which accused Sweden of entering into relations with a "band of robbers".

Mission "recognition": a Russian legation to Sweden

As the Russians saw it, the agreement opened the way for Swedish diplomatic recognition, and work began to send representatives to Stockholm. According to the arrangement, these would be called "trade delegates", but Moscow viewed them as government officials. The task of building up a foreign affairs administration had recently begun there. The number of employees in the Commissariat for Foreign Affairs quickly quintupled from 250 in 1918 to 1,300 three years later. The geographical division in the prerevolutionary Foreign Ministry remained, with one department for Western countries and one for the Orient. The man in charge of diplomatic activities in the West was Deputy Commissar of Foreign Affairs Maksim Litvinov, with whom we shall become acquainted below.

Moscow began putting forward possible representatives to Sweden. A few years earlier, Vatslav Vorovsky had been declared persona non grata by the British government. He was now rejected by Sweden. The next candidate was Maksim Litvinov, but Sweden rejected him as well. Litvinov had also been declared persona non grata by the British. Erik Palmstierna, the Swedish ambassador to London, wrote in his diary: "No, no, Mr. Finkelstein will have to wait, we don't want any propagandists here".[2] Litvinov was called Moses Finkelstein in the Swedish and foreign press at this time—a manifestation of the anti-Semitic public discourse in general and the linking of communism to Jews in particular.[3] The right-leaning evening newspaper *Aftonbladet* described "Moses Finkelstein" as a man with "the puffy red face of a wholesale merchant in which a pair of gimlet eyes glittered behind a gold-rimmed pince-nez".[4]

Moscow then proposed Platon Kerzhentsev, about whom the Swedish authorities knew nothing. The secret police had no information, so they turned to Scotland Yard, which informed them that Kerzhentsev was "more interested in propaganda than he was in trade issues". The British Foreign Office told the Swedish ambassador in London that he was not particularly regarded as persona non grata, while the Swedish consul in Estonia noted that Kerzhentsev was a "dedicated communist" and "half-Jewish", but was thought to be "less dangerous". He was said to have refrained from political agitation during the recently concluded Russian-Finnish peace negotiations in Helsinki. The Swedish government approved Kerzhentsev as the Soviet Russian trade delegate.

One February morning in 1921, Platon Kerzhentsev disembarked in Sweden, accompanied by his wife Maria, two children, his secretary and servants. He and his retinue, arriving on the Egil from Tallinn, were met on the quay at Stadsgården by members of the Social Democratic Left Party, a faction that had broken away from the Social Democrats in 1917, and the Swedish lawyer for the Soviet government. Journalists were also in attendance. "The press greeted me quite amiably. They said I was more like an Englishman or a German than a Russian. The only unpleasant thing was the claim in a tabloid that I was carrying communist literature in my baggage", Kerzhentsev wrote to the Commissariat of Foreign Affairs.

At the time of Kerzhentsev's arrival, Sweden was ruled by a so called caretaker government pending the upcoming special election to the Riksdag. Led by Oscar von Sydow, the government was formally apolitical, but it had a conservative slant and took a cautious approach toward the Russians' attempts at contact. About a week after arriving in Stockholm, Kerzhentsev met with Foreign Minister Herman Wrangel, to whom he maintained that although his title was "trade representative", he spoke for a foreign government and would "in the future surely have to do with Wrangel diplomatically". Their meeting was not a success: "Wrangel expressed doubt that we would be interacting as diplomats", Kerzhentsev wrote to the Commissariat of Foreign Affairs in Moscow, which instructed him to "insist" on meeting the foreign minister himself, instead of civil servants in the Ministry for Foreign Affairs. In a communication to Moscow in March 1921, Kerzhentsev complained about the difficulty of establishing contact with top-level Swedish officials. "I really don't know how long I can manage this boycott policy; I may quite simply be forced to turn to Grönwall[5] for negotiations. If I had had a secretary, I could have sent him".

The Russian foreign affairs leaders had several ideas about what Kerzhentsev could accomplish in Sweden. "Dear Comrade! It is time to launch efficient information operations abroad", wrote Foreign Commissar Grigory Chicherin to him in April 1921.

> Here from Moscow we constantly send telegrams on current issues, but the information arrives too late, if at all, to the foreign press. You must investigate why it has been so difficult to publicize information about us in the English, French, German press.

Stockholm, Chicherin maintained, was geographically the best place to establish an information center that could supply Moscow with news on the world situation and convey information from Moscow on Soviet Russian policies and economics to the rest of the world. In Moscow's eyes, Stockholm was a hub for diplomatic activities,[6] and Kerzhentsev was ordered to contact diplomats from countries with which Soviet Russia had managed to establish political relations. Again there arose the problem of Kerzhentsev's status. "They look upon me as a businessman," he wrote of the diplomatic corps in Stockholm.

One senses in the internal Russian correspondence a certain irritation with the von Sydow government, which in various ways demonstrated its reluctance to recognize the Bolshevik regime and its representatives abroad.

Moscow now decided that Kerzhentsev should leave his mission in Stockholm and move to Helsinki. Retaining an experienced representative like him in Sweden would be a waste of resources. "We must, of course, staff the more important outposts with experienced and competent people. And we must consider Helsinki to be such a post", wrote Vice Foreign Commissar Litvinov. For the time being it was impossible to count on doing "any serious political work" in Sweden.

New winds breathe life into the Russian question

A Social Democratic government assumed power in September 1921. Sweden had arranged special elections due to a bill recently adopted by the Riksdag introducing universal suffrage for both men and women. The percentage of the population with the right to vote rose from twenty percent in the preceding parliamentary election to fifty-four percent in the 1921 election. The Social Democrats became the largest party, supported by thirty-six percent of the electorate, and they formed a minority government with Hjalmar Branting as both prime minister and foreign minister. Branting was widely known for his strong interest in questions having to do with international peace and security, and he was awarded the 1921 Nobel Peace Prize for his "pioneering work for the cause of international peace".[7] The Social Democratic Statement of Government Policy declared that the new regime would work to activate commercial relations "eastward" as soon as possible.

Platon Kerzhentsev stayed in Stockholm, and Maksim Litvinov also arrived to "speed up trade with Sweden".[8] Hjalmar Branting met with Litvinov the very first day. It was a positive reception, Litvinov wrote to Chicherin: "Met Branting today, who from the outset maintained that he in principle supports diplomatic recognition but since he does not have a majority in the Riksdag, he has to toss a bone to the bourgeois parties, which would be that the Soviet Russian side acknowledge the Swedish economic claims as a matter of principle."

Litvinov also met the Swedish press. "Litvinov speaks of the communist reorientation", wrote *Svenska Dagbladet*, by which was meant the market-oriented change that had occurred in economic policy since the spring of 1921. The "New Economic Policy," NEP, had been proclaimed, and there were discussions within the Communist Party as to how foreign claims should be addressed. Internally among the Soviet Russian leadership, however, it had already been decided that none of the Swedish claimants would be able to get monetary compensation. "We have seized so many goods and so much property that at this stage we are unable to compensate the owners", Chicherin had written to Kerzhentsev as early as April. One project that was high on the agenda in discussions among the top Bolshevik leaders, however, was to offer concessions to foreign companies that had been confiscated in 1917, which meant that the former owners would be able to resume production in Russia, sell their products there, and import goods at preferential tariffs, but that they would not recover right of ownership, but would merely have right of disposition. Litvinov declared in Stockholm that Swedish businesses had prospects of acquiring economic concessions in Russia.[9]

Negotiations began, and Platon Kerzhentsev reported self-confidently to Moscow: "Everything clearly indicates that the Swedish government is prepared to make considerable compromises. The struggle and agitation we have been conducting for many months is bearing fruit". The compromises did not become as extensive as Kerzhentsev had promised, however. After three months the parties had reached an agreement whereby Sweden recognized the Soviet regime *de facto*, which compared with the 1920 trade agreement meant an expansion of the right to communicate with the homeland via coded cables and diplomatic couriers and that Soviet Russian citizens would be allowed to transit through Sweden to other countries. The parties were in addition granted the mutual right to conduct economic activity on each other's territory, a provision that was especially useful to Sweden. An important stipulation by the Russian side was that the Soviet delegate to Sweden be regarded as the only legitimate representative of the Russian state, which was a step closer to the coveted diplomatic recognition. Finally, there was the so called propaganda clause, which banned the legations from conducting political propaganda in the counterpart country. Great Britain, which in many respects served as a guide in the Russian question, had concluded a trade agreement with the Soviet government which specified the geographical areas where propaganda, or "hostile actions against British interests in the British Empire" would be forbidden, namely in India and Afghanistan. Thus in the British case the propaganda clause applied above all to the interests of the Empire. Sweden had no such interests: the liberal daily *Göteborgs-Posten* compared the soil for communist propaganda there to "a rocky Arabia for Bolshevik seed".[10]

The Branting government proposed the Russian treaty to the Riksdag in March 1922. The right-wing press complained that the Russian side had been given too many advantages. "It must have been encouraging for the Russian negotiators to be able to 'permit themselves a little bit of everything' vis-à-vis the Swedes", wrote the conservative *Svenska Dagbladet*.[11] *Nya Dagligt Allehanda*, which stood to the right of *Svenska Dagbladet*, expressed fears of a "Russian invasion"—the treaty would allow Russians to enter Sweden in unlimited numbers.[12] *Stockholms Dagblad*, a right-wing newspaper with a more pragmatic approach than that of *Svenska Dagbladet*, considered, to be sure, that there was a real risk for a "Russian invasion", but underscored that the treaty was also a win for Sweden, since Swedish citizens would be allowed to conduct trade in Russia.[13] There were various opinions in the liberal press. The danger of a Russian invasion was real, but it could be neutralized through government control, maintained *Dagens Nyheter*. *Svenska Morgonbladet*, the mouthpiece for liberals critical of the military, considered that it was important to resume official relations with Russia.[14] *Svenska Handelstidningen* was the most positive of all the bourgeois publications, asserting that "The fact that individual Swedes will be allowed access to Russia is a remarkable step forward".[15]

The Riksdag referred the agreement to one of its committees. The period 1920–32 has gone down in Swedish history as the era of minority parliamentarism. During these twelve years Sweden had on average a new government every year. This greatly increased the power of the Riksdag at the expense of the constantly changing minority governments, and work in the committees sometimes resembled work of the executive branch. The bourgeois majority of the committee recommended that the Riksdag not approve the agreement, citing, among other reasons, the unresolved claims against the Russian state. Sweden should wait for an international stance to be taken in the question: "The feeling of solidarity that has always inspired Sweden in its relations with other states should refrain us just now from concluding treaties with Russia", the committee majority declared.

Thus the Riksdag did not approve the proposed trade agreement between Sweden and Soviet Russia. Platon Kerzhentsev stayed on in Stockholm for another six months and continued networking among diplomats and journalists and conveying information between Moscow and the rest of the world. When he left Sweden in the spring of 1923 the press was well disposed toward him. The leading conservative paper *Svenska Dagbladet* wrote that Stockholm's diplomatic corps would surely "... miss Mr. Kerzhentsev, whose homey manner and jovial smile they have learned to appreciate, not to mention the good Russian cigarettes to which the soviet republic of workers and peasants treated the representatives of the bourgeois Swedish press. It must be admitted that the Bolshevik diplomats are often a very pleasant phenomenon".[16] The liberal *Svenska Morgonbladet* stated that Kerzhentsev did not at all seem like a Russian Bolshevik, but was on the contrary "extremely congenial, a fine person" who we did not want to believe had anything to do with "blood-and-guts Red tsarism".[17]

The Russian question: fluctuating political conditions

During the year that followed there was a shift in the political situation in Europe with respect to the Russian question. Things were happening in especially Great Britain. In the spring of 1923 a conservative government succeeded the earlier liberal one. The interests of the Empire overshadowed projects for rebuilding a Europe that included Russia. Prime Minister Curzon spoke of the "wretched regime in Moscow" and how the Russian threat to India from tsarist times had survived but had now become a new kind of challenge: the Russians had made friends with the "Asiatics" and supported them in their struggle with the British Empire via Afghanistan and Persia. This, Curzon maintained, was a breach of the propaganda clause in the British-Russian trade agreement. Sharply worded British complaints were sent to Moscow. In Sweden at this time a new government had been formed, with the conservative Ernst Trygger as prime minister. Under pressure from the

British-Russian crisis, the government held off on Moscow's proposals to replace Kerzhentsev. Eventually, however, Valerian Osinsky was approved. He arrived in Stockholm in late July 1923. Again the Swedish press encountered a person who failed to fulfill the expectations or apprehensions about the behavior of a Russian communist: "Osinsky hardly corresponds to the images that people in general have of a Bolshevik diplomat. He seems highly intellectual, is tall and slim, has brushed-back hair and nearsighted blue eyes that can, however, become quite piercing behind his thick glasses. He could be a Swedish professor".[18]

Prime Minister Trygger's attitude during Osinsky's first meeting with him was reminiscent of Foreign Minister Wrangel's reception of Kerzhentsev two years earlier. Trygger called the agreement Branting had reached with the Russian negotiators (which had not been approved by the Riksdag) a "scrap of paper" that could not serve as a platform for further negotiations.

When the new British Labour government recognized Soviet Russia diplomatically in January 1924, the situation for Sweden changed. Norway and Italy followed with recognition in February. In March Sweden extended diplomatic recognition without having gained anything beyond what Branting's agreement had achieved. Diplomatic delegations were established in Stockholm and Moscow. The first Soviet Russian ambassador was Valerian Osinsky, who remained another year in Stockholm. In Moscow it was Carl von Heidenstam, who had previously had business interests in Russia, who became Sweden's first ambassador to the new Russia.

Three delegates, three different fates

Three prominent Bolsheviks negotiated in Stockholm over the course of several years in the 1920s: Platon Kerzhentsev, Maksim Litvinov, and Valerian Osinsky.

Platon Kerzhentsev's biographical profile resembled that of several other top leaders in the Bolshevik Party in the 1920s: born in the 1870s–1880s in a provincial city into a middle-class family headed by a father who was a doctor or teacher. They had studied at the universities in Moscow, Petersburg or Kiev, been active socialists and at the beginning of the century had joined the leftist Bolshevik faction of the Social Democratic Party. In the 1910s until the 1917 revolution, some of them had gone into exile due to the tsarist regime's repressive policies toward left-wing parties. Many of them also had pseudonyms, in some cases, several.

Born in 1881 in Smolensk, Platon Kerzhentsev was forty years old when he arrived in Sweden. His original surname was Lebedev; he took his pseudonym from the Kerzhenets Forest outside Nizhny Novgorod, where he worked for a time as a journalist. His father was a doctor and a member of the first Russian parliament after 1905. Kerzhentsev joined the Russian Social Democratic Party early in the century and became a Bolshevik when it split into the two Bolshevik and Menshevik wings. He studied history and philosophy at Moscow University and went into exile in 1912 at the age of 31, living for five years in London, Paris and the United States. In 1917 he returned to Russia to work for the party. He was active primarily as a journalist and writer, and had authored books on the British Empire and the history of revolutionary Ireland. He also wrote about practical journalism and the theater.

Maksim Litvinov, whose real name was Meir Wallach, was born in 1876 into a Russian Jewish merchant family in Belostok in western Russia (present-day Poland). He attended secondary school and worked for several years as a bookkeeper. He joined the Social Democrats at the end of the nineteenth century and became active politically in Kiev, Riga, and elsewhere. He took part in the 1905 revolution and the same year helped start the Bolsheviks' first legal newspaper, *New Life*, in St. Petersburg. Litvinov was given various tasks by the Bolshevik Party, especially abroad. He went into exile in 1906 and until the revolution in 1917 lived mostly in England, where he married an Englishwoman, Ivy Low. In 1918, while still living in London, the Soviet Russian government appointed him as a diplomatic representative in Britain. He was arrested there, however, and was not able to return to Russia until the British representative, Bruce Lockhart, who had been arrested by the Soviet Russian police, was allowed to leave Moscow. In 1921 Litvinov became deputy foreign commissar and thereafter had various posts connected with foreign and security policy. In the 1930s he was the Soviet foreign minister until being succeeded by Vyacheslav Molotov in 1939. He died in Moscow in 1951.

Valerian Osinsky was thirty-six years old when he came to Stockholm. He was born in 1887 into the noble Obolensky family in a small community in Kursk Province. His father was a veterinary. He studied economics and law at Moscow University, joining the Bolsheviks in the early 1900s, when he adopted the pseudonym Osinsky. He was repeatedly arrested for his political activities and was exiled from Moscow to various places around the country. After the Bolsheviks came to power he held different posts in the government and administration, including head of the State Bank and later chairman of the powerful Supreme Soviet of the National Economy. Osinsky's political qualifications were based more on domestic issues than on foreign policy. He had been a delegate to five consecutive Communist Party congresses from 1918 to 1922. As a leader of fluctuating oppositional factions, he had been active in party work during the years following the revolution. In 1918, as the leader of the "Left Communists", he had opposed Lenin's plan to conclude peace with Germany, which involved significant territorial concessions. In 1920–21 he was a member of the "Democratic Centralists", who criticized the top-down control of the Communist Party.

Two of the Soviet Russian delegates to Sweden, Maksim Litvinov and Valerian Osinsky, belonged to the stratum of the political hierarchy immediately below the most powerful men (there were no women), that is, members or candidate members of the Communist Party Central Committee. Litvinov, who died at the age of seventy-five, was one of only seven persons in the old guard of the Bolshevik Party to survive Stalin's terror. Also, among these seven was Aleksandra Kollontai, another diplomatic representative in Sweden. There has been speculation as to why Litvinov and Kollontai were spared, but no one knows for sure. Valerian Osinsky was arrested and executed in 1938 during Stalin's attack on the top leaders of the party and government. Osinsky, who had long since abandoned factional pursuits and at the time of his arrest was the head of the Institute for the History of Science and Technology of the Soviet Academy of Sciences, was accused of "terrorist activities". He was fifty-one years old when he was executed.

Platon Kerzhentsev died in Moscow in 1940 at the age of fifty-nine, by all indications of natural causes.

The portraits of Kerzhentsev, Litvinov and Osinsky included here were done by the Swedish artist and writer Albert Engström in 1923, and can be found in *Moskoviter* (*Muscovites*), a lightly satirical portrayal of Moscow in the NEP period.[19]

[1] My article is based on Russian and Swedish archival materials. The Swedish sources are from the archives of the Swedish Ministry of Foreign Affairs, 1920 dossier system HP 32 B, HP 32 H, HP 64 Er, HP 80A/Russia, state committees such as the Customs and Treaty Committee 1919 and the Russian Investigation Commission, as well as the archive of the Swedish General Export Association and the archives of various companies such as Nohab, Munktells and ASEA. The Russian documents are in two archival institutions in Moscow: the *Russian Center for the Preservation and Documentation of Contemporary History* (RTsKhIDNI), fund 6 (Lenin's secretariat) and the *Archive of the Ministry of Foreign Affairs of the Russian Federation* (AVPRF), funds 0140 (Swedish Desk) and 0140a (Soviet Legation in Sweden). I have also used Helene Carlbäck, *Att byta erkännande mot handel: svensk-ryska förhandlingar 1921–1924* [Exchanging Trade for Recognition: Swedish-Soviet Negotiations 1921–1924 (PhD. diss. Uppsala University, 1997) and works on Swedish, Russian and other European history dealing with the Russian question (see Carlbäck 1997, 270–284).

[2] Erik Palmstierna, *Dagjämning: politiska dagboksanteckningar, 1920–21* (Stockholm: Tiden, 1954), 65.

[3] See Håkan Blomqvist, *Myten om judebolsjevismen: antisemitism och kontrarevolution i svenska ögon* (Stockholm: Carlssons, 2013).

[4] *Aftonbladet*, 13 June 1921.

[5] Fredrik Grönwall headed the Trade Department of the Ministry for Foreign Affairs.

[6] This can be viewed as a continuation of the situation during WWI, when Stockholm, as the capital of a non-combatant, neutral state, became a central place for diplomats, journalists and some politicians from other countries. The city rather quickly lost that position, however, as life in Europe returned to normal.

[7] Branting shared the prize with Christian Lange from Norway.

[8] *Svenska Dagbladet*, 11 November 1921.

[9] Some large Swedish firms—among them ASEA and SKF—obtained concessions to run their former businesses. L. M. Ericsson was considered for such an arrangement until their telephone company was awarded as a concession to the German firm Siemens a year later. SKFs and ASEAs concession activities ceased in the early 1930s, when Stalin reintroduced a state-controlled economic policy.

[10] *Göteborgs-Posten*, 6 March 1922.

[11] *Svenska Dagbladet*, 5 March 1922.

[12] *Nya Dagligt Allehanda*, 4 March 1922, 6 March 1922.

[13] *Stockholms Dagblad*, 5 March 1922.

[14] *Svenska Morgonbladet*, 6 March 1922.

[15] *Svenska Handelstidningen*, 4 March 1922.

[16] *Svenska Dagbladet*, 10 March 1923.

[17] *Svenska Morgonbladet*, 10 March 1923.

[18] *Stockholms Dagblad*, 21 June 1923.

[19] Albert Engström, *Moskoviter* (Stockolm: Bonnier, 1924).

Kergentzeff.

LITVINOFF

Minister Ossinskij.

The Return of the Clerk, the Sovietologist and the Eccentric – Irina Sandomirskaja as a mirror of Swedish–Russian Expertise

JOHAN ÖBERG

> Historical and economic conditions explain both the inevitable beginning of the revolutionary struggle of the masses and their unpreparedness for the struggle, their Tolstoyan non-resistance to evil, which was a most serious cause of the defeat of the first revolutionary campaign.[1]

Was it really that sublime faith in freedom, progress and everlasting peace that tore down the Iron Curtain and dismantled the Soviet Union some thirty years ago?

Or could it have been more primitive beliefs? Like faith in the panacea of new information technologies, new public or private management?

Or, if not faith in these, just the Leninist way: new machinery, managerialism and network society themselves, their own discourses, their self-worship?

If the latter is true, and there are some reasons to believe it is, what, then, about the outcomes and results of the same process in Swedish society?

Was it early 1990s optimism about the future world, or was it the new, volatile worldview of new public management that stripped the Swedish army of its firepower and the Swedish universities and state institutions of the Russian language?

Writing on the impact of network society as early as the early 1990s,[2] Manuel Castells was able to show how the global processes of horizontality, deterritorialization and globalization were—also in Russia—challenged by countercurrents such as identity and reterritorialization, which meant the return of language as fetish, of *rodina* and *otechestvo*, of asymmetry, incompatibility and the necessity of new forms of difficult, intercultural dialogue.

The Russian historian Yuri Afanasiev—himself an active participant in the reformation of the Soviet system and in the political debates of the 1990s—clarified on several occasions that this was not the end of history, especially not in Russia, but instead the beginning of history in the form of an even sharper conflict between the tendencies of globalization and renewed efforts to build statehood in Russia.[3]

And now, as the underside of globalization—its resistance to itself, so to say—seems to prevail, and volatile cycles go in quite a different direction than they did in the early 1990s, public debate in Sweden is being teased by a pessimism which is as superficial as the former optimism. Today the country declares itself in need of all that old stuff again: security, an army, a fire brigade, border checkpoints and a new generation of Russian-speaking Swedes and "Russia experts". But can insecurity, or frights, of this kind foster good reflective students and research?

The new Cold War seems nevertheless to attract the old solutions. Its heritage is surging. This return is surely something real, but what is its meaning, its functionality today, except as a reassurance, proof that today's world is the same as yesterday's: palpable, controllable and genuine?

One example of this current 'return of the real' by way of the heritage is the effort by the Swedish government to reinstitute knowledge of Russian and Russia in Swedish universities. But the contemporary perspective is, once again, a volatile market-driven one: a competent workforce is needed, for the time being. This is not about the foundation of independent cultural studies research or deepened dialogue or understanding. To put it bluntly, it is about the re-creation of a disappearing species that wants to reproduce itself: the Swedish Russia expert.

This is heritage. This is memory.

When I began my studies in Russian in a Swedish gymnasium back in the 1970s, I had an eccentric teacher who taught Russian in a funny, unsystematic way. And this is an understatement. He taught me how to order vodka in restaurants where there was no vodka, but especially: how to take a pause.

In fact, the most repeated phrase in this class (where I was often the only student) was: "*a teper', sdelaem pereryv*" ("And now, let's take a break"). I was sure this man must have had some kind of experience in Russia that he never talked about. He was *secret*. He was *trained*. For the exam, he offered me Alfred Jensen's work *Slavia* (the 1897 edition) as a present. Or as an excuse. I don't know. I had learned almost nothing from him, but I was still fascinated by what he had neither said nor taught.

A year or two later, he was exposed in a leftist journal for having been a Swedish spy in Russia who observed railway communications under the auspices of one of the Swedish Russia agencies: ÖEB—the *Eastern Economic Bureau* and the IB, the *Information Bureau*. He had by then submitted a small dissertation on Soviet railroads for the Department of Cultural Geography at the University of Gothenburg.

Unfortunately, he did not have the gift for teaching of a Jim Prideaux, and I had initially great difficulties in taking up Russian at the university. But I was fascinated by this character, this spiritually glowing and yet contourless cold warrior. The silences, the eccentric appearance, his exquisite knowledge and sharpness as far as Russia was concerned. But outside of that context he faded out. *Natura creata quae non creat.* Zero.

My teacher was also, it appeared, a quite distinguished collector of Russian icons and, later, a promotor of Soviet art events in Sweden, the biggest of which became the exhibit *Russian Painters 1850–1900. Artworks from Museums in Leningrad and Moscow* at the Gothenburg Museum of Fine Art; I think it was in 1981. And that was still after he had been exposed in the press! To my knowledge, he was subsequently mostly busy with social care for the elderly. How could that be? I have never understood. But this humility surely had some connection to Russia. He died rather young. Of course.

I understood later that he had once belonged to a special group of Swedes, the "Soviet experts". He was a clerk, a Sovietologist, an eccentric and a collector. But he was neither a thinker, nor a theoretician, nor a pedagogue. Soviet experts rarely have their own questions—they ask other people's. Holding their practical knowledge, like artists, they fade out into the 'Land of Eternal Darkness", like the hero of Swedish author Sven Delblanc's first novel *The Hermit Crab* (1962).

The Swedish dragoman

As Latin could not be used to communicate with Russians, specific interpreters were, as we know from Tarkianen[4] and Birgegård[5], necessary partners in Sweden's communications with Russia. They were necessary in all kinds of military and civil contacts for both offensive and defensive needs. They formed an indispensable infrastructure and contact channel. Sometimes they were powerful, sometimes they were flies on the wall. Structurally, they seem to have fulfilled the same functions as the dragomans did in the Ottoman Empire.[6]

The systematic training of interpreters had begun back in the seventeenth century, and was kept in several different formats until it was restructured in the 1950s within a special, scientific, modern department for military translators and interpreters, which also became the cradle of Swedish expertise on the

Soviet Union. During the Cold War there were also similar educational structures for Russian within other parts of the Swedish Armed Forces.

Over the years, and after a multitude of readings and encounters with this milieu, some general characterological traits have crystalized for me: these people were *practicing* the Soviet Union with the same enjoyment as others practice church organs or violins. And of course, they were no dragomans: socially and economically, they belonged to the Swedish establishment. But still, they had a double matrix: on one hand, they were journalists, government officials or politicians, cultural personalities, ambassadors, military men, businessmen, economists, police and secret police. Generally (with exceptions such as my teacher of Russian) they were solidly anchored and strongly influential within their respective fields, and on the other hand, they shared a strong identity as members of a select group of Russian-speaking Swedes. It is not pure coincidence that it was sometimes possible to recognize in their conversation the tones of *The Red and the Black* with its repeated mentions of *la belle latinité*. This Russian expertise was an imprint, a shared ideology uniting rich and poor, influential and powerless.

The inner circle of experts—more often men than women—rarely disagreed on important matters. They shared a well calibrated and elaborate doxa about the Soviet Union. They identified themselves as the responsible bearers of the language, the culture and the political analysis, but they also, in fact, managed many of the existing contact channels that Sweden sustained with the Soviet Union and its child—The Russian Federation—and they were in this sense important messengers and representatives of Swedish neutralism in relation to the Soviet Union in the dark and threatening times of the Cold War.

But there was more to the picture. Because relations with the Soviet Union were at the center of attention in Swedish politics, Sweden was also at the center of international attention, and so were the Russia experts. In consequence, they had a strong position in Swedish society and, with some exceptions, formed an important network of highly qualified people. One of the most influential representatives of this group once told me, back in the 1990s, that this elite of 300-400 people was so influential in Swedish society that it was the only group which stood any chance of making a successful coup.

As public figures, they were fundamentally anti-communist and anti-Soviet, but they were also specific; they were "realists" because of the knowledge about Russia and Russian that had been inculcated in them, they also knew what kind of place Sweden had in the world, and they knew exactly what could be said, and when, and what could not be said to the Russkies.

With the help of a discursive practice developed over many years, they could perfectly well negotiate and renegotiate a commonsensical identity of Sweden in the eyes of their Soviet partners: yes we are Christians, yes, we belong to the West, we are a strong capitalist economy, but we are also socialists, we have Swedish socialism, which is better than the Soviet version, don't you agree, we love sports, we produce high-quality cars, and we are very neutral. No one, and everyone, believed them.

Of course, the judgements of his select group of Russia experts—who also worked as influential policy makers in the political parties—was criticized now and then by academics, politicians, human rights and religious activists, who overtly challenged what they perceived as the culture of silence and cowardice which dominated our relations to the Soviet Union during the Cold War. This culture was reminiscent of Swedish policies with regard to Nazi Germany in the 1930s and 1940s. It was realistic and hence shameful.

And this was not Finlandization. The discursive practices and competencies of the Soviet experts were rarely built on any concrete experience of resistance to or more intimate familiarity with the great neighbor. There was no trauma of hatred-fierceness-silence in Sweden similar to the blockage Irina Sandomirskaja analyzes in her amazing book *Blokada v slove*.[7] But there were other kinds of traumas, among them a "bystander" trauma from the neutrality years of WWII and a residue of shame that has persisted in Swedish society since those years, a specific heritage which was also digested and integrated into the relations between Sweden and the Soviet Union (we perceive this specificity in the way the Raoul Wallenberg case has been managed over the years).

Both conservatives and Social Democrats were certainly fearful of a third world war and the consequences of a possible Soviet attack,[8] but in my experience this fright among Social Democrats was intertwined and mixed with a secret admiration for several features of the calm and slowly but steadily working socialist bureaucracy and the big scale of everything Soviet, from sports arenas to the large literacy and vaccination campaigns.

The conservatives were fascinated by Soviet conservatism. They saw how the Bolshevik system had preserved large parts of eighteenth- and nineteenth-century culture, including old-fashioned designs of theatre plays, ballets, operas and romances. When the ideological veil and the red flag were lifted, the Soviet Union was also able to showcase an unambivalent conservative magnificence. In the Soviet Union it was still possible to salute the flag, to sing hymns to the fatherland, the motherland and the homeland, to a place where discipline reigned in the army and where stylish parades could still be organized.

Empathies mixed with frights. And during the early 1990s the time came for many representatives of the group to start practicing Russia in a new way: in collaborative projects to support the development of democracy, economy, infrastructure. To test all that knowledge that had been built on observation, on the bystander position. During these years the group of Russia experts lost its former structure and coherence, and in some cases frustrated empathy changed into participant observation, participation and activism; some people went even further and began going native or became talking heads for the new, self-proclaimed democratic Russia appearing on the horizon.

What was peculiar, or notable at least, was that almost none of the group took up an intellectual career. No one wrote an independent, self-critical or critical book. The immense knowledge and practice accumulated over the past decades was rarely reinvested in reflexive processes in order to deepen our understanding of historic change.

Where would self-reflexivity regarding the conditions of possibility of their expertise-doxa have led this group? Maybe into an understanding of the cognitive and ideological relevance of this knowledge, not of the Soviet Union or Russia as broad historical phenomena, but instead of parallel endeavours inside the cognitive object itself. In the land of the Soviets there were also schools of military translators, where Swedish was taught. There was also a group of very influential Sweden experts with a perfect command of the language and Swedish-Russian history and culture.

They too worked in academic institutions and ministries, in the armed forces and security services, in the Central Committee of the CPSU, as diplomats and ambassadors. The two groups knew each other and knew about each other, sometimes as friends, which enhanced stability in their bilateral relationships.

To what extent, finally, did the two groups of experts also produce and reproduce each other? And to follow up, to what extent might we even here see some form of Russian/Soviet cultural influence on Sweden?

If this form of "cultural dialogue" is relevant, it is also relevant, as a part of understanding the processes of recovering Sweden's heritage of the Cold War, to try to introduce and project onto Swedish reality a similar biopolitical analysis that Irina Sandomirskaja has developed in relation to the Leningrad Blockade and more generally to the creation of the new communist human being.

It might, finally, be relevant to ask the question to what extent the phenomenon of the blind-deaf writer, pedagogue and researcher Ol'ga Skorokhodova[9] investigated and analyzed by Sandomirskaja, is also relevant for our understanding of the "Soviet expert"?

After the dissolution of the Soviet Union and the Warsaw Pact, and as a closer and officially declared relationship between Sweden and NATO developed, things changed in the Swedish expert group. With the marginalization of the communist and Soviet threat, this group became less cohesive and was also gradually marginalized. Dissent occurred between adherents of transatlanticism and self-proclaimed bearers of historical reason and neutralist doxa from the Cold War…

"… and this last thought of thine that all things will return".

It was a cold and grayish afternoon in March 2018, and the doors of the Press Room of the Ministry for Foreign Affairs in Stockholm had been thrown open to representatives of Swedish universities and research institutes. Clearly, no flowers were budding in Mosebacke Park. Outside, in the blustery and cold afternoon, you could see freezing ambassadors and officials with dispatch cases trying to keep their documents safe and their suits and ties in order in the wind.

A meeting had been announced by three ministers—Defense, Education and Foreign Affairs—in order to discuss what over several years had come to appear as a serious problem to Sweden's administration: the lack of expertise in the Russian language. Swedish missions to Russia and elsewhere could no longer be staffed with diplomats and specialists in Russia who were fluent in Russian—experts who once were the pride and glory of Swedish diplomacy.

But it was not only the Foreign Service that was lacking linguistically competent—or Russia competent—collaborators. Also, the Ministry of Defense (with the Defense Research Agency, Defense University), the Ministry of the Interior, the Institute for Foreign Policy, the Customs Service and the private sector seemed to be in need. Relations with Russia were gradually deteriorating.

The Minister of Higher Education stared at us, asking universities about their future plans for promoting Russian in their institutions. *Pari passu*, this was a rather Russian situation, and *pari passu*, she made it perfectly clear that there would be no extra funding. National interests are usually shared. Depending on how you perceive Swedish governance, it was kindly asked, assumed or suggested that universities *prioritize*.

Still, I reckon that the delegates from the Higher Education Institutions might have understood her message in the opposite way. There is always money somewhere, if one shows eagerness. In Uppsala there was an upcoming multi-disciplinary master exam. In Stockholm, maybe a Master's degree in Social Science that would include Russian or perhaps a new translator's degree; in Gothenburg, a web-based course in Russian for the Customs Service, the police and other stuff.

Maybe, I thought, the minister's fierce message may actually have been directed to her own, present or absent colleagues, asking them to open their wallets and "share".

The talk went on. One of the last speakers, a leading expert and distinguished representative of the Swedish Cold War foreign policy generation, proposed the building of a new "Russia House" tasked with producing new, useful expertise in Russian affairs. This would guarantee the eternal return of the "Soviet experts" we so badly need.

This imperative request seemed to be outvoted immediately by the multitude of academic representatives in attendance.

A new meeting was announced for the future. Now, go home and do your homework.

After the ball

It was dark outside. I walked the 200 meters back to the Central Station thinking that this had been a typical dysfunctional Swedish meeting between bureaucracies, seasoned with terrible coffee and strong vested interests. Entities that are supposed to cooperate, but whose thinking is full of contemporary Leninism: volume, money and power. Intentions were good but deeply problematic.

Good, of course: academic, critical Russian studies on a high international level ought to be a compulsory component in Swedish universities, considering that Sweden and Russia are close to each other geographically and have a long shared history.

But problematic, in a moral sense. It never ends well when universities use current, resource-driven security agendas and, as in this case, promise to revive the old Cold War "Soviet expert", who is in his or her essence the contrary of the slow, critical reflection, culture, art, history, philology and philosophy which make up the kernel of a serious university.

This kind of strategy—producing expertise out of fright—will lead to the production of something that we have learned so much about from Irina Sandomirskaja's work on the Leningrad Blockade. There, it has a name: *khaltura*.

[1] https://www.marxists.org/archive/lenin/works/1908/sep/11.htm
[2] Manuel Castells, *The Power of Identity, The Information Age: Economy, Society and Culture Vol. II.* (Cambridge, Massachusetts; Oxford, UK: Blackwell, 1997).
[3] http://gefter.ru/archive/15955.
[4] Kari Tarkiainen, *Moskoviten. Sverige och Ryssland 1478–1721* (Helsingfors: Svenska litteratursällskapet, 2017).
[5] Ulla Birgegård, "En ständig huvudvärk i relationerna mellan Sverige och Ryssland: Tsarens och kungens titlar," *Slovo. Journal of Slavic Languages, Literatures and Cultures*, No. 55, 2014, 34–46.
[6] A perfectly irrelevant yet interesting reference here, from an existential point of view at least, to the dragoman mood of existence is found in Georges Simenon's "Turkish" novel, *Les clients d'Avrenos* (Paris: Éditions Gallimard, 1935).
[7] *Blokada v slove: Ocherki kritihceskoi teorii i biopolitiki iazyka* (Moscow: Novoe literaturnoe obozrenie, 2013).
[8] One doxic reference here is the Swedish movie *Skymningsläge – Sverige under kalla kriget* (*Dusk, Sweden during the Cold War*, 2016) by Melker Becker and Veronica Martinson, which is based on films produced by the Swedish Armed Forces in the 1960s and 1970s.
[9] http://www.aif.ru/dontknows/file/clepogluhaya_pisatelnica_i_uchenyy-defektolog_olga_skorohodova_spravka p

Irina Sandomirskaja: A Bibliography

COMPILED BY MÄRTA BERGSTRAND

Scholarly works

1991

Emotivnye glagoly so znacheniem povedeniia (Emotive Verbs Denoting Behavior). Dissertation defended at the Institute of Linguistics, the Russian Academy of Sciences, Moscow, 1991

1992

Writing and the Magic of Power, in: *Heresies: a Feminist Publication on Art and Politics*, 1992: 26, pp. 44–61

1995

Old Wives' Tales: Notes on the Rhetoric of the Post-Soviet Intelligentsia, in: *Intelligentsia in the Interim: Recent Experiences from Central and Eastern Europe*, Lund: Slaviska institutionen, 1995, pp. 55–71

1996

"Ia tak khochu nazvat' kino". "Naivnoe pis'mo": opyt lingvo-sotsiologicheskogo chteniia, Moscow: Gnozis, 1996. 255 p. Together with Natalia Kozlova.

Russian Restricted Collocations: an Attempt of Frame Approach, in: *Euralex '96 Proceedings I–II: Papers submitted to the Seventh Euralex International Congress on Lexicography in Göteborg, Sweden*, ed. by Martin Gellerstam..., Göteborg: Dept. of Swedish, 1996, pp. 273–282. Together with Elena Oparina.

Novaia zhinz' na marshe. Stalinskii turizm kak 'praktika puti', in: *Obshchestvennye nauki i sovremennost'*, 1996: 4, pp. 163–172

1997

Walter Benjamin's Moscow Diary: A Mission to the Margins of History, in: *Reciprocal Images: Russian Culture in the Mirror of Travellers' Accounts*, ed. by Peter Ulf Møller, Oslo: Scandinavian University Press, 1997, pp. 93–113

1998

Phraseology as a Language of Culture. Its Role in the Representation of a Cultural Mentality, in: *Phraseology: Theory, Analysis, and Application*, ed. by A.P. Cowie, Oxford: Clarendon Press, 1998, pp. 55–78. Together with Veronica Teliya, Natalya Bragina and Elena Oparina.

Ojczyzna w polskim i rosyjskim obrazie świata, in: *Z polskich studiów slawistycznych. Językoznawstwo.* Seria XI, Warszawa, 1998, pp. 21–29. Together with Jerzy Bartmiński and Veronika Telija.

Idioma i kul'tura: v poiskakh obshchego osnovaniia, in: *Etnolingwistyka*, 8, 1998, pp. 9–23

Proletarian Tourism: Incorporated History and Incorporated Rhetoric, in: *Soviet Civilization Between Past and Present*, ed. by Mette Bryld & Eric Kulavig, Odense: Odense University Press, 1998, pp. 39–52

1999

Writing on the Wall: Remont, Restoration, and Identity, in: *Through a Glass Darkly: Cultural Representations in the Dialogue between Central, Eastern and Western Europe*, ed. by Fiona Björling, Lund: Department of Slavonic studies, 1999, pp. 113–129

2001

The Rehabilitation of Bad Poetry. Crickets, Children, and 'Cruel Language', *Slavica Lundensia*, 21, 2001, pp. 151–166

Kniga o rodine: opyt analiza diskursivnykh praktik, Wien: Wiener Slawistischer Almanach, 2001. 281 p.

Obol'shchenie Rodinoi: kommercheskii iazyk i simuliatsiia "svoego", in: *Kultur, Sprache, Ökonomie*: Beiträge zur gleichnamigen Tagung an der Wirtschaftsuniversität Wien, 3.–5. Dezember 1999, ed. by Wolfgang Weitlaner, Wien: Wiener Slawistischer Almanach, 2001, pp. 399–412

2002

Heimatbegriff in der sowjetischen und postsowjetischen diskursiven Praxis, in: *Europa und die Grenzen im Kopf,* ed. by Karl Kaser, Dagmar Gramshammer-Hohl & Robert Pichler, Klagenfurt: Wieser-Verlag, 2002, pp. 395–415

Vtoroi epigraf: (popytka raznochteniia), in: *Wiener Slawistischer Almanach,* Wien: Institut für Slavische Philologie, Universität München, 2002: 50, pp. 133–151

2004

In Search of an Order: Mutual Representations in Sweden and Russia during the Early Age of Reason, ed. by Ulla Birgegård & Irina Sandomirskaja, Huddinge: Södertörns högskola, 2004. 202 p.

[Introduction]: Two Empires and the Sea: Change and Exchange in Search of an Order, in: *Mutual Representations in Sweden and Russia during the Early Age of Reason,* ed. by Ulla Birgegård & Irina Sandomirskaja, Huddinge: Södertörns högskola, 2004, pp. 7–20

A Cosmopolitan in Search of a Fatherland: Admiral Shishkov and the Linguistic Myth of the Russian Empire, in: *In Search of an Order: Mutual Representations in Sweden and Russia during the Early Age of Reason,* ed. by Ulla Birgegård & Irina Sandomirskaja, Huddinge: Södertörns högskola, 2004, pp. 155–172

Golaia zhizn', zloi Bakhtin i vezhlivyi Vaginov: tragediia bez khora i bez avtora, in: *Telling Forms: 30 Essays in Honour of Peter Alberg Jensen,* ed. by Karin Grelz & Susanna Witt, Stockholm: Almqvist & Wiksell International, 2004, pp. 340–356

Opravdanie slovobludiia: nomadologicheskaia lingvistika Zhan-Zhaka Leserklia, in: *Poetika iskanii, ili Poisk poetiki: materialy mezhdunarodnoi konferentsii...,* ed. by Natal'ia Fateeva, Moscow: Institut russkogo iazyka im. V. V. Vinogradova, 2004, pp. 180–196

2006

Iazyk-Stalin: "Marksizm i voprosy iazykoznaniia" kak lingvisticheskii povorot vo vselennoi SSSR, in: *Landslide of the Norm: Language Culture in Post-Soviet*

Russia, ed. by Ingunn Lunde & Tine Roesen, Bergen: Dept. of Russian Studies, 2006, pp. 263-291

Kak ne "zavershit'" Bakhtina: perepiska iz dvukh elektronnykh uglov, in: *Novoe literaturnoe obozrenie*, 2006: 79, pp. 7-38. Together with Mark Lipovetskii.

On the Archaeology of the Wall, in: The Imprints of Terror: the Rhetoric of Violence and the Violence of Rhetoric in Modern Russian Culture. In memoriam Marina Kanevskaya, ed. by Anna Brodsky, Mark Lipovetsky & Sven Spieker, München: Sagner, 2006, pp. 241-262

2008

A Glossolalic Glasnost and the Re-Tuning of the Soviet Subject: Sound Performance in Kira Muratova's *Asthenic Syndrome*, in: *Studies in Russian and Soviet Cinema*, 2008: 1, pp. 63-83

Cinema Thinking the Unthinkable: Cold War Film and the Non-Reality of Russia, in: *Russia and its Other(s) on Film: Screening Intercultural Dialogue*, ed. by Stephen Hutchings, London: Palgrave, 2008, pp. 130-147

One Sixth of the World: Avantgarde Film, the Revolution of Vision, and the Colonization of the USSR Periphery during the 1920s (Towards a Postcolonial Deconstruction of the Soviet Hegemony), in: *From Orientalism to Postcoloniality*, ed. by Kerstin Olofsson, Huddinge: Södertörns högskola, 2008, pp. 8-31

Skin to Skin: Language in the Soviet Education of Deaf-Blind Children, the 1920s and 1930s, in: *Studies in East European Thought*, 2008: 4, pp. 321-337

The Poetics of Memory and the Politics of Reading: Fourteen Episodes of Remembering, in: *The Poetics of Memory in Post-Totalitarian Narration*, ed. by Johanna Lindbladh, Lund: CFE, 2008, pp. 81-94

2010

A Politeia in Besiegement: Lidiia Ginzburg on the Siege of Leningrad as a Political Paradigm, in: *Slavic Review*, 2010: 2, pp. 306-326

L'engage, or The Faculty of Unnecessary Things, in: *En annan humaniora – en annan tid = Another humanities – another time*, ed. by Carl Cederberg & Hans Ruin, Huddinge: Södertörns högskola, 2010, pp. 23-31

Return to the Motherland, in: *The Russia Reader: History, Culture, Politics*, ed. by Adele Barker & Bruce Grant, Durham: Duke University Press, 2010, pp. 735–742

2011

Derrida on the Politics and Poetics of Witnessing, in: *Rethinking Time: Essays on History, Memory, and Representation*, ed. by Hans Ruin & Andrus Ers, Huddinge: Södertörns högskola, 2011, pp. 247–255

2012

'Bez stali i leni': Aesopian Language and Legitimacy, in: *Power and Legitimacy: Challenges from Russia*, ed. by Per-Arne Bodin, Stefan Hedlund & Elena Namli, London: Routledge, 2012, pp. 188–198

Rage, Body, and Power Talk in the City of Hunger: the Politics of Womanliness in Lidia Ginzburg's *Notes from the Siege of Leningrad*, in: *Embracing Arms: Cultural Representation of Slavic and Balkan Women in War*, ed. by Helena Goscilo & Yana Hashamova, Budapest: Central European University Press, 2012, pp. 131–151

The Leviathan, or Language in Besiegement: Lydia Ginzburg's Prolegomena to Critical Discourse Analysis, in: *Lydia Ginzburg's Alternative Literary Identities: a Collection of Articles and New Translations*, ed. by Emily Van Buskirk and Andrei Zorin, Oxford: Peter Lang, 2012, pp. 193–234

Naivnoe pis'mo piatnadtsat' let spustia, ili Na smert' soavtora, in: *Neprikosnovennyi zapas*, 2012: 2, pp. 206–219

Ot avgusta k avgustu: dokumental'noe kino kak arkhiv pokhishchennykh revoliutsii, in: *Novoe literaturnoe obozrenie*, 2012: 5, pp. 231–248

2013

Blokada v slove: ocherki kriticheskoi teorii i biopolitiki iazyka, Moscow: Novoe literaturnoe obozrenie, 2013. 425 p.

Tudo podia ter sido diferente, tudo poderia ser diferente, tudo pode ser diferente, in: *Viso: Cadernos de estética aplicada*, 2013: 14, pp. 56–63

2015

Aesopian Language: The Politics and Poetics of Naming the Unnameable, in: *The Vernaculars of Communism: Language, Ideology, and Power in the Soviet Union and Eastern Europe*, ed. by Petre Petrov & Lara Ryazanova-Clarke, London: Routledge, 2015, pp. 63–88

Catastrophe, Restoration, and *Kunstwollen*: Igor Grabar, Cultural heritage, and Soviet reuses of the past, in: *Ab Imperio: Theory and History of Nationalities and Nationalism in the post-Soviet Realm*, 2015: 2, pp. 339–362

Disoriented Names: Benjamin and Kierkegaard on Politics and History in Language, in: *Dis-orientations: Philosophy, Literature, and the Lost Grounds of Modernity*, ed. by Marcia Sá Cavalcante Schuback & Tora Lane, London: Rowman & Littlefield International, 2015, pp. 187–218

2016

"Där en människa inte bör vara": poeten framför det förflutna utan mine, in: *Historiens hemvist. 2. Etik, politik och historikerns ansvar*, ed. by Patrizia Lorenzoni & Ulla Manns, Göteborg: Makadam, 2016, pp. 177–191

Welcome to Panorama Theresienstadt: Cinematography and Destruction in the Town Called "As If" (Reading H. G. Adler), in: *Apparatus*, 2016: 2–3

Bad Girls, Apocalyptic Beasts, Redemption: A tribute to Helena Goscilo, in: *Transgressive Women in Modern Russian and East European Cultures: From the Bad to the Blasphemous*, ed. by Yana Hashamova, Beth Holmgren & Mark Lipovetsky, New York: Routledge, 2016, pp. 192–208

2017

Den fördömda lyckan, eller socialismens ekonomiska problem i Moskva, in: *Revolution och existens: läsningar av Andrej Platonov*, ed. by Tora Lane, Stockholm: Ersatz, 2017, pp. 133–156

Clarice and Photogeny, or, "Not Knowing the Concept of 'Enough'", in: *Ad Marciam*, ed. by Hans Ruin & Jonna Bornemark, Huddinge: Södertörns högskola, 2017, pp. 199–209

After the End of the World: Panorama, in: *The End of the World: Contemporary Philosophy and Art*, ed. by Marcia Sá Cavalcante Schuback & Susanna Lindberg, London: Rowman & Littlefield International, 2017, pp. 235–256

Ahasuerus on an Excursion: *Austerlitz*, 2016. Directed by Sergei Loznitsa, in: *Mémoires en jeu: Revue critique interdisciplinaire et multiculturelle sur les enjeux de mémoire*, 2017: 4, pp. 9–11

Bakhtin in Bits and Pieces: Poetic Scholarship, Exilic Theory, and a Close Reading of the Disaster, in: *Slavic and East European Journal*, 2017: 2, pp. 278–298

2018

Von … bis …: Etappen einer Bildformel im Dokumentarfilm über die Sowjetunion: Visuelle Erinnerungskulturen in Osteuropa, in: *Bildformeln: Visuelle Erinnerungskulturen in Osteuropa*, ed. by Susanne Frank, Bielefeld: Transcript Verlag, 2018, pp. 63–88

Miscellaneous

1998

"Landskap med vandringman" (review of: Boris Gasparov, *Iazyk, pamiat', obraz – lingvistika iazykovogo sushchestvovaniia*, Moscow: Novoe literaturnoe obozrenie, 1996), in: *Dialoger* 1998, 46, pp. 37–39

1999

Self-Critical Narcissus: On Language and Power in the Mode of Seduction, in: *Shaking Hands and Making Conflicts* (Catalogue), ed. by Mika Larsson, Partnership for Culture: Stockholm, 1999

2000

Dressing, Undressing, Cross–Dressing, in: *The Memory of the Body. Underclothes During the Soviet Era*, Moscow, 2000 (exhibition catalogue)

IKEA i Moskva, in: *Moderna tider*, 2000: 121 (November), pp. 54–57
Der politisch-ökonomische Aspekt der russischen Geduld: Und für den Kefir ein Extra-Dankeschön an alle, in: *Podium Literatur*, 2000, 113/114, pp. 5–9

2001

Blind, Mute, Dead, and Melancholy, in: *Bra mot melankoli = Remedy for melancholy*, curators Anders Kreuger & Evaldas Stankevičius, Sollentuna: Edsvik konst och kultur, 2001

Moscovia Felix: An Obscene Discourse about an Abscene Place, in: *Yearbook*, Malmö: Konsthögskolan i Malmö, 2001

"Public Artist, Go Away": Pathfinding in the Citadel of Necessity, in: *Konst på SÖS: essäer om konst på sjukhus och i annan institutionsmiljö*, ed. by Susanne Andersson, Ann Magnusson & Ulla Parkdal, Stockholm: Konstnämnden, Stockholms läns landsting, 2001

2004

Tedium Vitae, Curriculum Vitae, in: *Faster Than History*. Catalogue for the art exhibition, Helsinki: Kiasma, 2004

2005

Antropofagi utan metaforer: fallet Leningrad, in: *Glänta*, 2005: 3, pp. 115–122

2007

Det nakna livet – en läroplan, in: *Glänta*, 2007: 1, pp. 3–17

2009

Babusjkan som sådan och som kulturpolitik, in: *En bok om böcker och bibliotek: tillägnad Louise Brunes*, ed. by Erland Jansson, Huddinge: Södertörns högskola, 2009 pp. 193–199

2012

The end of La Belle Époque (text in Russian and English), in: Misha Pedan, *The end of La Belle Époque*, Stockholm: Khimaira Publishing, 2012, 96 unnumbered pages

2013

Allt kunde ha varit annorlunda, in: *Glänta*, 2013: 2–3, pp. 156–160

Pussy Riot: Reflections On Receptions: Some Questions Concerning Public Reactions in Russia to the Pussy Riot's Intervention and Trial, in: *Baltic Worlds*, 2013: 1, p. 56. Together with Yulia Gradskova.

2016

Review of: Steven Maddox, *Saving Stalin's Imperial City: Historic Preservation in Leningrad, 1930–1950*, Bloomington: Indiana University Press, 2014, in: *Slavic Review*, 2016: 3, pp. 787–788

2017

Review of: Emily Van Buskirk, *Lydia Ginzburg's Prose: Reality In Search Of Literature*, Princeton: Princeton University Press, 2016, in: *Tulsa Studies in Women's Literature*, 2017: 1, pp. 233–235

2018

Det olikas likhet, det likas olikhet, in: *Glänta* 2018: 1, pp. 26–27

Södertörn Philosophical Studies

1. Hans Ruin & Nicholas Smith (eds.), *Hermeneutik och tradition: Gadamer och den grekiska filosofin* (2003)
2. Hans Ruin, *Kommentar till Heideggers Varat och tiden* (2005)
3. Marcia Sá Cavalcante Schuback & Hans Ruin (eds.), *The Past's Presence: Essays on the Historicity of Philosophical Thought* (2006)
4. Jonna Bornemark (ed.), *Det främmande i det egna: Filosofiska essäer om bildning och person* (2007)
5. Marcia Sá Cavalcante Schuback (ed.), *Att tänka smärtan* (2009)
6. Jonna Bornemark, *Kunskapens gräns, gränsens vetande: En fenomenologisk undersökning av transcendens och kroppslighet* (2009)
7. Carl Cederberg & Hans Ruin (eds.), *En annan humaniora, en annan tid/Another humanities, another time* (2009)
8. Jonna Bornemark & Hans Ruin (eds.), *Phenomenology and Religion: New Frontiers* (2010)
9. Hans Ruin & Andrus Ers (eds.), *Rethinking Time: Essays on History, Memory, and Representation* (2011)
10. Jonna Bornemark & Marcia Sá Cavalcante Schuback (eds.), *Phenomenology of Eros* (2012)
11. Leif Dahlberg & Hans Ruin (eds.), *Teknik, fenomenologi och medialitet* (2011)
12. Jonna Bornemark & Hans Ruin (eds.), *Ambiguity of the Sacred* (2012)
13. Brian Manning Delaney & Sven-Olov Wallentein (eds.), *Translating Hegel* (2012)
14. Sven-Olov Wallenstein & Jakob Nilsson (eds.), *Foucault, Biopolitics, and Governmentality* (2013)
15. Jan Patočka, *Inledning till fenomenologisk filosofi* (2013)
16. Jonna Bornemark & Sven-Olov Wallenstein (eds.), *Madness, Religion, and the Limits of Reason* (2015)
17. Björn Sjöstrand, *Att tänka det tekniska: En studie i Derridas teknikfilosofi* (2015)
18. Jonna Bornemark & Nicholas Smith (eds.), *Phenomenology of Pregnancy* (2016)

19. Ramona Rat, *Un-common Sociality: Thinking Sociality with Levinas* (2016)
20. Hans Ruin & Jonna Bornemark (red.), *Ad Marciam* (2017)
21. Gustav Strandberg, *Politikens omskakning: Negativitet, samexistens och frihet i Jan Patočkas tänkande* (2017)
22. Anders Bartonek & Anders Burman (eds.), *Hegelian Marxism: The Uses of Hegel's Philosophy in Marxist Theory from Georg Lukács to Slavoj Žižek* (2018)
23. Lars Kleberg, Tora Lane, Marcia Sá Cavalcante Schuback (eds.), *Words, Bodies, Memory: A Festschrift in honor of Irina Sandomirskaja* (2019)

Södertörn Philosophical Studies is a book series published under the direction of the Department of Philosophy at Södertörn University. The series consists of monographs and anthologies in philosophy, with a special focus on the Continental-European tradition. It seeks to provide a platform for innovative contemporary philosophical research. The volumes are published mainly in English and Swedish. The series is edited by Marcia Sá Cavalcante Schuback and Hans Ruin.

www.ingramcontent.com/pod-product-compliance
Lightning Source LLC
Chambersburg PA
CBHW041438300426
44114CB00026B/2918